THIRD EDITION

IMPLEMENTING CHANGE

Patterns, Principles, and Potholes

GENE E. HALL

University of Nevada, Las Vegas

SHIRLEY M. HORD

Southwest Educational Development Laboratory

Boston   Columbus   Indianapolis   New York   San Francisco   Upper Saddle River
Amsterdam   Cape Town   Dubai   London   Madrid   Milan   Munich   Paris
Montreal   Toronto   Delhi   Mexico City   Sao Paulo   Sydney
Hong Kong   Seoul   Singapore   Taipei   Tokyo

Vice President and Editor in Chief: *Jeffery W. Johnston*
Senior Acquisitions Editor: *Meredith D. Fossel*
Editorial Assistant: *Nancy J. Holstein*
Senior Marketing Manager: *Christopher Barry*
Project Manager: *Holly Shufeldt*
Senior Art Director: *Jayne Conte*
Cover Designer: *Suzanne Duda*
Cover Image: *Fotolia*
Full-Service Project Management and Composition: *Sudip Sinha/Aptara®, Inc.*
Text and Cover Printer/Binder: *R. R. Donnelley & Sons*
Text Font: *Times*

Credits and acknowledgments borrowed from other sources and reproduced, with permission, in this textbook appear on appropriate page within text.

Every effort has been made to provide accurate and current Internet information in this book. However, the Internet and information posted on it are constantly changing, so it is inevitable that some of the Internet addresses listed in this textbook will change.

Library of Congress Cataloging-in-Publication Data
Hall, Gene E.
   Implementing change : patterns, principles, and potholes / Gene E. Hall, Shirley M. Hord.—3rd ed.
     p. cm.
   Includes bibliographical references and index.
   ISBN-13: 978-0-13-701027-1
   ISBN-10: 0-13-701027-3
   1. School improvement programs—United States.   2. Educational leadership—United States.
I. Hord, Shirley M. II. Title.
   LB2822.82.H355 2011
   371.2'070973—dc21

                              2010006670

10 9 8 7 6 5 4 3 2 1

www.pearsonhighered.com

ISBN 13: 978-0-13-701027-1
ISBN 10:   0-13-701027-3

CONTENTS

iv

CHAPTER THREE

―――――――――

Clarifying the Change: Innovation Configurations   42

CHAPTER FOUR

Understanding Feelings and Perceptions About Change: Stages of Concern   67

CHAPTER FIVE

Exploring the Use of Innovations: Levels of Use   92

CHAPTER SEVEN

CHAPTER EIGHT

The Construction of Understanding: Intervention Mushrooms   164

CHAPTER TEN

Diffusion: Communication and Change Agents   211

CHAPTER ELEVEN

Organization Development: Team Building, Action Research, and Process Consultants   232

CHAPTER TWELVE

Implementing Change: Assessing and Facilitating the Process
from Individuals to Whole Systems   260

FOREWORD

About five years ago I was enjoying dinner one evening with my daughter, Leslie, an education major at The University of Texas at Austin, and my dear friend Shirley Hord. Leslie shared what she was learning in her education classes as well as through her practice teaching assignments. She was adamant in her views on what schools needed to do to help her and her colleagues be more successful. Shirley listened intently, asked probing questions, and affirmed Leslie's feelings. To this day I think about that evening from many perspectives. I remember thinking that Shirley was using the Concern-Based Adoption Model (CBAM) and Stages of Change (SoC) to guide her questions to help Leslie clarify her learning. She inspired Leslie to speak with confidence, and her affirmation of her views made the evening a night to remember. I wait for the moment when Leslie is taking a graduate course and comes across the name Shirley Hord and remembers the evening we all shared together. I wonder if, as an experienced teacher, she might wish to revisit some of the "pearls of wisdom" she shared with one of our nation's change experts.

That moment hasn't arrived for Leslie, but every time I have the wisdom to consult the enduring work of Gene Hall—initial architect of this work—and Shirley Hord, I am awestruck by their propensity and persistence to keep pushing until the rest of us get change right.

In 1980, I worked as my district's free-enterprise consulting teacher—a very early model for instructional coach. I had the responsibility to ensure that the "characteristics and benefits of the free enterprise system" were integrated throughout the K–12 social studies curriculum. I was engaged in my doctoral program and was given permission to use my work as the basis for my dissertation study. I decided I would explore how a district successfully helps all teachers infuse a new curricular program into an existing curriculum. During my review of the literature, three names surfaced over and over again: Gene Hall, Shirley Hord, and Susan Loucks-Horsley. Their research provided a structure for my study, and these leaders would continue to influence my work in profound ways for the next three decades.

After completing my doctorate, I attended my second National Staff Development Council (NSDC) Annual Conference in Atlanta, Georgia. I had a new job assignment: part-time district staff developer and part-time free-enterprise consulting teacher. I chose a preconference session led by one of those researchers who had influenced my dissertation study: Susan Loucks-Horsley. She was also scheduled to deliver a keynote address to the conference audience. In a small-group setting, we spent an entire day examining the implications of the change research. In her keynote she addressed more than 800 educators on the same subject. In both sessions she demonstrated deep understanding of her subject, concern for the questions of her participants, and enthusiasm for a subject she seemed confident would reshape education.

I later learned the subject was not a new one for her. She had been working for several years with a team of colleagues at The University of Texas at Austin R & D Center for Teacher Education studying how educators implement change. Since the early 1970s these researchers were concerned about the support educators need to successfully transition into teaching and to implement changes in schools, such as introducing new curricula or teaching strategies.

Three years later, I found myself working for NSDC while launching an academy for other new staff developers. I worked with others to design a curriculum that addressed the foundational knowledge of our burgeoning field. Of course the research on change would be included, and Hall, Hord, and Loucks-Horsley became members of the Academy faculty.

The conversation focused on how to help individuals change in those early years. Over time, the stakes got higher, new entities took an interest in the outcomes of education investments, and Hall and Hord expanded attention from individuals to organizations, from individual classrooms to schools, from changing alone to changing with the support of community, and finally from changing for oneself to changing to benefit students. In the course of our relationship, Shirley Hord and I arrived at the realization that professional development and change were synonymous ideas—or as Shirley prefers to say, opposite sides of the same coin. Professional learning is always designed to support any kind of change, and change does not occur without professional learning. And as a result, the suite of change and professional development tools grew from CBAM to include SoC, Levels of Use (LoU), and Innovation Configurations (IC).

It seems that everything a district administrator, external assistance partner, or school leader needs to facilitate successful change is embedded in this research and these tools. But individuals willing to dig into the research and use the tools must be prepared for the hard work these tools necessitate. They are not panaceas; they do not work overnight; and they do not work with absolutely everyone.

Decades have passed since I was first introduced to this seminal research, and its meaning increases for me every day. I join with the countless educators who rely on the commitment and wisdom of Hall and Hord whenever they are faced with a new educational challenge—we know where to turn first to start our change journey. I think of the brand-new educational leader being introduced to the SoC for the very first time and feeling like he has discovered a tool that will help him multiply his success countless times over. I picture the early-stage central office person charged with implementing a new curriculum and being exposed to her first IC and understanding the importance of investing the resources necessary to create an IC for her program. In both cases, I know how outcomes will be dramatically different because these educators benefit from the wisdom and strategies captured brilliantly in this third edition of Hall and Hord's classic work.

As the stakes for educational improvement increased and most of the silver bullets failed to hit their targets, more and more educators asked, What do we really know about helping educators to change? They soon learned that making change was hard work—no silver bullets. If they were to invest in such an effort, they needed to know they were approaching it correctly. These educators would turn to an edition of Hall and Hord's *Implementing*

Change. Those who recognized the seriousness of their charge to change would appreciate the research, the explanations, the cautions, the details, and the tools. They could sense that they would get the results they sought if they followed Hall and Hord's wisdom with fidelity. Thousands of educators have stories to share of their significant outcomes. With the third edition of this groundbreaking publication, educators once again have the definitive resource for guiding their change efforts.

Stephanie Hirsh, Ph.D.

Executive Director
National Staff Development Council
Dallas, Texas

PREFACE

Welcome to this the third edition of *Implementing Change: Patterns, Principles, and Potholes.* We are pleased that so many found the earlier editions to be worth reading. This text has been an important source of ideas for understanding, facilitating, and studying change processes. We have learned from writing it and having the many exchanges with our readers of ideas and stories.

With so much change happening all around us, it makes sense that a book on change would need change, too. In writing this new edition, a challenge for us authors has been to make important changes and updates while preserving the foundational content that was so useful in the first two editions. We think we have accomplished both objectives.

NEW TO THIS EDITION

Important changes to this edition include:

- As before, the major construct that is the topic of each chapter is *evidence-based.* For this edition, up-to-date citations from research have been inserted with each construct, tool, and application.
- Providing the newest version of the *Stages of Concern Questionnaire (SoCQ) (Form 075),* which replaces the form that had been used for thirty years.
- Adding another measure, the *Change Facilitator Style Questionnaire (CFSQ),* which is proving very useful in understanding critical dimensions of change leadership.
- Inserting *Reflection Questions* at the end of each major section. These questions challenge readers to immediately relate the ideas they have been reading to their real world experiences.
- Another new feature within each chapter is three or four *Pothole Warnings.* These are our way of pointing out a danger or caution related to the topic that is being described. The Pothole Warning is followed by a *Pothole Repair,* which describes a way to avoid or deal with the problem that the warning has identified.
- At the end of each chapter is a new feature, *Conduct a Study*, which identifies two or three topics for which future research is needed.
- Each chapter has 20% to 80% new content.
- The chapters have been resequenced so that the flow is from individuals engaged in change, to organization-level change, and on to large system change.
- There are new examples from research and from experience.
- Also new is a heavy emphasis on use of the Implementation Bridge in thinking about facilitating change and conducting research and evaluation studies.

WHY IMPLEMENTING CHANGE CONTINUES TO BE SO IMPORTANT

The ideas, research findings, and case examples presented here represent the cumulative understanding of researchers and those who have experienced change firsthand as leaders and participants. For 40 plus years we and our colleagues have been contributing to this developing understanding through our own research, offering presentations and workshops, evaluating change efforts, and serving as coaches and mentors.

One clear conclusion that we have offered in the past still holds. Those who initiate change and those who study it should be able to predict much more about what truly happens during this process than is typically the case. We also should be much better at attending to the needs of the people involved and preventing much that often goes wrong. Hopefully, our attempt to pass on some of what we have learned will be of help to you and the others with whom you are engaged during change.

THE TITLE

The title of this book—*Implementing Change: Patterns, Principles, and Potholes*—is fittingly representative of its content. One of the problems in the field of change is that there is no agreement on the meaning of commonly used terms. For example, the word *change* can be a noun (e.g., the change that is being attempted) or a verb (e.g., changing the culture). The word also can be used to represent the whole of a change effort (e.g., "We have a big change underway!"). Having the term *implementing* as the first word in the title adds an important emphasis. Most changes require some time and effort to make them operational—in other words, to implement them. As you will read throughout this book, we see that successful change begins and ends with understanding the importance of implementation constructs and dynamics.

The terms *patterns, principles,* and *potholes* have been carefully chosen as well. There are patterns in change processes, and most of this book is about describing and naming those patterns. In the study of change, as in the so-called hard sciences, there is widespread agreement on a number of points, or principles. We certainly do not know all that we should; however, some elements of change are understood and agreed on by many of us. All of us know full well that "potholes" may be encountered throughout a change process. While too often the inclination is to give too much attention to these problems, it is foolish to ignore them.

PART I: THE CONTEXT FOR IMPLEMENTING CHANGE

Part I opens by introducing a set of *change principles* that should be accepted as givens. Once you read each you will likely say, "Well, of course. I knew that." However, you also can think of change initiatives where that change principle was ignored. Just because we know something, doesn't mean we always act accordingly. Incorporating these change principles alone should lead to fewer surprises and more success in your change efforts.

Over the last 50 years the trend definitely has been toward the impetus for change coming from outside the organization. This trend is easily documented in education. Just chart the increasing role of the federal government between the original Elementary Secondary Education Act (ESEA) of 1965 and the 2001 version, No Child Left Behind. The increasing demand for change in schools, school districts, and states is unprecedented. Many have argued that, ideally, change should be initiated from within. However, this requires special conditions as well as opportunity.

In Chapter 2 we describe characteristics of organizational culture that foster internal initiation of change. The chapter focuses heavily on the characteristics of Professional Learning Communities (PLC), which represent an ideal culture for initiation, implementation, and sustaining of change.

PART II: TOOLS AND TECHNIQUES FOR UNDERSTANDING IMPLEMENTATION AT THE INDIVIDUAL LEVEL

As you will discover, our particular perspective for viewing change, the Concerns-Based Adoption Model, or CBAM (pronounced "see-bam"), offers a number of important ways for understanding what change is about, especially as it relates to the people involved. This perspective is based in our developing understanding of the efforts of individuals to learn about and become skilled and confident in using innovations. Part II introduces the three diagnostic dimensions of CBAM. Each is a research-based construct with related tools that can be used to facilitate, evaluate, and research implementation initiatives.

Chapter 3 introduces ways to think about and appraise the change itself. There can be dramatic differences between what the developer of an innovation has in mind and what is actually implemented. These differences are called *Innovation Configurations*. A second CBAM diagnostic dimension addresses the personal side of change. Even when change takes place in organizational settings, personal feelings, moments of joy, and frustrations are part of it. Understanding these *concerns* is addressed in Chapter 4. Chapter 5 is about use and nonuse of innovations. This is not a dichotomous phenomenon. Instead there are different *Levels of Use*. Change Facilitators and program evaluators should pay close to attention to these different ways of "using" an innovation.

PART III: THE IMPERATIVE FOR LEADERSHIP IN CHANGE

One of the areas in which our research has advanced the most since the last edition has been in understanding and documenting the significant difference that change leaders can make. In Chapter 6 three Change Facilitator (CF) Styles are described. A number of studies have documented the differences in innovation implementation success that are related to how leaders lead. We now have our first study documenting relationships between CF Style and student test scores. In Chapter 7 conceptual frameworks and research strategies for describing and understanding what change facilitators do, (i.e. *interventions*) are introduced.

A large portion of this book was written with the assumption, and the expectation, that it is possible to be proactive in facilitating the change process. However, even the change leaders do not control all parts of the process. We call one key component of the uncontrollable *Intervention Mushrooms,* which is the topic of Chapter 8. Some change facilitators are skilled at detecting and addressing Mushrooms, while others fail to see them at all. Although we think that this chapter will be of particular interest, an important caution is necessary. The chapter on Mushrooms comes after seven other chapters, each of which presents a construct that needs to be understood *before* it is possible to explore the dynamics of Mushrooms and what can be done about them.

PART IV: DIFFERENT PERSPECTIVES FOR UNDERSTANDING THE BIG PICTURE OF CHANGE

The chapters in Part IV introduce three perspectives for understanding change that are classics. Each has an extensive history of research, model building, and applications. Each also offers a number of tools that can be used to facilitate, study, and evaluate change efforts. In Chapter 9 *systems and systemic thinking* are the topic. This approach became particularly important when the U.S. government needed a way to manage very large projects, such as construction of nuclear submarines and putting a human on the moon. Across the years of these massive undertakings, each piece had to be designed, fit together with the other pieces, and arrive at the assembly line at the right time. Chapter 10 introduces another of the classics: *Diffusion.* This perspective had its beginning early in the 20th century with studies of the varying rates and willingness of farmers and others to adopt innovative practices. It very quickly became obvious that not everyone adopts an innovation at the same time. In Chapter 11 another perspective is introduced: *Organization Development (OD).* This approach focuses on group dynamics and the process skills that can help teams be more effective. Organization Development offers a number of techniques and ways to facilitate change that can be useful.

PART V: COMBINING VIEWS AND TOOLS

Chapters 1 through 11 build from the individual to the group to the whole organizational setting. In the last chapter, Chapter 12, we review and extend applications of the constructs that were introduced in the previous chapters. The importance of building implementation factors into the conduct of evaluation and research studies is one important topic. Another is using recent research to focus more on the importance of leadership to change success. The themes of thinking holistically and systemically are reinforced in this chapter as well.

CHAPTER ORGANIZATION

Each chapter begins with presentation of a basic change construct. There are examples of what it looks like, descriptions of how to measure it, and implications for achieving change success. Each chapter also has a number of purpose-built features that are intended to help you draw connections between what you know now and what we would like you to understand when you have finished reading each chapter.

To help ground the basic pattern being presented, every chapter begins with several quotes, which will probably be familiar to you. The ideas presented in the chapter illustrate how these quotes can be analyzed in terms of their meaning for change process success. To help you focus on some of the key topics in each chapter, a set of Focus Questions is offered near the beginning. Each chapter, except Chapter 12, also contains a short case study, or vignette, that illustrates its pattern in action.

To aid in remembering key points, a set of Guiding Principles is presented as well, except for Chapters 1 and 12. A feature that we have carried over is the "Implications for Facilitating Implementation" box. This feature lists several succinct suggestions for ways to use the ideas introduced in each chapter. At the end of each chapter are a number of Discussion Questions and Fieldwork Activities designed to bring each of the patterns to life and to provide opportunities for you to test the constructs presented. For this edition, we have added a new feature at the end of each chapter, *Conduct a Study*. This is where we identify one or two important topics that we know less about and where research studies could be very informative.

*****

So here it is. The new *Implementing Change* book! We hope that it will help you improve your understanding of the change process and how to facilitate change in ways that are responsible and beneficial. The constructs and tools also have important applications in program evaluation studies. If you are interested in research, plenty of ideas are scattered throughout that need to be systematically examined. Let us know what you are thinking of studying and what you learn.

We gratefully acknowledge the encouragement and support of our editor at Pearson/Allyn and Bacon, Steve Dragin. Steve knows firsthand about the challenges of implementing change. Hopefully his reading of our manuscript will help him in his leadership role. He certainly has helped us with developing this edition. We also wish to thank the following reviewers: Martha Burger, Midwestern State University; Francis Ann Kayona, St. Cloud State University; Christopher J. Quinn, Azusa Pacific University; and Karen Tankersley, Arizona State University. We have considered and attempted to incorporate nearly all of their suggestions.

G. E. H.

S. M. H.

ABOUT THE AUTHORS

Gene E. Hall, Ph.D., University of Nevada, Las Vegas, has been a full professor at four universities and served as the Dean of the College of Education at two universities. Dr. Hall is internationally recognized for his career-long focus on developing new understandings about the change process in organization settings. He regularly serves as a consultant for schools, school districts, businesses, and state leaders on the implementation of various innovations and change processes from a Concerns-Based perspective. In addition to his work in the United States, he regularly collaborates with colleagues in other countries in relation to facilitating, evaluating, and studying change processes. His more recent research has examined relationships between extent of implementation and outcomes such as increases in student learning. Dr. Hall has had a parallel academic career in regard to innovation in and national accreditation of teacher education. He is a co-author of *The Foundations of American Education,* now in its 15th edition, and the lead author of *The Joy of Teaching: Making a Difference in Student Learning.*

Shirley M. Hord, Ph.D., Southwest Educational Development Laboratory, is Scholar Laureate, in association with the National Staff Development Council. She authors articles and books on school-based professional development, school change and improvement, and professional learning communities. In addition to co-authoring *Implementing Change: Patterns, Principles, and Potholes*, she has published *Learning Together, Leading Together: Changing Schools Through Professional Learning Communities,* Teachers College Press (2004); with Patricia Roy, *Moving NSDC's Staff Development Standards Into Practice: Innovation Configurations,* National Staff Development Council (2003); and *Leading Professional Learning Communities: Voices from Research and Practice,* Corwin Press (2008). In addition to working with educators at all levels across the United States, Canada, and Mexico, Dr. Hord serves as an educational consultant worldwide, particularly in Asia, Europe, Australia, and Africa.

PART I

THE CONTEXT FOR IMPLEMENTING CHANGE

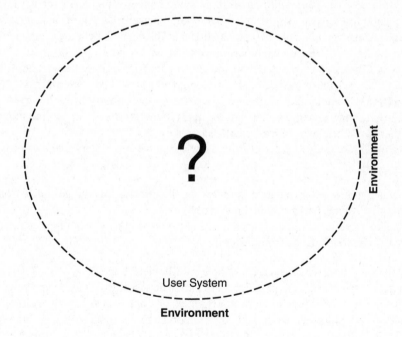

?

User System

Environment

ORGANIZING FRAMEWORKS FOR PARTS

The chapters of this text have been organized into five parts. The parts and chapters are sequenced to unveil key concepts and themes about change that are understood and well researched. The introduction to each part describes the main themes of that part. Each part begins with a graphic for help in visualizing the key themes and concepts that will be introduced. These frameworks become more complex as the reader moves through the parts and chapters.

The graphic for Part I contains little detail. It presents the dotted outline of a shell with the words *User System* inside the shell and *Environment* outside. Your attention should be drawn to the question mark at the center. This symbolizes all that could be known about implementing change. In another way, the question mark is intended to be a question to you, the reader: What do you know about change from your experiences?

CHAPTERS 1 AND 2

One of the major dilemmas at this time has to do with the large number of change efforts that are being demanded by external sources. Instead of the members of organizations having the autonomy to consider, plan, and launch their own change initiatives, over the last several decades outside forces such as state and federal policymakers, the courts, and various experts have set the change agenda. For example, high-stakes testing and the multiple mandates in No Child Left Behind (NCLB) are examples of external forces requiring change in schools. The Environmental Protection Agency (EPA) and the Occupational Safety and Health Administration (OSHA) are requiring businesses to implement changes. The Department of Homeland Security (DHS) demands that we remove our shoes when going through airport security. Rather than initiating change, organizations and individuals are having to implement many changes that have been determined by outsiders.

Two important questions result from this tension between internal and external change forces:

1. How is implementing change different when the impetus for change comes from the environment versus being initiated internally?
2. What characteristics of an organization and the environment make it more likely to successfully initiate change from inside?

Addressing these questions are the topics in Chapters 1 and 2.

Chapter 1 will describe 10 **principles of change** that most would agree apply regardless of whether the impetus for change is internal or external. Of course, there are some differences, and these will be noted. Still, this set of principles is important to successful change in both situations. Chapter 2 will introduce constructs and research related to **organization culture**. There will be more, or less, implementation success depending on the condition and shape of the culture. Change success depends less on whether the source of the change is internal or external and significantly more on the degree to which the culture of the organization is open and ready to consider what is currently being done and continually examining ways to improve. The ideal condition is to have a professional learning community (PLC). Chapter 2 will focus on characteristics and the importance of facilitating the construction of a PLC-type organization culture.

CHAPTER 1

IMPLEMENTING CHANGE
Patterns, Principles, and Lessons Learned

Learning means you are adjusting to change.
—Art Linkletter on the *Larry King Show,* July 20, 2002

Change means you are adjusting your learning.
—Director of professional learning

We know from past experience that it is important to stay the course. It takes time to institutionalize new practices.
—High school principal

After all this research on classrooms, the inescapable conclusion is that school-based leadership makes a big difference.
—Assistant superintendent, urban district

When everything comes together right, change is an energizing and very satisfying experience.
—Sales manager, a real estate company

Here we go again. You know how change is. It is like a pendulum, swinging back and forth.
—Teacher, middle school history department

WHY A BOOK ON "IMPLEMENTING CHANGE?"

Are you a teacher, an assistant principal, an inner-city district superintendent, a state-level director of traffic or highways, a campus-based school principal, a college dean, or the dad in a family? Regardless of your role, chances are you have had experiences in suggesting or introducing changes of some sort in your organization. How many times have you been successful in accomplishing those changes, most especially if the changes were not readily agreeable to your constituents?

Or perhaps you are the human resources manager of a large company. How do you manage the training and development of employees so that they productively take on new and improved behaviors that contribute to the company's bottom line while maintaining employee satisfaction on the job? Perhaps you are responsible for research and evaluation for your school district, or a large corporation, or installation of a new approach in the military or government. Your responsibility is to ascertain the effectiveness of new classroom and production floor practices. These new activities require change. Each must first be in place (implemented) before its effectiveness can be assessed.

For decades—no, millennia (think Machiavelli, *The Prince,* originally published in Italian in 1532, currently available translated, 2005)—leaders have been delivering suggestions, invitations, mandates, and legislation in hopes of changing behaviors, attitudes, knowledge, and understanding. These leaders also have a need to know if their improvement strategies are working. Such actions of introducing, accomplishing or implementing, and assessing change have occurred erratically in the corporate sector, in schools, in medical practice, and in almost every other area of human endeavor. A large part of the required implementation activities have gone unheeded or have resulted in superficial, modest, or poor installation. Too many end with the participants observing, "See, I told you so: This too would pass."

One of the districts we studied encountered this situation (based on years of not providing intervention support for the various change efforts). When administrators realized the feelings of the staff, they immediately planned for, announced, and delivered assistance and support for the current change. They designed and put in place a monitoring system that provided bimonthly feedback on the status of implementation. These actions sent strong signals to the staff that the new program was here to stay and that the administration would back it over time.

In an era of abundant research findings and examples of tested and improved practices that have led to better products and processes, there is a surprising and woeful lack of finding these new ideas, products, and processes employed in our homes, schools, and workplaces. Advertising and marketing activities extol the virtues of everything from the latest fad diet to how to teach phonics. Many of these products and processes are discarded after a brief period of experimentation and no immediate or visible success.

So what is the problem here?

For the past 40 years, the authors have been leaders of an international team of researchers studying the change process in schools, colleges, businesses, and government agencies. We have been systematically charting what happens to people and organizations when they are involved in change. We have learned a lot about the challenges, the problems, and what it takes to be successful. Our research approach is different from that of others in a number of ways, including our primary focus on the people at the front lines who have to implement the expected change. Our secondary focus has been on how leaders can and do facilitate change.

In our 65 combined years of research and practice efforts to discover, support, and assist schools and other organizations in their efforts to improve, we have observed and shared the successes of those schools and businesses that have managed and guided change efforts from their abstract promise to their successful reality. We have observed also, despite our most urgent and encouraging support and assistance, organizations adopting new programs and processes year after year, and quickly rejecting each as they failed to deliver on their promise.

Our keen observations, rigorous studies, and multiple experiences have led us to articulate some basic principles about the process of change.

The original team for these research efforts came together in the late 1960s at the University of Texas at Austin. From 1970 to 1986, this group studied the change process in schools and universities as part of the agenda of the Research and Development Center for Teacher Education. Along the way, researchers from around the United States, Belgium, the Netherlands, Australia, Canada, Taiwan, Hong Kong, and several other countries joined in verifying the concepts and extending the research agenda. Now in place is an international network of change-process researchers who have conducted studies related to the concepts and principles presented here. We initiate the discussion of change and implementation in this book by a brief explication and review of these time-tested principles.

REFLECTION QUESTIONS

As you think about your experiences, what have you learned about change? What is one principle of change that you would put forth?

FOCUS QUESTIONS

1. How are change and learning related?
2. What role is required of school leaders in the process of change?
3. Why are interventions so significant to the success of change efforts?
4. Can top-down mandates really work?

PRINCIPLES OF CHANGE

One important result of our long-term collaborative research agenda is that we now can draw some conclusions about what happens when people and organizations are engaged in change. A number of patterns have been observed repeatedly, and some have developed into major themes, or basic *principles,* and we do mean *principles.* As in the so-called hard sciences, enough is now known about some aspects of the change process that we can state a series of principles that will hold true for all cases.

The change principles presented in this chapter are the givens underlying all that will be presented in subsequent chapters. From our point of view, these principles are no longer debatable points, for they summarize predictable aspects of change.

Before introducing selected principles about change, a caveat is needed: Each principle is not mutually exclusive, and at first reading some may seem inconsistent with others. Also, these principles do not cover all aspects of change. (Otherwise we would not need the other chapters in this book.) Instead, they address selected aspects of the change process in which the patterns are clear. Acknowledging that these principles are foundational to our way of thinking about change will save you time in trying to discover our implicit assumptions. In addition, understanding them should help you in predicting key aspects of change efforts with which you are engaged.

Also, we need to emphasize that at all levels—individual, organizational, and system—change is highly complex, multivariate, and dynamic. If it weren't so complicated, it would not be nearly as much fun to study, facilitate, and experience. So let's begin our journey of bringing order to change by introducing a set of principles about change that each of us has understood implicitly but probably not verbalized. Interestingly, we predict that you will be able to describe personal change experiences in which each of these principles has been ignored or violated. Certainly, your future change efforts can be more successful if these principles are acknowledged.

Change Principle 1: Change Is Learning—It's as Simple and Complicated as That

To *improve* the speed of transportation from one place to another, one might decide to make a *change* and use a bicycle; to become a skillful bicycle rider requires *learning* about the pedals, handlebars, balance, the rules of the road, and laws governing the conduct of persons using public highways and neighborhood paths and sidewalks. This is an example easy to understand and to visualize. It is also easy to understand that having a caring dad or big brother to guide the learning, to provide feedback about how to sit astride the vehicle, how to rotate the pedals so that the wheels turn efficiently can add measurably to the quality and time required of the learning.

In the marketplace, matters are not quite so simple. A shoe store manager, noting that the quality of her merchandise and the appeal of the salesroom equaled those of her nearest competitor, which was besting her in shoe sales, wondered if her sales staff lacked in their approach to customers. She engaged a colleague to check this and discovered that the competing store's staff expressed a warmer attitude toward customers and expressed and conveyed more knowledge about the merchandise to customers. It was obvious to this manager that something must be done to *improve* staff/customer relations.

Her first attempt to *change* her staff's knowledge and skills was to bring them together for coffee before the store opened and share a report from the Business League about research that had been done that identified how sales personnel should act to make successful sales. The staff appreciated the fine coffee and rolls but expressed a lack of knowing what to do to behave as the research findings indicated. Well, the manager contemplated, I guess they will need *to learn* how to act in these new ways.

In three successive meetings, the staff met to study new behaviors, to see them demonstrated, to practice them on each other, and to receive feedback from the business consultant who was instructing them. Everyone was delighted when shoe sales increased, as did the commissions of the staff.

To make things better (improved) in the family setting, in the marketplace, and in the classroom, *change* is introduced and *learning* makes it possible to make the change (see Figure 1.1). In the two examples provided, the changes and their learning needs are fairly easy to understand and to accomplish. But let's visit a mathematics classroom and a school improvement effort—one expected to enable students to increase their abilities in critical thinking, in problem solving, and in teamwork. Before these new outcomes (changes) can be realized in the students, the instructional staff must change their teaching. Changing to a new way of teaching mathematics is not an easy effort.

One of the authors still vividly recalls a long-ago classroom teaching experience. The district mathematics curriculum coordinator introduced and expected that all teachers would

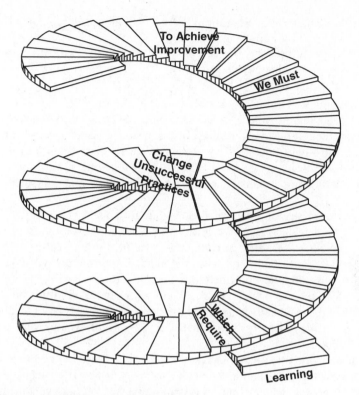

FIGURE 1.1   Learning: The Basis for Improvement

Source: Created by James L. Roussin, Generative Human Systems

implement and use a new inquiry-oriented math curriculum that provided students with a large degree of self-guided instruction. To support the teachers in this new approach to teaching math, teacher's guides for the curriculum were distributed, and teachers were directed to access staff development/learning about how to teach the new program by sitting alone in front of their residential televisions—not a very powerful learning strategy.

Subsequently, this teacher's mathematics guide became permanently affixed to her left arm. Following this "teacher-proof" set of teaching directions worked okay when the students responded with understanding and the correct answers. However, when students didn't understand or respond correctly, the teacher did not know what to do for she had little depth of understanding of the process for this kind of instruction. Fortunate for all in this classroom, one of the intellectually gifted sixth-grade students understood the situation and the curriculum and taught the teacher! *Learning* enabled the teacher to *change* her practices and to use the *improved* and more effective program with students. (As a side note, in this same vignette, many teachers did not have access to the learning that enabled them to use the program. After trials and frustration with the program, they reverted to their old practices—a common result in such scenarios.)

Professional learning is a critical component embedded in the change process. Research focused on change process and on professional development reveals parallel findings, both of which identify the imperative of learning in order to use improved programs, processes, and practices.

Change Principle 2: Change Is a Process, Not an Event

The very first assumption in our studies of change in the early 1970s was that change is a process, not an event (Hall, Wallace, & Dossett, 1973). In other words, change is not accomplished by having a one-time announcement by an executive leader, a two-day training workshop for teachers in August, the delivery of the new curriculum/technology to the office, or all of these. Instead, change is a process through which people and organizations move as they gradually learn, come to understand, and become skilled and competent in the use of new ways.

Our research and that of others documents that most changes in education take three to five years to be implemented at a high level (for example, see George, Hall, & Uchiyama, 2000; Hall & Loucks, 1977; Hall & Rutherford, 1976). Further, for each new unit (e.g., school, business, or state) that undertakes the change, the process will take three to five years. For each new adopting unit, the clock begins at the beginning. There are very few shortcuts. However, the use of the constructs and tools presented in this book will significantly reduce the time needed to achieve a higher level of implementation. Failure to address key aspects of the change process can either add years to, or even prevent, achieving successful implementation.

Unfortunately, too many policymakers at all levels refuse to accept the principle that change is a process, not an event, and continue to insist that *their* changes be implemented before their next election, which typically is within two years. This "event mentality" has serious consequences for participants in the change process. For example, the press to make change quickly means that there is neither time to learn about and come to understand the new way nor time to grieve the loss of the old way.

Have you ever realized that grief is a key part of change? Chances are that when people must change, they have to stop doing some things that they know how to do well and in fact like doing, which creates a sense of sadness. What many leaders see as resistance to change may in large part be grief over the loss of favorite and comfortable ways of acting. We recall following a new science program implementation, in which the second-grade teachers literally wept over losing their egg-hatching unit. This personal side of change will be examined in depth in Chapter 4.

Although many other implications of this principle will also be developed in subsequent chapters, one that is important to note here has to do with planning for change. The strategic plan for change will look very different, depending on whether it is assumed that change is a process or an event. If the assumption is that change is a process, then the plan for change will be strategic in nature. It will allow at least three to five years for implementation and will budget the resources needed to support formal learning and on-site coaching for the duration of this phase. There will be policies that address the need for multiyear implementation support, and each year data will be collected about the change process to inform the leaders in supporting planning for and facilitating implementation in subsequent years.

If the assumption is that change is an event, the plan for implementation will be tactical in nature. It will have a short-term focus typically centering on one formal training session for teachers before school begins, no on-site coaching or follow-up, and perhaps a first-year summative evaluation to see if the new approach is making a significant difference. As will be described in later chapters, one typical consequence of not finding any significant differences in the first or second year of implementation is the mistaken conclusion that the new approach does not work, when in fact there was not enough time and support for implementation so that it might work.

Examples of an event mentality also can be seen in the formal steps taken in the typical school improvement process. Developing the plan utilizes several steps and implementation requires just one. If school improvement were being thought of as a process, instead of an event, it would be called school "improving." Such an event mentality was well expressed by one assistant superintendent who exclaimed in the spring of the first year of implementation, "What do you mean that teachers need more training!? We bought them the books. Can't they read?"

Change Principle 3: The School Is the Primary Unit for Change

Although we have emphasized and will continue to emphasize the importance of understanding the dynamics of individuals in change, the key organizational unit for making change successful is the school. The school's staff and its leaders will make or break any change effort, regardless of whether the change is initiated from the inside or outside. However, the school is not an island; rather, it is part of district, state, and/or federal systems of education. The school can and must do a lot for itself, but it also must move in concert with and be supported by the other components of the system.

Note the assertion that schools need outside support. Change is a complex, dynamic, and resource-consuming endeavor. No single organization, be it a school or a national corporation, is likely to have all the expertise and resources needed to succeed in change. As will be emphasized in later chapters, *external* change facilitators, as well as supports from other parts of the system, are necessary. This is why the concept of local control does a disservice to organizations such as schools. Change processes are easier and chances of sustained success are increased as the school staff understands more about how to use external resources and as those external to the school recognize the importance of their roles in facilitating change success in each school.

Everyone—teachers and principals in the school and personnel in the district office—must consider and view how a school learns and advances as a change process unfolds. Many of the same interventions, such as providing teachers (and principals) with professional learning about their role with the innovation, can in fact be made throughout a district, especially during the first year of implementation. However, by the second year, different schools will be moving at different rates and will have different change successes and challenges. Thus, at least some of the key interventions will need to be uniquely targeted for each school.

Change Principle 4: Organizations Adopt Change—Individuals Implement Change

Although everyone wants to talk about such broad concepts as policy, systems, and organizational factors, successful change starts and ends at the individual level. An entire organization does not change until each member has changed. Another way to say this is that there is an individual aspect to organizational change. Even when the change is introduced to every member of the organization at the same time, the rate of learning to make the change and of developing skill and competence in using it will vary individually. Some people will grasp the new way immediately, although most will need some additional time, and a few will avoid making the change for a very long time. Rogers (2003) has called this third group "laggards." Even when the change is mandated, some individuals will delay implementation. One implication of this principle is that leaders of organizational change processes need to devise ways to anticipate and facilitate change at the individual level.

This principle does not mean that all of the interventions (e.g., on-site coaching or a telephone hotline to address specific questions) in a change process must be addressed at the individual level. Nor does it mean that every individual will be at a different point in the process. People respond to and implement change in typical patterns that will be described in the following chapters. Change process leaders can and should anticipate many of these patterns. Many interventions should be targeted toward subgroups (e.g., principals training in what the change entails), and many others should be aimed at the organization as a whole. Still, since there is an individual element to how the change process unfolds, many of the interventions must be done with and for individuals, for there can be no change in outcomes until each individual implements the new practice.

Organizations are under heavy pressure to increase performance. In business, the press is to increase productivity, quality, and sales. In schools, the bottom line is the expectation to have ever-increasing student scores on standardized tests. To improve performance, many policymakers and executives are placing heavy emphasis on evaluating the end results. For schools, this is seen in the widespread focus on high-stakes testing. Annual testing of students has been mandated, and NCLB mandates negative consequences for schools that do not show adequate increases in test scores. An implicit assumption with this approach to change seems to be that schools will incorporate the necessary changes to make test scores go up. However, little support is being made available to schools to implement these changes.

Figure 1.2 illustrates this problem. Imagine a setting where there is a very large and deep chasm with schools engaged in current practice located on the left cliff. On the right side of the chasm are the increases in student outcomes that are desired. Strategies that focus only on the right side fail to acknowledge several implementing change realities. First, if there are no changes in practice, there is little reason to expect a change in outcomes. As principals often observe, "If you always do what you have always done, you will continue to get what you always have gotten." The second failure is in relation to Change Principle 2: Change is a process, not an event. If it takes three to five years to implement new practices to a high level, then it is highly unlikely that positive increases in outcomes will occur during the first or second year of implementation. In the scene shown in Figure 1.2, practitioners are being asked to make a *Giant Leap*. They are being directed to improve outcomes without any support for learning how to change their current practices, and thus improve.

In order for change to be successful, an Implementation Bridge is necessary. Each member of the organization has to move across the Implementation Bridge. As they learn to change their practices, there can be changes in outcomes. Without an Implementation Bridge, there is little reason to expect positive change in outcomes. Instead, there are likely to be casualties as attempts to make the giant leap fail. Individuals and whole organizations may fall into the chasm.

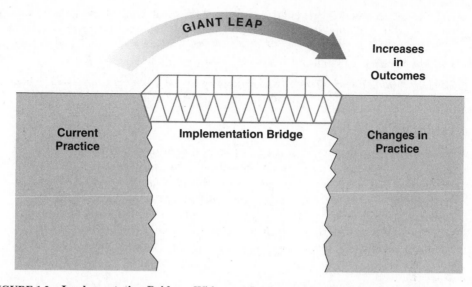

FIGURE 1.2   Implementation Bridge   Without an Implementation Bridge, individuals and organizations must make a giant leap.

Each chapter in this book will present research-based constructs and tools that can be used to facilitate individuals and organizations in moving across the bridge. The constructs and tools also can be used to measure the extent to which they have moved across the bridge. These implementation assessment data can then be correlated with outcome measures. Ideally, outcomes should be higher for those individuals and organizations that have moved further across the bridge. This was the case in one large study of implementation of standards-based teaching of mathematics (George, Hall, & Uchiyama, 2000). Students in classrooms with teachers who had moved further along with implementation had higher test scores.

REFLECTION QUESTIONS

Why would you wish for your children (or grandchildren) to be assigned to a teacher who is a continuous learner, one who is consistently updating his/her knowledge base? In what ways might it be useful if the school supplied the resources for this learning?

Change Principle 5: Interventions Are Key to the Success of the Change Process

As individuals plan and lead change processes, they tend to be preoccupied with the innovation and its use. They often do not think about the various actions and events that they and others could take to influence the process; these actions are known as *interventions*. Training workshops are perhaps the most obvious type of intervention. Although workshops are important, the research studies cited in this book document that many other kinds of interventions are significant also—and that some are even more crucial to achieving change success!

Pothole Warning

The term training workshops is used with great frequency. If we train horses and dogs, what do we really mean by a training workshop for educators?

Pothole Repair

It seems to us that the term training is not very appropriate for its application to the human species. On the other hand, the knowledge and skills that are required for some designated task must be "developed" in each individual. And what about the term workshops? Here, it appears that we are really using this term to refer to large group learning sessions. In the case of either term, what is needed is an understanding that these activities are interventions that support individuals in gaining the requisite capacities for behaving in new ways. Without these interventions, whatever they are labeled, the change is doomed unless attention is given to them.

Interventions come in different sizes. Interestingly, the most important interventions are the little ones, which most leaders forget to do or forget about having done. When change is successful, it is the quantity of the little things that makes the final difference. One of the major types of small interventions is what we call the *one-legged interview*. One frequent opportunity for one-legged interviews occurs when a teacher and a principal meet in the corridor as each is headed to a different classroom. If they do not interact or if they have a social chat, these encounters are lost opportunities for innovation-related interventions. However, if the principal or teacher initiates a brief discussion about the innovation—"How's it going with _____?"—then a one-legged interview type of intervention has taken place.

We use the term *one-legged* to indicate that these interventions are brief (most people can't stand on one leg very long), since both the teacher and the principal probably have to be somewhere else when the next bell rings. Yet a moment was taken to talk about the teacher's involvement with the innovation. The research reported in later chapters consistently indicates that teachers are more successful with change in schools where there are statistically significantly more one-legged interviews.

We will present more about one-legged interviews in Chapter 7 on interventions. Here, the point is that it is critical to distinguish between the concepts of *innovations* and *interventions*. Change leaders tend to think only about innovations and not to think sufficiently about interventions in terms of an overall plan for and during the unfolding of the change process; and many fail to appreciate the value of small interventions.

Change Principle 6: Appropriate Interventions Reduce Resistance to Change

One of the big questions about change has to do with dealing with resistance. In most change efforts some people will *appear* to be resisting and some may be actively sabotaging the effort (note "appear to be" and "may be"). The first step is to determine the reason for the apparent resistance. Often what appears to be resistance is the individual working through the sense of loss for having to stop doing something that was comfortable. A second form of resistance is grounded in having serious questions about whether the change will really be an improvement. This questioning may be due to limited understanding about the new, or it may be based in solid reasoning and evidence. Some see a third form of resistance. Several contemporary writers have stated in one way or another that change is painful, and they assert that this pain must be endured as a natural part of the change process. These authors might leave you feeling that only the masochist likes change, but this does not have to be the case.

Each of the three cases for apparent resistance has very different underlying reasons. In most situations, addressing the resistance requires attending to individual differences (Change Principle 4). To address these concerns requires very different interventions. *If* the process is facilitated well, learning about the change and its implementation can be productive, and it certainly does not have to hurt or even be dreaded. Of course, there are moments of frustration and times of grieving over what is being lost. However, if there is major pain in change, chances are strong that the leadership for the change process has not understood what is entailed and required to facilitate the process well. In each of the following chapters, basic constructs, measures, research findings, and case examples will be introduced and used to describe ways of more effectively facilitating change. If these tools are understood and used well, there should be little resistance or pain—and large gains.

REFLECTION QUESTIONS

Think about a change effort in which you have been involved. Were any individuals involved who were resistant to the change? Which of the three explanations might apply to these individuals? Or, is there a fourth explanation for their attitude?

Change Principle 7: Administrator Leadership Is Essential to Long-Term Change Success

A central theme of advocates for bottom-up change is that those nearest the action have the best ideas of how to accomplish the change. Many implementers believe that they do not need any involvement from or with those above them. But here again, the findings of research and experience argue for a different conclusion.

Many of us have had firsthand experience with trying to implement some sort of innovative effort from the bottom. A classic example for the authors of this book was when we first worked together as teacher education faculty members. We were hired to create and implement an experimental teacher education program based on the teacher concerns model of Frances Fuller (1969). We and several others formed a multidisciplinary faculty team that developed and operated an experimental teacher education program that was truly an innovation bundle, one that included innovations such as professors teaming, an all-day blocked schedule for teacher education candidates, early field experiences, and a partnership of principals and teachers. In short, it incorporated many of the innovations that are found in what are now called professional development schools.

Although the teacher education program was very successful and became well known nationally and internationally, it died after five years. It did not become the regular teacher education program at our university, nor did it have much direct influence on the traditional teacher education program. Why was that?

As faculty, we were at the proverbial bottom of the organization. As long as we had the energy, we were able to work collaboratively to develop and implement our innovation bundle. Although that bundle turned out to be successful, over time our faculty colleagues in the regular programs and the administration of the university did not actively support the continuation of the bundle, nor the implementation of any of the specific innovations into the regular programs. Without their direct support, in the end the innovation withered and was forgotten.

The point here is not to analyze what we might have done to garner more administrator support (which we will do in other chapters). Rather, our goal is to use a firsthand experience to show that although the "bottom" may be able to launch and sustain an innovative effort for several years, if administrators do not engage in ongoing active support, it is more than likely that the change effort will die.

In many ways Change Principle 7 is a corollary of Change Principle 8, since everyone along the policy-to-practice continuum has a role to play if change is going to be successful. Yes, teachers and professors can create, share with others, and implement new practices. Yes, administrators have to do things on a day-to-day basis that are supportive and provide continuous learning about the innovation opportunities. (Remember those one-legged-interviews?) Administrators also have to secure the necessary infrastructure changes and long-term resource supports if use of an innovation is to continue indefinitely. And finally, yes, policymakers need to design polices that legitimize infrastructure changes and innovative practices and encourage continued use of the innovation.

Change Principle 8: Facilitating Change Is a Team Effort

In this book we will emphasize repeatedly the importance of facilitating the change process, which means that leadership must be ongoing for change to be successful. In Chapter 6 we will describe different change facilitator styles and the significance of each. Embedded in all of this and in many of the principles presented here is the core belief that change is a team effort. Just as in Change Principle 3 we stress that no school is an island, we argue here that collaboration is also necessary among those responsible for leading change efforts.

Although in Change Principle 7 we describe the crucial role of the school principal, we want to emphasize that many others also have a responsibility to help change processes be successful. Indeed, other administrators play important roles, as do front-line users and nonusers of the innovation. Teachers, for example, play a critical leadership role in whether or not change is successful. We really are in this phenomenon together, and all must help to facilitate the process.

Team leadership for change extends far beyond the school site. In many ways all of the actors across the Policy-to-Practice Continuum (see Table 1.1) are contributors to change success. Each of these role groups has the potential to strongly influence what happens at the local site and

TABLE 1.1   The Policy-to-Practice Continuum

FEDERAL	STATE	DISTRICT	SCHOOL	CLASSROOM
President	Governor	Superintendent	Principal	Teacher
Secretary of Education	Commissioner of Education	Board of Education	Site Council	
Congress	Legislature			

with individual users. State and federal executives and policymakers obviously have the potential to affect change in schools. Each time there is an election, voters hear about the "education" governor/president. Administrators and staff in the school district office can make important contributions to efforts to move across the Implementation Bridge. Each of these "external" roles can, and do, make significant differences in the degree of success of change. Colleagues in a school make a difference, too, as they learn about the change together. When teachers and others inside the organization share successes and challenges, implementation efforts can be more successful.

REFLECTION QUESTIONS

Consider a change project in which you were part of the team supporting and facilitating the effort. Who/what roles did you and the other team members represent? What support and assistance did you/they offer that contributed to the success of the project?

Change Principle 9: Mandates Can Work

Change Principle 5 introduced the concept of interventions and gave special attention to a category of small interventions called one-legged interviews. Among the number of other types of interventions that will be described in later chapters, one of the more common is known as a *strategy*. A mandate is one kind of strategy that is used widely. Although mandates are continually criticized as being ineffective because of their top-down orientation, they can work quite well. With a mandate the priority is clear, and there is an expectation that the innovation will be implemented. The mandate strategy fails when the only time the change process is supported is at the initial announcement of the mandate. When a mandate is accompanied by continuing communication, ongoing learning, on-site coaching, and time for implementation, it can work. As with many change strategies, the mandate has garnered a bad name—but not because the strategy itself is flawed but because it is not supported with the other necessary interventions.

Change Principle 10: The Context Influences the Process of Learning and Change

In considering the school as the unit of change, we can think of it as having two important dimensions that affect the change efforts of the individual and the organization:

1. The *physical features,* such as the size and arrangement of the facility, and the resources, policies, structures, and schedules that shape the staff's work
2. The *people factors,* which include the attitudes, beliefs, and values of the individuals involved as well as the relationships and norms that guide behavior

An increasing body of literature on the influence of workplace culture has evolved from both educational writers who study school improvement and from members of the corporate sector who are concerned with quality and its relationship to profits. Interestingly, these two rather disparate worlds share common views about desirable organizational conditions that result in effective staff performance and customer satisfaction/high-level learner outcomes (in the school setting).

In schools that have created such organizational conditions, the staff collectively reflects on its work with students and assesses its influence on student performance. In this collegial inquiry, the staff may identify areas for improvement. Interestingly, addressing these improvement targets begins with the staff's identification of what *they* must learn in order to more effectively help students become more successful learners. This community of "professional learners" (Hord, 2004) embodies individuals who value change and who seek change in order to increase their efficacy as teachers. Having such a learning-oriented staff can contribute profoundly to how the change process unfolds and ultimately succeeds in a given school. One attribute of these change-ready staffs is shared and supportive leadership. Such a professional learning community demands a sharing principal who is working participatively with teachers in their quest for high-quality learning.

Pothole Warning

With no interaction with the staff, the administrator/principal of the school determines that the staff should adopt a new mathematics curriculum that targets students' self-initiated learning. The program is announced to the staff, and they are provided with two days of staff development to support this adoption. The principal announces that there will be an evaluation of the new program at the end of the current semester.

Pothole Repair

Wow! Do you feel revolution in the air? This is a mandate that will fail. Alternatively, the professional learning community school is one in which the entire staff—administrators and teachers—come together to study student performance data in order to decide collectively where attention needs to be given for increasing student learning, and what innovation or new programs/processes will be selected to address the needs of the students. Related is the attention needed for the staff to adopt the innovation and the interventions necessary to support their learning to use it—implementation.

In Chapter 2, we will review the literature and describe additional characteristics of these communities of professional learning, whose culture embodies those conditions that are conducive to and supportive of change. The operationalization of these factors in a school makes a significant difference in the staff's concerns about change and in the amount of success in moving across the Implementation Bridge.

This chapter's vignette presents a brief change story as a way to summarize what the change principles are like in action.

■ ■ ■ ■ ■ ▬▬▬▬▬▬▬▬▬▬▬▬▬▬▬▬▬▬▬▬▬▬▬▬▬▬▬▬▬▬▬▬▬▬▬

VIGNETTE

A DISTRICTWIDE CHANGE INITIATIVE: PRINCIPLES ADDRESSED, PRINCIPLES MISSED

During the writing of this book, one of the authors was invited to conduct a Concerns-Based Adoption Model (CBAM) workshop for a medium-size school district. Although the district leaders were facilitating change in ways that were consistent with most of the principles outlined in this chapter, several of the principles were being violated, with predictable results.

■ ■ ■ ■ ■

VIGNETTE CONTINUED

The district teachers had been engaged in implementing a well-known model of teaching for three years (Change Principle 2). This initiative was a districtwide mandate of the superintendent (Change Principles 7 and 9). The teachers, as well as the district office curriculum and staff development personnel, had received extensive professional development in the use of the teaching model (Change Principles 4 and 5).

As in most school districts, a number of other change initiatives and mandates were being advanced in the district at the same time. For example, each school was engaged with school improvement plans, annual standardized testing, inclusion, technology, and a new mathematics curriculum; and the elementary schools were engaged in restructuring the primary grades. Ironically, even with all of these change initiatives at work in the schools, the principals were allowed only to leave their schools for professional development in the teaching model; they had not received information or skills development in what any of the other innovations entailed. Learning about how to facilitate change was done with all the central office professionals but no principals (Change Principles 7 and 8). The teachers received extensive professional development through workshops, but no specialized interventions took place to help teachers individually (Change Principles 5 and 6).

Further, although implementation of the teaching model had been underway for three years, the district leadership made no effort to adjust change-facilitating interventions on a school-by-school basis. All schools were treated in the same way (Change Principle 3).

As could be predicted, an undercurrent of talk ensued about how too much attention had been given to the teaching model and not enough to a number of the other priorities. Dismay was also felt over the fact that principals were not permitted to leave their buildings to learn how to help teachers implement any of the other innovations (Change Principle 6).

Two principles were not supported in this situation: Change Principle 3, which argues that each school be seen as a unit of change, and Change Principle 8, which underlines the need for a team to facilitate change. Change Principle 10 was ignored completely. As a result, the teaching model was being used well in some classrooms and some schools but not in others. The failure to address Change Principle 7 meant less understanding and support by the principals for each of the other innovations.

What was needed next was a process that would help all of the system's professionals—the district staff, principals, and teachers—realize that they were part of the same system and that they all had role responsibilities. The vertical character of the superintendent's centralized directives was not allowing for a horizontal policy-to-practice perspective to develop. The need for each role group to do its own jobs well was being eroded. Staff development was available for some, but the sense of a team effort was not being developed. The key to forming a horizontal/teaming approach was missed by prohibiting principals from participating in learning about what teachers were doing with the other innovations and about how to use change-facilitating concepts. An additional change leadership objective was missed by not ensuring that all district change facilitators developed a common language about the change process and ways to facilitate it. A shared language gives those who have the opportunity to facilitate change a better understanding of how to do so and results in teachers having more success in implementing the various innovations that have been introduced.

VIGNETTE CRITIQUE QUESTIONS

1. If Change Principles 3, 5, 6, and 8 had been in place in this district, what specific differences would they have made?
2. What should be done next in this district?
3. If an innovation requires three to five years for quality implementation, how would you manage the six initiatives in this district?

SUMMARY

The main reason for writing this book is to describe what has been learned about facilitating the process of change. This knowledge, if used well, can reduce, if not avoid altogether, the apprehension and dread associated with change and can lead to successful results. Nearly all of the ideas and suggestions made are derived from research. In this chapter we have created the foundation by summarizing a set of change principles that represent some of the predictable patterns of change in organizational settings. The metaphor of the implementation bridge should help in visualizing many of the change principles.

A very important next step is to develop an understanding and appreciation of the personal side of change, which we will address with the concept of *Stages of Concern*. The fact that leaders do make a difference in supporting participants in learning how to use new programs and processes will be addressed through our research on *Change Facilitator Style*. The leaders' actions, known as interventions, will be reviewed as well. Don't forget that the change process we describe is taking place inside an organizational setting. Individuals in organizations construct an organizational culture based on values and norms. Understanding the importance of organization culture is the beginning step for achieving long-term change success. Consideration of this culture will be explored in Chapter 2.

We will be consistently asking you to think about situations that you are experiencing and about how you can facilitate change. This is done throughout to help you tie the various ideas together, to relate them to your context, and to learn how to make them useful in your setting.

We are living in a time of change. Rather than viewing change as a painful course of action, let's develop an understanding of how it works, how to facilitate the process, and how to learn from our experiences. To accomplish these outcomes, the following chapters will be organized around key change process concepts. Each chapter will include research findings and examples of how a research-verified construct can be used to facilitate change and to monitor how well it is going. Each chapter includes a number of features, such as Pothole Warnings, that can be of help in anticipating things that can go wrong. Occasionally we point out areas where more research is needed. The primary purpose, though, is to increase your understanding about how the change process works and how to be most effective in influencing, facilitating, and monitoring that process.

DISCUSSION QUESTIONS

1. With which of the change principles presented in this chapter do you strongly agree? Are there any with which you strongly disagree? Why?

2. Can change be successful? Explain your answer.

3. Change Principle 6 addresses resistance to change. Is resistance present in every change effort? Is resistance ever appropriate?

4. Describe a change process that you have had or are experiencing. Point out where the different principles fit. Do any of them explain why certain things have gone well and what is, or was, problematic?

FIELDWORK ACTIVITIES

1. Interview a person in a leadership role in a school district or other type of organization. Ask the person to propose three to five principles he or she has learned about change. How do their principles compare with those presented in this chapter? How do they compare with yours?

2. Select a school or other type of organization and learn about the effort to implement a major innovation. Make a chart of the internal and external leaders of the change process. What types of facilitating interventions is each person making? To what extent are the individuals working as a team?

CONDUCT A STUDY

1. In a school district where a districtwide innovation such as a new curriculum or perhaps a new technology has been introduced, conduct a survey of six schools expected to be implementing it and randomly selected. Construct a chart on a large piece of chart paper, listing the 10 principles with a brief description of each principle down the left (vertical) side. On the horizontal continuum, place the name of each of the surveyed schools at the top of the column. Under the name of each school, make two columns labeling one *Principal* and the second *Teachers*. This prepares your chart, on which you will record your findings by filling in the cells with information obtained from the principal and the teachers that you interview.

2. Interview the principal and two teachers individually (this should be done confidentially–do not reveal your sources), soliciting from them indicators of the presence or absence of each principle. Compare the responses of the teachers with the administrator. Share the results with the administrator and other persons responsible for facilitating the implementation effort.

3. Conduct a follow-up study. Share the results (above) with the central office staff responsible for implementation. Using the same chart, interview these subjects every month (for the next four months) to ascertain if/what interventions have been provided that address the ignored principles. At the conclusion, share the results with this group.

ADDITIONAL READINGS/RESOURCES

Abrahamson, E. (2004). *Change without pain*. Boston: Harvard Business Press.

Deutschman, S. (2007). *Change or die*. New York: HarperCollins.

Kotter, J. (2005). *Our iceberg is melting*. New York: St. Martin's Press.

Kotter, J. (2008). *A sense of urgency*. Boston: Harvard Business Press.

Reigeluth, C. M., & Garfinkle, R. J. (1994). *Systemic change in education*. Englewood Cliffs, NJ: Educational Technology Publications.

Sarason, S. B. (1996). *Revisiting "The culture of the school and the problem of change."* New York: Teachers College Press.

CHAPTER 2

DEVELOPING PROFESSIONAL LEARNING COMMUNITIES

I am so happy in my new job. I am part of the cheese department team for our largest market. Our team meets to decide on purchases, pricing, and such. We know that we are successful because of customers' satisfaction and the profit and loss sheet.

—Staff person in a Whole Foods store

Our principal expects us to work together on instruction but provides no time in our schedule to do this; furthermore, he makes all the decisions about our classrooms anyway.

—Fifth-grade teacher

Can you believe it? The school board added several days to our contract year, and spread those days across the school year, so our middle school teachers have time to meet share and learn new instructional strategies.

—Middle school principal

Did you know? The faculty and administrators in my children's schools get together regularly just like my medical doctors do to learn the latest and most effective ways to teach children. And to review individual student learning problems. Are we lucky in this district, or what?

—Parent in a local school district

Our dean is encouraging faculty to meet, to assess how we are impacting our students, and to engage, ourselves, in learning new ways to enable all students to be successful in the new workplace demands for employment.

—College history professor

Numerous researchers and practitioners agree: The culture in which organizations function, whether they are public sector schools, private corporate entities, or others, has a profound influence on the individual in the organization and on his or her individual and collective productivity. A growing literature has been developing, as researchers and writers strive to understand this phenomenon and to promote the professional learning community (PLC) as the ideal cultural context. Is your organization's culture one of "continuous assessment," "continuous learning," "continuous improvement of effectiveness," or "laissez faire—we've done it this way for forty years and it works." Hmm, does it work well? And, what exactly is *culture?*

Scholar/practitioner Edgar Schein (1992) maintains that "the culture of a group can now be defined as a pattern of shared basic assumptions that the group learned as it solved its problems . . . that has worked well enough to be considered valid and, therefore, to be taught to new members as the correct way to perceive, think, and feel in relation to those problems" (p. 12).

In today's social, economic, and educational environments, it is difficult—nay, impossible—to ignore the assessment and consequent adjustment, modification, or change of one's organizational culture.

According to Trice and Beyer (1993), it is imperative for leaders of change efforts to be conscious of their organizations' cultures, to recognize dysfunctional elements, and to attempt to guide cultural evolution so that the organization can survive. Schein (1992) argues that leaders must manage cultures or "the cultures will manage them. . . . Cultural understanding is essential to leaders if they are to lead" (p. 15). Guiding, leading, or managing culture is not yet well understood, but much attention is being given to it. More research in today's schools and businesses begs to be done, so that we might have better understanding of it and how a PLC culture can be initiated, "managed," and assessed for continuous improvement in the operation and productivity of the corporate and public sectors.

FOCUS QUESTIONS

1. What are the origins of the learning organization or PLC culture?
2. What is a research-based definition of PLC?
3. What values can be gained in a culture that is conducive to change and improvement?
4. How would the professionals, and all staff, interact in such a context?
5. What would the leadership of a school or business enterprise be like where the focus is on the professional development of all, and the norm is continuous improvement in teaching and learning?
6. How would the change process work in the learning organization/PLC culture?

For a long time, organizational culture has been a subject of inquiry in the corporate world. Although schools have been likewise interested, until recently educators have given little attention to this topic. To provide simplicity and for purposes of this chapter, we offer this everyday garden-variety definition of culture:

> *Culture is the individually and socially constructed values, norms, and beliefs about an organization and how it should behave that can be measured only by observation of the setting using qualitative methods.*

Boyd (1992b) points out that the culture (people or human factors) and the situational variables (physical or structural factors) interact to make up the context and that these two sets of variables are difficult to separate in terms of their individual and collective effects during the change process. Nonetheless, these concepts are important for understanding change in organizational settings. They can offer very important and useful additions to the change facilitator's portfolio of knowledge, skill, and understandings.

This chapter looks at the school organization's culture embedded in its context and how it interacts with the individuals engaged in the organization's work. We know that institutions, or organizations, do not change; individuals do. We know also that, although the individuals change the organization, the organization has a profound influence on its people.

REFLECTION QUESTIONS

Think of these three words: *professional, community, learning.* **What kind of mental pictures does each stimulate for you? Describe your pictures.**

ORIGINS OF ORGANIZATIONAL CULTURE AND PROFESSIONAL LEARNING COMMUNITY

Obviously organizational productivity is affected by individual staff members' productivity. Consequently, most organizations are encouraged to remain open to the creative talents of their members and to implementation of innovations and improvements that will best serve their clients. These expectations are assumed to be true for schools as well as the corporate sector. Therefore, whether in the corporate sector or in schools, attending to the staff's work-related needs is imperative. Those studying workplace cultures of both schools and business have identified important messages for school improvers.

Five Disciplines

Senge (1990) was not the first to study and write about organizational culture, Argyris (1982), Deal and Kennedy (1982), Likert (1967), McGregor (1960), Schein (1985), and others have analyzed and commented (sometimes profusely) about the organizational culture of corporations and how people in particular settings can work more effectively. In addition. Deal and Peterson (1990), Boyd (1992b), and Boyd and Hord (1994) have identified factors that describe school organizational cultures that support the current, and likely the future, unprecedented demands on schools to change.

Senge's (1990) thinking about work in the corporate setting, reported in *The Fifth Discipline,* captured the attention of educational leaders struggling to persuade schools to become interested in change and improvement. Senge, looking to the work of Argyris (1982), identified factors that individuals and their organizations collectively need in order to establish a predisposition for change and to become a learning organization. Five disciplines, or ways of thinking and interacting in the organization, represent these factors.

The first discipline is *systems thinking,* a consideration of the whole system that also recognizes the parts and their patterns and interrelationships (see Chapter 9). The systems approach makes it possible to structure interrelationships more effectively. This discipline integrates the other four, fusing them into a coherent body.

Building a shared vision, the second discipline, is the construction of compelling images shared by the organization's members and focused on what the organization wants to create. These shared pictures of the future foster genuine commitment.

Personal mastery, the third discipline, is the practice of continually clarifying and making personal vision more precise, identifying what each individual wants in his or her personal participation in the organization. Senge believes that unless all personal visions are included, there can be no shared vision.

The fourth discipline, the use of *mental models,* involves separating what has truly been observed from the assumptions and generalizations that people make based on their observations. Here, individuals reveal their assumptions for all to examine.

The final discipline, *team learning,* is the activity of coming together to discuss and to learn with and from each other. Developing team learning skills involves each individual balancing his or her own goals and advocacy to achieve collaborative decision making that serves the well-being of all.

This description of the interactive, collegial, vision- and decision-sharing learning organization can be found in the educational setting (Boyd & Hord, 1994)—and it is this new and infrequently found school culture that commands our attention and challenges our action.

Seventeen Factors

Boyd (1992a), reviewing a wide range of the literature on organizational context in the public and private sectors, identified 17 indicators that describe an educational context conducive to change. These 17 factors were clustered into four functional groupings by Boyd and Hord (1994): (a) reducing isolation, seeking to bring staff together into closer proximity so that interacting and working together is supported; (b) increasing staff capacity, which uses professional development to increase the staff's knowledge and skills to work together collaboratively; (c) providing a caring, productive environment that addresses not only the factors that support productive work but also the affective factors that contribute to the staff feeling valued and cared about; and (d) promoting increased quality, in which the staff members continuously assess their work in order to increase their own effectiveness and that of the school. Figure 2.1 shows how the 17 indicators relate to the functional groupings.

These factors were found actively operating in the Driscoll Square School, which was being studied by the Leadership for Change (LFC) Project of the Southwest Educational Development Laboratory (Hord, 1992b, 1993). The LFC staff was interested in understanding how schools and their leaders go about the work of school change. The Driscoll School

---

GUIDING PRINCIPLES OF ORGANIZATIONAL CULTURE

1. Organizations adopt change; individuals implement change.
2. The organizational culture influences the work of individuals.
3. Organizations must value and support individuals in change efforts.
4. There are identifiable factors that describe the context of the learning organization culture.
5. Leadership for change facilitation is shared among all participants of a PLC.
6. The unceasing quest for increased effectiveness drives the PLC.

FIGURE 2.1   Indicators of a Context Conducive to Change

REDUCING ISOLATION

Schedules and structures that reduce isolation
Policies that foster collaboration
Policies that provide effective communication
Collegial relationships among teachers
A sense of community in the school

INCREASING STAFF CAPACITY

Policies that provide greater autonomy
Policies that provide staff development
Availability of resources
Norm of involvement in decision making

PROVIDING A CARING, PRODUCTIVE ENVIRONMENT

Positive teacher attitudes toward schooling, students, and change
Students' heightened interest and engagement with learning
Positive, caring student–teacher–administrator relationships
Supportive community attitudes
Parents and community members as partners and allies

PROMOTING INCREASED QUALITY

Norm of continuous critical inquiry
Norm of continuous improvement
Widely shared vision or sense of purpose

strongly exemplified the descriptors of Senge's (1990) "learning organization" and Boyd's (1992a) 17 indicators of a context conducive to school change. The Driscoll School can be characterized as a PLC (Boyd & Hord, 1994), which is one whose professional staff meets regularly and frequently to reflect on and inquire into its practices and to learn together and take action on that learning for the benefit of students. The brief picture of this school's culture and other elements of its context presented in *The Driscoll Square School Difference* vignette is illuminating.

■ ■ ■ ■ ■ ▬▬▬▬▬▬▬▬▬▬▬▬▬▬▬▬▬▬▬▬▬▬▬▬▬▬▬▬▬▬▬▬▬

V I G N E T T E

THE DRISCOLL SQUARE SCHOOL DIFFERENCE

The Driscoll Square School, an elementary school built in 1923, is located in a large city on the fringe of the downtown industrial area. Like many schools in older urban cities, its population decreased as more and more people moved to the suburbs. Because of the decline in enrollment, the school was slated to be closed. However, a few tenacious parents prevailed, and it was saved—but as an open enrollment school, which meant that it had to generate an enrollment large enough to justify keeping the doors open.

A new principal brought the vision of a child-centered school and shared authority for those working with the children. The formerly ill-maintained school soon sparkled with children's art,

VIGNETTE CONTINUED

music, singing, and dance. Each day now starts with Morning Meeting, when all children and staff meet in the basement to celebrate children's birthdays and accomplishments: a first-grader reading his first primer aloud to the audience, third-graders demonstrating a Native American dance, and fifth- and sixth-graders modeling how peer mediation helps to solve disagreements without fisticuffs.

Another regular event is Faculty Study on Thursdays, during which all faculty get together as a total group some weeks and as grade groups on others. This 2-hour block of time was gained by extending the instructional day 4 days a week and abbreviating it on Thursday, an arrangement that was reached after much lobbying and the signing of documents that declared that no teacher was coerced into accepting this agreement. These structures and schedules form the basis of the school's "learning community" in which all individuals refer to themselves as "family." They proclaim that the "Driscoll Difference" represents their essence. And what does this essence—their philosophy, values, and beliefs about children—look like operationally?

ANALYSIS

Morning Meeting has established a feeling that "we are all together in this enterprise," meaning that all adults and all children are involved. Further, since all teachers "own" all children, no teacher hesitates to take whatever kind of action seems appropriate with any of the children. Most of the faculty eat lunch in one room, where they share interests, concerns, and congratulations about all the children and themselves. Because the school is crowded, there was some consideration of using this area for a classroom. But after much soul searching, the faculty determined that their program and ways of operating would not be able to continue as effectively without this common meeting space.

Faculty Study makes it possible for the entire staff to be in one place at one time on a regular basis, with enough time to study and learn together, identify and solve problems, consider issues, and stay together on any and all matters. This has resulted in the development of the following important cultural norms:

1. A widely held vision of what the school should be
2. Broadly based decision making across the faculty that includes a management team that energetically represents the teachers' views
3. Widely distributed and inclusive leadership wherein everyone takes responsibility to bring new ideas, help each other implement the ideas, and share the leadership function, so that the group operates differently from an organization with a "hero leader"
4. A pervasive attachment to critical inquiry that challenges faculty to regularly say to themselves:
   - What are we doing for our children?
   - Is there a better way?
   - Let's try it! (This is an expression of Little's [1982] "norms of collegiality and experimentation.")
5. A norm of continuous, seamless improvement

In this culture, there is no fear about introducing and implementing change. Change is valued and sought as a means of achieving improved effectiveness; change and improvement are introduced by everyone and are a way of life. However, adoption and implementation are not done frivolously. Much thought and study are given to changes and whether their implementation will support and/or enhance the school's mission.

(continued)

■ ■ ■ ■ ■ ▬▬▬▬▬▬▬▬▬▬▬▬▬▬▬▬▬▬▬▬▬▬▬▬

V I G N E T T E   CONTINUED

VIGNETTE CRITIQUE QUESTIONS

1. Do you know of a school that exemplifies the kind of culture described at Driscoll? How did this culture develop at the school?
2. What is the role of the principal and/or key teachers in the development and operation of a school that acts as collegially as Driscoll does?
3. Discuss the advantages and disadvantages, in terms of change process, for schools that operate as Driscoll does.

THE PLC CONTEXT AND CULTURE

Rosenholz (1989) first brought teachers' workplace factors into the discussion of teaching quality by maintaining that teachers who felt supported in their own ongoing learning and classroom practice were more committed and effective than those who were not supported. Such support was manifested as teachers worked together, sharing their craft and wisdom, learning from each other, and collaborating on problems and issues of concern to them. This support increased teacher efficacy, which meant that they gave more attention to students' needs and adopted new classroom behaviors more readily.

Darling-Hammond (1996), Lieberman (1995), Little (1982), and McLaughlin and Talbert (1993) agreed with Rosenholz and have been increasingly clear and insistent about the need to provide teachers with a context that supports their professional endeavors and nurtures their collaborative efforts. Their research has revealed the influence of the work-place culture on teachers' practices and, consequently, on outcomes for students. Darling-Hammond observed that workplaces that are supportive of teachers are few and far between and that attention must be focused on rethinking the organizational arrangements of the work setting.

Typically, schoolwide change efforts have been short term and lacking in participation by the entire staff. Encouraging the staff's motivation to change so that improvement in the school is ongoing has been a formidable challenge to school change leaders. If the context of the school affects teachers' ability and inclination to change, what does the research tell us about such school settings?

Dimensions of a Professional Learning Community

The PLC has become widely heralded as the way for professional staff of schools to work for student benefits. The norms of collaboration and democratic participation in decision making, as well as sharing power and authority, contribute to a culture in which the staff grows in professionalism and efficacy. This efficacy instills a confidence that each faculty member is influential in the learning process of his or her students, persuading faculty that each student can learn with the appropriate material and strategies. The PLC is one such approach to a school's culture. In a review of the research on this topic, Hord (2004) identified the five dimensions of

FIGURE 2.2   Dimensions of Professional Learning Communities

Shared values and vision: The staff's unswerving commitment to students' learning, which is referenced for the staff's work

Collective learning and application: The identification and implementation of staff's learning in order to more effectively address students' needs

Supportive and shared leadership: Jointly held power and authority that involve the staff in decision making

Supportive conditions: Physical and human capacities that promote collaborative organizational arrangements and relationships

Shared personal practice: Feedback and assistance from peers that support individual and community improvement

PLCs as follows: (a) shared values and vision, (b) intentional collective learning and application, (c) supportive and shared leadership, (d) supportive conditions, and (e) shared personal practice (see Figure 2.2).

Shared Values and Vision.   In the schools where the professional staff—administrators and teachers—is organized in learning communities, staff shares an undeviating focus on student learning. The staff assumes that students are academically able and create visions of the learning environment that will enable each student to realize his or her potential. In this community, each individual member is responsible for his or her own actions, but the common good is uppermost. The relationships of the individuals are described as caring, and they are encouraged by open communication and trust. The vision of the PLC maintains a focus on quality in the work of the staff and the students.

Intentional Learning and Application.   In the PLC, individuals rigorously study student performance data from a wide variety of sources. They determine where students have succeeded and work together collaboratively to identify areas where students have not performed well. These areas become the focus of attention and exploration of new practices to address the students' learning needs. This approach requires the staff's engagement in intentional learning in how to use the new practices effectively. The conversations that staff has about students, learning, and teaching form the basis for decisions about what to learn and how to learn it, so that staff's learning addresses students' learning needs. As a result of these learning conversations and interactions, decisions are made collectively and new content and instructional strategies are used in classroom practice. The intentional collegial learning and widely shared decision making are in turn applied to action and new practice, thus expanding the repertoire of all. Schools where the staff is sharing, learning, and acting on its learning produce increased learning outcomes for students.

Supportive and Shared Leadership.   If a school staff is working collaboratively and making decisions, the role of the principal remains a highly significant one, with the principal participating with the staff as a learner and contributing democratically to decision making. This new relationship leads to a collegial leadership in which all staff members are growing and playing on the same team. Three factors are required of principals whose school staff is operating as a PLC: a need to share authority, the ability to facilitate the work of the staff, and the capacity to participate without dominating. Key characteristics of principal leadership will be described in detail in Chapter 6.

Supportive Conditions.   Supportive conditions provide the infrastructure and basic requirements of the when, where, and how the staff can collectively come together as a whole to learn, to make decisions, to do creative problem solving, and to implement new practices—actions that are characteristic of the PLC. Two types of conditions are necessary: (a) physical or structural conditions and (b) the human qualities or capacities of the people involved. Examples of each type follow.

Physical Conditions.   These factors include the time to meet and interact, the size of the school and proximity of the staff to each other, communication procedures, and resources. Schedules and structures that reduce isolation of the staff are important so that they can come together. Policies that foster collaboration and provide for staff development should be in place. Time is a vital resource and the hardest to find. This factor is bedeviling and currently being explored so that more creative ways may be found to create time for staff to meet and to learn collaboratively.

People Capacities.   Positive teacher attitudes toward students, schooling, and change are found among staff in PLC arrangements. Staff's heightened interest in continuous learning and norms of critical inquiry and improvement are routinely in place. Staff's openness to feedback, which typically assumes trust among the individuals involved, must be developed for the PLC to operate optimally.

In one of the early schools that we discovered operating as a community of professional learners, multiple activities were created by the staff to support its learning and working together, along with social activities that allowed staff members to know each other and to develop positive relationships and trust. One of these was a regular once-every-2-weeks, Thursday, after-school volleyball game in the school's basement gymnasium. On the alternate week on Friday after school, the staff convened at the local ice cream parlor to share the week's successes and concerns. Not to create the staff's social agenda, but to provide a forum for interaction, food, and brotherhood/sisterhood, was a monthly potluck supper served on a rotating basis in a staff member's home. These venues made opportunities for getting acquainted, learning about each other, breaking the barriers of isolation, and promoting comfort with each other.

Shared Personal Practice.   In the PLC, teachers visit each other's classrooms to review their teaching behavior. This practice is in the spirit of peers supporting peers. In these visits, teachers observe, script notes, and discuss observations after the visit. Making time for these activities is difficult, but the process contributes to the individual's and the community's improvement. Mutual trust and respect are imperative. The staff must develop trust and caring relationships with each other. These relationships develop through both professional problem-solving activities and social interactions of the staff. As a result, the staff finds support for each other's triumphs and troubles.

In terms of the change process, when a school staff learns and works collaboratively in a PLC culture, the outcomes for the staff are significant, as reported by Hord (2004) in the literature review. Not only do teachers express more satisfaction and higher morale (school climate factors), but they also make teaching adaptations for students, and these changes are done more quickly than in traditional schools. In such a context, teachers make a commitment to making significant and lasting changes, and they are more likely to undertake fundamental, systemic change.

Structure of the PLC Dimensions

The end result of the PLC dimensions is the intentional learning of the participants and their application of the learning in their classrooms or other organizational settings. These dimensions are interactive, and to identify one as more important than others is frustrating, as all serve to support and sustain the work of the PLC as it goes about its self-initiated work. In Figure 2.3 (Hord & Hirsh, 2008), we see Shared Values and Vision, Shared and Supportive Leadership, Supportive Conditions (detailed here as Structural Conditions and Relational Conditions), and Peer-to-Peer Support (Shared Personal Practice) combined as a frame that encloses the heart and soul of the PLC, the learning of its participants. This collective learning, intentionally determined by the PLC members and based on their study of student performance data, vitally and without ceasing contributes to quality teaching and student learning. The frame of the five dimensions supports the PLC in its targeted dimension: professional learning.

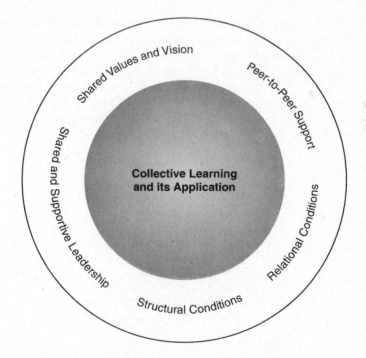

FIGURE 2.3   Two Dimensions of Professional Learning Communities

Source: From Corwin Press, *Sustaining Professional Learning Communities.* (2008). A. M. Blankstein, P. D. Houston, & R. W. Cole (Eds.), p. 35.

Who Is the Professional Learning Community?

As noted earlier in relation to the dimensions of a PLC, sharing of ideas and responsibilities is important. The bringing of ideas and taking responsibility are assumed by the community of professionals in schools at the campus setting or at the district level. Essentially, all professional staff—administrators, teachers, counselors, and others—are involved in reflecting on their practice and its benefits for their clients—in this case, students. They assess what they do for students and whether their various instructional practices are or are not resulting in appropriate effects. If not, they identify what they need to learn to do differently in order to change so that their students are successful learners. As noted in Figure 2.4, students are always at the heart of the community's conversation and efforts, but it is the campus professionals who have the responsibility and are accountable to serve students well. In addition to the professional community, increasing circles of individuals influence by their actions and policies (school board, parents, district office, community citizens) the work of the campus professionals. This structure is depicted in Figure 2.4.

Benefits of a Professional Learning Community

The research that has been conducted on PLCs reveals benefits that accrue to the staff and to students in a variety of settings and arrangements.

Schools.   Lee, Smith, and Croninger (1995) conducted an extensive study, sharing findings on 11,000 students enrolled in 820 secondary schools across the nation. In the schools characterized as PLC, the staff worked together and changed its classroom pedagogy. As a result, students were engaged in high intellectual learning tasks, and they achieved greater academic gains in math, science, history, and reading than those in traditionally organized schools. In addition, the achievement gaps among students from different family backgrounds were smaller in these schools, students learned more, and, in the smaller high schools, learning was distributed more equitably.

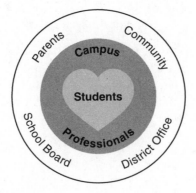

FIGURE 2.4   Who Is the Community?

Source: Achieving Learning Success for Each Student: Transforming Intentions into Reality. Northwest Regional Educational Laboratory for the Association Partnership including AASA, NAESP, NASSP, Portland, Oregon.

The schools in the study were communally organized, and this arrangement promoted staff and students to commitment to the mission of the school; staff and students worked together to strengthen the mission. In these schools, teachers envisioned themselves as responsible for the total development of the students, and they shared a collective responsibility for the success of all students. In addition, the teachers and other staff expressed more satisfaction and higher morale, students cut fewer classes, and the dropout rate was lower. Both staff and students contributed to lower rates of absenteeism.

In a study by Bobbett, Ellett, Teddlie, Olivier, and Rugutt (2002), the researchers found in a study of Louisiana schools that a strong positive relationship existed between teachers' professional commitment found in the professional culture of the schools and school performance of the students. The school's professional culture was the strongest predictor of school performance in the elementary schools in the study. After statistically controlling for the effects of poverty, teachers' professional commitment and collegial teaching and learning in the school culture accounted for a large amount of the variation (23%) among schools in school effectiveness and outcomes (on school test scores).

Leadership Teams.   In an evaluation study in Louisiana, the external evaluator and external facilitators noted that in Louisiana Alliance schools the principal, external facilitators, and leadership team supported the faculty's implementation of the Collaborative School Reform model. These leaders provided abundant guidance and assistance to the teachers in using the model. (For further discussion, see "Leadership and Interaction in a Professional Learning Community.") In those schools where there was more support, and subsequently more frequent meetings of the teachers in subgroups and the whole group engaging in community conversations occurred, the degree of implementation of the process was greater. This higher level of implementation was associated with increased student gains on the state accountability measures (Rood & Hinson, 2002).

REFLECTION QUESTIONS
In which setting do you believe that the PLC could be most beneficial: schools, leadership teams, or university? What is your rationale for your belief?

University.   In yet a different setting, Gonzalez, Resta, and De Hoyos (2005) looked at the barriers and facilitators related to the implementation of policy initiatives to transform the teaching-learning process in higher education. The transformation required a different approach to classroom instruction, and this was mandated by the highest level of the university's administration. After several years of staff development to support the faculty in changing their instructional practices and an effort to develop PLCs of the faculty, a study showed that faculty members who perceived they were part of a PLC expressed concerns about their impact on students. Those teachers who did not view themselves as having membership in a PLC expressed concerns for managing their classrooms and other time and logistical management issues. If these outcomes can be attributed to the presence of a PLC culture, what roles can leaders play, or what strategies do they employ to create and maintain a PLC?

LEADERSHIP AND INTERACTION IN A PLC

In a series of articles for the National Staff Development Council's journal, *Journal of Staff Development*, Hord traced the development of teachers' roles from that of individual entrepreneur, to collaborator with other teachers in project work, to participant in PLC decision making about adult learning necessary to support students' successful performance (Hord, 2007; Hord, 2008; Hord, 2009). For this latter role to become possible, school administrators and teachers will experience a shift in their relationship so that they work on a more level plane in a more collegial environment. Although Hargreaves (1997) does not use the term *PLC*, he suggests that "the central task in creating cultures of educational change is to develop more collaborative working relationships between principals and teachers and among teachers themselves" (p. 2). According to Schmoker (1997), school personnel are being asked, many of them for the first time, to be "thinking contributors who can generate solutions to emergent problems and obstacles. This is something new . . . [to be] brought together—regularly—to be asked for their suggestions, to develop real solutions to the most pressing concerns students face" (p. 143). Similarly, Zmuda, Kuklis, and Kline (2004) have maintained that a competent system necessitates several important changes that resonate here, "from an environment of isolation to one of collegiality . . . from individual autonomy to collective autonomy and collective accountability" (p. 1).

Collegial Learning

Collegial learning provides a means for enabling the culture of educational change. Thus, in their study of change, Caine and Caine (1997) quoted a teacher as saying that "actively processing in a social context is increasing my learning" (p. 197). And, in a poetic form, Wheatley and Kellner-Rogers (1996) exclaimed "that life leaps forward when it can share its learning" (p. 34). By supporting individual members, organizational learning can offer a very promising avenue to more successful change processes. This kind of organizational culture fosters mutual respect and regard, high levels of trust, and innovative solutions to problems. The faculty experiences the social and emotional support that these cultures produce. The staff is intellectually challenged by its peers and work and develops higher intellectual learning tasks for students. Teachers' conversations with other staff strengthens their content knowledge and broadens the repertoire of instructional strategies teachers bring to their students.

In schools where the staff exemplifies the learning organization, the principal is not "the sage on stage," as some have suggested, but "the guide on the side." The requirement to understand and consider the implementer's concerns and evolving use of new practices does not diminish. And the leadership actions and strategies necessary to support implementation remain de rigueur. It is how the leadership role plays out that differs.

Sharing Responsibilities

In the learning organization context, all members of the staff share the leadership role, although the nominal leader remains the point person. Ultimate responsibility must not be abandoned, and the positional leader (principal, superintendent, etc.) assumes and maintains this responsibility—but operationally in a less visible and more democratic way. Everyone on the staff contributes ideas for change, and everyone contributes to the interventions or strategies needed for high-quality implementation (discussed in Chapter 7). The staff participates with peers in these strategies and facilitates implementation:

Developing a shared vision

Planning and providing resources

Investing in professional learning

Checking on progress

Providing continuous assistance

Creating a context conducive to change

With the sharing of tasks, the obligation of any one individual is lessened—and strengthened. Each individual has the opportunity to be involved in a highly active, committed way. Over time, the opportunities are accepted, and expectations and norms are established for continuing this kind of behavior. The staff values its role of involvement as decision makers and facilitators of improvement. They experience a new dimension of their efficacy as professionals. In this way, the entire staff develops facilitating leadership that supports change. The first step in making such a support structure possible is for school and district leaders to declare high-quality professional learning for all faculty as part of the daily work. They make it a priority goal within their settings.

Using Conversations

It has been suggested that the PLC is a network of conversations. This being the case, the role of leaders is to support the conversations with the physical conditions necessary for the staff to meet: time, a location, and policies that support the time that the staff invests in its community of conversations. Change leaders must also attend to the emotional and interpersonal needs and skills of the participants. Thus, developing the skills of the staff in active listening, setting aside assumptions while in the conversation, and trying to understand each other's comments and making meaning of them are all necessary skills to be developed.

Additional attention must be given by leaders to enabling the community to articulate a shared system of beliefs, explanations, and values, which is continually sustained by further conversations (Capra, 1997). In a study that asked hundreds of executives and employees to describe the quality of conversations (as a Core Business Process) that had a powerful impact on them, Brown and Isaacs (1997, cited by Capra) reported about respondents' comments:

There was a sense of mutual respect between us.

We took the time to really talk and reflect about what we each thought was important.

We listened to each other, even if there were differences.

I was accepted and not judged by the others in the conversation.

We explored questions that mattered.

We developed a shared meaning that wasn't there when we began.

Types of Leadership

Capra (1997) clarified that two types of leadership are needed for conversation and community work. The first is the traditional idea of a leader—the person who is able to formulate the mission of the organization, to sustain it, and to communicate it well. The other kind of leadership is what facilitates the development and evolution of the community. This latter type is not limited to a single individual but is distributed, and its responsibility becomes a capacity of the whole. This means that the building up and nurturing of conversations occurs in a climate of warmth, mutual support, and trust, with continual questioning and rewarding of innovation. Thus, leadership means creating conditions, rather than giving directions, and includes the freedom to make mistakes. Although the spirit of disagreement and debate is present, these communities are caring communities as well as learning communities.

Other Leadership Ideas to Be Considered

Positional leaders model the democratic participation that they hope to engender in staff. They hire new staff with strong values of collaboration and collegiality, and they reward continuous learning among teachers. They identify and support the acquisition of additional skills and models that focus on resolving conflict, using data for decision making, using criteria for making selection of new practices, and using criteria for selecting research results to be used by the group in improving its practice.

In *Educational Leadership* (February, 2009), Hord and Hirsh identified the approaches that principals use to support strong learning communities of professionals: emphasize to

IMPLICATIONS FOR LEADERS FACILITATING CHANGE

The local board of education must support, encourage, and persuade the school staff to engage in collaborative work. They do this by providing districtwide time across all schools for the staff to meet as a community. Further, the board communicates to the district community the purpose and benefits to be derived for their children when the professional staff meet and work in this way.

The superintendent of a district and the principal of a school are key to the creation and maintenance of any culture; most certainly this is true of PLCs. Therefore, these positional leaders must make certain that logistical and organizational arrangements are available to support the PLC.

Skills for operating as a PLC must be developed across the entire staff; otherwise, the PLC will not be productive. This suggests that the central office staff has roles to play in developing the capacity of campus-based administrators and teachers to work collaboratively.

An enduring focus should guide the PLC's work, and that focus is always on student results.

There should be accountability measures for the PLC's work (i.e., objectives that focus on outcomes for students, an agenda, activities to reach objectives, minutes of the meetings).

teachers that you know they can succeed—together; expect teachers to keep knowledge fresh; guide the communities toward self-governance; make data accessible; teach discussion and decision-making skills; show teachers the research; take time to build trust. Obviously, the principal will need to be current with regard to the research and up to date on data analysis skills. The administrator will also be required to share authority, power, and decision making; participate democratically in the learning community with the teachers; and help them develop discussion and decision-making skills.

In collaborative learning school cultures, principals remain key to shaping the norms, values, and beliefs of the staff. Principals shape culture in the multiple daily interactions they have with the school community. Kent Peterson (Allen, 2003), who has studied and written about school culture for many years, has described the principal as a potter who builds culture through hiring, budget, and supervisory decisions; the principal is a poet whose written and oral messages can reinforce a healthy culture; the principal is an actor on all the stages of school events; and the principal is a healer who can help repair the culture when tragedy, conflict, or loss occurs. Such actions by the principal and other leaders produce schools that are anchored in relationships and intellectual tasks that stimulate and challenge each member of the community to be his or her very best.

REFLECTION QUESTION

What are the most effective means for developing these skills and becoming effective in using the tools in the PLC membership?

Pothole Warning

The ultimate and most important question for a PLC is how the culture or work ethic of a PLC affects student learning results. Beware of this focus becoming skewed and slipping.

Pothole Repair

One of the middle schools that we have studied uses a lens through which it examines every decision to be taken: "Is it good for students? If not, forget it."

STRATEGIES FOR FACILITATING A PROFESSIONAL LEARNING CULTURE

We know a retired high school principal and central office curriculum specialist, hired to "turn a poor performing high school around," who addressed his urban high school staff at its initial meeting in this way:

> This year . . . the conversation . . . will be about students . . . and learning . . . student learning and staff learning.
>
> *Note:* The ellipses (. . .) indicate pauses.

This simple message was delivered in a clear, well-modulated voice, with a calm but smiling demeanor. This principal knew that a single statement would not gain desired results; therefore, this first pronouncement was followed by consistent questions, comments, and interactions daily with staff and students:

- Mrs. Falkland, what did you learn about John Smith's reading challenge?
- Mr. Kaiser, I've been reading this book on physics instruction and wondered if you've tried this strategy on page forty-six?
- Mary Alice, how is it going with the journalism course you're taking at the community college? Last week you shared with me about learning to create interest-piquing headlines.
- Josh, are you learning about colleges for a football scholarship that have a well-reputed engineering program that you're interested in?
- Mr. Albrecht, how is your algebra department's study of constructivist teaching and learning progressing? How can I help?

Another high school principal in a rural area we know "snuck up on the blind side" of staff to initiate a PLC. Calling the staff together, he announced that the school board was asking the school to provide a recommendation on whether to require students to wear standard uniforms to school. Soliciting a discussion, the principal encouraged commentary. After lengthy sharing, the staff members volunteered that they were expressing their own points of view and that they recognized they didn't know enough about student uniforms to make a recommendation. After discussing this acknowledgment, the staff and principal determined that they needed to reorganize themselves into small teams to access more information from parents, students, the small business community, and any research studies that had investigated this matter. They agreed to meet in 2 weeks to share their learning.

When they met again and reported, they realized they had no solid knowledge about the expenses they would be imposing on parents. Thus, they reorganized to inquire of clothing suppliers and other schools that had experienced such a change. Staff members noted that they were surprised they did not have adequate knowledge to make an immediate decision. Not long thereafter, the staff agreed on a recommendation, sharing its sources of information used in the process. The principal noted that

> they had collaborated in identifying what they needed to know, and where to seek it in order to learn about required student uniforms.

Further, he noted that in engaging in these activities, the staff members had engaged with each other as a PLC. Thus, he labeled their activities after they had experienced them—and strongly applauded their efforts. Before he adjourned this meeting, he announced that in 2 weeks they would meet for a half day to study their just-arrived student data so that they might celebrate those academic areas in which students had been successful learners and identify where focused attention was required. In this way, he was leading them to further exploration of students needs—and what they would do about it.

REFLECTION QUESTIONS

Would one of these approaches work for you? What would be a good alternative to launching staff into the work of a PLC?

We have seen a wide array of strategies and techniques that leaders may use to launch and develop a culture of collaboration. A final set of ideas, from Knapp, Copland, and Talbert (2003), contributes to the knowledge base of school leaders who build work cultures around learning:

- Create structures for regular staff interaction about learning and teaching.
- Set up cycles of schoolwide inquiry into learning and teaching performance.
- Identify and address staff assumptions about norms, values, and beliefs related to learning.
- Recruit teachers who work from a values base consistent with the culture that leaders seek to develop.
- Create opportunities for staff to have a voice in decisions about issues related to teaching and learning.
- Celebrate accomplishments in student and teacher learning.

Clearly, there is much to be done to build a collaborative culture—that is, a PLC—that is focused on continuous improvement.

REFLECTION QUESTIONS

We have consistently promoted the idea of intentional collegial learning for the professionals in our schools and school systems. What could this look like ideally, and how might you start to turn your mental image into reality?

OUR CLOSING PITCH

Joyce, Wolf, and Calhoun (1993) contend that the design and operation of the organization, rather than the staff, have been the major problem in improving schools. This idea can be inferred from our description of the PLC as a preferred arrangement. Further, they maintain that changing the organization will result in increased creativity and vitality of teachers and students. The challenge, then, is to create organizational settings (the school) that honor all individuals (children and adults) in a caring, productive environment that invites and sustains a continuous quest for improvement.

We, the authors, have lived and worked in a "learning organization" of the type that Senge (1990) has described; we have observed and studied a few schools that have the cultural attributes of a learning organization; and we profoundly believe that schools must develop this kind of context if real and continuous change and improvement are to occur. We see this as the educational challenge for the immediate future—and it is our own personal challenge as researchers and improvers. As Wheatley (1992) has suggested,

> We are beginning to look at the strong emotions that are part of being human, rather than . . . believing that we can confine workers into narrow roles, as though they were cogs in the machinery of production. . . . We are focusing on the deep longings we have for community, meaning, dignity, and love in our organizational lives. (p. 12)

SUMMARY

There is wide agreement that the professional culture described in this chapter—one with an efficacious and caring staff, whose *heart* and *mind* are focused on children—is what is needed in schools today. In this chapter we have shared commentary from a wide array of school and organizational theorists and reformers, all of whom extol the virtues of paying attention to organizational culture in the workplace. We have promoted the concept of the PLC as an ideal form of culture in any workplace and in any context. (We have seen such a culture operating in a context of authoritarian, hierarchical decision making, as a subculture that guided the norms and behaviors of a small group of staff members.)

Pothole Warning

Many school leaders assume that providing time for learning teams and the whole faculty learning community to meet will "do the trick." It ain't so. Neither has the abundant emphasis that has been placed on collaborative work as the defining characteristic of the PLC been beneficial. Nor is electing to study and learn about the latest hot topic or innovation du jour a good idea.

Pothole Repair

If the construction of a PLC in your organization seems to be stuck and lacks direction, bring student performance data to a meeting. Ask the members to identify where students are performing well—then celebrate these results. But, also, examine the data for areas where student results are not favorable. Focus on these data and use them to stimulate conversations and actions on what to do about the disappointing outcomes.

Although time and a place for the community to meet is, obviously, vital, it is what goes on in the meeting of the PLC that is important. Consider the three words: *professional* refers to the certified or licensed staff in the school who have the responsibility and accountability for delivering an effective learning program for students; *community* indicates that these people come together in a group whose shared purpose is to *learn*—this adult learning is directly related to the learning needs of students. Thus, the time and place is not for any activity but for the learning of the staff. Similarly, the PLC's purpose is not collaborative work per se, although working collaboratively could be an activity of interest. It is possible that collaborative work could produce learning results for the participants, but whether this by-product provides the learning necessary for the staff to become more effective with their students is problematic.

We have described the PLC in terms of its five dimensions, or ways of operating, as identified from the literature. These dimensions are shared values and vision, intentional collegial learning and its application, supportive and shared leadership, supportive conditions (both physical structures and human capacities), and shared personal practice. We also reported the values and benefits to both the organization's staff and to its clients (in the case of schools and districts, the clients are the students). Frequently, some staff members suggest that their learning should focus on instructional topics under study by a school in the next neighborhood, rather than the area of need dictated by examining their students' performance data. If this topic does not respond to the needs of the staff's students, then staff leadership should guide staff to re-examine student data so that decisions are made based on the data.

Of prime importance, suggestions were made, based on the literature on this topic, about the role, strategies, and actions that leaders must take to initiate, develop, and maintain a PLC. One set of those strategies must focus on supporting the staff members in transferring, or implementing, their learning into their classrooms. Learning how to teach in a constructivist mode is far easier learned in the community than is using these instructional practices in one's classroom when the door is closed. Thus, leaders must be conversant with change process tools and techniques—which, of course, is what the rest of this book is about.

DISCUSSION QUESTIONS

1. Why would you want a school staff to be organized as a PLC?

2. What difference would it make to a school's change efforts if the school's culture were that of a PLC?

3. Discuss the "balance of power" in a staff organized as a PLC.

4. Describe key characteristics of the leadership needed for facilitating change in the learning organization school.

5. What functions does a context that supports change play? Explain why these functions are important.

FIELDWORK ACTIVITIES

1. Identify a school that appears to be developing a PLC culture. Make an instrument of the 17 Boyd and Hord (1994) indicators by adding rating scales to each one. Administer the instrument to the school's leadership or management team. Lead a discussion with them of their results, focusing on where the school is strong and where attention is needed.

2. In the district or region, identify a low-performing and a high-performing school and conduct a qualitative (ethnographic) study that identifies elements of the culture in the organizations. Or conduct this study in your local fire department, tailor shop, or elsewhere, looking for descriptors or indicators of the culture of this workplace.

3. Find a school that has become a PLC. Interview longtime and new staff to solicit (a) current descriptions of the school, (b) descriptions of what the school was like before it changed, and (c) explanations of how it became a PLC.

4. Find a school that is amenable to becoming a PLC. Use interviews with several staff members to describe their vision of such an organization. Conduct a meeting with the school improvement council to plan strategies for recreating the school as a learning organization.

CONDUCT A STUDY

There is a need for additional rigorous research studies that will lead to understanding the contribution of the PLC to the successful planning and implementation of change efforts. Consider one of these topics for study:

1. What skills must the community of professionals develop in order to learn and work together effectively? In addition, what resources are needed to support the community in providing the most effective strategies and the highest-quality instructional programs for students?

2. The most important question for continued study is this: How does the culture of a PLC affect student learning results?

ADDITIONAL READINGS/RESOURCES

Assessment Instrument

Of interest to many people who are working to maintain a PLC in their organizations and to dissertation students who are studying the PLC in schools is the School Staff as Professional Learning Communities instrument. This brief instrument uses the five dimensions of the PLC described in this chapter and enables leaders to assess the degree to which the five dimensions are present in their organizations. For permission to use this copyrighted instrument, contact the Southwest Educational Development Laboratory, www.SEDL.org, (800) 476-6861.

Recent Books

Hord, S. M., Roussin, J., & Sommers, W. A. (2010). *Guiding professional learning communities: Inspiration, challenge, surprise and meaning.* Thousand Oaks, CA: Corwin Press.

Hord, S. M., & Sommers, W. A. (2008). *Leading professional learning communities: Voices from research and practice.* Thousand Oaks, CA: Corwin Press.

Huffman, J. B., & Hipp, K. K., with contributing authors A. M. Pankake, G. Moller, D. F. Olivier, & D. F. Cowan. (2004). *Reculturing schools as professional learning communities.* Lanham, MD: Scarecrow Education.

McLaughlin, M. W., & Talbert, J. E. (2006). *Building school-based teacher learning communities.* New York: Teachers College Press.

Stoll, L., & Louis, K. S. (2007). *Professional learning communities: Divergence, depth and dilemmas.* Berkshire, UK: Open University Press.

PART II

TOOLS AND TECHNIQUES FOR UNDERSTANDING IMPLEMENTATION AT THE INDIVIDUAL LEVEL

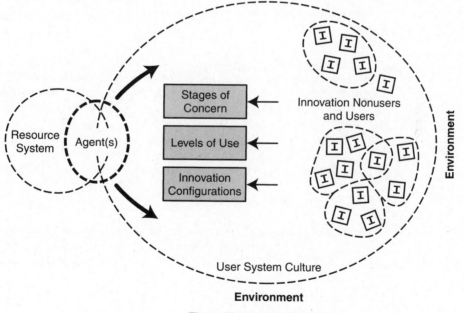

Environment

Three Diagnostic Dimensions

CHAPTER 3

CLARIFYING THE CHANGE
Innovation Configurations

I have just visited three third-grade classrooms to observe the teachers using the new curriculum. Two of them are operating as expected, but the third is way off base.

—Elementary school principal

Why can't they [instructors] just read the lesson as written and do what it says? When you go out in the field, you will not believe some of the things that are going on.

—Curriculum developer

The district mathematics liaison stopped by yesterday and said I was doing a good job! To tell you the truth, I still don't know what I am supposed to be doing, so I just make it up as I go along.

—Middle school teacher

Well, the teacher's guide is so clear and the training gave me the opportunity to practice, so I understand what is expected. I am able to do all of the activities in each lesson just as they are described in the guide and how I saw them in the video examples.

—Social studies teacher

My hospital volunteer group is trying hard to explain to new members what our roles are as nurses' aides—what can we do to describe it better?

—County hospital volunteer

A frequent problem for teachers and others who are expected to implement new practices is that they are not clear about what they are being asked to do. Even when training and materials are provided, there is a big leap from preparing to do something to actually doing it. In the end, what teachers do in the classroom may bear little resemblance to what the creator(s) of the change had in mind originally. All of the teachers may call it the same thing, but in practice what they do may look very different. In this chapter we will examine the *innovation*;

the change itself. How to describe an innovation and how to measure it in classroom use are central themes. A key purpose of this chapter is to identify a concept and tool that can be used to construct a common understanding of what a change can look like for everyone involved.

FOCUS QUESTIONS

1. Should all teachers in a school be doing the same thing in their classrooms relative to reading, science, mathematics, and other subject areas?
2. How can you specify what an intended change is supposed to look like?
3. What key issues result from a lack of clarity about how to use an innovation?
4. How can a clear vision of a change serve as a road map to successful implementation?
5. How can you determine which classroom practices really make a difference in student learning, or which organization's practices contribute best to clients' satisfaction?
6. What is an Innovation Configuration (IC) Map? Who should be involved in developing one?
7. How many components and variations are needed to make a really good IC Map?
8. What are some of the uses of an IC Map?

THE CHANGE: WHAT IT IS AND IS NOT

A major reason that widespread change often occurs only modestly across a school is that the implementers, change facilitators, and policymakers do not fully understand what the change is or what it will look like when it is implemented in the envisioned way. When there is such confusion, principals and other facilitators may give conflicting signals, and teachers will create their own versions of the change as they try to understand and use the materials and/or processes that have been advocated. Evaluators then have serious difficulties in appraising whether the new way is better than the old. This is particularly problematic when what is being done under the name of the innovation is different in various classrooms. This phenomenon led those of us working with the Concerns-Based Adoption Model (CBAM) to add a third diagnostic dimension to the paradigm—Innovation Configurations (IC)—and that is the topic of this chapter.

Before describing Innovation Configurations, a definitional issue must be addressed. For any change or innovation there will be one or more architects, or creators. They may be national expert(s) or local developer(s). Frequently the creators of an innovation are curriculum experts from outside the school or district, such as a national project or publishing house. Other changes emerge when a local team or committee of teachers, who have experimented in their classrooms, develop an approach that they wish to share with others. Still other changes are driven by local school boards, state legislatures, and federal policies; some are even initiated by court decisions. In the CBAM approach to change, we have used the term *developer* to represent any and all of these sources.

REFLECTION QUESTIONS

What difference would it make, if any, whether a new program or practice— innovation—was created by a local or external developer? Have you had the experience of working with both a local and a national developer? What comparisons can you make about these two sources of the change?

INNOVATION ADAPTATION

The concept of IC addresses both the idealized images of a change created by a developer as well as the various operational forms of the change that can be observed in classrooms. The focus in the IC diagnostic dimension is on developing and applying word-picture descriptions of what the use of an innovation can look like—that is, how does it look in *operation,* what are individuals *doing* related to the innovation.

Previously, a typical means of determining whether a new program or process was being used in classrooms was to count how many classrooms contained the program materials. Alternatively, *use* of the new way would be assumed because the teachers had participated in a workshop or the principal would report that teachers were doing it.

The uncertainty of whether there was high-quality use of a new program or process was discovered early in the original CBAM verification studies. The implementation of two innovations was being studied: teacher teaming in elementary schools and college professors' use of instructional modules. In each case, when the so-called users were asked to describe what they were doing, a surprising range of practices was outlined, but in all cases the interviewees would claim to be using the same innovation. For example, when teachers in Texas, Nebraska, and Massachusetts were asked to describe their teams, they provided very different pictures of the innovation of teaming:

> *Team Texas*   consisted of three teachers and two aides who served approximately 110 students. They "teamed" all day and were housed in a pod that was equivalent in size to three classrooms. The students were taught by all of the teachers, and each teacher took the lead in planning for one subject area.
>
> *Team Nebraska*   consisted of three teachers, each of whom had a homeroom class. For half the day, students would move from classroom to classroom as they were grouped and regrouped for lessons. Teachers kept their own students for the afternoon. Teachers specialized in teaching all students particular subjects.
>
> *Team Massachusetts*   consisted of two teachers, each of whom had a regular classroom with 25 to 30 students. The teachers exchanged lesson plans once a month, but each kept and taught his or her own students all day.

As these examples illustrate how the change is thought about in theory may bear little resemblance to the activities that are done in classrooms under the name of that innovation. In each of the schools just described, the teachers were quick to say "Oh, yes, we are teaming," but what they were doing under the name of teaming was very different.

An early conclusion in our studies was that users of innovations tend to adapt and in some cases mutate innovations. In other words, the innovation *in action* can take on many different operational forms or configurations. Once the phenomenon of IC is recognized and accepted as a natural part of the change process, a number of implications emerge. For example, the outcomes from the use of different configurations of an innovation will likely vary. Users of some configurations will be associated with higher outcomes than those using other configurations. Also, to further their implementation, training, and coaching, users will need to target different aspects of the innovation, depending on which configuration is in use. There is a philosophical issue here, too. To what extent is there a need to advocate for close adherence to the developer's intended model (i.e., a "fidelity" approach)? When, or should, all users be doing the same thing? In other words, how necessary and appropriate is a fidelity model of change? The concept of IC and its related measurement procedure help address these questions.

The purpose here is not to make judgments about how good or bad it may be to adapt an innovation. Instead, the goal is to point out that (a) in most change efforts innovation adaptation will occur, (b) there is a way to chart these adaptations, and (c) these adaptations have direct and indirect implications for facilitating and assessing change processes. In the concluding section of this chapter we return to issues related to fidelity and some of their implications, but first, we describe IC as a concept and its Mapping procedure.

REFLECTION QUESTIONS

Have you been an implementer in a change project and found yourself adding to or not doing some parts of the new program? What motivated your making these changes?

INNOVATION CONFIGURATIONS AS A CONCEPT

Anyone who has been involved in change recognizes the phenomenon of IC. The tendency to adapt, modify, and/or mutate aspects of innovations is a natural part of the change process; it is neither malicious nor even explicitly planned. It happens for a number of interrelated reasons, beginning with uncertainty about what is supposed to be done. Most people, especially teachers, want to do the "right" thing. Therefore, when teachers are asked to use an innovation, they will try. The problems begin when the details of how to do it are not made clear.

In nearly all cases the innovation as operationalized by different users will vary along a continuum from being very close to what the developer had in mind to a distant zone where what is being done is nearly unrecognizable. Creating different configurations of an innovation is not unique to education. For example, consider cars as the innovation. As Figure 3.1

FIGURE 3.1   A Continuum of Innovation Configurations for a Car

illustrates, and as any parking lot confirms, a car can be and has been significantly adapted from the initial conception of a two-door sedan. A whole range of "configurations" can be observed, ranging from changes in color, to the addition of mag wheels, to rebuilding as a race car, to some forms that some might claim are cars about which the rest of us would say, "No, those are not cars!"

REFLECTION QUESTIONS

Think of an innovation that you were expected to put into practice. Where did you start, and how did you know when you had full implementation? Did you have any uncertainty about the expectations for your implementation effort?

This same continuum of configurations exists for educational innovations, except that determining what is and is not the innovation is more difficult than with the car example. All too frequently the developers of an educational innovation have not thought clearly about what use of their change will really entail. They have thought more about what is needed to support its implementation, such as training and materials. In addition, because teachers, like the rest of us, are always short of time, they will tend to reduce the amount of change and effort they have to invest whenever they can. If there is limited training and support for the change, it is likely that it will not be fully or faithfully implemented. Although the teachers may genuinely believe that they are using the innovation, an expert observing their classroom may conclude "Hmm, the way they are doing it is not what the developer intended."

The different configurations of educational innovations are easy to picture. Take, for example, the innovation of integrated use of technology. What is envisioned here is classroom use by students and teachers of various forms of technology for information retrieval, processing, and communication. Some of the relatively simple configurations that could be observed include (a) classrooms with only a few computers with no Web access, which are used mainly for drill and practice, (b) classrooms with computers that are linked within the school and include CD-ROM databases but no Web access, (c) classrooms with computers with Web access, projection devices, and video, where students work individually with their own laptops and in groups to research, plan, develop, and communicate presentations about their learning, and (d) schools in which all computers are in a lab or media center and used on an assigned schedule for groups of students.

Once it is recognized and accepted that there will be different configurations of an innovation, an important next issue is how to describe those configurations. Answering this question entails development of an IC Map.

MAPPING INNOVATION CONFIGURATIONS

The scenarios described in the previous section are very familiar to teachers, principals, and other leaders. The situation in which teachers are not sure about what they are to do occurs in part because innovation developers have a hard time imagining the extent to which their innovation can be adapted. Another reason for the uncertainty is that change facilitators and teachers do not have clear images and descriptions about what the use of the innovation can look like. To address these needs, we have developed a process and tool that can be used to

GUIDING PRINCIPLES OF IC MAPPING

1. Always type the word *DRAFT* on each page of your IC Map.
2. Always type your name and the date of the current draft on each page. This will reduce confusion over whether someone is referring to the most recent version of the IC Map.
3. Watch out for IC Map components that simply taper off as they move from the *b* or *c* to the final variation. If this is happening to one dimension, make sure you have a second dimension that increases from *c* to the final variation. After all, if the ideal dimension is decreasing, some other practice is taking its place.
4. Remember that the *d* and *e* variations are not "bad" or simply pejorative descriptions; they should be descriptions of alternatives that represent other ways of doing things.
5. A completed IC Map should serve as a record of how an innovation is being used; its purpose is not to explain how the information about practice is to be collected, which may be done by interview, observation, or user self-assessment. Some caution is needed in terms of reliability and validity, especially for certain types of IC Map components. For example, there will be much lower validity for a teaching process component that is self-assessed than one that is recorded by a trained observer.
6. An IC Map is only good for the innovation for which it was designed. With a different innovation, the map-building process will have to be done again.
7. Strive to have very descriptive word pictures for each variation. Address the presence or absence of each dimension in each variation.
8. Be careful about having too few and too many dimensions in a component. Very rarely should a component consist of only one dimension or more than four.
9. Remember that the consensus-building process and debate among the mappers is key. The talk about "what you mean" and "what I mean" is critical to developing a useful and valid IC Map.
10. Do not insert fidelity lines until after the IC Map has been through several generations of drafts and there are clear reasons to do so.

visualize and assess the different configurations that are likely to be found for any particular innovation. We call the process *Innovation Configuration Mapping* and the resultant tool an *Innovation Configuration Map.*

Elements of Innovation Configuration Maps

The concept of a map was deliberately chosen for this work because, just as a road map shows different ways for getting from one place to another, so does an Innovation Configuration Map. A highway map will picture interstate highways, U.S. highways, and county roads. These are alternate routes, all of which make it possible to complete the trip. The IC Map does the same thing for change facilitators and users of innovations by identifying the major components of an innovation and then describing the observable variations of each component. The IC Map is composed of "word picture" descriptions of the different operational forms of an innovation or change.

FIGURE 3.2   A Simple IC Map Component (from the Science Program)

COMPONENT 1: UNITS TAUGHT

(A)	(B)	(C)	(D)	(E)
All units and most activities are taught.	Most units and activities are taught.	Some units are taught.	A few selected activities are taught.	No units or activities are taught.

Pothole Warning

Do not assume that just because every staff member attended the two-hour session where the innovation was described that they all hold the same image of what it is—especially if it was described in general terms.

Pothole Repair

How to enable every one to hold a common, and authentic, vision of the new practice is the challenge. Precision in describing what use looks like is the key, and the operable term. Read on. The IC tool can address this challenge.

IC Map Components.   Consider the very simple IC Map component presented in Figure 3.2, which describes the units that a teacher presents. In the *a* variation, all units and most activities are taught. The quantity of units and activities that are taught decreases in the other variations, with the *e* variation describing the classroom where none of the units or activities are taught. Even without naming a specific program, it is possible to use this component with its different variation descriptions to visualize different degrees of coverage of units and activities. It is part of the "map," just as is a highway map.

The purpose of the IC Map is to present carefully developed descriptions of different ways of doing the innovation. An IC Map will have a number of components (typically 6 to 12), and each component will have a number of variations (typically 2 to 6). The number of components will vary depending on the complexity of the innovation and the amount of detail needed. There is a dynamic trade-off between the number of components and the level of detail represented. In an IC Map with fewer components, each component will have more information, which at some point makes the descriptions so very dense that it is not easy to visualize because of the detail. On the other hand, an IC Map with many components may be too finely ground to be practical. In the end, the team that develops an IC Map has to decide what is best for its situation.

The major goal in writing each component description and each variation description is to be as visual as possible. The better the word pictures, the easier it will be for teachers, principals, and others to see what successful use of the innovation entails. This cannot be overstated.

Developing Clear Word-Picture Descriptions.   The IC Map component presented in Figure 3.2 was deliberately chosen because of its simplicity. A more typical IC Map would have much richer component descriptions, as shown in Figure 3.3. These components were

FIGURE 3.3   Two IC Map Components for the Instructor's Role in the Fast Trac II Course for Business Entrepreneurs

FAST TRAC II COURSE INNOVATION CONFIGURATION MAP

Site _____   Session _____   Instructor _____   Observer _____   Date _____

A. FULL COURSE OVERVIEW

2) Balanced Coverage of the Six Core Modules   —Entrepreneurial Mind-set   —Management & Organization   —Finance [*6 covered, equal emphasis*]
—Legal Entities   —Marketing   —Negotiations

(a)	(b)	(c)	(d)	(e)	(f)
All six modules are developed and with equal emphasis.	All six modules are developed but with one or more given less emphasis.	One or more modules are not systematically addressed.	One or two modules become the course.		

LECTURE SEGMENT

11) Use of Examples by the Instructor During the Lecture (Variety, Type, Relevance, and Length)

(a)	(b)	(c)	(d)	(e)	(f)
Examples are used throughout. Examples are interesting, varied, to the point, and congruent with the issue or topic at hand. Examples include retail/service/manufacturing and participants' expertise with examples from their businesses.	Examples presented are to the point and congruent. Variety is limited in terms of retail/service/manufacturing and participants' businesses.	Examples and stories are not always relevant to the issue or topic at hand and tend to be drawn out, or a few businesses are overused as examples. Examples may not be clearly explained.	So many examples and war stories are shared that complete coverage of the points is hindered.	So many examples and war stories particular to the instructor's personal experience are shared that there is little variety and complete coverage of the point is hindered.	There are few examples and/or all of the examples are based in one or two businesses.

Source: Reprinted by permission from the Kauffman Center for Entrepreneurial Leadership at the Ewing Marion Kauffman Foundation.

selected from the Instructor Profile for Fast Trac II (Novak, 1992), a 10-week course for business entrepreneurs. In this project, which was done by the Center for Entrepreneurial Leadership of the Kauffman Foundation, there was interest in developing an IC Map that depicted the role of the course instructor that could be used as part of the quality control check as the course was disseminated nationally. The resultant IC Map also was used to select content for instructor training since instructors were to be skilled in doing each of the map's components. The map was also used by the instructors in planning and self-reflection and by trained assessors in determining instructor certification by viewing videotapes of their classes.

One of the interesting aspects of the Fast Trac IC Map was that the innovation was the role of the course instructor. An IC Map also could have been developed around the role of workshop participants or around what they, as entrepreneurs, applied from the course to their businesses. Deciding which innovation user to focus on for IC Mapping is a critical first step.

Note in Figure 3.3 how the component and variation descriptions in Component 2 are stated. The basic component is the same, but more information is presented for the component than in Figure 3.2. However, as IC Mapping expert Paul Borchardt would say (personal communication, November 10, 2003), this is still a "boring" component, since it basically just evolves from "all" (*a*) to "a little" (*d*). A component of this type could be made much richer by adding a second dimension, or practice, that increased in occurrence from *b* to *d*. For example, the dimension of excessive time being spent on one or two modules could gradually increase across the variation descriptions. Alternatively, a "small and skinny" continuum could be used, indicating "all" to "little" than can be easily checked off.

A much higher quality example of an IC Map component and its variations is Component 11 in Figure 3.3. Note how the word-picture descriptions of each variation are richer and how four different dimensions—variety, type, relevance, and length—are addressed in each variation. An IC Map notation technique is to present a key word for each dimension within brackets following the component label.

Indicating Ranges of Quality and Fidelity.   Figures 3.2 and 3.3 illustrate a number of additional features of IC Map components as well, including the implicit value in the sequencing of the variations. As one moves from the *e* variation toward the *a* variation, the behaviors and practices described increasingly approach the more ideal practices as viewed by the innovation developer or some consensus group, usually those who developed the IC Map. This sequence, having the ideal/"a" variation to the left is the reverse of what is done with most scoring rubrics. One of the reasons for this is to have the map reader learn about the ideal variation first. Laying the component variations along such a continuum from more to less desirable can be very helpful. Note that this IC Mapping technique can be used only to implicitly signify when some variations are valued more highly than others. The authors of this text are not arguing for or against such a fidelity perspective but merely showing how it can be noted on the IC Map.

Another IC Mapping technique that can be helpful with a fidelity perspective is use of what we call *fidelity lines,* which are represented by the vertical dashed and solid lines between certain variations of the components in Figure 3.3. A solid line signifies that all of the variations to the right have been judged to be "unacceptable" ways of doing that component; all of those to the left of a dashed line are considered "ideal" practices, whereas those between the solid and dashed lines are viewed as "acceptable." Determining the placement of these lines in this case was done by the Fast Trac course developers. Whether to have lines and where to place them are important decisions for IC Mapping groups. No matter who is to make the decision about the inclusion of fidelity lines, *no lines should be added until after the IC Map has been through several revisions and has been used in data collection.* The insertion of fidelity lines should not be arbitrary or capricious. The rationale should be very good, and, hopefully, empirical data should support their placement.

On the other hand, over time, the lines could be shifted to represent goals (for accomplishment) as the innovation users become more familiar and experienced with using the innovation and are ready to move to the more sophisticated or ideal variations on the left of the map. Being flexible with the lines in this way also reduces the users' anxiety, for it communicates that they are not expected to become expert immediately but that they may move through the variations with the help of their facilitator and colleagues.

Student Roles in IC Maps.   One of the first decisions in IC Mapping is to determine which role(s) will be the focus of the map. For example, as mentioned, the Fast Trac map shown in Figure 3.3 could have focused on the participants or the regional dissemination administrators instead of the instructors. Normally, IC Maps will deal not just with the role of the teachers and their use of the materials but also with the role of the students. For example, Figure 3.4 describes one aspect of student performance in a constructivist approach to teaching mathematics (Alquist & Hendrickson, 1999), which is based on the National Council of Mathematics Standards. Figure 3.5 is a student component from the IC Map for standards-based education of the Douglas County School District in Colorado. The rich and observable descriptions of each variation in these examples were the result of intense and sustained effort.

For the clearest and most straightforward depiction of each of the role groups (i.e., students, others), making a map for that unique role group is advised. This gives those individuals an immediate and complete picture of expectations for them. Of course, the various IC Maps for the various role groups can be shared so that there is understanding across the organization about *who* is expected to do *what.* This approach was taken in the creation of IC Maps to represent/reflect what each of five groups (principals, teachers, central office staff, superintendent, and school board) were expected to be doing in implementing the National Staff Development Council's (NSDC) standards for staff development. For an extended period of time (years) these standards had languished in their printed documents, then the NSDC executive director suggested that maps be constructed to give each of the "players" rich word-pictures of their role (Roy & Hord, 2003).

Other Roles in IC Maps.   The NSDC created IC Maps of five role groups of educators (Roy & Hord, 2003) to describe expectations for their activities when conducting staff development that exemplified the 12 NSDC standards for staff development (NSDC, 2001). Figure 3.6, the Cross Walk, is the result of organizing all the desired outcomes (in these maps, *desired outcomes* is the term used for *components;* there are no variations in the Cross Walk) of all five role groups of educators.

The desired outcomes of teachers are presented as the first column in the Cross Walk. Then the desired outcomes of the other role groups are placed horizontal to the teachers in order to show which desired outcomes relate to each other. This depiction suggests how the four role groups (principal, central office staff members, superintendent, and school board) support and enable the achievement of the desired outcomes for teachers.

52

FIGURE 3.4 Student IC Map Components

INNOVATION CONFIGURATION MAP FOR THE TEACHING AND LEARNING OF MATHEMATICS
DODDS-HESSEN DISTRICT SUPERINTENDENT'S OFFICE, RHEIN MAIN, GERMANY

DRAFT   DRAFT   DRAFT

B. Engagement with Task/Investigation

3) Student Engaged in Mathematical Tasks Throughout the Lesson [Engagement, Time]

a	b	c	d
Most students are engaged in mathematical tasks, most of the time.	Most students are engaged in mathematical tasks, part of the time.	Some students are engaged in mathematical tasks. Many are off task most of the time.	Few students are engaged any of the time.

4) Students' Understanding of Problem-Solving Strategies [Knowing Your Goal, Where You Are Now, Knowing the Steps to Get to the Goal, Reflection]

a	b	c	d	e
Students view the open-ended problem as a whole and analyze its parts. They create, select, and test a range of strategies. Students reflect upon the reasonableness of the strategies and the solution.	Students grasp the open- and close-ended problem as a whole and analyze its parts. Students pick an established/traditional strategy to try to solve the problem, which is applied without considering alternatives. Students reflect upon the reasonableness of the solution but not the strategy.	Students approach the open-ended problem as a whole but do not have a clear understanding of the parts. The primary focus is on getting an answer. The students' reflection is on whether the answer is right rather than the reasonableness of the strategy.	Students approach open-ended problems as unconnected/unrelated parts and do not see the problem as a whole. Students may manipulate materials and numbers, but they are not clear about the reason/purpose. If observable, reflection is about procedures.	Students calculate and compute using rote and routine procedures. Students are not clear about the final goal or the relationship of the tasks to that goal. There is little or no reflection about what is being learned.

DRAFT

Property of Hessen DSO, Unit 7565 Box 29, APO AE 09050—Contact the authors of the IC Map for the latest version.

Source: From "Mapping the Configurations of Mathematics Teaching" by A. Alquist and M. Hendrickson, 1999, *Journal of Classroom Interaction, 34*(1), 18–26. Reprinted by permission.

FIGURE 3.5   Student IC Map Component for Standards-Based Education (Douglas County School District, Castle Rock, Colorado)

DOUGLAS COUNTY SCHOOL DISTRICT—LEARNING SERVICES STANDARDS-BASED EDUCATION—CONFIGURATION MAP

Component #5—Student Ownership and Understanding of Learning (Understanding of Standards or Checkpoints, Understanding of Progress in Relation to Standards or Checkpoints, Understanding of What Is Needed to Improve Performance in Order to Achieve Standards or Checkpoints):

(I)	(II)	(III)	(IV)	(V)
Students' focus is on the **current activity**.	Students' focus is on **the requirements of the class and grade** they receive.	Students can use the **"language" of standards.** They can state the **standards and checkpoints** that they are expected to learn, but they are **unclear about where they are** in meeting the standards or checkpoints or about what **to do** to achieve them.	Students **understand** what they are **expected to know and be** able to do and can **articulate in specific terms** what it means to reach the standards or check-points. They can **describe where they are** in regard to the standards or checkpoints but are **unclear what they need to do** to achieve them.	Students **understand** what they are **expected to know and be able to do** and can **articulate in specific terms** what it means to reach the standards or checkpoints. They can **describe where they are** in regard to the standard and know what they **need to improve** to achieve it.

Examples:

"We are reading *The Diary of Anne Frank*, and I will be writing some kind of report when we are finished."	"We are studying how to use primary source materials. I need to get at least a B on the final report."	"I know that we are studying how to select and evaluate primary source materials as related to the Holocaust. I'm not sure exactly what I'll need to know about primary sources, or if I am any good at using them."	"I know that we are studying primary source materials as related to the Holocaust, and that's why we are reading *The Diary of Anne Frank*. I know that we will be evaluating and interpreting sources for their usefulness in understanding the Holocaust. I can find sources, but I am not sure how to evaluate their relevance and quality. I am not sure what I'll need to do to become proficient in evaluating these sources."	"I know that we are studying primary source materials as they relate to the Holocaust and that's why we are reading *The Diary of Anne Frank*. I know that we will be evaluating and interpreting sources for their usefulness in understanding the Holocaust. I am pretty good at locating primary sources, but I have trouble knowing whether they are really quality sources. My teacher has shown some interesting ways to judge the quality of a source, but I need some more practice with them."

April, 1999 |

Douglas County School District Re-1

Source: Douglas County School District Re-1, Castle Rock, Colorado. Reprinted by permission.

FIGURE 3.6 Cross Walk of Five Role Groups for National Staff Development Council's Standards for Staff Development

STANDARD: LEARNING COMMUNITIES

TEACHER	PRINCIPAL	CENTRAL OFFICE STAFF MEMBERS	SUPERINTENDENT	SCHOOL BOARD
	1.4: Creates and maintains a learning community to support teacher and student learning			1.2: Takes collective responsibility for the learning of all students
	1.3: Understands and implements an incentive system that ensures collaborative work		1.1: Understands and implements a recognition and incentive system that rewards collaboration that achieves district goals	1.1: Supports a recognition and incentive system that rewards collaboration that accomplishes districtwide goals for student learning
		1.1: Prepares administrators and teachers to be skillful members of learning teams	1.3: Ensures district administrators are prepared to be skillful leaders and members of learning teams	
1.1: Meets regularly with colleagues during the school day to plan instruction		1.1: Prepares teachers for skillful collaboration		

FIGURE 3.6 *(Continued)*

STANDARD: LEARNING COMMUNITIES

TEACHER	PRINCIPAL	CENTRAL OFFICE STAFF MEMBERS	SUPERINTENDENT	SCHOOL BOARD
1.2: Aligns collaborative work with school improvement goals	1.2: Creates an organizational structure that supports collegial learning	1.2: Maintain and support learning teams	1.2: Creates policies and structures that support the implementation of learning communities within the district	1.3: Functions as a learning community
1.3: Participates in learning teams, some of whose membership extends beyond the school	1.5: Participates with other administrators in one or more learning communities	1.3: Participate with others as a member of a learning team	1.4: Participates in learning communities that focus on continuous improvement	1.4: Supports individual, team, school, and systemwide learning at the local, regional, state, and national levels
		1.4: Support learning team use of technology		

Source: From *Moving NSDC's Staff Development Standards into Practice: Innovation Configurations*, by Shirley Hord and Pat Roy (Roy & Hord, 2003). Reprinted with permission of the National Staff Development Council, www.nsdc.org.

The idea is to read horizontally, beginning with the teacher, paying no attention to the numerals of any of the outcomes (unless you wish to refer back to the ICs presented in the book of maps). Notice that in some rows of desired outcomes, all squares are not filled. This effort with the Cross Walk is to illustrate the systemic approach to professional development and the role that all educators play.

More Complex and Richer IC Map Components.   When the need and available time are present, IC Map components can be made even more complex and richer. In one such project the innovation itself was very subtle and complex, and developing each component had to be done in ways that built in the nuances of the philosophy of the developer as well as clear descriptions of how this approach would be seen in classroom practices. The innovation, the Essential Curriculum, is an educational program that provides children and young people with the knowledge and skills that will directly assist them in their development as capable and ethical people (Dunn & Borchardt, 1998). Although the program contains lessons and activities, its philosophy of how people should treat each other is expected to be expressed in the classroom throughout the day. Because of this, the IC Map includes components that describe practices during a lesson as well as others that address practices to be used throughout the day.

To help teachers, change facilitators, and evaluators who assess implementation of the Essential process, the IC Map components became much more complex. One of those components is presented in Figure 3.7. This IC Map component contains a number of readily apparent differences compared to our previous examples. First, the range of variations is greater, with a common dimensionality built into each one that deals with how holistically the teacher is integrating use of the program's principles. The f variation, for example, describes the case when nothing that is related to that component is observed. The g variation addresses behaviors and actions that are actually antithetical to the intent of the program, which is information that can be very helpful. Another important addition to this component is the open-ended list of examples under each variation description. Although they will not represent all that is in a particular variation, nor will they necessarily be exclusive to that variation, they do describe the kinds of behaviors that are indicative of it.

Here is something for you to consider: You have undoubtedly tried to read and understand highly detailed road maps that make it frustratingly difficult to plainly see the bigger and clearer picture. You may want to consider two or three iterations of an IC Map—that is, a first map of an innovation might provide the major components and their variations in rich language so that one develops an initial mental image of the innovation in action. This map then may also serve as a monitoring instrument to track where and how the individual implementers are progressing. Then, on the reverse side of the document page, a more detailed map may be portrayed that provides to the implementer and the facilitator further information and useful explanation, and so on. Using this approach reduces user and implementer anxiety and frustration.

REFLECTION QUESTIONS

Whew! There's a lot of information here about IC Maps. Take a moment to recall a time when you were expected to change your practice by implementing a new way of "doing." Was there clarity about the new way, and, if so, was that helpful to you? How? If not, what were your results?

FIGURE 3.7 A Dense and Complex IC Map Component with Indicators

THE ESSENTIAL CURRICULUM IC MAP

II. All Day in the Classroom

D. Teacher

6) The Principles and Concepts are applied throughout the day by the teacher [*Teacher Application, All*].

Consistent reliance on and integration of program	*Deliberate and conscious application of principles and concepts*	*Emphasizes selected principles and concepts*	*Program delivery as designed*	*Presentation of parts and pieces at random*	*Non-use*	*Opposition to principles and concepts*
(Complete Integration)	(Deliberate Application)	(Selected Emphasis)	(Motions)	(Parts and Pieces)	(Nothing)	(Antithesis)
(a)	(b)	(c)	(d)	(e)	(f)	(g)
Principles and concepts are integrated without conscious effort into activities of the day. ■ Teacher and students acknowledge mistakes in words, including "Oops, I goofed." ■ Teachers teach students through steps of correcting errors seamlessly. ■ Students have "driver's licenses" and "drive" to other parts of the building using self-control. The license can be suspended for lack of self-control.	All principles and concepts are developed and consciously applied throughout the day. ■ When opportunities arise, teacher and students draw connections to and apply specific principles and concepts. ■ When faced with opportunities, teacher and students talk out loud about the relevant principle or concepts.	Selected principles and concepts are emphasized and applied appropriately throughout the day. ■ Teacher leads students in applying principles of "self-control" but does not refer to other concepts. ■ Teacher recognizes opportunities around "making mistakes" but misses opportunities related to other principles and concepts.	Lessons are taught, but no extrapolations to situations outside the Essential lesson context. ■ When obvious opportunities to refer to principles and concepts arise, teacher does not make connection. ■ Teacher handles fight on playground without reference to any Essential principle.	Some activities are purposefully selected to teach the concept. ■ Tap and Trade game is played without principles being taught. ■ Social studies curriculum happens to lend itself to the selection of Essential lessons.		Principles and concepts applied in classroom are antithetical to Essential curriculum. ■ Praise is used indiscriminately (unearned). ■ Self-esteem activities teach principles and concepts counter to Essential's principles. ■ "In this classroom we will not make mistakes." ■ "I can give my students self-esteem." ■ Mistakes are punished without any processing.

Source: From *The Essential Curriculum*, The Teel Institute, Kansas City, Missouri. Reprinted by permission of the Kauffman Center for Entrepreneurial Leadership at the Ewing Marion Kauffman Foundation.

The Process of Developing an IC Map

Developing an IC Map is a challenging endeavor. It also is energizing for those who really are interested in successful implementation of an innovation. The process includes moments of discovery about the intent of a particular innovation and how it should be used as well as the initial struggle to figure out what the components are and then how to develop useful word-picture descriptions for each variation. Additional rewards come when the first draft of the IC Map is shared with interested teachers, principals, and other change facilitators. Often, this is the first time they will have seen written descriptions of what they will be doing when using the innovation.

Frequently, the first reaction of people who examine an IC Map is to do a self-assessment of where they would place themselves on each component's variations. A second reaction is to consider some of the other variation descriptions and whether they should try them. The IC mappers receive very helpful feedback from these dialogues, which can be used in further refining the map.

Developing an IC Map is definitely an interactive process. An individual working alone is very unlikely to construct a map that is as useful as one that evolves from a team effort. Typically, three to seven key people (who are to some degree knowledgeable about the innovation) work together and over time (in total five or six days will be needed) to devise a complete first draft of an IC Map. One of the major outcomes of this interactive process is that the IC mappers develop a consensus about what the innovation should look like when it is in use. Up to that time, they likely will not have been using the same terms and detailed images of use. This regularly observed lack of explicit agreement in understanding adds greatly to teachers' confusion about what they are supposed to be doing. Teachers have a difficult time when their principal, district office staff, and outside experts work off different implicit mental images of what ideal use looks like.

When it is reasonable for IC Mapping, have a larger number of the school staff and relevant district personnel in the room (comfortably). There will be less confusion when more individuals are privileged to participate in the dialogue and consensus building about the ideal form and other variations. Through the process and dialogue, clarity increases among about what use of the innovation looks like and how they are to use it. This results in participants having precise expectations, a feeling of contributing to the innovation that they will use, and commitment to the innovation's implementation. In other words, the staff will have "buy-in."

REFLECTION QUESTIONS

Have you had the opportunities to experience both of these initial processes: (a) being part of the construction team and (b) having an IC Map handed to you with instructions for following it? How does this compare with your not being provided with a clear image of what ideal use should look like? Which approach did you prefer? What advantages did each approach provide? What different reactions and feelings did each of the approaches stimulate?

The general process that is followed in developing an IC Map is presented in Figure 3.8. The beginning steps entail reviewing all of the available printed material and then interviewing the innovation developer and/or experts. Following this, a range of classrooms where the

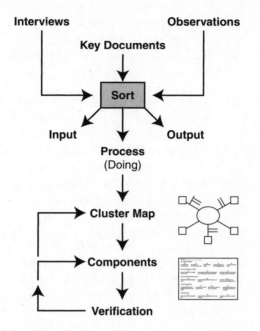

Note: This is a dynamic, interactive, consensus-building process.

FIGURE 3.8   The IC Mapping Process

innovation and similar practices are in use should be observed. It is important to observe a variety of classrooms because an IC Map needs to have word-picture descriptions that cover all possible variations. Three key questions that should be asked throughout this process:

1. What does the innovation look like when it is in use?
2. What would I see in classrooms where it is used well (and not as well)?
3. What will teachers *and* students be doing when the innovation is in use?

A key part of IC Mapping is the orientation that is taken. The focus is on developing pictures of the operational forms of the innovation, not statements of its philosophy or a listing of its implementation requirements. Innovation creators have a tendency to focus on implementation requirements. They may say something like "You have to use these materials and spend at least thirty minutes doing so every day." However, this is the wrong answer for those building the IC Map. Instead they need to know *how* those materials are being used and *what* happens in the classroom when they are.

A separate list (in the margin or on the reverse side of the IC document) of Implementation Requirements may be created to care for these items and keep them from becoming lost in the process.

The initial document review, interviews, and observations should lead to generating possible components that represent the major parts of the innovation. These ideas for possible components are listed without assessment or judgment on chart paper. Mappers then delete suggestions that are irrelevant and add others deemed significant. The suggestions that are similar or alike are clustered, and one statement is created to represent each set of the suggestions. These component statements are clear, crisp, and communicate well. The first goal is to develop a holistic organizing scheme of possible components that represent what the innovation is like when it is used.

Following this comes the task of agreeing on which components are key and should be developed. The selected components should represent critical aspects of innovation use, not those typical to good teaching in general. Then comes the intense work of negotiating the wording of components and component variations. Once a draft is complete, it should be tested in what we call the first "dose of reality." Without exception, when IC mappers try out their first full draft, they discover a number of points that need clarification. They also are likely to discover that other components need to be mapped.

Developing an IC Map is a highly interactive and iterative process. Our experience has been that innovation developers cannot develop high-quality IC Maps by themselves. Also, it is always best to have three or more people drafting an IC Map. An earlier technical document on IC Mapping (Heck, Stiegelbauer, Hall, & Loucks, 1981) may be of some help. A more significant resource is the more current technical manual (Hord, Stiegelbauer, Hall, & George, 2006). The Guiding Principles of IC Mapping also provide additional technical information and tips to consider in reviewing map drafts.

INNOVATION CONFIGURATIONS: APPLICATIONS AND IMPLICATIONS

The Innovation Configuration concept and IC Maps have many applications and implications. We have selected a few to introduce here to stimulate further thought about this important aspect of the change process. The points that are included address some facets of facilitating change processes, conducting research, and drafting IC Maps.

Using IC Maps to Clarify the Change

Once an IC Map is developed, it should be shared with all of the potential and current users of the innovation and with all change facilitators. This was done, for example, for the nine innovation bundles in the Kentucky Education Reform Act. Under the leadership of Roger Pankratz and the Kentucky Institute of Education Research, nine cross-state constituent teams of 6 to 10 members each met for a week to develop the first drafts of the IC Maps. Each team was assigned one bundle. The resulting copies of their IC Maps were then sent to all 1,230 schools in the state. This was the first time that teachers and principals had word-picture descriptions of what they could be doing under the labels of each of the reform initiatives.

Using IC Maps to Guide Construction of a Professional Learning Community

In Professional Learning Communities (PLCs), the concept and the work (Chapter 2) involve command of substantial information and understanding about how to create the desired structures in schools. Although some information about each structure may be accessible, much more would be desirable. One tool for increasing understanding would be for the change facilitators to create IC Maps of PLC (or other reform structures or practices). The resultant maps could be used to guide and support development of the PLC and also used to assess the extent of implementation by both staff and students at various points in time. In this way, interventions that support participants could be related to how far they have moved on the map in terms of the variations of the components. For example, interventions could be cataloged as they relate to the development of each of the five dimensions of PLC (components) in the map.

Using IC Maps to Plan Implementation Supports

An IC Map is also a diagnostic tool for planning professional development. For example, a large number of teachers could be observed and an IC Map marked for each to indicate their progress in implementation, with the information then summarized by component. The summary would be a tally of how many teachers were at each of the variations for each component. Then it would be possible to identify those components for which implementation was going well (i.e., many teachers using *a* and *b* variations) and any components where implementation was lagging (i.e., many teachers using *d* and *e* variations). This information could be used to plan a large group learning session to address less well-implemented components.

Coaching with IC Maps

IC Maps can be a useful coaching tool as well. Principals and other change facilitators observe classrooms to provide help to teachers, but often they are not given guidelines and specifics about what to look for. The IC Map provides a set of descriptions that can be used to focus their observations. There might also be a pre-observation discussion during which the teacher and the facilitator agree that certain IC Map components will be targeted during the observation. If a student IC Map is used that focuses on what the students are doing, teachers are less likely to perceive the use of an IC Map as an evaluation threat. In all cases, if the focus is kept on the innovation instead of the teacher, personal concerns will be lower.

Using IC Maps for Self-Reflection

One of the most important uses of IC Maps is for self-assessment and reflection. Each component variation should be a word picture description of one way that component could be made operational. As was suggested above, unlike most rubrics, with an IC Map the *d* and *e* variations are not merely on less of the *a* variation; instead they represent other possible practices. When an implementer, such as a teacher, compares his or her current practice with the variation descriptions, she or he will be able to place themselves at one of the variations along the continuum. In addition, by studying the other variations they can see what they can do differently to get closer to the *a* variation. The vignette illustrates how useful self-reflection with an IC Map can be.

■ ■ ■ ■ ■ ■

VIGNETTE

USING AN IC MAP COMPONENT FOR REFLECTION AND PEER OBSERVATION

Two teachers are discussing their understanding of standards-based education (SBE) and what they think their students understand about it.

JOSÉ: I think I'm finally understanding what SBE is about. It really has been a big change for me. I've been used to providing information and teaching with the discovery approach. The idea that I should make sure up front that the students understand the desired outcome has been a big change for me.

MARY JO: I know what you mean. I've always wanted my students to learn, but I too thought that they should have to figure it out from scratch.

JOSÉ: I still don't think my students get it. They can give me a general idea about the standards and the specific benchmarks we are working on, but they don't seem to be very clear about it. I wish I could somehow get them to understand what their responsibilities are.

MARY JO: I know what you mean. Do you remember that implementation rubric handout our district SBE coordinator gave us last August? There was a student component. Maybe we should look at that.

JOSÉ: I know what you mean. I just happen to have a copy in my file. I am going to look it over and see if it gives me any ideas.

MARY JO: Why don't you pull a copy and then tomorrow, when you have your break, you can come observe my physical science class and see what you think? Don't use the whole thing—just the component that focuses on student learning.

This story points out two important applications of an IC Map. First, it can be used by teachers for self-reflection. Teachers can read each component, assess where they are, and then think about what they wish to continue doing and what they might want to change. An IC Map can also be used for peer observation as teachers observe each other's classrooms using an IC Map as the rubric. They can focus the observation through pre-observation discussion and then debrief each other afterward.

Note that in this case only one component of the IC Map was used as the focus for the planned peer observation. This is a very efficient and useful way to go about it. The selected component was one that dealt with student behaviors, which was a very good choice. When teachers focus on what they would like students to accomplish, there can be a very direct connection back to what the teachers need to do to help students succeed in the desired ways.

VIGNETTE CRITIQUE QUESTIONS

1. Think about using an IC Map for teacher self-improvement. Under what conditions would you want to use the whole IC Map? When would it be best to use one or two components?
2. Would you ever want to share the IC Map with students? Why or why not?
3. Would you ever consider sharing an IC Map with parents? Why or why not?

REFLECTION QUESTIONS

Have you been involved in one of the five application activities cited above? What were your struggles and triumphs? Did you and your colleagues achieve practical results from your endeavors? Or, have you been left pretty much on your own to figure out the details of innovation use? Either way, how far did you get?

Pothole Warning

The preceding situation is a real stickler. It leaves the black box of implementation, the giant leap, to the imagination or to assumptions. How do we know if individuals have adopted and implemented new programs? Do we know to what degree they have reached the ideal state of implementation? How can we attribute student gains to new programs when it is possible that the programs were not fully operational in each classroom?

Pothole Repair

Of course, we have been in this same situation of not knowing. Thus was born the construct of Innovation Configurations. Summative evaluation studies must begin with assessing extent of implementation of the innovation in each classroom. This assessment must be done in comparison classrooms, too.

USING IC MAPS IN RESEARCH, EVALUATION, AND IMPLEMENTATION ASSESSMENTS

A serious problem in most research and evaluation studies has been the failure to document implementation before making judgments about the effects of various treatments, programs, and innovations. Typically, implementation is assumed to have occurred if teachers were trained or the materials were purchased. Our view is that without direct determination of the extent of implementation by each implementer, any study findings will be suspect. Also, any comparison classrooms have to be checked to see if components of the innovation are in use. Without direct measurements of presence and absence of components of the innovation, it is highly risky to be drawing inferences about the effects of a particular program or innovation. An IC Map provides one clear and direct way to record the actual extent and quality of what has been implemented in treatment and comparison classrooms and schools.

Testing Fidelity of Implementation Against Student Outcomes

In a number of earlier research studies, IC Maps were developed and data collected to assess the extent of implementation. For example, Bridge (1995) conducted a number of studies of the implementation of the Integrated Primary program in Kentucky. The *a* variations were formulated using the state's reform initiative and the standards of the National Association for the Education of Young Children. Bridge found that children had higher achievement in primary-grade classrooms with higher levels (i.e., more *a* and *b* variations) of implementation of the developmentally appropriate practices. Koon (1995) had similar findings in a study of the extent of implementation of YESS! Mini-Society (Kourilsky, 1983), an innovation designed to introduce concepts of business and entrepreneurship to students.

THE FIDELITY ENIGMA

The work of both Bridge (1995) and Koon (1995) had a fidelity orientation—there was an established vision of which practices were more preferable. In both studies, the IC Maps were developed accordingly, and higher student outcomes were associated with higher fidelity implementations. An issue that merits discussion is whether it is appropriate to ask for or insist on high-fidelity use of an innovation. From one point of view, teachers are being told what to do, which reduces their teaching freedom. On the other hand, if student gains are higher when the innovation is used in specified ways, should not teachers be expected to use the verified practices? Although we do not have a simple or universally applicable answer to this critical question, we believe that it must be openly asked, discussed, and addressed in each change effort.

Identifying Critical Components and Their Relationship to Student Outcomes

In a study of standards-based teaching and learning of mathematics, the relationship between fidelity of implementation, particular IC Map components, and student outcomes were examined (George, Hall, & Uchiyama, 2000). In the first analysis, classrooms were grouped as being of high (a and b variations), medium (c variations), or low (d and e variations) fidelity. The highest fidelity implementations had significantly higher student test scores. A further statistical analysis by IC Map component identified one component in particular as being associated with higher student test scores ("Teacher use of direct instruction"). Empirical findings of this type could be used by the change facilitators to design key workshops and other forms of support that would enhance implementation of the most critical component(s).

SUMMARY

In this chapter we introduced the idea that an innovation can be made operational in many different forms or configurations. We advocated developing IC Maps and openly sharing the drafts with all parties. Along the way we pointed out some of the conceptual, operational, and philosophical implications of this process. Key points to remember from this chapter are summarized as Guiding Principles.

One of the important benefits of developing an IC Map is the consensus building that it encourages. Without such agreement, the various leaders and change facilitators all too frequently deliver different messages to the nonusers and users, which adds to the confusion and frustration about the change. It sometimes also leads to early adopters of the innovation establishing practices (i.e., configurations) that are later determined to be inappropriate or even not in keeping with the original design. Change processes will be more efficient and effective when from the outset careful consideration is given to what ideal implementation should look like. What are the possible components and variations? This is not to say that images and values of the innovation cannot change with time. In fact, this is one of the reasons why it is important to type *DRAFT* on each page of the IC Map. Still, it is better to begin with the best possible estimate of a shared vision rather than starting with conflicting conceptions.

In conclusion, efforts to implement changes in schools—new processes, practices, organizational structures, and the like—have long been highly ambiguous. We believe that the typically elusive visions of what use of an innovation entails has been a primary reason for the lack of widespread successful change. When a variety of configurations is implemented, it is unlikely that significant gains in student learning will be detected across all classrooms. As has been described in this chapter and illustrated in the vignette, the IC Map is a multipurpose tool that change leaders and implementers can use to improve this situation. Also, don't forget the importance of documenting the configurations that have been implemented when conducting research and evaluation studies. Evaluators and researchers need to have firsthand documentation of which configurations have been implemented in the so-called treatment groups and in any comparison groups. As one constituent enthusiastically reported, "The IC Map is the best thing since sliced bread!"

DISCUSSION QUESTIONS

1. Describe an experience that you have had during which the innovation as used was different from what the developer had intended. Why did this occur?

2. What key steps would you take to introduce the idea of developing an IC Map to a school/district staff?

3. How could a teacher use an IC Map?

4. How could a principal use an IC Map?

5. How could a corporation or private sector manager use an IC Map?

6. What do you see as an important implication of IC for evaluation and research studies?

FIELDWORK ACTIVITIES

1. Develop two or three configuration components, with their variations, for an innovation that you know. Try out the draft of your IC Map by observing or interviewing someone who is using the innovation. What did you learn about the innovation and its implementation from this experience?

2. Critique an IC Map that someone else has developed. Can you visualize the ideal use of the innovation from studying the map? Which variation descriptions present clear word pictures? What are the dimensions within each component? Does each component contain a reasonable number of variations? Which would you suggest be changed or clarified?

3. After studying all of the available materials related to a particular innovation, sketch a cluster map of possible components and some of the variations. Then interview or observe someone who is using the innovation. How do you need to change your cluster map?

4. Make a presentation to your CEO and/or board of directors about the desirability of creating IC Maps to support use of your new golf ball promotional strategies by the sales teams. In addition to the teams, what other individuals should have an IC to guide their work in this promotion? Explain why.

CONDUCT A STUDY

1. Create an IC Map of an impending curriculum to be implemented. Share it with the principal, instructional coaches/facilitators, and the teachers. Use the map to track the implementation progress of six to eight teachers for a 2-month period. Identify any interventions that the facilitators are providing to the teachers. Correlate the progress of participants and the interventions that they received. Report your conclusions to the participants involved. If the subjects are agreeable and interested, continue the study for another 2 months.

2. Identify one parent in each of two families whose teenager students cannot seem to maintain a tidy bedroom, despite regular demands, scoldings, bribes, and threats. Invite the two parents to write a paragraph describing their typical interactions with their children, related to the condition of their bedrooms. Engage the parent and his/her child in constructing an IC Map of a "reasonably" tidy bedroom. The following are examples of possible components:

   a. Makes the bed daily
   b. Places soiled clothes in the hamper
   c. Takes uneaten food, dishes, and utensils to the kitchen and garbage container

   Additional components could be added, but keep it fairly simple. Develop variations for each of the components. The maps of the two families could be quite different; they should represent the components of interest in each family. Coach the parents in how to introduce the maps to their children, indicating that each student will use the "map" collaboratively with his/her parent to record the journey to a tidy personal living space. After 2 weeks, interview the parents to ascertain how the map is working. Is the student using it? Has the appearance of the room changed? Now ask the parents to leave the monitoring in the students' hands with no parental interference for 2 weeks. Interview the parents to learn if progress continues or decreases. The idea is to learn how an IC Map might be applied to family life and to discover if this is a reliable means for changing behavior with less stress and trauma.

ADDITIONAL READINGS/RESOURCES

Killion, J., & Harrison, C. (2006). *Talking the lead: New roles for teachers and school-based coaches.* Oxford, OH: National Staff Development Council.

Killion, J., & Roy, P. (2009). *Becoming a learning school.* Oxford, OH: National Staff Development Council.
    For accessing training in the use of and creation of IC Maps, contact the authors or Southwest Educational Development Laboratory, 211 East Seventh Street, Austin, Texas 78701, (800) 476–6861.

CHAPTER 4

UNDERSTANDING FEELINGS AND PERCEPTIONS ABOUT CHANGE

Stages of Concern

My kids have been doing terrific things with manipulative materials in mathematics. Now José and I are talking about bringing our two classes together to do some cooperative groups.

—One teacher's thoughts in the third year of use of a new approach to teaching mathematics

I don't have time to go see what she is doing. I still have to plan for how I will work with this new approach tomorrow.

—Very busy teacher who has been engaged with the new approach for half a year

Oh, oh! What is the principal talking about now? Will I have to stop using what I have been doing and start doing this new stuff?

—Thoughts of one teacher upon hearing that something new is being proposed

I haven't thought about it. I have so many other things going on.

— High school department chair who also has yearbook staff to advise and a new prep to prepare

The preceding quotes are all too familiar to those of us who have spent time in schools working with teachers and other workers as they have been engaged in change. Many feelings and perceptions are expressed, and many more are only whispered or left unspoken. No matter how promising and wonderful the innovation, no matter how strong the support, implementers will still have moments of self-doubt about whether they can—and even whether they want to—succeed with this new approach. Moments of euphoria are experienced when the change works well, and at other times success seems impossible.

We all know what it is like during a first year of doing something new and different. We tire more easily. We need more time to prepare. And we can't predict everything that will happen. We never feel like we are really on top of matters.

Yet after several years the new becomes familiar and readily doable. Our thoughts shift from the struggles of figuring out what to do to the satisfactions of seeing what happens with students and of talking with others about the benefits of the change and about how to fine-tune it to work even better.

Across all of these experiences an affective dimension can be observed, for we are not just doing but continually thinking and feeling about how the change is working, how well we are doing, and what effects it is having. This Personal side of change is experienced by everyone—executives, parents, students, sales representatives, secretaries, and governors—whenever we are involved in implementing change.

FOCUS QUESTIONS

1. How do you handle those personal feelings and perceptions that come out as part of the change process? Should any of them be ignored?
2. Do all of the implementers in a building or region have the same types of concerns, or are they different for everyone?
3. When you are talking to someone, how can you discover what his or her concerns are?
4. In terms of the feelings and perceptions that people have as the change process unfolds, is a pattern predictable?
5. Do the Stages of Concern always move forward, or can they be arrested or move backward?
6. How fast can implementers move through the Stages of Concern?

THE PERSONAL SIDE OF CHANGE

Pothole Warning

Personal feelings and perceptions can very easily upset a change process.

Pothole Repair

Sometimes it is more important to attend to the Personal aspects of change than it is to singularly focus on use of the innovation.

Feelings and perceptions about an innovation and/or a change process can help or disrupt. When people are excited about a promising change they will try it. But if they perceive threat or loss, people will hold back from engaging with the process. These feelings and perceptions can be sorted and classified into what we call *concerns.* In fact, extensive research is available about how our feelings and perceptions evolve as the change process unfolds. We have named this process the *Stages of Concern* (SoC). These stages give us a way of thinking about people's feelings and perceptions about change. In addition, through research and experience, a set of techniques have been established for assessing concerns.

Understanding the SoC and using the assessment techniques can result in significantly more effective one-on-one coaching sessions, more relevant workshops, and strategic plans that take into account the Personal side of the change process. In this way, the process can be both facilitated and increasingly personalized. A description of the SoC, the assessment techniques, and their applications will be the central topic of this chapter. In subsequent chapters, examples of how the SoC construct can be used with other diagnostics to assess and/or facilitate the change process will be described.

Different Types of Concerns

The idea of calling one's feelings and perceptions *concerns* was originally proposed by Frances Fuller (1969), a counseling psychologist at The University of Texas at Austin who took an interest in student teachers as a result of teaching their required educational psychology course. When she started teaching the course, she worked diligently to make it a good one, but the evaluations at the end of the semester showed that 97 out of the 100 students rated the course "irrelevant" and "a waste of time."

Fuller was an exceptional educator. As Howard Jones, a colleague of ours from the University of Houston likes to tell, she did not react as you might expect to the students' evaluation of her course. Instead of being completely discouraged, she asked, "What did I do that turned those 3 students on?" This was a breakthrough question. When she looked at the 3 students who had rated the course positively, she found that they, unlike the other 97, had had some sort of previous experience with children. They had either taught a church class or were parents already. Thus, they had a different background with which to understand and appreciate the introductory course on educational psychology. Fuller hypothesized that their *concerns* were different as a result of their experiences.

Fuller's Unrelated, Self-, Task, and Impact Concerns

Fuller proceeded to conduct a series of in-depth studies of the concerns of student teachers. She then proposed a model outlining how, with increasing experience in a teacher education program, the student teacher's concerns moved through four levels: Unrelated, Self, Task, and Impact.

Unrelated concerns are found most frequently among student teachers who have not had any direct contact with school-age children or clinical experiences in school settings. Their concerns do not center on teaching or teaching-related issues. Instead, they more typically focus on college life (e.g., "I hope I can get a ticket to the concert") and college studies removed from professional education courses (e.g., "I hope I pass that geography course"). These students do have concerns, but they are not teaching-related concerns.

Self-concerns tend to be most prevalent when teacher education candidates begin their student teaching or more intense clinical work. Now they have concerns about teaching but with an egocentric frame of reference in terms of what the experience will be like for "me" and whether "I" can succeed. Beginning student teachers with Self-concerns will be asking questions such as "Where do I park my car when I get to the school?" "Can I go in the teachers' lounge?" and "I hope that I can get along with my cooperating teacher so that I get a good grade." These expressions indicate concerns about teaching but with a focus on themselves rather than on the act of teaching or the needs of children.

Task concerns show up quite soon after the start of student teaching, as the actual work of teaching becomes central. Typical expressions include "Oh! I am so tired, I had to stay up until midnight grading papers." "When three groups are going at once, my head is spinning, and I don't know where to turn next!" "These materials break too easily—there are pieces everywhere, and they just play with them!"

Impact concerns are the ultimate goal for student teachers, teachers, and professors. At this level the concerns focus on what is happening with students and what the teacher can do to be more effective in improving student outcomes. Improving teaching and student learning are what the talk and thought are about: "My kids are doing great; they understood what I was trying to do!" "I am thinking of adding some new interest centers. They might attract those children who don't seem to get it this other way." "There is a workshop next Saturday on involving kids with special needs in cooperative groups. I am going to take it."

In her studies, Fuller found that over two thirds of the concerns of preservice teachers were in the Self and Task areas, whereas two thirds of the concerns of experienced teachers were in the Task and Impact areas. She also observed that at any given time teachers may have concerns at several levels but that they tend to concentrate in one particular area.

Connecting Concerns to Teacher Education

Fuller (1970; Fuller & Bown, 1975) proposed a different model for the content and flow of a teacher education program, which she named *personalized teacher education.* In such a program, the courses and field experiences are linked with the developing concerns of the students. She believed that becoming a teacher entailed *personalogical development,* or the development of one's own style and philosophy, and that the best way to achieve this end was to address the student's concerns when she or he had them. In the design of a teacher education program, this means offering the courses and field experiences in a sequence that parallels the developing concerns of the students, rather than a sequence that parallels the professors' concerns.

Thus, when teacher education students have Self-concerns, this is the time for early field experiences, low-ratio teaching activities, and educational psychology courses on children of the same age as those being observed. For students with Task concerns, the timing is ripe for the how-to components of methods courses. The history and philosophy aspects of teacher education are seen by the students as being much more relevant when offered to parallel the development of their Impact concerns, which typically occurs near the end of their program. This personalized approach does not mean that all content that is important from the professors' point of view is left out. Instead, the information is provided when it is most relevant to the students' developing interests and perceived needs. In terms of cognitive psychology it means that the students have accumulated sufficient prior knowledge, or they have schema constructed so that they are able to draw connections between what they currently understand and what they need to be learning next.

CONCERNS AND THE CHANGE PROCESS

As you may have already seen, our research on the concepts and issues related to change has clearly documented that the concerns phenomena that Fuller identified are limited neither to college students going through teacher education programs nor to teachers. In fact, everyone involved in change exhibits the same dynamics seen in the education students confronted with the innovations of student teaching.

The same *Unrelated, Self, Task,* and *Impact* pattern of concerns is found in people involved with all types of innovations and change processes. In addition, choosing the types of interventions that are to be done to facilitate the change process is based on the same personalization model. What facilitators of the change process do needs to be reflective of the concerns of those engaged with the innovation and those considering its use. In fact, if the example is simply changed from teaching to a school innovation, the same types of concerns are typically heard:

Unrelated (now called *Unconcerned*): I am not really interested in _____ [this innovation]. My mind is on. . . .

Self: I don't know if I can do this. Also, I am concerned about what my boss thinks.

Task: Using this material is taking all of my time. You can't imagine all the pieces and steps that are entailed in just doing one activity!

Impact: Yesterday, I was talking with Mary Beth. Both of us have found that with the new approach, all of the students (clients) are engaged in and picking up on the concepts much more quickly.

As these quotes illustrate and the findings from our research and that of our colleagues document (see, for example, Persichitte & Bauer, 1996; Shieh, 1996; Van den Berg & Vandenberghe, 1981), the same types of concerns exist when people are engaged with any change. Further, the personalized idea about what the leaders need to say and do is the same. Interventions to facilitate change must be aligned with the concerns of those who are engaged with the change. For example, when teachers are in the first year of implementing an innovation such as standards-based education, and they have many Task concerns, the most valued and effective facilitator is a teacher or consultant who is highly experienced with the details and mechanics of using the innovation and can offer specific how-to tips. Teachers with intense Task concerns don't want to hear about the philosophy; they want help in making the innovation work more smoothly. The more abstract and subtle aspects of innovation use are of greater interest to teachers with Impact concerns.

Pothole Warning

What should a leader do when a teacher says, "Why should I do this anyway? It too will pass."

Pothole Repair

This may be a hint of Self-concern ("I don't know what it is" or "What will it mean for me?"), or perhaps it is an indication of more intense lack of concern ("I have a lot of other things on my plate right now"). Either way, rather than telling the teacher "This is different," first ask them to explain why they feel the way they do.

Identifying the Stages of Concern

Through our research, we have identified and confirmed a set of seven specific categories of concerns about the innovation that we call *Stages of Concern* (SoC, pronounced "ess-oh-see"

FIGURE 4.1   Stages of Concern: Typical Expressions of Concern About the Innovation

	Stages of Concern	Expressions of Concern
IMPACT	6 Refocusing	I have some ideas about something that would work even better.
	5 Collaboration	I am concerned about relating what I am doing with what my co-workers are doing.
	4 Consequence	How is my use affecting clients?
TASK	3 Management	I seem to be spending all of my time getting materials ready.
SELF	2 Personal	How will using it affect me?
	1 Informational	I would like to know more about it.
UNRELATED	0 Unconcerned	I am concerned about some other things.

not "sock"!), as presented in Figure 4.1. We also have developed a more comprehensive definition of the term *concern:*

> The composite representation of the feelings, preoccupation, thought, and consideration given to a particular issue or task is called *concern.* Depending on our personal make-up, knowledge, and experiences, each person perceives and mentally contends with a given issue differently; thus there are different kinds of concerns. The issue may be interpreted as an outside threat to one's well being, or it may be seen as rewarding. There may be an overwhelming feeling of confusion and lack of information about what "it" is. There may be ruminations about the effects. The demand to consider the issue may be self-imposed in the form of a goal or objective that we wish to reach, or the pressure that results in increased attention to the issue may be external. In response to the demand, our minds explore ways, means, potential barriers, possible actions, risks, and rewards in relation to the demand. All in all, the mental activity composed of questioning, analyzing, and re-analyzing, considering alternative actions and reactions, and anticipating consequences is *concern.*
>
> To be concerned means to be in a mentally aroused state about something. The intensity of the arousal will depend on the person's past experiences and associations with the subject of the arousal, as well as [on] how close to the person and how immediate the issue is perceived as being. Close personal involvement is likely to mean more intense (i.e., more highly aroused) concern which will be reflected in greatly increased mental activity, thought, worry, analysis, and anticipation. Through all of this, it is the person's perceptions that stimulate concerns, not necessarily the reality of the situation. (Hall, George, & Rutherford, 1979, p. 5)

With further study and application in schools, colleges, and, to a lesser extent, business, we and our colleagues developed paragraph definitions for each of the SoC, which are presented in Figure 4.2. Note that the original ideas of Unrelated, Self, Task, and Impact have been preserved, but, based on the research findings, the Self and Impact areas have been clarified by distinguishing stages within each. Self-concerns are now divided into two

FIGURE 4.2   Stages of Concern About the Innovation: Paragraph Definitions

Impact	**6 Refocusing:** The focus is on the exploration of more universal benefits from the innovation, including the possibility of major changes or replacement with a more powerful alternative. Individual has definite ideas about alternatives to the proposed or existing form of the innovation.
	5 Collaboration: The focus is on coordination and cooperation with others regarding use of the innovation.
	4 Consequence: Attention focuses on impact of the innovation on "clients" in the immediate sphere of influence.
Task	**3 Management: Attention is focused on the processes and tasks of using the innovation and the** best use of information and resources. Issues related to efficiency, organizing, managing, scheduling, and time demands are utmost.
Self	**2 Personal:** Individual is uncertain about the demands of the innovation, his/her inadequacy to meet those demands, and his/her role with the innovation. This includes analysis of his/her role in relation to the reward structure of the organization, decision making, and consideration of potential conflicts with existing structures or personal commitment. Financial or status implications of the program for self and colleagues may also be reflected.
	1 Informational: A general awareness of the innovation and interest in learning more detail about it is indicated. The person seems to be unworried about himself/herself in relation to the innovation. She/he is interested in substantive aspects of the innovation in a selfless manner, such as general characteristics, effects, and requirements for use.
Unrelated	**0 Unconcerned:** Little concern about or involvement with the innovation is indicated. Concern about other thing(s) is more intense.

Source: George, A. A., Hall, G. E., Stiegelbauer, S. M. (2006).

stages—Informational and Personal—and Impact concerns into three—Consequence, Collaboration, and Refocusing.

If you think about it, these stages make intuitive sense, and you certainly hear people express these kinds of concerns. For example, at the beginning of the change process teachers (and others) say:

> *Well, at this point I don't know much about it, other than we have been told that we will be adopting it (Stage 1 Informational). I don't know what the principal thinks about our doing this (Stage 2 Personal), or if he even knows about it (Stage 1 Informational). I just hope that I don't have to stop doing what I have been doing and start all over again (Stage 2 Personal). I hope that we learn more at the next faculty meeting (Stage 1 Informational).*

All of these concerns are in the *Self* area, but they represent two component parts. The person knows a little but would like to know more (Stage 1 Informational) and is concerned about where he or she stands in terms of the principal's knowledge and position and what he or she will have to give up when the innovation arrives (Stage 2 Personal).

Pothole Warning

Don't forget about those who are enthusiastic about the change.

Pothole Repair

Having intense Impact concerns is ideal. Unfortunately, all too often leaders overly focus on those with Self and Task concerns. Be sure to take time to compliment and support those with Impact concerns.

Impact concerns are even more complex. Stage 4 Consequence deals with increasing effectiveness and impact in one's own use of the innovation; Stage 5 Collaboration focuses on concern about working with one or more colleagues so that together there can be more impact; and Stage 6 Refocusing indicates that the person has ideas about a more effective alternative. Remember, that the overarching theme of Stages 4, 5, and 6 is always concern about improving the *impact* of the innovation on clients/students.

REFLECTION QUESTIONS

How does the SoC idea fit with your feelings about change? What are some examples from your experiences?

WHY ARE THEY CALLED "STAGES" OF CONCERN?

The research studies clearly document a quasi-developmental path to the concerns as a change process unfolds. However, the ideal flow to concerns is not always guaranteed, nor does it always move in one direction. *If* the innovation is appropriate, *if* the leaders are initiating, and *if* the change process is carefully facilitated, then implementers will move from early Self-concerns to Task concerns (during the first years of use) and, ultimately, to Impact concerns (after three to five years).

Unfortunately, all of these *ifs* are not always present. More often than not, the support needed for the change process over time is not forthcoming, or the leaders fail to facilitate effectively, or, in the case of schools, the district, state, and federal governments annually add more innovations to the point that none is being fully implemented. In these situations, concerns do not progress from Self to Task to Impact. Instead, progress is arrested, with Stage 3 Management concerns continuing to be intense. If these conditions do not change, in time many teachers return to Self-concerns.

In the first conception of the Concerns-Based Adoption Model (CBAM), the term *Stages of Concern* was deliberately chosen to reflect the idealized, developmental approach to change that we value (see Hall, Wallace, & Dossett, 1973). Unfortunately, in most instances, as we pointed out in Chapter 1, change is not viewed and treated as a process but as an event. When this event mentality is applied, the stages model breaks down, and people are forced into sustained Self and/or Task concerns. This is why we call the stages "quasi" developmental.

CAN THERE BE CONCERNS AT MORE THAN ONE STAGE?

When presenting the SoC, we are frequently asked if it is possible to have concerns at more than one stage at the same time. Of course it is possible. In fact, most of the time a person will have intense concerns at more than one stage. For example, although a teacher may have intense Task (Stage 3 Management) concerns, concerns about students are still influencing his or her instructional decision making. In general, teachers will have a conglomeration of concerns representing several of the stages, with some more strongly felt than others and some absent all together.

Graphically, we represent this conglomeration or array of concerns of varying intensities by using a concerns profile. By representing the SoC on the horizontal axis and the relative intensity of concerns on the vertical, a general picture of a person's concerns can be displayed. The peaks indicate stages that are more intense, and the valleys show those that are less intense.

Different, commonly observed scenarios can be envisaged using concerns profiles. For example, we have already described the first-year user of an innovation with intense Stage 3 Management concerns. That person's concerns profile would have a peak on Stage 3, whereas the other stages would be lower. If the person were also a first- or second-year teacher, he or she might have more intense Stage 2 Personal concerns about surviving the evaluation process and receiving tenure. In this case the concerns profile would likely have two peaks, one for Stage 3 Management concerns and a second peak for Stage 2 Personal.

GUIDING PRINCIPLES OF CONCERNS THEORY

1. We all have Personal concerns (Stage 2) when first confronted with change. Rather than condemning someone who has a high level of Personal concerns, you first need to be empathetic and work to determine why these concerns are so intense. Then efforts can be made to resolve them.

2. When you find teachers with Impact concerns, be sure to take time to encourage them. Although these are the types of concerns that we wish educators had all the time, they are unfortunately less frequent than we would like. Spend more time with teachers who have Impact concerns. They will find your interest supportive, and you will feel better by being around such positive teachers.

3. Stage 5 Collaboration in combination with Stage 4 Consequence concerns are very rare in any organization, including schools. When a number of employees have such concerns, it strongly indicates that the leader has been doing something special. In terms of interventions, do all that you can to nurture and support Impact concerns. A school where both Stage 5 concerns and Stage 4 Consequence concerns are intense truly exhibits an interest in students and collegiality about teaching. This is a very strong indicator that a Professional Learning Community (PLC) type of organizational culture is in place.

4. The SoC can be applied to both individuals and to groups. In fact, this chapter deliberately does not identify which are being discussed. The concepts and thinking are the same for both. However, because group SoC Questionnaire (SoCQ) profiles are by definition an average, they can mask individual differences.

IMPLICATIONS FOR LEADERS FACILITATING CHANGE

1. Assume that all change processes will begin with most everyone having more intense Self (Stage 1 Informational and Stage 2 Personal) concerns. From the very beginning, before implementation, interventions should address these concerns.
2. Early and frequent offering of information is the key to reducing the potential for aroused Stage 2 Personal concerns. Once aroused, Personal concerns must be addressed in ways that facilitate their resolution; this often means dealing with issues that are not directly related to the innovation.
3. The first time an innovation is used is when Task (Stage 3 Management) concerns will become most intense. Strategies, such as providing an on-site implementation facilitator, technical manuals, and Web sites with how-to-do-it tips, should be established that directly anticipate and address Task concerns.
4. An important condition for the arousal of Impact (especially Stage 4 Consequence, Stage 5 Collaboration) is first facilitating the resolution of Self and Task concerns.
5. Concerns-based interventions can be targeted toward all implementers, especially during the early phases of the change process. As implementation progresses, key organization units, such as individual schools and departments, will increasingly need to be the targeted units for interventions. Each unit is likely to change at its own pace, and interventions must be customized to address each unit's unique concerns profile.
6. The SoC Questionnaire (SoCQ) can be overused, which results in resistance to filling it out "again." Being skilled at using the one-legged interview and interpreting open-ended concerns statements are much more useful for those engaged in the daily activity of facilitating change processes.

Another teacher might be very experienced and truly a master teacher. His or her concerns profile could be most intense on Stage 3 Management concerns, too, relative to first-year use of the innovation. But her or his second-highest stage could be Stage 4 Consequence, indicating more concern about how use of the innovation is affecting his or her students.

Many combinations of concerns can be imagined and have been observed. In each case, once the profile of concerns has been identified, the important work can begin. As interesting as it is to see and attempt to analyze a concerns profile, the crucial step is in using it to make *concerns-based interventions* that will resolve the concern and move the person toward more advanced use of the innovation. Examples of relevant and inappropriate interventions for each SoC are presented in Appendix C.

ARE THERE TYPICAL CONCERN PROFILES?

SoC profiles are a very informative way to illustrate movement and nonmovement during a change process. When concerns profiles are collected at different points in time, each is a snapshot of that moment. The time series of profiles becomes a motion picture of how concerns evolved and, hopefully, developed. These snapshots represent one way of assessing how far across the Implementation Bridge a particular unit or individual has progressed.

As the term *stages* implies, and as the numbering of the stages suggests, there is a hypothesized pattern to the evolution of concerns profiles when the change process unfolds successfully. This progression takes the form of a "wave motion" of intensities that begins with Self-concerns being more intense prior to first use of the innovation. Then, as implementation begins, Task concerns become more intense, and Self-concerns gradually reduce in intensity. With time (three to five years), Impact concerns can increase in intensity as the Self and Task concerns decrease. A graphic representation of this wave motion pattern is presented in Figure 4.3.

As we have pointed out, this idealized evolution does not always occur. Attempting to change humans in an organizational context is a very complex, dynamic, and, in many ways, subtle enterprise. However, by looking for the patterns, being knowledgeable about what has

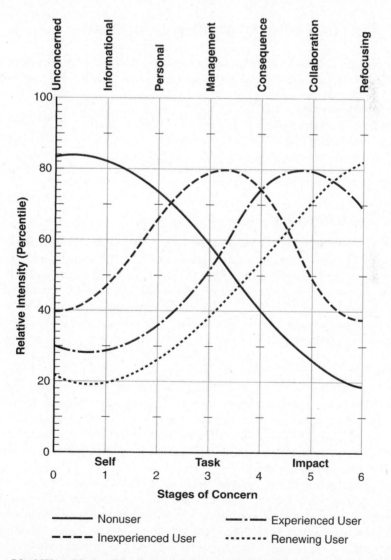

FIGURE 4.3   Ideal Wave Motion Development of Stages of Concern

been learned about change, and being grounded in the uniqueness and intricacies of the situation, it is indeed possible to plan and facilitate a change process that will unfold in the manner shown in Figure 4.3. But since there is a high likelihood that convoluted turns and unexpected happenings will occur along the way, Change Facilitators must continuously engage in monitoring and adjusting.

REFLECTION QUESTIONS

In your experience, how long has it taken to move in increasing intensity from Self, to Task, and ultimately to Impact concerns? What were the keys to getting there— or not getting there?

TECHNIQUES FOR ASSESSING STAGES OF CONCERN

The monitoring of the change process should include regular and ongoing assessment of the SoC of all participants, including the Change Facilitators. There are three ways to assess concerns:

1. One-legged interview (OLI)
2. Open-ended concerns statement (oeSoC)
3. SoC Questionnaire (SoCQ)

Each of these techniques has its strengths and appropriate uses, as well as its inherent weaknesses.

The One-Legged Interview

Many of the CBAM research studies have carefully documented the numerous interventions that school principals, school improvement teams, lead teachers, staff developers, and others have used to facilitate an innovation (Entrekin, 1991; Hall, Hord, & Griffin, 1980; Schiller, 1991a and 1991b; Shieh, 1996; Staessens, 1993; Vandenberghe, 1988). One of the major findings has been that schools that are more successful in change have statistically significantly more of the very small, almost unnoticed interventions that we call *incidents* (see Chapter 7 for more information about interventions). Most of these take the form of a brief conversation between a Change Facilitator and an implementer about use of the innovation, which we call *one-legged interviews* (OLIs).

The busy work of schools leaves little time for extended conversation; everything happens on the run. The clock is ticking, the bells are ringing, and the students are moving. When the adults do meet, their available time is short. Maybe a couple of minutes allow for a quick chat as they pass in the hall, go to the office to pick up their mail, or gather in the lounge during the lunch period.

CBAM research shows that these brief moments are *critical opportunities* whose frequency will determine the final degree of implementation success. Because the time available is so brief, you must make it count.

One interesting insight into the concept of one-legged interviews came when a principal suggested that we should call them "flamingo interviews." This seemed like a good idea until, when telling a Floridian about the suggestion, she pointed out that, yes, a flamingo does stand on one leg, but it also puts it head under its wing! This would not be a very effective way to assess concerns.

The important beginning of a one-legged interview is to encourage the client (e.g., a teacher) to describe what he or she is doing and how the client feels about what he or she is doing, or thinking of doing, with the innovation. The facilitator should not assume that he or she understands the situation but instead should ask and listen.

How's it going today with _____?
What do you see as strengths and weaknesses of this approach?
Tell me more.

The trained facilitator can quickly hear and, if necessary, probe lightly to clarify the concerns. Following this quick diagnosis, the second part of the OLI is for the facilitator to do something to address in some way the indicated concerns. This is an important time to keep the "wave motion" in mind. The focus of the intervention must be on helping to resolve current concerns while anticipating the potential arousal of others.

Using the one-legged interview to assess concerns has advantages and disadvantages. Advantages include that it can take place whenever you are in conversation, whether it is face to face or by telephone. Also, it is unobtrusive, with none of the obvious probing involved in paper- and-pencil methods. Another strength is that the facilitator shows interest in what the teacher is doing, which in and of itself is supportive. This is a very useful technique for sales representatives as they assess customer needs.

The major disadvantage is accuracy. Different facilitators can hear the same words and offer very different interpretations. So be very careful about leaping to conclusions based on a diagnosis derived from a one-legged interview. Specifics must be checked out and, as with all concerns-based diagnoses, treated as tentative until more is known.

The Open-Ended Statement

The first systematic measure of concerns that Frances Fuller used was to ask teacher education students to write a description of their concerns, which was then content analyzed. This open-ended statement has continued to be helpful, and collecting the information is straightforward. Respondents are given a blank piece of paper that has the following written at the top:

When you think about [the innovation] what concerns do you have?
Please be frank, and answer in complete sentences.

1.

2.

3.

These papers are then collected and content analyzed as described in a manual by Newlove and Hall (1976). The first step is to read the statement to determine if the overall theme is Unrelated, Self, Task, or Impact concerns. The statement is then reread, and an SoC is assigned to each sentence in order to make a holistic assessment. Note that the individual sentence scores are not totaled and averaged. There is no such thing as a "3.5 concern" or a "5.7 average concern." Instead, the entire statement is judged.

This technique has a number of strengths. An obvious one is that the concerns are in the respondents' own words. Also, this technique can be used at any time. For example, if a staff meeting or workshop is coming up, ask the participants to submit an open-ended concerns statement two weeks in advance. This information can then be used to plan the meeting or workshop so that it responds to the expressed concerns. Participants can thus have input in a nonthreatening way.

As with the one-legged interview, the open-ended format has disadvantages. One is that different respondents will provide different amounts of information. One person may write three paragraphs, whereas another may write only one sentence. Some people will only provide a list of topics instead of complete sentences, which means no concerns statement is available to be scored. Some people will turn in a blank page, which is very hard to interpret. The other major problem with open-ended concerns statements is reliability. Even thoroughly trained judges have difficulty in agreeing on how to rate some statements. But for most staff-development and meeting situations, for which an estimate of concerns is useful, the open-ended statement is an excellent tool.

The Stages of Concern Questionnaire

The most rigorous technique for measuring concerns is the Stages of Concern Questionnaire (SoCQ) (Form 075), which is a 35-item questionnaire that has strong reliability estimates (test/retest reliabilities range from .65 to .86) and internal consistency (alpha-coefficients range from .66 to .83). The SoCQ was constructed to apply to all educational innovations. The questionnaire items stay the same, with the only change being the insertion of the name of the specific innovation on the cover page.

It is possible to use the SoCQ to construct concerns profiles. Because the questionnaire has been designed so that a raw score is calculated for each stage, a graphic representation of the data can be made using a percentile table for conversions. Study and practice, as well as training, will develop one's skill in interpreting these profiles.

Copies of the SoC Questionnaire and the SoC Quick Scoring Device are included as Appendices A and B in this book. A technical manual, *Measuring Implementation in Schools: The Stages of Concern Questionnaire* (George, Hall, & Stiegelbauer, 2006), includes additional scoring and interpretation information, as well as guidelines for appropriate applications. *An important caution:* No one should consider using the SoCQ without study and direct access to this important reference.

The original SoCQ was developed several decades ago (Hall et al., 1979). It has had extensive use in studies, as a guide for staff development, and for facilitating implementation processes. In 2006 the SoCQ items and statistics were revisited and the new version (Form 075) was established. This form has an even stronger record of effectiveness.

The advantages of the SoCQ technique for assessing concerns include strong reliability and validity and the capability of using it to develop concerns profiles. The SoCQ is particularly useful for formal implementation assessment efforts. One disadvantage is that respondents often do not want to fill out this, or any other, questionnaire. This most formal way of assessing SoC should thus be used sparingly. Normally in our school studies we will use the SoCQ twice a year (e.g., early October and late April). Sometimes we have gone to a third assessment in January. We always include space for an open-ended statement on the last page to give the respondents another opportunity to point out something they may think is being missed.

Change Facilitator Stages of Concern Questionnaire

A special form of the concerns questionnaire, *Change Facilitator Stages of Concern Questionnaire* (CFSoCQ), was developed for use with principals, staff developers, and others who have a role in facilitating implementation (Hall, Newlove, George, Rutherford, & Hord, 1991). This questionnaire is not for use with those who are the front-line implementers of the innovation. The CFSoCQ is designed to assess the concerns from the perspective of the leaders and other supporters of the implementers. The CFSoC stages have been defined, and these definitions are used to interpret CFSoCQ profiles in the same manner as is done to interpret SoCQ profiles.

REFLECTION QUESTION

When in a change process would you want to use each of the three ways of measuring SoC?

Characteristic Stages of Concern Profiles

Many of the commonly observed SoC profiles are easy to interpret by studying the technical manuals and developing an understanding of concerns theory. Some profiles are in fact "classic"; we have seen them many times, and their meaning is well understood. A couple of these are presented here to illustrate our thinking about diagnosis and implications for concerns-based intervening.

Remember that one of the keys to interpreting concerns profiles is to look for the peaks and valleys. It does not matter if the overall profile is at the 80th percentile or the 20th; it is the overall shape that must be considered first. It is the high and low points on that profile that serve as the beginning frame of reference.

The second step is to study closely the full definitions of each stage presented in Figure 4.2. A peak on a profile indicates that the type of concerns that are described for that stage are intense, whereas a valley shows that there is little or no concern for that stage. When there is a peak at more than one stage, the profile must be interpreted by combining the definitions for those stages. In most cases this level of interpretation will serve well.

However, to illustrate that there is always more to be learned about concerns theory and assessment, a couple of the more interesting variations in concerns profiles are described next. For each profile we offer a brief interpretation and ideas about the types of interventions that would make sense.

The "Big W" Concerns Profile

The "Big W" Concerns Profile (so named for its configuration of peaks and valleys) has been observed all too frequently (see Figure 4.4). In this profile Stage 3 Management concerns are very intense, whereas Stages 1 Informational, 2 Personal, 4 Consequence, and 5 Collaboration

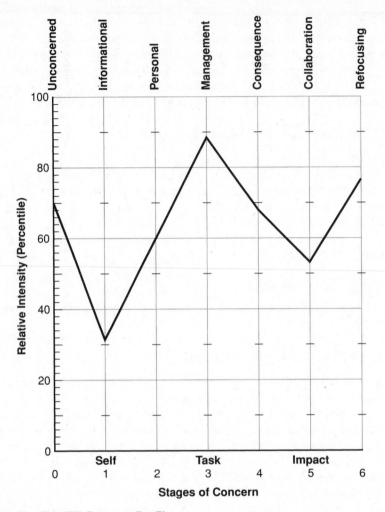

FIGURE 4.4   The "Big W" Concerns Profile

are of much lower intensity. This profile would not be so significant if it were not for the "tailing up" on Stage 6 Refocusing. This combination of peaks and valleys indicates some ideas are strongly held about what ought to be done differently with this innovation (Stage 6 Refocusing) that are related to the very high (and unresolved) Stage 3 Management concerns. Teachers with this profile can be quite adamant about their situation and how things should be changed.

More than a one-legged interview will be needed to address the underlying cause of such high Task concerns. We know from a number of studies that this concerns profile is frequently found in schools where the principal has displayed the Responder Change Facilitator Style (see Chapter 6). Part of the strategic action may thus be to strengthen the principal's support of the teachers' use of the innovation.

High Stage 4 Consequence and Stage 5 Collaboration in a concerns profile (see Figure 4.5) represent the ideal goal of a concerns-based implementation effort. After all, the essence of good schooling is teachers with high Impact concerns about the effects of the use of

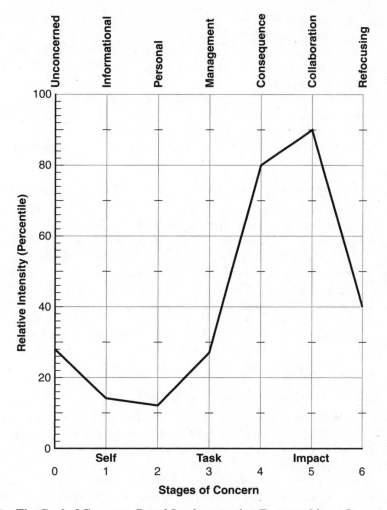

FIGURE 4.5   The Goal of Concerns-Based Implementation Expressed in an Impact Concerns Profile

the innovation in their classroom (Stage 4 Consequence) and about linking with other teachers in using the innovation (Stage 5 Collaboration). These are characteristics of a PLC at its best. The early research of Judith Warren Little (Little & McLaughlin, 1993) on teacher collegiality confirms the importance of this dynamic for teachers and their students. Unfortunately, finding individual teachers and school staffs that reflect this concerns profile is very rare. To develop to this point means that change truly has been treated as a process, that the innovation has been given sufficient time to be implemented, that there has been a principal with an Initiator Change Facilitator Style, and that the innovation, or more likely an innovation bundle, was significant and matched the school's vision well.

Intervening on this profile should include a celebration. Clearly the teachers and the principal have been hard at work and doing some special things. They should be congratulated, supported, and cherished. Also, this is a fragile system state. A change in a key player (e.g., the superintendent or the principal) or the arrival of some new mandate from the school board, state, or federal government can sidetrack and undercut the synergy and momentum that have been built. Therefore, a second set of interventions should be designed to protect and encourage the continuation of the Impact concerns, with a special emphasis on facilitating the sustaining of Collaboration concerns.

When a large number of SoC profiles are available they can be sorted into subgroups according to common characteristics. For example, Matthews, Marshall, and Milne (2000) had in excess of 700 SoC profiles from teachers engaged in their first year of use of laptop computers. Nearly all of the SoC profiles could be placed in one of six subgroupings.

IMPLICATIONS OF RESISTANCE IN STAGES OF CONCERN PROFILES

We haven't yet talked about resistance, which is a natural part of change. In the CBAM work, most of what is called *resistance* will show up in the SoC diagnostic dimension, especially Self-concerns. Here again, we advocate listening before intervening. Often, what Change Facilitators see as resistance are aspects of Stage 2 Personal concerns. There is an uncertainty about what will be expected and self-doubts about one's ability to succeed with the new way. There may also be some grieving over the loss of things that were currently being done successfully. Another aspect of this, which is all too frequently overlooked, is the failure to have addressed, early on, Stage 1 Informational concerns. When people don't know what is happening, it is perfectly normal for Stage 2 Personal concerns to become more intense. The less information provided, the higher the Stage 2 Personal concerns will be.

At the beginning of a change process, when Self-concerns are more intense, be sure to use many channels to communicate what is coming. Communication must start during the spring, before implementation is to begin. Also, don't simply make a one-time announcement and expect everyone to get the message. People with Stage 1 Informational concerns need to receive small bits of information, repeated across time. They do not want all of the details at once. And don't forget their Stage 2 Personal concerns; they want to hear enthusiasm and promises of continuing commitment to and support for the change.

Of course, there can be real resisters. The reasons for their position are varied. Some may simply not understand the proposed innovation. Others may have a different agenda or a real philosophical disagreement with the innovation. Sadly, there may be one or two who have serious problems elsewhere in their lives, which none of us are equipped to handle. In a concerns profile, especially high Personal concerns (Stage 2) in what would otherwise be a nonuser profile (remember Figure 4.4), and a slight "tailing up" of Stage 6 Refocusing, are indications of what typically is called a "hostile" nonuser.

Pothole Warning

Mandates automatically lead to significantly higher Stage 2 Personal concerns. Failure to anticipate this condition can be fatal to change initiatives.

Pothole Repair

As was pointed out in Chapter 1, mandates can work but only when greater attention is given to addressing Self (Stage 1 Informational and Stage 2 Personal) concerns. More effort must be given to providing information that is clear and consistent.

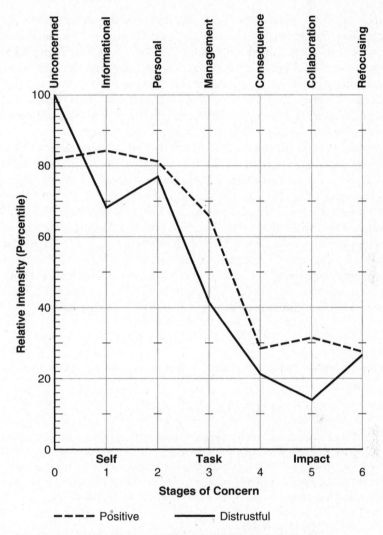

FIGURE 4.6   Comparison of Positive and Distrustful Nonuser SoC Profiles

Let's look more closely at these dynamics. Figure 4.6 presents both the typical positive nonuser profile and the typical hostile nonuser profile. Consider some of the standard comments of the hostile nonuser:

"Where is the research to show that this is better?"

"We've always done it this way. All you have done is put a new name on it."

"Ah. This is just old wine in new bottles. You know how education is. It's just a pendulum swinging back and forth from fad to fad."

The tendency of Change Facilitators is to react to such attitudes by saying something like "Oh, no. This really *is* different." However, from a concerns profile perspective, this is the wrong intervention. What the facilitator is hearing is the "tailing up" on Stage 6 Refocusing—that is, strongly held ideas about how things ought to be different. But which SoC is the highest? Stage 2 Personal, and right behind these is Stage 1 Informational. This indicates that the so-called resister actually does not have enough information about the innovation and thus is personally uncomfortable about it. So telling this person that this innovation really is different is *interpreted* (see Chapter 8) as follows: "You are telling me that I don't know what I am talking about and that further threatens me." The result is less ability to listen, still higher Personal concerns, and probably stronger "tailing up" on Stage 6 Refocusing.

A better intervention approach (although there is no quick cure once this profile is established) would be to express empathy and understanding for the person's concerns. Don't attempt to explain a lot in the first contact. Try to have a series of one-legged interviews to get a sense of what is producing this concerns profile, and then gradually provide pieces of information about the change, the change process, and how they will be supported. There is no simple remedy for this, or for many other concerns profiles. However, what needs to be done to facilitate change in most cases is relatively straightforward: provide information, resources, and support that are aligned with the person's concerns.

Much of the discussion of SoC to this point has focused on individuals. SoC also can be applied to groups, a whole school staff, or a larger system. As one example, read the vignette presented here to see how SoC can be used in a districtwide change process.

■ ■ ■ ■ ■ ■▬▬▬

VIGNETTE

DISTRICTWIDE USE OF STAGES OF CONCERN

In one large suburban school district, the science department coordinators and staff developers engaged in a collaborative project with CBAM researchers to do a concerns-based implementation of their revised science curriculum. Ultimately, this project was very successful in terms of teacher success in implementing the curriculum and was recognized with a special award from the American Educational Research Association based on the practitioner-researcher partnership.

THE IMPLEMENTATION GAME PLAN

From the beginning, an accepted assumption was that change is a process, not an event. Further, the SoC were used as the guiding dimension when planning training workshops, newsletter content, and other interventions. The SoCQ was administered twice a year (in early October and late April) for three years, and science facilitators were trained in doing one-legged interviews.

Due to the large size of the district (80 elementary schools plus many secondary schools), it did not seem reasonable to expect that all schools could be supported in implementation at the same time. So the district was divided into thirds, and implementation was phased for one third of the schools at a time, beginning at six-month intervals. (Many year-round schools were in this district, so the traditional nine-month school year did not apply throughout.)

ADDRESSING TASK CONCERNS

The school board had budgeted for three all-day in-service sessions. Rather than holding all of these at the beginning, they were distributed over the first year and a half of use of the curriculum. This

V I G N E T T E   CONTINUED

made great sense from a concerns-based perspective, since Stage 3 Management concerns last for at least a year. Also, Task concerns are most clear and intense when teachers are engaged in teaching specific lessons. By stretching the time between the in-service days, it was possible to offer each near the time when teachers would have questions about specific lessons they were about to teach.

A cadre of lead teachers was identified and trained to design and conduct the in-service workshops. These teachers had field-tested the materials and were experienced science teachers. They were trained in the SoC, in how to interpret SoCQ and open-ended data, and in doing one-legged interviews.

The lead teachers established an overall design for workshop days as well as a special version for each grade level. Then teachers from across the district were brought together by grade for the workshops. A newsletter was used to guide teachers in pacing themselves from lesson to lesson and to alert them about upcoming logistical steps. A special class of interventions was the "comfort and caring" sessions, which were hosted by an experienced science teacher after school. Here again, face-to-face opportunities were provided to address the "how-to" questions (Stage 3 Management) as they arose.

SELF-CONCERNS AND THE PRINCIPAL

The important role of the school principal was anticipated as well. All too frequently the principal is bypassed, and only teachers are trained. Most principals, however, like to know what their teachers are being asked to do. In addition, the change-facilitator role that the principal assumes makes a major difference in how successful teachers will be with implementation (see Chapter 6). Remember, one of the early concerns is Stage 2 Personal, when a common question has to do with principal support. Having principals know what is expected and anticipated can help them be more supportive.

Thus, early in the district project it was decided that principals should be given information first, before their teachers, although they did not receive as much information nor the same information. A half-day session was held with the principals, who were shown the materials, the teacher's guide, and sample lessons. All of this addressed their Self-concerns. They were also told about some of the questions and problems that their teachers would likely have. They were introduced to the lead teachers and to the special telephone hotline and the other implementation support resources that were designed to help them and their teachers implement the revised science curriculum.

EARLY SELF-CONCERNS OF TEACHERS

According to concerns theory, teachers are likely to have some kinds of Self-concerns in the school year prior to implementation of the innovation. (Remember the "wave motion" shown in Figure 4.3.) To address these early nonuser Stage 1 Informational and Stage 2 Personal concerns, a 1.5-hour after-school meeting was held in the spring before implementation was to begin. As the staffs from two neighboring schools met at one of the schools, one of the science department coordinators and a lead teacher hosted an introductory session about the new curriculum, what would be expected, the timeline, and the availability of supplies.

These briefing sessions were conducted in an upbeat tone. "We really like this program." The expectation was made clear: "Use of this curriculum is board policy." The timeline for in-service sessions and the resources that would be available to help teachers were described briefly. Remember, at this point teachers do not want all of the details. They instead need positive reinforcement and a general picture of what will be happening. At this time, Stage 1 Informational concerns are being addressed and Stage 2 Personal concerns are being anticipated. If the dispersing of information is paced well, and if the support is in place, the intensity of Stage 2 Personal concerns should not increase disproportionately.

(continued)

■ ■ ■ ■ ■ ▬▬▬▬▬▬▬▬▬▬▬▬▬▬▬▬▬▬▬▬▬▬▬▬▬▬▬▬▬▬▬▬▬▬▬▬▬

V I G N E T T E   CONTINUED

At the end of the introductory sessions, teachers were offered the opportunity to take the teacher's guide with them: "I know that some of you will want to do some preplanning this summer. In case you do, here is a copy of the teacher's guide. You don't have to look at it before the first workshop, but it is here if you would like it."

IMPACT CONCERNS FOR SOME

It was expected that more intense Impact concerns would be felt by some teachers, such as those who had field-tested the innovation and those who were experienced science teachers. Although they still had to learn about the curriculum, they were ready to consider some of the more advanced and subtle aspects of innovation use. Interventions for them had to be different in some ways.

To address the varying levels of teachers' concerns, the workshops were designed with alternate routes for parts of the day. One route, which allowed teachers to stay in a small-group setting and to work with an experienced teacher on specifics of lesson preparation, materials, and activities, was chosen by teachers with more Self and Task concerns. The second route, which gave teachers the choice to work independently or in pairs through a series of self-paced modules, films, and exercises, was selected by teachers with higher Impact concerns.

Another strategy that focused on Impact concerns was to wait three years before training all teachers in some of the more subtle aspects of the innovation. It was decided at the outset that the first goal was to have all teachers teaching science, instead of having just some teaching science very well. Given the limits on resources and the large size of the district, it would not have been possible to achieve both outcomes at once. It was also not possible from a concerns perspective. As a result, a new round of workshops was started in the third year to prepare all teachers to use cooperative groups in science teaching. Although this had been planned from the beginning, it was not emphasized until after the Task concerns about materials, lessons, and scheduling had been resolved.

In summary, the first three years of the implementation were designed to have all teachers teaching science by addressing their Self and Task concerns. During the fourth year, other innovations (e.g., cooperative learning), in what was now an innovation bundle, were introduced and supported. With this phasing approach an entire district came to have quality science teaching in most of its elementary classrooms.

VIGNETTE CRITIQUE QUESTIONS

1. What characteristics of the interventions used in this district made them especially relevant to each identified SoC?
2. What would need to happen in a school that continued to have Task concerns?
3. Typically, it takes three years for a school staff to resolve their Task concerns. What could be done in the third year of implementation to facilitate the arousal of Impact concerns?

REFLECTION QUESTION

For most innovations, such as new curriculum approaches and new technology, it typically takes three to five years for the SoC wave motion to unfold with a whole school/district staff. What would you see happening with a transformational innovation such as changing from teaching-centered to student-learning-centered instruction?

Pothole Warning

If the Personal side of change is not seen as important or needing to be addressed as a change process unfolds, then the entire effort may be lost.

Pothole Repair

Not only is there likely to be increasing doubts about the change, there can be more resistance. Attending to Stage 1 Informational concerns early and often is very important.

SUMMARY

In this chapter we have examined the Personal side of change. There is a construct, Stages of Concern, and tools to assess the feelings and perceptions of individuals, groups, and whole staffs. SoC is first and foremost a heuristic and diagnostic tool for understanding the feelings and perceptions that are part of all change processes. As interesting as assessing SoC can be, the most important part is to make Concerns-Based interventions. Examples of interventions have been inserted throughout this chapter. Additional examples, along with inappropriate interventions, are provided in Appendix C. The SoC construct also is useful for predicting what will happen next and planning for future interventions. In addition, SoC is an important tool for diagnosis, program evaluation, and research.

We know that SoC is a cross-cultural phenomenon. For example, Shieh (1996) was the first to systematically identify the same categories of concerns in teachers in Taiwan. Earlier Van den Berg and Vandenberghe (1981) developed Dutch language measures and documented SoC in Belgium and the Netherlands. Hargreaves, Moyles, Merry, Paterson, Pell, and Esarte-Sarries (2003) studied teacher concerns in the United Kingdom. In a large study in Cyprus, Christou, Eliophotou-Menon, and Philippou (2004) documented relationships between teacher SoC and implementation of a mathematics curriculum. Also, Cheung, Hattie, and Ng (2001) and Cheung & Yip (2004) have examined SoC in Hong Kong. Also, SoC has been studied extensively in regard to the implementation of technology (see, for example, Yuliang & Huang, 2005).

Failure to attend to concerns as people are experiencing the change process can lead to several kinds of potholes. For example, teachers who believe "this too will pass" could develop the Hostile Nonuser SoC profile (see Figure 4.6). Mandates can lead to resistance, especially if Self-concerns are not addressed. As a review revisit the Pothole Warning features that have been inserted at several points throughout this chapter.

When concerns are addressed it is possible to have Impact concerns increase in intensity. Be sure to support and encourage people with these concerns. Unfortunately they are often the most lonely and neglected since they are not demanding of time and attention. After all, in a Concerns-Based world the arousal and sustaining of Impact concerns, especially at Stage 4 Consequence and Stage 5 Collaboration, is the goal.

As a last reminder, be sure to obtain the technical manual (George et al., 2006) and if possible participate in a training session before initiating a major effort using SoC. Also, be sure to refer back to the "Guiding Principles" for key suggestions about facilitating change processes.

DISCUSSION QUESTIONS

1. Which of the SoC have you found to be most important to attend to?

2. What was done to address your concerns when they were really intense at a particular stage? What would have happened to your concerns without this intervention?

3. If the ideal is having teachers with Impact concerns, what can be done to support the arousal and sustaining of Stage 4 Consequence concerns? What would need to be added to address Stage 5 Collaboration?

4. What happens to your concerns when your supervisor has intense Stage 2 Personal concerns? How do your interactions change?

5. Think about one of the great teachers you have had. Generally, what where his or her most intense SoC?

6. In your experience, which workshops have you considered to be the best and the worst? How did each match with your concerns at the time?

FIELDWORK ACTIVITIES

1. Attend a workshop and observe the concerns of the participants. How well did the content and process of the workshop match those concerns?

2. Collect and analyze open-ended concerns data from people who are attending a staff meeting or workshop. Analyze the statements. (Obtain a copy of Newlove and Hall's [1976] manual to help with this.) Develop a recommendation about what should be done and how to address the participants' concerns.

3. Conduct a one-legged interview with a person, and then ask someone else who understands SoC to do the same, with the same individual. See how well your assessments of the person's concerns match.

CONDUCT A STUDY

Note: Before conducting any study, be sure to obtain a copy of the appropriate technical manual and study it closely. Also, contact one of the authors of this text when you have questions.

1. *Evaluating a Workshop:* Measure the SoC before and after a week-long workshop. Think about how the SoC changed, or did not change, as a result of what was done.

2. *Monitoring Implementation Progress:* At a key time, such as halfway through the first year of implementation, assess SoC using the SoCQ and an open-ended concerns statement. Use these data to plan the next steps of implementation support.

3. *Longitudinal Study of a Major Change Effort:* Plan for and collect SoC data once or twice a year for several years. Use the findings to plan next steps and to review how far across the Implementation Bridge each individual department and a whole school have progressed.

4. *Summative Evaluations:* A key issue that must be addressed in evaluation studies has to do with determining the extent of implementation. Before judgments can be made about the value of an innovation in terms of outcomes such as student learning, an assessment should be made of how far along implementation has progressed. SoC is one important indicator. In theory, outcomes should be higher as each implementer moves from Unconcerned, to Self, to Task, and ultimately to Impact concerns.

5. *Research Question:* A basic area for research would be to learn more about what is entailed in arousal and resolution of concerns. Frances Fuller (1969, 1970) hypothesized that arousal of a concern was more of an affective experience and resolution came about through cognitive experiences. We need to know a lot more about this topic.

ADDITIONAL READINGS

For measuring teacher SoC, use the Stages of Concern Questionnaire (Form 075). George, A. A., Hall, G. E., & Stiegelbauer, S. M. (2006). *Measuring implementation in schools: The Stages of Concern Questionnaire.* Austin, TX: Southwest Educational Development Laboratory.

For measuring leaders of change efforts, use the Change Facilitator Stages of Concern Questionnaire (CF-SoCQ). Hall, G. E., Newlove, B. W., George, A. A., Rutherford, W. L., Hord, S. M. (1991). *Measuring change facilitator Stages of Concern: A manual for use of the CFSoC Questionnaire.* Austin, TX: Southwest Educational Development Laboratory.

For measuring written descriptions of concerns, refer to Newlove, B. W., & Hall, G. E. (1976). *A manual for assessing open-ended statements of concern about the innovation* (Report No. 3029). Austin: The University of Texas, Research and Development Center for Teacher Education. (ERIC Document Reproduction Service No. ED 144 Also available from the Southwest Educational Development Laboratory, Austin, TX. 207).

CHAPTER 5

EXPLORING THE USE OF INNOVATIONS

Levels of Use

Mercy! Is this new software product useful! They are always bringing new tools, but this one sounds good, and I am going online to see if I can learn more about it, and if it will do anything for our department.

—Central office social studies coordinator

I am happy to report that I have worked the bugs out of how to use math manipulatives with third-graders, and I have a system that works!

—Third-grade teacher

Can you help me order the equipment for the sophomore earth science units? I'm getting things ready to start in September.

—High school science teacher

My marketing director told me to find out how our sales staff is working with the new product; we may need to give them more training if they are not pitching the new product in a well-organized and consistent way.

—Head of sales for Futura Kitchen Co.

I telephoned a colleague at another school to inquire about the problem-based mathematics program his school is using and whether it stimulates the kids in critical thinking.

—Middle school math department chair

Another teacher and I have worked together with this approach. The changes that we have made this year are really helping students to succeed.

—Teacher in the fifth-grade team

There is a prevailing assumption that if individuals have a new program, process, or product, they will be employing it in an effective way. Through our research studies we have learned that use of a new program is not automatic, nor is it a matter of some persons using it and others not. Using new programs or processes is not a simple case of "Yes, he's using it" or "No, she is not." In any given change effort, implementers will be operating in very different ways with new practices—thus, the real question is "*How* is she or he using it?"

Before we began our exploration of this question, use of new curriculum, instructional methods, or the implementation of new organizational structures were assessed in terms of whether the materials and/or equipment required were present in the classroom. Little attention was given to whether the materials ever left the storage closet or, instead, held up a flower pot.

The implicit assumption was that initial professional development plus materials equaled use. Our observations and studies have documented a number of different behavioral patterns for nonusers and users. To understand this phenomenon of the change process, the Diagnostic Dimension of Levels of Use was born.

Stages of Concern. Levels of Use. The terms have a deceptively similar ring. However, we are about to make a significant conceptual switch, for whereas Stages of Concern (SoC) addresses the *affective* side of change—people's reactions, feelings, perceptions, and attitudes—Levels of Use (LoU) has to do with *behaviors* and portrays *how* people are acting with respect to a specified change.

This chapter will explore the behaviors of people as they seek to learn about new practices for their classrooms and schools or, perhaps, ignore such matters entirely. It also will examine behavior as individuals adopt and implement new ideas and innovations. Eight LoU will be explained, and examples and applications will be given. LoU is a third Diagnostic Dimension of the Concerns-Based Adoption Model (CBAM). The behaviors of so-called users and nonusers is another frame for describing where people are along the Implementation Bridge and for diagnosing their progress in implementing a change.

Further, the LoU framework makes it possible to understand and predict what is likely to occur as a change process continues to unfold. Facilitators who understand and apply the LoU concept and its measures are able to provide appropriate interventions that will be relevant and helpful to those involved, or expected to be involved, in change. In addition, LoU is a very important concept for evaluators and researchers. A critical step in determining whether a new approach is making a difference is to determine first if the innovation is being used. Otherwise, as Charters and Jones (1973) observed, there is a risk of evaluating "nonevents."

FOCUS QUESTIONS

1. What is the concept of LoU?
2. What benefits does LoU provide in evaluation of change efforts?
3. How can an individual's LoU be assessed?
4. How can a person be further described by Categories at each of the LoU?
5. What does a person look like at each of the LoU?
6. How can LoU be applied to facilitating change efforts?

THE LEVELS OF USE CONCEPT

Eight classifications, or behavioral profiles, of how people act or behave in relation to an innovation have been identified and verified through research. Since LoU deals with behaviors, it was possible to develop operational definitions for each level (see Figure 5.1). These definitions enable a change facilitator or evaluator to make clearer distinctions within the traditional dichotomy of use/nonuse (Hall, Loucks, Rutherford, & Newlove, 1975). These individual measurements can be aggregated for a school- or systemwide view of the extent of use of a particular change.

The first distinction to be made is whether the individual is a user or a nonuser. Three nonuse and five use levels have been identified. Each is described briefly in the following subsections, along with suggestions about appropriate interventions.

FIGURE 5.1   Levels of Use of the Innovation

Users	**VI**	**Renewal:** State in which the user re-evaluates the quality of use of the innovation, seeks major modifications of or alternatives to present innovation to achieve increased impact on clients, examines new developments in the field, and explores new goals for self and the system.
	V	**Integration:** State in which the user is combining own efforts to use the innovation with related activities of colleagues to achieve a collective impact on clients within their common sphere of influence.
	IVB	**Refinement:** State in which the user varies the use of the innovation to increase impact on clients within immediate sphere of influence. Variations are based on knowledge of both short- and long-term consequences for clients.
	IVA	**Routine:** Use of the innovation is stabilized. Few if any changes are being made in ongoing use. Little preparation or thought is being given to improving innovation use or its consequences.
	III	**Mechanical Use:** State in which the user focuses most effort on the short-term, day-to-day use of the innovation with little time for reflection. Changes in use are made more to meet user needs than client needs. The user is primarily engaged in a stepwise attempt to master the tasks required to use the innovation, often resulting in disjointed and superficial use.
Nonusers	**II**	**Preparation:** State in which the user is preparing for first use of the innovation.
	I	**Orientation:** State in which the user has recently acquired or is acquiring information about the innovation and/or has recently explored or is exploring its value orientation and its demands upon user and user system.
	0	**Nonuse:** State in which the user has little or no knowledge of the innovation, no involvement with the innovation, and is doing nothing toward becoming involved.

Source: LoU has been described and presented in many publications. An important resource for obtaining more detailed information about LoU is Hall, Dirksen, & George (2006).

GUIDING PRINCIPLES OF LEVELS OF USE

1. With any innovation, each person exhibits some kind of behaviors and thus can be identified as being at a certain LoU.
2. The Decision Points that operationalize the levels and the information related to Categories contribute to the overall description of an individual's LoU.
3. It is not appropriate to assume that a first-time user will be at Level III Mechanical Use. Nor should it be assumed that a person who has used the innovation several times will not be at LoU III.
4. A focused interview protocol has been established for efficiently collecting LoU information. A written format will not work to measure behavior. The only alternative to the LoU Interview would be extended ethnographic fieldwork using the LoU Chart as the observation and interview guide, which is what was done in the original LoU Interview validity study (Hall & Loucks, 1977).
5. Informally gathered information about an individual's LoU can be used for facilitating implementation of change; more rigorously collected LoU data can be used for conducting research studies and for evaluating the extent of implementation.
6. The LoU are presented in a logical sequence, but this is not always followed by everyone. Typically, people move sequentially from LoU 0 to LoU IVA and then may move up, down, or stay at LoU IVA.

Nonusers

Three very different types of nonusers have been identified. It is important to understand the behavioral distinctions between them, since the support and assistance that is appropriate for each will vary accordingly. In addition, although the behaviors of each are quite different, all three describe nonusers of the change from an evaluation perspective.

Level of Use 0 Nonuse.   When a person knows very little or nothing at all about an innovation or change, and exhibits no behavior related to it, that person is said to be at LoU 0 Nonuse. Further, if the LoU 0 person has any knowledge of the innovation, it may be inaccurate. If such a person receives a brochure in the mail, it is not read. If there is an orientation presentation about the innovation, he or she does not attend or, if required to attend, grades papers or engages in some other form of off-task activity. Again, no action is taken related to the change.

If it is not important for such an individual to become involved with the particular change, a facilitator may ignore this person. However, if the person is expected to be involved, the facilitator's challenge is to design and deliver interventions that stimulate interest and support movement to learn about the change. LoU 0 Nonuse people are potentially an excellent source of data for the evaluator who is looking for a comparison or control group. However, much to the chagrin of change facilitators and evaluators, significant proportions of LoU 0 people are regularly found in the *treatment* group.

Level of Use I Orientation.   When a person takes action to learn about an innovation, or exhibits interest in knowing more about it, he or she is characterized as being at LoU I Orientation. Typical LoU I behaviors include attending an overview session about the innovation, examining a Web site or materials displayed by a vendor, asking questions of colleagues, or e-mailing a vendor to obtain descriptive materials about various approaches that might work. The behaviors of the individual are related to learning more about the innovation, but no decision has been made to use it.

The facilitator will find it easy to respond to such a person, since he or she is actively looking for information. Thus, relevant interventions include providing information in the most provocative and interesting manner possible, so that adoption and use will be encouraged.

Level of Use II Preparation.   An individual who has decided to use the new program or process and names a time to begin is at LoU II Preparation. At this level, use has not started, but the intention and a specific start-up time have been indicated. The person typically is studying and preparing materials for initial use.

It could be that the decision to begin use has been made for the individual—for instance, by a state or district policy that mandates action or by the principal in concert with faculty peers who are pressing for use. In any case, although how the decision is made is of interest, it does not figure into LoU, which focuses on behaviors. Obviously, the facilitator's role is to be as supportive as possible, providing assistance so that when use does begin, it can proceed as efficiently and smoothly as possible.

The three classifications of nonusers have been verified through studies of change efforts in K–12 schools, universities, medical schools, and business settings. Because the three levels represent three different behavioral profiles, they provide understanding and guidance to change facilitators in supporting each individual in his or her actions to learn about, consider, and prepare for first use of an innovation. Strategic planners should keep in mind that in order for an entire organization or macrosystem to change, the individual members will need time and appropriate interventions to move beyond these nonuse levels.

Users

Implementation may be said to start in earnest when users and their clients (i.e., company staff, teachers, and students) begin use of the innovation. Five LoU of users have been identified and described. A key in making these distinctions is the type of adaptations that are being made by the user in relation to his or her use of the innovation or in the innovation itself. How this plays out will be discernible as each of the five levels is described in the following subsections. Keep in mind that although these descriptions are presented in a sequence that is logical, each person will not necessarily follow the sequence. Each LoU is independent of the other; LoU is not a straight-line hierarchy.

Level of Use III Mechanical.   At this level, use of the innovation is disjointed and inefficient. This LoU is characterized by experimentation in schedules and organization in order to make the innovation work more easily for him or her. There is continual referral to the users' manual, and planning is day to day and minute to minute. Adaptations are made in managing time, materials, and other logistics. The short-term, day-to-day focus is on planning and a general inefficiency in how the innovation is used. Very likely, the implementer is making adaptations in his/her use or in the innovation itself in order to master their use of the new practice.

The facilitator's task is to help LoU III Mechanical use implementers with the frequently harrowing experiences of finding and organizing materials, and having time to plan for use while managing classrooms and students. The lack of knowledge about what will happen next affects such users' efforts to make innovation use more efficient for them.

Successful facilitators of LoU III users are those who are willing to do all sorts of seemingly low-level, nitty-gritty tasks to help the implementer achieve short-term success in use. They offer many how-to tips. They send out e-mails with organization suggestions. They may publish a Web site or set up a telephone hotline to answer mechanical-use questions as they arise.

Successful facilitators have been known to organize materials in the closet, co-plan with the teacher, run and fetch what is needed, bring in substitute materials when glitches occur, and co-teach or demonstrate teaching in the LoU III teacher's classroom. As noted in the discussion of adaptations, LoU III implementers typically make changes in their use of the innovation in order to find a system that works for them. A knowledgeable and experienced facilitator can be a highly significant source of help.

Level of Use IVA Routine.   If the user has been given sufficient time and adequate help, LoU IVA Routine may be reached. At this level, the implementer has mastered the innovation and its use and has established a regular way of working with it. At this level, users do not plan to make any adaptations or changes; instead, use is stabilized. These users may be heard to comment "Why should I change? My way is working fine." Thus, the LoU IVA person is making no adaptations. Note that this does not mean that the Configuration they are using is of high fidelity. LoU IVA users have routines in place and are not making any changes at this time in their use of the innovation.

The facilitator may conclude that this user needs no help, since use is established. In this case, congratulations and some celebratory symbol from the facilitator could be a wise response. On the other hand, a discussion with the user, or an observation to determine how this person's use aligns with the ideal variation on an IC Map (see Chapter 3), could be very informative and ultimately lead to a new set of actions, perhaps a move toward LoU IVB.

Level of Use IVB Refinement.   Some users begin to observe and wonder how well their use of the innovation is working for the benefit of their clients (in the case of classrooms, this would be students). Based on their reflection and assessment, they make adaptations in the innovation or in their use of it with the intention of increasing client benefits. These actions signify LoU IVB Refinement. The key here is making adaptations for the client's benefit (not for the benefit of the user, as in LoU III). Note again how the types of adaptations help to understand and distinguish each LoU.

The facilitator is typically welcomed warmly by the LoU IVB person, who is looking for new ways to make the program as successful as possible for students. Since the LoU IVB user is wondering how well the program is working, a key action of the facilitator could be to suggest or to help the teacher find assessment or evaluation tools or rubrics to use in checking student work. Conversation about the adaptations or adjustments that are under consideration also would be helpful to the LoU IVB user. Providing journal articles and examples of what other users have done will be useful, too.

Level of Use V Integration.   The LoU V Integration person, like the LoU IVB individual, is making adaptations for purpose of increasing benefit for clients, but the LoU V action is done in concert with one or more users. The collaboration is between users, not between a user and a resource person such as a counselor, librarian, or principal. The two or more users collegially plan and carry out adaptations in their use of the innovation that will benefit their students.

LoU V is a significant phase for the evolution of a change process and for the professional culture of the school. Change facilitators should do all that they can to nurture and facilitate its development and continuation. The facilitator's task is to make it possible for people who wish to work together to do so. Thus, making accommodations in the schedule so that the LoU V users can have concurrent planning periods, changing office or classroom assignments, and other logistical arrangements should be done in order to support two or more users working together.

It should be noted that some users wish to work together to better manage the new program and its demands and to increase the users' efficiency and decrease the workloads that new programs frequently demand. This can be a wise means of providing additional help and support to peers. However, this reason for working together is part of LoU III Mechanical Use, not LoU V, which entails collaborating to make adaptations in use for *client* benefits, not *user* benefits.

Level of Use VI Renewal.   At LoU VI Renewal, the user is exploring or implementing some means to modify the innovation in major ways or to replace it altogether. The modification may constitute one very significant addition or adjustment, or it may comprise multiple small adaptations that add up to significant change. In either case, the adaptation is intended to benefit clients. Again, making the adjustments is central, and it is the size or number of adaptations that places a person at this level. Curiously, persons at LoU VI comprise a small part (2.5%) of the CBAM database.

Facilitators for persons at this level may applaud them and stay out of their way. These users may be called on or may offer to provide additional materials or resources that will translate their adaptations into reality. For example, the LoU VI individual might be invited to provide professional development activities for and with others to share a possible new direction. Or the user may be asked to join a design team that is planning an entirely new replacement program or a revision of the current program. On the other hand, if the program is meant (through the decision of someone in authority) to be used without changes in its design, the facilitator may find himself or herself in the position of having to tactfully explain that the proposed LoU VI adaptations are not in line with the expectations of the school, district, or state.

In summary, the operational definitions for each LoU are behavior based and action oriented. LoU does not focus on attitudes or feelings; SoC does that. Because these actions can be observed, facilitators find the LoU construct and definitions useful for observing and analyzing what users are doing, for better understanding their needs, and for further facilitating implementation. Assessing LoU is critical in evaluation and research studies. Otherwise, there is no certainty that the so-called treatment group only contains users and that there really are no users in the control group.

REFLECTION QUESTIONS

Consider the eight LoU. At which levels do you think a facilitator's support would be most critical? Why would that be the case?

ASSESSING AN INDIVIDUAL'S LEVEL OF USE

Whereas information about a person's SoC may be obtained in several ways (see Chapter 4), LoU may be assessed only through long-term observation or use of a specially designed focused interview protocol (Hall, Dirksen, & George, 2006; Loucks, Newlove, & Hall, 1975). Various researchers and others have attempted to develop a paper-and-pencil measure to determine LoU, although we have consistently stated that it will not work. Measuring behaviors through self-report (as is done in assessing feelings through the SoC Questionnaire) is like trying to decipher semaphore signals by listening to a radio. In summary, using a questionnaire to rate one's behaviors and to make the distinctions across the levels is not possible.

Using Decision Points to Distinguish Each LoU

The two Configurations of LoU Interviews are (a) the LoU branching interview and (b) the LoU focused interview. In both, the person's placement at his or her LoU is determined by referring to a set of Decision Points, which distinguish between each LoU.

In our previous descriptions, the factor of adaptations was used as an abbreviated way to introduce each Decision Point. Figure 5.2 offers a fuller explication of each LoU and the Decision Points that are used to define them.

The LoU Branching Interview

In a one-legged interview, the facilitator visits with the user in a brief and casual way to gain a broad view of an individual's LoU in order to offer appropriate assistance. In a word, the outcomes of this conversation are for facilitation purposes: to make a quick assessment of a person's LoU and to do something that will facilitate further use of the innovation.

The branching interview is constructed so that the facilitator, through a series of questions, gains information about the user's innovation-related behaviors (see Figure 5.3). To gain this quickly assessed estimate of the overall LoU of the individual, the initial question is "Are you using the innovation?" The response separates nonusers from users, and depending on the response, the "no" or "yes" branch is followed. Then the facilitator must ascertain which of the three types of nonusers or five types of users the individual may be. The key in the interview is to stimulate the person to describe and provide examples of behaviors that he or she is taking in relation to the innovation. The interviewer then refers to the Decision Points and LoU definitions to estimate the person's LoU, which provides the diagnostic guidance for structuring support and assistance.

Pothole Warning

Use of the branching interview exclusively cannot provide the rigorously gained information required for careful evaluation of an implementation effort. Nor can this data collection tool produce results that are acceptable for research studies. Beware of this temptation.

Pothole Repair

To gain more reliable and valid data for research and evaluation purposes, read on!

FIGURE 5.2   Levels of Use of the Innovation with Decision Points

Decision Point F: Begins exploring alternatives to or major modifications of the innovation presently in use.

Level VI, Renewal: State in which the user re-evaluates the quality of use of the innovation, seeks major modifications of or alternatives to present innovation to achieve increased impact on clients, examines new developments in the field, and explores new goals for self and the organization.

Decision Point E: Initiates changes in use of the innovation for benefit of clients based on input from and in coordination with colleagues.

Level V, Integration: State in which the user is combining own efforts to use the innovation with related activities of colleagues to achieve a collective impact on clients within their common sphere of influence.

Decision Point D-2: Changes use of the innovation to increase client outcomes based on formal or informal evaluation.

Level IVB, Refinement: State in which the user varies use of the innovation to increase the impact on clients within his or her immediate sphere of influence. Variations in use are based on knowledge of both short- and long-term consequences for clients.

Decision Point D-1: Establishes a routine pattern of use.

Level IVA, Routine: Use of the innovation is stabilized. Few if any changes in use are made. Little preparation or thought is given to improving innovation use or its consequences.

Decision Point C: Makes user-oriented changes.

Level III, Mechanical Use: State in which the user focuses most efforts on the short-term, day-to-day use of the innovation, with little time for reflection. Changes in use are made more to meet user needs than the needs of clients. The user is primarily engaged in an attempt to master tasks required to use the innovation. These attempts often result in disjointed and superficial use.

Decision Point B: Makes a decision to use the innovation by establishing a time to begin.

Level II, Preparation: State in which the user is preparing for first use of the innovation.

Decision Point A: Takes action to learn more detailed information about the innovation.

Level I, Orientation: State in which the individual has acquired or is acquiring information about the innovation and/or has explored its value orientation and what it will require.

Level 0, Nonuse: State in which the individual has little or no knowledge of the innovation and no involvement with it, and is doing nothing to become involved.

Source: LoU has been described and presented in many publications. An important resource for obtaining more detailed information about LoU Hall, Dirksen, & George (2006).

The LoU Focused Interview

For research, implementation, assessment, and evaluation studies, more rigorous and detailed data are needed. For these purposes, the prospective LoU interviewer undergoes a three-day training and certification program to prepare for using the full formalized LoU

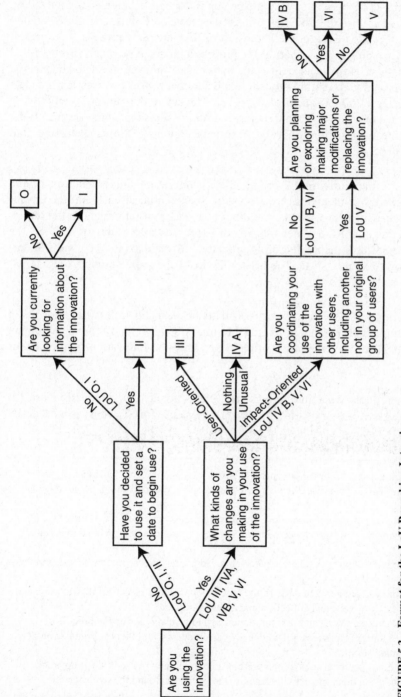

FIGURE 5.3 Format for the LoU Branching Interview

Source: LoU has been described and presented in many publications. An important resource for obtaining more detailed information about LoU is Hall, Dirksen, and George (2000).

101

Interview protocol. A full LoU Interview takes 30 minutes or less and appears to the interviewee to be an interested discussion of what the person is doing in relation to an innovation. The LoU Interview is based in the LoU definitions, the Decision Points, and more detailed indicators of each LoU called Categories. The result of this interview process is an overall determination of the person's LoU. As part of the process a matrix-type rating sheet is filled out that becomes a more descriptive account of the individual's innovation-related behaviors. The LoU Interview protocol and rating procedure are summarized in two training manuals (Hall, Dirksen, & George, 2006; (Loucks et al., 1975). The key to this process is employing questions that are based on a set of seven Categories or dimensions that compose each LoU: Knowledge, Acquiring Information, Sharing, Assessing, Planning, Status Reporting, and Performing (see Figure 5.4).

Knowledge.   This is the individual's practical and theoretical understanding of the change: its characteristics or elements, how to use it, its potential effects, and the advantages and disadvantages of its use. Unlike the other Categories, which relate to the implementer's behavior, this cognitive dimension is not expressed as a behavior. Rather, the Knowledge Category reflects the degree of complexity and sophistication of one's understanding of the innovation and its use. The higher the LoU, the more complex the Knowledge schema.

Acquiring Information.   This Category focuses on actions taken to seek information about the innovation through such behaviors as questioning colleagues and others, reviewing printed materials supplied by a vendor, visiting sites where the innovation is in place, or searching Web sites.

Sharing.   Sharing reflects what individuals tell others about their innovation use (or nonuse), including related ideas, problems, successes, and plans. This Category is most easily

FIGURE 5.4   Levels of Use Categories

Knowledge: That which the user knows about characteristics of the innovation, how to use it, and consequences of its use. This is cognitive knowledge related to using the innovation, not feelings or attitudes.

Acquiring Information: Solicits information about the innovation in a variety of ways, including questioning resource persons, correspondence with resource agencies, reviewing printed materials, and making visits.

Sharing: Discusses the innovation with others. Shares plans, ideas, resources, outcomes, and problems related to its use.

Assessing: Examines the potential or actual use of the innovation or some aspects of it. This can be a mental assessment or can involve actual collection and analysis of data.

Planning: Designs and outlines short- and/or long-range steps to be taken during the process of innovation adoption (i.e., aligns resources, schedules activities, meets with others to organize and/or coordinate use of the innovation).

Status Reporting: Describes personal stand at the present time in relation to use of the innovation.

Performing: Carries out the actions and activities entailed in operationalizing the innovation.

---

learned about through observation. Sharing is when one person tells another what they are doing, or not doing, relative to the innovation. This Category is not for when the person is asking others something about the innovation. Those behaviors are placed under the Acquiring Information Category.

Assessing. Exploring actual or potential innovation use to determine its strengths and weaknesses is the focus of Assessing. Informally or formally collecting and analyzing data about what is being done and its effects are examples of Assessing. However, Assessing also may be only mental reflection about use of the innovation.

Planning. Thinking ahead to design and outlining short- and long-term actions to take relative to use of the innovation constitutes Planning. The individual is looking beyond today's use to next steps.

Status Reporting. This Category entails the individual's reporting his or her own views of their overall use of the innovation. The information derived from the interviewer's questions in this Category provides a general description of the person's LoU.

Performing. The Performing Category is for those concrete indicators of actions taken related to use or nonuse of the innovation. In the LoU Interview specific examples of behaviors will be rated in the Performing Category.

> ### Pothole Warning
> *Many students of LoU find understanding and verbalizing the distinction between Status Reporting and Performing difficult; consequently, they mix them up.*

> ### Pothole Repair
> *It might be prudent to carry a pocket index card with the definitions and an example of Status Reporting and Performing in order to have these descriptions handy but also to enable the facilitator in adding to his/her repertoire of examples of each.*

One of the interesting aspects of the LoU Categories is that all, with the exception of Performing, represent actions relative to innovation use that occur outside the actual moments of delivery in the classroom. As is obvious, much activity related to using innovations occurs beyond the classroom, or use site, and significant time and activity are invested in such behaviors.

How the Levels and Categories relate (for further explanation, see Hall & Hord, 1987) is depicted in the LoU Chart in Appendix C. For each LoU, the Category behavior that occurs is different. Description of these behaviors is found at the intersection of the horizontal row that describes a particular LoU with the vertical column that addresses each Category. The trained LoU interviewer is skilled at asking questions that allow the user to describe what he or she is doing in relation to each Category. The trained LoU interviewer can also relate information obtained in an interview to the Decision

Points. Each of these smaller ratings are then integrated holistically to determine the overall LoU.

REFLECTION QUESTIONS

How might you manage "differentiated" interventions for individuals who are exhibiting a range of LoU behaviors? Will you need to address each individual, or how can you group implementers who are behaving similarly?

APPLYING LEVELS OF USE

The three major ways in which LoU can be employed are (a) planning for the next steps in a change process, (b) facilitating the change process, and (c) conducting evaluation and research studies. The first two can be considered formative uses; the latter involves the summative domain.

IMPLICATIONS FOR LEADERS FACILITATING CHANGE

In this section there is significant discussion and multiple suggestions of interventions that may be employed at each LoU to support and enhance the effective implementation of new programs, practices, or processes. These ideas, however, should not be used in a cookbook fashion. Therefore, it is very important for the change facilitator to understand that it will take time and practice to become knowledgeable and skilled in facilitation of change using LoU:

- The facilitator should have deep content knowledge of the innovation, understanding its essential components and characteristics, as well as its philosophical (and historical, perhaps) basis, the assumptions that accompany it, and the purposes or goals for which it may be used (see Chapter 3). The facilitator's superficial knowledge base can provide only superficial support as each person and group move across the Implementation Bridge.
- In addition to knowing the innovation, the facilitator must have a deep understanding of the concept of LoU, and the operational definitions of each of the levels. This requires careful and thorough knowledge and skills development about the construct and its measurement. Being able to accurately recognize and identify users' (and nonusers') behaviors associated with the levels is obviously important. To do this, training followed by practice and feedback to refine such identification skills is needed.
- The effective facilitator not only knows well the innovation and the LoU tool but also uses appropriate interactions with individuals in the interview process in order to obtain useful information—and to supply or suggest relevant interventions that enable the individual to move to higher levels of use. These skills and qualities have direct implications for the preparation and competence of facilitators to use LoU in change efforts.

Facilitation of Change

LoU is not only an important tool for facilitators and evaluators; it also can be used to guide strategic planning. The plan can be placed on a timeline that best addresses each LoU. However, unlike SoC, which represents users' affect about innovations, LoU focuses on the implementers' behaviors. Thus, the LoU construct and its measures contribute in a second way to describing change at the individual and group levels. These descriptions enable planners to predict and change facilitator to understand the status of each group and individual and to determine appropriate support for advancing the change process.

For facilitating purposes, the first need is for an overall estimate of each individual's LoU, which can be obtained through one-legged interview that applies the informal branching format. Frequently, it is desirable to obtain an estimate for a group of persons—for instance, all the kindergarten and first-grade teachers, all the eighth-grade teachers, or an academic department in a high school. This is done by interviewing many of the individuals and aggregating the data. This assessment is followed by provision of interventions for the group. Similarly, data could be collected from all or a sampling of individuals to assess the LoU in a school or system. This may well be the case for Planning. If district and even state data are desired, representative sampling could be done across the unit.

We strongly believe that each person's LoU and success with a change is in large measure influenced by the facilitation he or she receives. If no support and facilitating interventions are offered, many will never fully implement the innovation, and others will remain nonusers. Further, those who are at LoU III Mechanical Use need interventions that will help them move beyond this level, or they may adapt the innovation to make it easier for them to manage, or they may stop using the new practice altogether. There are, however, effective actions that change facilitators can take to assist individuals in moving up the use levels.

From a strategic perspective, assuming that all potential implementers across a system should ultimately be users, the facilitator's first challenge is to plan for intervening in ways that support individuals in moving from LoU 0 Nonuse to LoU I Orientation. Although, hopefully, intended users would have been involved to some degree in deciding to adopt or to develop the innovation, this is frequently not the case. The facilitator, therefore, may need to begin by making people aware of the impending innovation and all expectations regarding the individual's role with it. The first objective is to stimulate people to actively seek information (Decision Point A), thus moving them to LoU I Orientation. Keep in mind, however, that each person must move through Decision Point A in order to be characterized as being at LoU I Orientation.

At LoU I Orientation and LOU II Preparation, information is needed from the facilitator about the purposes and requirements of the change as well as the timelines for implementation. This information should be general so as not to be overwhelming, yet specific enough to allow people to move to the next level. At these nonuse levels, individuals also need information about required materials and equipment—their purchase and preparation—and about how to get started. The advice should be practical, with only a moderate amount of attention to theory.

As use is initiated, most if not all first-time users of an innovation will be at LoU III Mechanical Use. Their typical behaviors reflect concerted effort to find and organize materials. Effort is invested in searching for time to plan for and put new ideas into practice. These users try multiple ways of handling various parts of the innovation. There are unanticipated innovation-related surprises as well as a short-term focus on Planning (e.g., for the next day). During this period, then, users typically need help in finding, ordering, and organizing themselves and structural aspects of innovation use.

Help in finding the time for managing these logistics and anticipating what comes next with use of the innovation is imperative. Facilitators who can do these coaching activities well will significantly reduce the amount time that implementers remain at LoU III. How-to workshops to develop management skills and to provide guidance in structuring tasks can help, as can Web sites and chat rooms. Making it possible for users with common problems to meet with an experienced user to ask technical questions is another effective intervention that will be effective and well received.

If people have appropriate facilitative assistance and time they typically move to LoU IVA Routine. They have established a way to use the innovation that they believe works for them and their students or other clients. By definition, LoU IVA users do not experiment with the program further, make no adaptations in the program or in their way of delivering it, and state that they plan to continue their current use in the same way. This is an especially important time to check on users' Innovation Configuration (see Chapter 3).

If the LoU IVA user's IC meets the expectations set forth in the goals of the change effort, one appropriate intervention is to celebrate. Give praise and other types of recognition to reinforce the person's efforts. If, on the other hand, a user is using a less-than-desirable Configuration of the innovation and has become stable (LoU IVA Routine) in this pattern, the facilitator may need to encourage further refinements in use. Interventions to help the user continue to change may be in order at the same time that encouragement is being provided.

Pothole Warning

Oh, dear! I will need to help these people get "unstuck" if they are stabilized in a pattern of using the new program that is not desirable. What a challenge!

Pothole Repair

One intervention to consider is taking these implementers to observe another person(s) who demonstrates exemplary practice. Before such a visit is arranged, consider how to discuss this with the "needy" user so that the visit will produce a positive effect on use.

LoU IVB Refinement users are typically a pleasure for facilitators. These people are searching for new materials, activities, or other refinements in use of the innovation that will benefit their students. Importantly, they are also mentally assessing how well the innovation and their use of it are working in relation to their students. Thus, these users welcome suggestions for assessing effectiveness and new ideas for improving varied aspects of the program or practice. Putting them in contact with others to access new information is a key intervention. Bringing others to visit them to see their ideas at work is confirming and rewarding. In addition, LoU IVB users may be potential facilitators.

If individuals are interacting with other users to coordinate their use and are making efforts to work together for their clients' benefits, they are diagnosed as LoU V Integration. Through collaboration, they are making adaptations in their use for client gains. In classroom innovations, an LoU V user may be working with another user to collectively regroup students in order to take advantage of their interests or reorganizing activities and/or materials to accommodate differing ability levels. The facilitator supports the LoU V users by making it possible for them to more easily coordinate their efforts (e.g., by restructuring schedules, space, etc.). Time for planning together will be of utmost importance. If the integration involves several people, developing their skills in shared decision-making could be relevant.

Normally, not a lot of a facilitator's time is directed to LoU VI Renewal users. In typical change processes, very few people reach this level, and those who do have typically done so by virtue of their own creative abilities and energy. Further, these users are interested in significantly modifying the innovation, which may or may not mesh with the planned goals of the change effort. These users can be a very positive force in change because they have ideas and because their ideas are focused on improved outcomes for their clients. They could, however, be moving in a completely different direction from the one the innovation's designer intended. Their work should thus be either supported and applauded, or channeled in more productive ways that are consistent with organization's goals.

Motivation for Movement in Levels of Use

One aspect of LoU that has been the source of interesting speculation, but little research, is the causes for change in LoU. Does change come about simply as a result of increasing experience with the innovation, or is it related to affective aspects of the person? What causes people to move to higher LoU? Are there particular keys to understanding why people move to lower LoUs and from use to nonuse? Do certain kinds of interventions make a significant difference in movement? Although each of these questions is intriguing, little research has been conducted to aid in developing answers. One reason for this is the multivariate nature of the questions, which means that they would be best answered with longitudinal study designs, a project few researchers are willing to undertake.

The simplest way to think about the motivational aspect of movement in LoU would be to assume a one-to-one correspondence with movement in SoC. There is an obvious correspondence between LoU and SoC. For example, Task concerns correspond to the LoU III Mechanical Use; Stage 5 Collaboration concerns correspond to LoU V Integration. But we know that this picture is too simplistic. Using large databases from cross-sectional studies, we have been able to predict one Diagnostic Dimension from knowing the other only at the extremes. In other words, if a person is a nonuser it can be predicted statistically that he or she is likely to have more intense Self concerns. If the person is at a higher LoU, it can be predicted that she or he is likely to have aroused Impact concerns. However, no statistical prediction of SoC has been possible when a person is at LoU IVA Routine, which means that any SoC profile may be found at this level.

Our preferred hypothesis about the relationship between movement in LoU and motivation is as follows. At the lower LoU, the actions cause the arousal of concerns. For example, when a person attends an orientation workshop, the Stage 1 Informational and Stage 2 Personal concerns increase in intensity; use drives concerns. At the higher levels, concerns would seem to drive LoU. A teacher who has concerns about certain students not doing well in mathematics will take action to learn about alternative approaches (LoU IVB Acquiring Information). A teacher who is developing concerns about working with a colleague so that more students can be served (Stage 5 Collaboration) will likely start talking with the colleague about what might be done (LoU V Integration). All of this is speculative, but it is very attractive. The simple linear relationship, although initially logical in an intuitive way, is too simplistic. Human emotions and behaviors are much more complex, especially when it comes to their dynamics during times of change.

Evaluation of Change

In using LoU for evaluation of implementation, the three-day formal training and certification in the rigorous LoU focused interview, data collection, and data coding are required Hall, Dirksen, & George, 2006; Loucks et al., 1975). The training programs result in evaluators and researchers ascertaining with reliability each individual's LoU in each of the Categories and the overall LoU. Having such a precise measure of LoU makes various interpretations possible: How effective was the implementation plan? How effectively has facilitation been conducted? How far has the change process moved? Has institutionalization been achieved? And, when connected with outcome data, such as test scores, how much gain results from use of the innovation?

For instance, if users are at LoU III Mechanical Use, student/client outcomes could be lower instead of higher than what is found in a control group. (Remember all those evaluation reports with no significant differences?) On the other hand, if teachers are at LoU IVB and are making changes in the innovation or in their use of it to increase student outcomes, there could be higher outcomes. Whether for facilitating the change process or evaluating implementation, LoU offers a critical tool for addressing the extent of implementation.

REFLECTION QUESTIONS

How will you decide whether to use the branching interview for LoU or to invest in three-day training to become certified to conduct full LoU Interviews? On what basis will you make this decision?

SIDELIGHTS ABOUT LOU

Two final little items: You might have noticed that SoC uses Arabic numerals for its naming system, whereas LoU employs Roman numerals. This is simply an effort to further differentiate the two concepts and their classifications. We are also careful to refer to SoC and LoU, as appropriate, and not vice versa.

You might have wondered why LoU IV is the only level divided into two sections, LoU IVA and LoU IVB. The answer is one of history and pragmatics. The initial LoU verification study was launched with only seven levels: 0 through VI. However, as the research team went about its explorations, the need for an additional classification became very apparent. A large number of people out there were users, but they were not making any changes in their use! Another LoU was discovered. Since we were into a large field study and had learned all that is in the LoU Chart, we decided to not try to relearn all the higher levels. Instead we split LoU IV into two levels: IVA Routine and IVB Refinement.

In the vignette that follows, we will use an individual teacher, rather than a school, as an example of LoU in a change process. And, rather than supplying analysis at the end of the vignette, we will analyze this individual as we learn her story.

■ ■ ■ ■ ■

VIGNETTE
TIME SERIES SNAPSHOTS OF A HYPOTHETICAL USER

Students of CBAM have suggested that it is easier to understand LoU if the example of a "real live person" is provided for each level. Therefore, we introduce Louise, a hypothetical language arts classroom teacher in a high school. We will trace Louise through all the LoU, describing her at each one, including the Decision Points. But please remain aware that in reality people do not move hier-archically from one level to the next. Sometimes an individual may skip a level, move back to a lower level, or reach a level and move no further. At other times a user may drop the innovation entirely (this is not rare, particularly at LoU III) if she or he receives no help and becomes increasingly un-able to make sense of the change or to use it efficiently.

Louise, who has been in the school for four years, is considered a good teacher by the students and is respected by her peers. Her principal told her that he had heard that the state board of educa-tion was recommending that schools think about including a service project in the curriculum, and he asked Louise what she thought. Louise expressed a lack of information and interest, as she was not sure what it was all about (LoU 0 Knowledge). Further, she had just purchased a new home, a new lawn had been planted, and she was busily occupied with preparations for the school year that would begin shortly. She gave no further attention to service learning (LoU 0 Performing) and asked the principal no questions (LoU 0 Acquiring Information).

[Overall, Louise is at LoU 0 Nonuse with regard to service learning.]

At the end of September, the gentle autumn rains had come to Louise's lawn, and to her class-room came a student from another high school in the city. This student asked Louise if the class would be doing a service learning project. Louise said, "No, I don't think we'll do that this year." However, the topic came up again on Saturday, when Louise was playing tennis with some colleagues, one who mentioned going to an orientation session on service learning and asked Louise what she thought. She described her student's question and borrowed materials from her tennis partner's workshop to review (LoU I Acquiring Information and Performing).

[Because Louise has taken action to learn more about service learning (Decision Point A), she has moved to Level I Orientation.]

The principal supported Louise's expression of interest and encouraged her to learn more. Louise found the materials to be highly interesting (LoU I Assessing). She talked with her language arts department chair and called her language arts coordinator to find out what was available in the school and district relative to service learning (LoU I Acquiring Information). The principal suggested that Louise visit the school's U.S. history teacher who had begun implementing service learning.

Subsequently, she attended a second district workshop/learning session on service learning and became quite excited about the ideas (LoU I Acquiring Information and Assessing). She shared what she was doing with her second-period junior-level language arts class, whose members asked questions and expressed interest (LoU I Sharing). Louise decided that she would attend a series of three sessions to learn more (more Acquiring Information and indications of Decision Point A).

Her principal said that the school's budget would support teachers who wanted to attend the workshops that focused on the philosophy of service learning and on how to use it with high school students. As a result, Louise said that she would begin to "do" service learning with the second-period class immediately after Thanksgiving.

(continued)

■ ■ ■ ■ ■ ■

V I G N E T T E   CONTINUED

[Because Louise has decided to use service learning and sets a specific time to begin (Decision Point B), she is at LoU II Preparation.]

Louise attended the workshops on service learning and considered them to be quite good. She thought that the philosophy and values of service learning were well articulated and that they provided a meaningful basis for selecting the materials and choosing activities for students (LoU II Assessing). She began to collect materials and to make lesson plans for her class that would engage in service learning (LoU II Performing). Further, Louise and the other workshop participants were networking and sharing tips on how to get started, even though some people were from rural areas some distance away from the city (LoU II Sharing and Acquiring Information).

On schedule, Louise initiated service learning with her second-period class after the Thanksgiving break. Since the holiday season of giving and sharing with others was in the air, Louise had thought this might be a good time to launch service learning.

It was a good time, but it was also a maddening time. Louise had prepared all the suggested materials to teach the first activities but was unsure about how (or with whom) to make contacts for doing service projects in the community (LoU III Knowledge). The students were excited by the plans and clamored to be quite independent in all phases of the service projects, whereas Louise was trying to keep up with finding and providing materials, activities, and ideas (LoU III Planning and Performing). She made a number of unproductive phone calls to community members to enlist their support and placement of projects. She commented, "Everything seems to take more time than I had anticipated" (LoU III Status Reporting). A crisis almost occurred one day when she had not prepared sufficiently for the class and a school board member stopped by.

Parents telephoned, and some came to the class, to find out what was going on, which was a mixed blessing for Louise in the midst of all that she was trying so hard to do. The parent inquiries were both useful and distracting. It took significant time to explain service learning and their children's role in it to each one, although after hearing about the projects, many parents offered their support, time, and resources. She tried to train one of the parents to make assignments for the students, but this required more of her time than was helpful, so she dropped this idea (LoU III Performing). The principal checked in regularly, providing support and some suggestions and ordering materials that were needed. Somehow Louise made it to the holiday break.

[Because Louise is using the innovation and making user-oriented changes (Decision Point C), she is at LoU III Mechanical Use.]

During the December–January break, Louise reflected on her work with service learning and how disappointing her use had been (LoU III Assessing). She decided that she definitely would not expand it to other classes until she had ironed out the wrinkles, and that in the spring semester the second-period class would do only two projects and that there would be a great deal of planning (LoU III Planning). Louise would invite the students to reflect on their experience, and together they would correct their errors and discuss frustrations. She would guide them to an area of language arts curriculum that would fit well with the projects, thus integrating service learning so that it and language arts were more meaningful. More importantly, this would save her valuable classroom time (LoU III Planning). She talked this over with the language arts coordinator, who supported her assessment and plans (LoU III Sharing).

At the end of the school year, Louise breathed a sigh of relief. She and the second-period juniors had accomplished the two projects, the second coming off more smoothly than the first (LoU III Assessing). Louise had asked the workshop leader and the history teacher to come into her classroom several times to give her pointers and ideas (LoU III Acquiring Information). This had helped a great deal. Having someone in the building who was more experienced with service learning

■ ■ ■ ■ ■ ■

VIGNETTE CONTINUED

had been especially meaningful. [Note this behavior is not indicative of LoU V Integration. The purpose is to address Louise's efforts and efficiencies.] Louise and the students assessed the triumphs and traumas of the two spring projects, and all felt that they had made significant strides in how to do service learning successfully (LoU III Assessing). Further, the principal congratulated the students and Louise publicly on their efforts.

In the fall, Louise continued to do service learning with that year's second-period junior class, using the improved methods that she and her students had developed during their spring projects. She made no adaptations in the projects nor in her way of working with students for the fall semester (LoU IVA Performing).

[Because Louise has determined a satisfactory way to do service learning and has repeated her approach in the fall (Decision Point D-1), she is at LoU IVA Routine.]

During the following spring semester, Louise and her class did two service projects, and each went well. But for the second one, after talking with her principal and carefully training and planning with the students, she gave the students the opportunity to make their own contacts to initiate their projects. She felt this additional responsibility would improve the students' understanding of the community and of how to go about making arrangements in the "real world" (LoU IVB Assessing and Performing). It did indeed make the students feel very empowered and capable. This move also was applauded by the parents, who saw it as an opportunity for their children to develop poise and confidence while giving service to others.

[Because Louise has adapted her use of the innovation to increase client outcomes (Decision Point D-2), she is at LoU IVB Refinement.]

In May, the principal dropped a hint to the local newspaper's editor, a friend in the Rotary Club, who picked up on the story of Louise's students and sent a reporter to interview the class. Louise suggested that the reporter also interview the history teacher (Thomas) and his class about their service learning experiences. The discussion between the two teachers and the reporter after the interviews focused on the local railroad museum and its need for exhibits, publicity, and docents to guide tours for lower-grade children.

Later that night, Louise had an idea—in the fall, why couldn't she and Thomas organize the senior students from their classes into task forces that would explore the museum's needs and determine how to address them (LoU V Planning). The senior students, who would have experienced service learning and who could offer the content and capacity of their history and language arts courses, would be allowed to develop plans and procedures for the various parts of the project, although they would be monitored carefully by their teachers.

At the beginning of the fall semester, Louise and Thomas and their classes began to meet together during second period in the media center, where there was space to accommodate them. Louise worked in depth with various groups of students while Thomas floated to facilitate and support the others. The two teachers did extensive planning for this team-taught, blocked cohort of students. They would frequently exchange assignments so that each played various roles with the students, keeping their work fresh and their ideas stimulating to the students (LoU V Performing). They occasionally invited the principal to actively participate in their project.

[Because Louise has initiated student-oriented change in the innovation in coordination with Thomas (Decision Point E), she is at LoU V Integration.]

Louise was quite pleased with her work with Thomas (LoU V Assessing). The history students had led the research among community "old-timers" to gain information about the early days of the railroad. The language arts students supplied leadership in designing publicity about the museum.

(continued)

■ ■ ■ ■ ■ ▬▬▬▬▬▬▬▬▬▬▬▬▬▬▬▬▬

V I G N E T T E   CONTINUED

All students developed scripts about the various exhibits and trained each other to deliver the information to younger children. They made schedules for the children's visits and assigned themselves as docents to guide the tours. Louise and Thomas were very excited about working in tandem with their students (LoU V Performance).

During the Thanksgiving holiday, Thomas moved to another state, which forced Louise to consider a new dimension to service learning. Stimulated by the gift of some computers and related equipment from her uncle, during the winter holiday she began to explore how her students might use e-mail to connect with students of the other teachers in her workshop network (LoU VI Assessing).

The language arts coordinator and principal conferred with Louise about the new idea. They decided that the students from various schools who would communicate by e-mail would select a common service topic for investigation in their respective communities and then use the technology to share information, report needs, brainstorm solutions, develop plans, critique each others' ideas, and share results of their projects.

[Because Louise has explored major modifications in how to plan for and execute service learning (Decision Point F), she is at Level VI Renewal.]

This is not the end of Louise's story, but it is quite enough for now.

VIGNETTE CRITIQUE QUESTIONS

1. Consider the time line of Louise's journey through LoU. What reaction, if any, do you have to the pace of her movement?
2. What, if anything, should Louise's principal and/or curriculum supervisor do with/for her now?
3. Does LoU give you a means for understanding the process of using new programs? Explain your response.

SUMMARY

In this chapter, LoU, a third Diagnostic Dimension of the CBAM, was introduced and described. The Decision Points, which differentiate the levels that include the nonusers and users of innovations, were presented as a means for precisely identifying individuals at the various levels. An additional means for illuminating the eight levels is the use of seven Categories, which were also described.

As outlined in this chapter, two procedures—one that is informal, which is used for facilitation purposes, and one that is more rigorous, which is used for research and evaluation purposes—may be used to assess individuals for their LoU. How LoU may be employed to facilitate the change process was discussed, as were abundant examples of interventions that can be applied to assist individuals and groups in their movement to higher LoU.

A vignette of a teacher's LoU as she learned about and used service learning was shared, along with rich descriptions of her use as she proceeded through her hypothesized journey. Similar to the work that a rater of LoU Interviews would do, codings of the level and Category were given to pieces of information and data that were revealed in the case story.

Although this case is purely an invention, it reflects real life and provides an intimate portrait of a user of an innovation at various LoU.

We also made reference to the importance of documenting LoU in research and evaluation studies. We will present more about applications of LoU in research and evaluation studies in Chapter 12. In doing such studies, it is crucial to assess LoU in the control/comparison group as well as in the treatment group. We almost guarantee that both groups will contain a mix of users and nonusers.

DISCUSSION QUESTIONS

1. Using LoU, describe a sequence for developing workers' knowledge and skills on the production line as they are introduced to and gradually become skilled at using a new machine, technology, procedure, or process.

2. Describe an experience you have had with a change wherein you can identify the different LoU levels.

3. Place the different LoU on the Implementation Bridge. Which LoU represent behaviors before one is on the bridge, and which represent being all the way across?

4. Use examples to illustrate and discuss how the Categories expand the descriptions of an individual's LoU.

5. What are the two major ways of measuring LoU? How are they similar and different?

6. Think of an innovation, such as technology- or problem-based learning. How could LoU be used as a diagnostic tool to plan for its implementation?

7. How might teachers' LoU of a new math program be used to explain student outcome scores across three years of implementing the program?

FIELDWORK ACTIVITIES

1. Interview three people (e.g., teachers) about an innovation. Use the LoU branching interview technique to estimate each individual's LoU, and then design an appropriate intervention for each. If you can't find three teachers, use classmates. Remember that they don't have to be users for you to assess their LoU.

2. Plan how LoU could be employed at the school district or state level to assess implementation of a systemwide school improvement project.

3. Identify a change effort that is in its early stages on your campus or in your workplace. Explain how you would use LoU to develop and guide a three-year implementation plan.

4. Consider the Innovation Configuration (IC) of your new product or practice (in operation) (see Chapter 3). Describe how you would use the IC in tandem with an LoU Interview to learn the status of implementation of your organization's latest process.

CONDUCT A STUDY

1. If you are a teacher leader (a grade-level team chairperson), an instructional coach, or a principal, consider interviewing a random sample of five or six teachers who are at the launch of a new curriculum. Plan to interview each individual every two to four weeks, using the Branching Interview. Keep a chart of the teachers' interview results, and make a note about the subsequent interventions that are supplied to each—the interventions' purpose is to move the respondents to a higher LoU. Study your chart each month to ascertain if movement has occurred in the teachers' LoU, and, if so, what generalizations you might make about your results.

2. Follow up the facilitator/informal study (if you accomplished this) with a summative study at the end of six or eight months, using the Focused Interview (of course, you will need to enroll in the three-day learning session to gain the skills and be certified to do this). Compare your results of the Branching Interview with those of the focus interview. Analyze to ascertain the extra detail and specificity that were gained through use of the Focus Interview (if it was used) and its ratings.

ADDITIONAL READINGS/RESOURCES

For accessing training in either the LoU branching technique or LoU focused interview, contact the authors.

Guskey, T. R. (2000). Participant use of new knowledge and skills, Chapter 7, in *Evaluating professional development*. Thousand Oaks, CA: Corwin Press.

PART III

THE IMPERATIVE FOR LEADERSHIP IN CHANGE

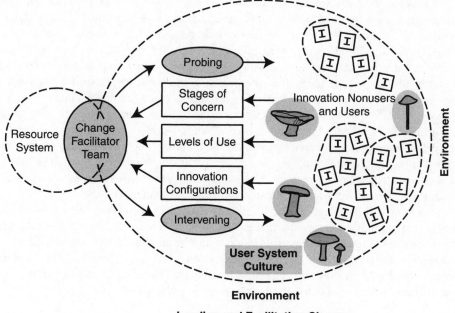

Leading and Facilitating Change

115

ORGANIZING FRAMEWORK FOR PART III

The shaded portions of this graphic emphasize the leader(s) and others who can influence the unfolding of a change process. Their actions can entail "probing" to assess the current extent of implementation, making "interventions" that affect the implementers and/or the culture. There also are "mushrooms" growing around the edges of the user system.

CHAPTERS 6, 7, AND 8

A continuing theme in business, government, and education is discussion, examination, and cries for effective leaders and leadership. Although it is not acknowledged as frequently, today's leaders must be able to lead change processes. The success of all organizations requires that they initiate changes and that they accommodate changes in response to their environment. Each of the earlier chapters in this book presented key theories, models, constructs, and tools that leaders can use to facilitate change. Up until this point the efforts of the formal and informal leaders of organizations have not been addressed directly. In the next three chapters the actions, approaches, and consequences of the leaders' efforts are examined.

In Chapter 6 the Change Facilitator Style of leaders will be the topic. The research on interventions has led to the identification of three different styles of leaders. These styles are correlated with varying degrees of success in implementing innovations. In addition, the more recent research has documented significant relationships between the style of the leader and student outcomes. An important point to keep in mind as this chapter is studied is that in most settings there will be more than one person with formal responsibility for leading a change initiative. The way these individuals work together as a Change Facilitator Team will be heavily influenced by the Change Facilitator Style of the leader.

In Chapter 7 the actions that leaders take, their interventions, will be examined in detail. Researchers have developed schemes for describing, classifying, and counting interventions. The resultant categories are useful for planning and reflecting on the various actions that leaders and others take as they are engaged in implementing change. Analysis of interventions has been informative in understanding how to better facilitate change processes.

Chapter 8 will introduce a very different category of interventions: mushrooms. Up to this point the explicit assumption has been that change leadership and change facilitating interventions are made by leaders, followers, trainers and consultants. Intervention mushrooms represent a very different source of interventions. Just as the name implies, mushroom interventions grow in the dark and can be nutritious to the change process. Intervention mushrooms also can be toxic and can cause serious drag on a change process.

CHAPTER 6

DESCRIBING LEADERS AND THE DIFFERENCES THEY MAKE

Change Facilitator Style

His attitude is so positive that it is often mistaken for expertise! You can't help but like him.

As she uses a finger to draw several loops that converge in the air, a staff person observes, "The principal draws in things I didn't even know were out there. She always is thinking about how all the pieces can fit together."

"Everything is so well organized and gets done on time. He always focuses first on resources. He is like a cook who follows the recipe."

"He was a wonderful man who did nothing."

"I empower them, but I monitor too."

Leaders and leadership are popular topics for discussion and research. People continually debate whether a certain person is a good leader and what the characteristics of effective leadership are. Literally thousands of research studies have examined characteristics and behaviors of leaders in a never-ending quest to answer the age-old question of how leaders can make a difference. In this chapter we will consider leadership in a special context: *implementing change*. We will examine recent studies that have focused on leadership during change processes and describe how different approaches relate to implementation success. By the end of this chapter, you will have a set of tools to assess yourself and leaders you have known. You also will have some clues about how to work with and influence different types of leaders.

FOCUS QUESTIONS

1. What are the important variations in how different leaders facilitate change?
2. How is the concept of style different from behavior?
3. What are the key differences between the Initiator, Manager, and Responder Change Facilitator Styles?

4. Which Change Facilitator Style will be most closely correlated with higher levels of implementation success?
5. What are some tips to working with supervisors with different styles?
6. Which Change Facilitator Style do you prefer to use when you are in a leadership role?

Each of us has our favorite stories about leaders who were great to work for, the ones who respected our skills and potential, who let us take on extra responsibilities, and who helped us to grow professionally and personally. We also have stories about the leaders who did not trust us, who maintained control over the smallest details, and who would not give genuine consideration to our ideas. And then there are those leaders who were very friendly, who always had time to chat, and who verbally encouraged us to try anything, but in hindsight we can see that they never made a definite decision and that each attempt at change seemed to fall apart during implementation.

These types of experiences with leaders are typical rather than atypical. There are varied approaches to leadership, and different people lead in different ways. Further, there are patterns and similarities among those leaders who do make a difference and among those who do not make a difference. Depending on how the leader leads, the followers and the organization will have very different change process experiences, and the ultimate results of the change effort will differ as well.

We have identified different approaches to leadership that we call Change Facilitator (CF) Styles. Each style is defined by what the leaders do and their different perspectives about how to support change processes. Depending on their style, leaders send different signals to their staff and spend their time doing different things. For example, some leaders are never seen. They are in their office or out of the building attending some sort of meeting. Other leaders are ubiquitous! They seem to always be present and know about everything that is going on. The effects of these different styles can be observed in the amount and degree of success that the followers have in implementing and using the change. Also, in our most recent research we have found significant differences in outcomes that are associated with how the leader leads.

We will introduce the concept of CF Style and its implications for followers in this chapter. Although the focus of our research has been on the formal heads of organizations—namely school principals—keep in mind that leadership in change efforts is not something that is done only by the designated administrator(s) at the top. *Everyone who is engaged in change has a responsibility to assist in facilitating the process.* In addition, everyone will have a particular style. In other words, although most of the research presented in this chapter was done with school principals, the findings have implications for anyone who is facilitating change.

Two sets of implications of this work on CF Style must be kept in mind: First, regardless of your position in an organization, you have a potential role to play in helping to facilitate the change process, and in doing this you will have your own CF Style. (What will it be?) Second, the formally designated leaders of the change process will have their own CF Style. (How can you best work with each?) Everyone, whether principal or teacher, plant manager or assembly-line worker, has a potential role in facilitating the change process. Whether they knowingly assume this role and how they go about it is the main topic to be addressed in this chapter. You also will be introduced to some ways to analyze CF Styles and to think about implications for working with others in change leadership.

Pothole Warning

Failure to understand and address the importance of leadership can reduce the likelihood of having change success.

Pothole Repair

As you will learn in reading this chapter, how leaders lead can make a major difference in implementation success. The style of each leader must be understood and planned for.

THE HISTORY OF RESEARCH ON LEADERS AND LEADERSHIP

> *Which way did they go?*
> *How many of them were there?*
> *I must find them!*
> *I am their leader!*

This oft-cited refrain summarizes much about leadership in general and especially as it relates to leadership in change. Too often leaders don't lead until they figure out which way the troops are moving. The refrain is used here to introduce you to a number of important questions: In what ways do you see that leaders make a difference? What do you believe are the important characteristics of "good" leaders? What kind of leader do you like to work with? And how do you lead?

We use the metaphor of a dog-sled team to introduce some of the important differences in the way that leaders lead. Some leaders are like the lead dog. They like to be at the front, checking out the view ahead and breaking trail for those behind them. Others like to lead from within the team. They often say that they are not comfortable with the visibility that comes with being at the front, whereas those who like the front position point out that the view is always the same for those behind. Still other leaders stay at the back of the sled, like the drivers, riding the rails of the sled, pushing the sled, and barking out commands to those on the team who are not pulling hard enough. Other leaders seem to be more like the spectators and race officials. They watch from the sidelines while the team, sled, and driver travel by. They are ready to evaluate, and occasionally cheer, the performance of the team and driver, but they do not enter the race themselves. So again, which kind of leader do you like to be with? How do you lead? And which type do you think makes the biggest difference?

The Legacy of Research on Leadership

Leaders and leadership have been the subject of study and theorizing for most of the twentieth and early twenty-first century. In fact, so much has been written about these subjects that there are major anthologies just to summarize the history of study and examination of leaders and leadership (see, for example Bass & Bass, 2008; Northouse, 2007). Some of the earliest studies of leaders examined particular traits, such as height and eye color. Over the course of the twentieth century many models of leadership were proposed, such as the important work by

Fiedler (1978) suggesting that the style of effective leaders is contingency dependent—in other words, a different style of leader is needed for different situations. In more recent times reviews have been conducted of the studies in relation to principal leadership (see, for example, English, 2004; Leithwood & Montgomery, 1982). Others have studied specific behaviors of leaders in the hope of identifying a critical set of needed skills and competencies (see, for example, Leithwood, Louis, Anderson, & Wahlstrom, 2004).

Many have proposed models of leadership that suggest that how a leader leads must be considered across two dimensions: a task dimension and a people, or relationship, dimension (see, for example, Blake & Mouton, 1964). According to some, the "best" leaders are those who exhibit high levels of both task and relationship behaviors. Others advocate shifting the balance of task and relationship behaviors depending on the "maturity" of the followers (see, for example, Hersey, Blanchard, & Johnson, 2000). This long and extensive legacy of research, theory, and model building about leaders and leadership has focused primarily on business and industry contexts. Very little has been done in education organizations, and even less with leaders and leadership during change processes.

Discovering in an Implementation Study That School Leaders Were Making the Difference

Nearly all of the research and models about leaders and leadership had their beginnings in studies of individuals in leadership positions or in theorizing about what people in leadership positions should be like. By contrast, our research on leaders and leadership in change had a very different beginning. Rather than starting with an agenda to look at change leaders, we stumbled onto the need to look at leaders because of some research findings about teacher success and lack of success in implementing change. In other words, our early work was on the ground with what teachers were experiencing.

Implementation Data That Were a Mystery.   As a research team, we were analyzing a very extensive set of data about teachers' Stages of Concern (SoC) (see Chapter 4), Levels of Use (LoU) (see Chapter 5), and Innovation Configurations (IC) (see Chapter 3). We had just completed a 2-year study of teachers' implementation of a very innovative science curriculum in a large (80 schools) suburban school district. All of the teachers had participated in carefully designed workshops that were presented by lead teachers. SoC, LoU, and IC map data had been collected twice a year, and the district office change facilitators had devoted themselves to coaching teachers. So we expected that at the end of two years all of the teachers in all of the schools would be at the same point in terms of implementation. Wrong!

In the SoC, LoU, and IC Map data we found very distinct variations that appeared to represent school-by-school differences. We were able to sort the schools into three groups according to how the implementation data differed. To use the SoC data as an illustration, in Group A were a few schools that exhibited a gradual lowering of Self and Task concerns and an arousal of Stage 4 Consequence concerns. This is the profile we expected for all schools. But there were two other groups, each of which had more schools. In Group B were schools that revealed generally flat concerns profiles that were low on all stages. In Group C were schools whose teachers had the "Big W" concerns profile—in other words, they had high Stage 1 Informational concerns, high Stage 3 Management concerns, and a serious "tailing up" on Stage 6 Refocusing concerns. These teachers were not pleased with having unresolved Task concerns and had some very strong ideas about what should be done to make things better.

What Would Explain the Differences?   We were puzzled about how to explain these data. All the teachers had received the same district workshops and the same curriculum materials. The schools were generally alike in terms of student socioeconomic status and the like, and they all had had two years to implement the new curriculum. So we decided to present the three lists of school names to our district change facilitator colleagues and ask how they would explain the clustering of the schools. With very little hesitation they said, "It's the principals! In the schools in Group A the principals are very active and supportive of teachers using the new curriculum. In Group B the principals are well organized, but they don't push their teachers to go beyond the minimum. In Group C schools, the principals don't help their teachers. They talk a good game, but they don't follow through."

Principal Leadership Is the Key.   The outcome of these discussions with our school-based colleagues was a set of in-depth studies to document and analyze the intervention behaviors of school principals to see if, indeed, what they did as school leaders could be correlated with the extent of teacher implementation success. From these and the earlier studies of teachers engaged in change processes, the concept of CF Style emerged. These studies did not originate with some a priori model of leadership or theories about what good leaders do. As with other Concerns-Based Adoption Model (CBAM) studies, the work on CF Style came out of what happens to real people living and working to implement change.

REFLECTION QUESTIONS
What have you seen leaders do that made a difference in change process success? What were some of the differences in their leadership styles?

THE CONCEPT OF CHANGE FACILITATOR STYLE

Interestingly, as obvious as it is, many school district leaders, staff developers, and researchers miss the fact that *all principals are not the same*. Principals view their role and priorities differently, and they operationally define their roles differently in terms of what they actually do each day. One implication of this fact was that in studying principals as change facilitators, we needed to sample schools so that we had representatives of different ways in which principals lead change efforts. Our emerging concept of CF Style provided the means for doing this. We could select study schools using the descriptions of principal leadership that had been discovered in comparing schools in Groups A, B, and C.

Note that so far we have been referring to *style*. For the rest of this chapter, it will be very important to understand that there is a big difference between the concept of style and the idea of leader behaviors. Style represents the overall tone and pattern of a leader's approach. Behaviors are a leader's individual, moment-to-moment actions, such as talking to a teacher in the corridor, chairing a staff meeting, writing a memo, talking on the telephone, and sending an e-mail. The overall accumulated pattern and tone of these behaviors form a person's style. Interestingly, more effective leaders understand that each of their individual behaviors is important in and of itself as well as a sign of their overall style.

Pothole Warning

To assume that all leaders will fully support implementation of the innovation, and to treat them all the same, is very risky.

Pothole Repair

Different leaders will have different views about the innovation and will approach their role in facilitating implementation in different ways. The views, styles, and behaviors of individual leaders should be understood, and system support strategies should take these differences into account.

Three Change Facilitator Styles

Our studies of principals revealed that there are three distinct CF Styles: the Initiator, the Manager, and the Responder. We know that these three do not represent all possible styles, but they do represent three contrasting approaches that are regularly seen in change processes. In this section, each of these CF Styles is described. To make the descriptions come alive, we have included some of our favorite examples and anecdotes from the studies. Formal definitions of each CF Style are presented in Figure 6.1.

While reading these descriptions keep these questions in mind:

1. How well do these descriptions match with leaders you have experienced?
2. Which CF Style do you think is most highly correlated with greater teacher success in implementing changes?
3. Which CF Style do you use?

Initiator Change Facilitators.   Initiators have clear and strongly held visions about what their school should be like. They have a passion for the school. They are motivators who are continually articulating what the school can become. When decision issues come up, they listen to all sides and quickly make decisions based on what they think will be best for students and what will move the school closer to their vision. Initiators set high expectations for teachers, they expect loyalty, and they push. They expect teachers to be engaged in teaching, supporting students, and contributing to the effort to continually improve the whole school. For example, one elementary school had a goal of children writing every week. To encourage teachers and students in this effort, the Initiator principal asked teachers to give him samples of all students' writing each week. He then displayed the samples around the school halls and common areas.

Initiators push teachers, students, parents, and personnel in the district office to support the things they believe will help students learn, teachers teach, and the school moves forward. They are the ones that implicitly, and sometimes explicitly, say "Lead, follow, or

FIGURE 6.1   Descriptions of Three Change Facilitator Styles

Initiators have clear, decisive, long-range policies and goals that transcend but include implementation of the current innovation. They tend to have very strong beliefs about what good schools and teaching should be like and work intensely to attain this vision. Decisions are made in relation to their goals for the school and in terms of what they believe to be best for students, which is based on current knowledge of classroom practices. Initiators have strong expectations for students, teachers, and themselves. They convey and monitor these expectations through frequent contacts with teachers and setting clear expectations of how the school is to operate and how teachers are to teach. When they feel it is in the best interest of their school, particularly the students, Initiators will seek changes in district programs or policies or will reinterpret them to suit the needs of the school. Initiators will be adamant but not unkind, they will solicit input from staff, and then decisions will be made in terms of the goals of the school, even if some are ruffled by their directness and high expectations.

Managers place heavy emphasis on organization and control of budgets, resources, and the correct applications of rules, procedures, and policies. They demonstrate responsive behaviors in addressing situations or people, and they initiate actions in support of change efforts. The variations in their behavior are based on the use of resources and procedures to control people and change processes. Initially, new implementation efforts may be delayed since they see that their staff are already busy and that the innovation will require more funds, time, and/or new resources. Once implementation begins, Managers work without fanfare to provide basic support to facilitate teachers' use of the innovation. They keep teachers informed about decisions and are sensitive to excessive demands. When they learn that the central office wants something to happen in their school, their first questions will be about available dollars, time, and staffing to accomplish the change. Once these questions are resolved, they then support their teachers in making it happen. As implementation unfolds, they do not typically initiate attempts to move beyond the basics of what is required.

Responders place heavy emphasis on perception checking and listening to people's feelings and concerns. They allow teachers and others the opportunity to take the lead with change efforts. They believe their primary role is to maintain a smoothly running school by being friendly and personable. They want their staff to be happy, to get along with each other, and to treat students well. They tend to see their school as already doing everything that is expected and not needing major changes. They view their teachers as strong professionals who are able to carry out their instructional role with little guidance. Responders emphasize the personal side of their relationships with teachers and others. They make decisions one at a time and based on input from their various discussions with individuals. Most are seen as friendly and always having time to talk.

---

get the hell out of the way." Sometimes they push too hard, which makes some feel pressured and uncomfortable. They also are knowledgeable about policies, rules, and procedures, but on occasion they will work with the philosophy that "It is easier to seek forgiveness than it is prior approval." For example, if several budgets have specific rules about how the funds can be spent, they will still commingle the funds so that a combined activity can take place.

Initiators consciously question and analyze what they and others do. They reflect on what others have told them, on what issues may be emerging, and on how well tasks are being accomplished. They listen to teachers and students. They not only make decisions but consciously work to make sure that all decisions and actions move people and the school in the desired direction. They are focused on assessment, instruction, and curriculum. Initiators also have a great deal of passion. They care deeply about their students, teachers, and the school. Their pushing, monitoring, and bending of the rules are done to support everyone in doing his or her best. They also have what we are calling *strategic sense,* which means that they do not lose sight of the big picture while they are doing the day-to-day activities. They anticipate what might happen and envision alternative responses that they may need to employ.

Manager Change Facilitators.   Managers approach the leadership of change efforts with a different set of behaviors and emphases. They are very organized and get things done efficiently. They are skilled at making their school run like a well-oiled machine. They focus first on what the formal policies, rules, and procedures say. Then they focus on resources, budgets, schedules, and logistics. The bells ring on time, everyone knows the procedures for getting supplies, schedules are planned well in advance, and the various forms are filled out correctly and processed promptly. There are procedures for everything.

As proposals for change are made by teachers or those outside the school, Managers do not rush in. When asked by an external facilitator or district administrator to try something different, their first response will likely be "Well, that is an interesting idea, but my teachers are real busy right now." Managers buy time, which they use to study and learn more about the change and to consider whether they should have the school engage with it.

When a change is proposed Managers are quick to ask "Well, we can't do this unless I have more budget or another staff line. Is there a grant for doing this?" An important consequence of this delaying is that teachers and the school are protected to some extent from random changes. This dampening of the initiation of change also buys time for the principal and teachers to learn about the proposed change and to prepare for an efficient implementation. As a result, when changes are implemented, they tend to proceed smoothly and to acceptable levels.

Manager CF Style leaders also try to do many things themselves rather than delegate to others. They arrive at school very early in the morning, stay late in the evening, and return on the weekends to do more of the administrative tasks. They work hard at having things organized and providing resources for the staff. In many ways, they demand more of themselves than they do of others. When one principal was asked about why she had written the School Improvement Plan rather than asking the AP or SIP Team leader to do it she replied, "Well, it is easier for me to do it right the first time than to have someone else do it and then have to fix it."

Responder Change Facilitators.   Responders approach leadership with a primary focus on what is happening now. They do not have many ideas about what the school should be like in the future or where education is going. Instead their attention is on others' present concerns, feelings, and perceptions. Therefore, when they do one-legged interviews with teachers and others, their purpose is to discover concerns and perceptions about current topics and issues. Responders also spend time on the phone and with e-mail checking with other principals about their perceptions of what the assistant superintendent was talking about in the last principals' meeting "when she said. . . ." They engage in the same sort of discussions with parents, community members, and students. The pattern to their talk is chatty, social, and always willing to listen to concerns.

Responders are most willing for others to take the lead. For example, if a teacher wants to try a different curriculum approach, the Responder principal will say, "Go ahead. You know we always like to be innovative in this school." If someone from the district office or a nearby university wants to start a new project in the school, the Responder will welcome that person as part of the overall goal of trying to keep everyone happy. As a result, many disparate projects and activities can be going on in different parts of the school.

In contrast to Initiators, Responders delay making decisions. They want to have first heard from everyone about their concerns and perceptions. When they do have to make a major decision, such as cutting a staff position or reassigning a classroom, they struggle and in the end tend to make it at or shortly after the deadline. And the decision will be most heavily influenced by the last person with whom they talked. Thus, it is possible for a teacher or someone else to influence a decision right up to the last moment.

Another part of the Responder CF pattern is the tendency to minimize the size and significance of proposed changes. They often feel that a change proposal is not as innovative as its advocates claim. A Responder may say, "So what's the big deal? We have been doing most of this already—you just have a different name for it." Also, Responders tend to hire strong and independent teachers because they believe "They know more about teaching than I do. It is my job to work with the community and do the other things so that they can teach." Another theme with Responder CF Style leaders is their wish for everyone to get along and be happy.

REFLECTION QUESTIONS

Which of these CF Styles have you experienced? What was it like to work with each? Which one do you prefer to have as your supervisor?

INDICATORS OF CHANGE FACILITATOR STYLE

1. CF Style is the overall pattern that is derived from accumulated observations of individual leader behaviors.
2. CF Style provides the context for understanding and interpreting the actions of a change leader.
3. Initiators focus on doing what will be best in the long term for students and the school, rather than primarily on making people happy in the short term.
4. Schools with Manager leaders attain implementation success. However, little effort is made to move beyond the acceptable minimums.
5. Responders ask about concerns but are less active in attempting to resolve them and in facilitating change. They just tend to keep checking on how people are feeling about issues in general.
6. Influencing leaders with different CF Styles requires customized approaches. Responders are most interested in staff feelings, Managers focus most on administrative and organizational rules and procedures, whereas Initiators want to hear the facts and reasons about how the school will be improved.

DISCUSSION AND IMPLICATIONS OF CHANGE FACILITATOR STYLE

Now that the different CF Styles have been introduced, it is important to think about some of the implications, issues, and questions. The different CF Styles described here do not represent all principals, nor do all principals fit perfectly into one of these styles. However, they do appear to represent three more commonly found approaches to change leadership. If the CF Style descriptors offer nothing else, they can help you think about leaders with whom you have worked. Also, what about your style? Which one are you most like? And, what do you think are important characteristics of leaders during change processes?

A Continuum of Change Facilitator Styles

One way to think about the relationship of one CF Style to the others is to place them on a 100-point number line (see Figure 6.2). The stereotypic Responder is positioned at point 30, the stereotypic Manager at point 60, and the Initiator at point 90. Then, by using the paragraph definitions (Figure 6.1), it is possible to envision what persons who are combinations of the three styles would be like. For example, one principal might behave somewhat like a Responder but overall tend to be more of a Manager. That person could be placed around point 50 on the number line. A leader who is developing a clearer vision about the school and is sometimes thinking of more long-term goals might be somewhere between the Manager and Initiator CF Styles, maybe around point 75.

Other CF Styles can be imagined by envisioning what people would be like at the extreme ends of the continuum. For example, a leader who scores above 100 would be a despot who does not listen and just decrees, whereas a person at the 0 end would display an extremely laissez-faire approach, neither taking a position nor helping with the change. Off the chart, far to the left, would be the covert saboteur who works behind the scenes to scuttle the change effort.

Metaphors for Change Facilitator Styles

Metaphors can be a useful way to summarize a great deal of information and ideas. A metaphor that should help in thinking about the totality of each CF Style is that of a game. What type of board game would symbolize each CF Style?

The Initiator is a chess player. Just as chess has many pieces, each with its own rules for being moved, the Initiator sees the individual differences in the school's people and activities. And just as good chess players use strategies and anticipate many moves ahead, Initiators not only engage in doing the day-to-day activities of change leadership but are also constantly

FIGURE 6.2   A Continuum of Change Facilitator Styles

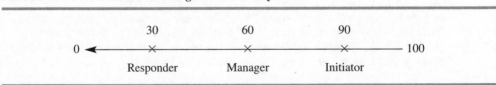

thinking about what needs to be done next. Most importantly, Initiators will have several alternative strategies in mind in anticipation of possible scenarios that could unfold.

Manager leaders play a board game, too, but it is a simpler one—checkers—with different pieces and rules of movement but a less complicated view of the organization. Although all the pieces look and move the same, there are tactics and strategies, but they are simpler. Still, in checkers, as in chess, the actions have a sustained purpose.

The game metaphor for Responders is that of flipping coins. Each flip of the coin is an act that is independent of the one that came before and the one that will follow. To a surprising degree, this is the case for the intervention behaviors of Responders. Each action tends to be taken independently. Much less consideration is given to stringing together such actions as individual one-legged interviews, faculty meetings, announcements, and e-mail notes to teachers. Each task and issue is addressed independently. For example, a teacher may be told at the beginning of the school year that she or he is responsible for maintaining the materials closet, but the Responder principal never follows up to see if the teacher is doing the task or if anything needs to be adjusted. As a result, interventions do not accumulate to make tactics and strategies or to develop coherent themes that teachers can see.

Additional Research and Support for Change Facilitator Styles

One could question whether these different CF Styles actually exist. How can we be assured that they are not just figments of the authors' imaginations? Also, do we know anything about the relationship of these CF Styles to teacher success in change or, even more importantly, student learning? Addressing these questions is one of the important purposes of research. This is also one reason we took the time in the introduction to this chapter to explain the background studies that led to the hypothesis that there are different CF Styles. In this section, some of the related and more recent research studies will be introduced.

Research Findings: Intervention Behaviors of Each Change Facilitator Style

Principal.   The first research study on CF Styles was the Principal/Teacher Interaction (PTI) Study (Hord & Huling-Austin, 1986). In this study, full-time ethnographers systematically documented the interventions of nine elementary (three in each of three districts in different states) school principals for an entire school year. What they said in staff meetings, their one-legged interviews, their memos, and their time in classrooms were documented and described. Implementation was assessed by measuring teachers' SoC, LoU, and IC. Statistically significant differences were found in the quantity and quality of the principals' interventions. For example, the interventions most related to innovation implementation took place in the Initiator schools, whereas the fewest occurred in the schools with Responder principals. Although the total number of interventions made by all facilitators was observed in schools with Initiator principals, Manager CF Style principals did the most interventions themselves (Hall & Hord, 1987); Hall, Rutherford, Hall, & Huling, 1984).

Since that first study, a number of other researchers in the United States have independently confirmed that principal intervention behaviors can be clustered according to these three styles (see, for example, Entrekin, 1991; Hougen, 1984; Trohoski, 1984). In addition, studies have been done in Belgium (Vandenberghe, 1988) and in Australia (Schiller, 1991)

FIGURE 6.3   Summary Characteristics of Three Change Facilitator Styles

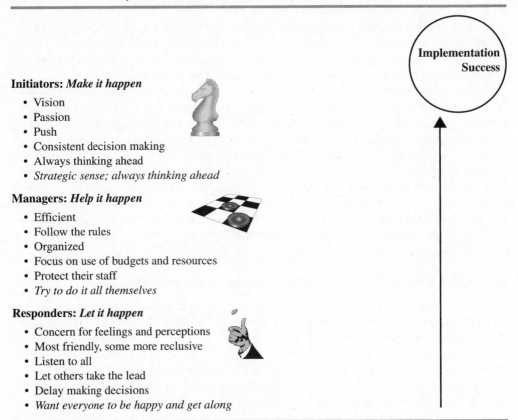

Initiators: *Make it happen*

- Vision
- Passion
- Push
- Consistent decision making
- Always thinking ahead
- *Strategic sense; always thinking ahead*

Managers: *Help it happen*

- Efficient
- Follow the rules
- Organized
- Focus on use of budgets and resources
- Protect their staff
- *Try to do it all themselves*

Responders: *Let it happen*

- Concern for feelings and perceptions
- Most friendly, some more reclusive
- Listen to all
- Let others take the lead
- Delay making decisions
- *Want everyone to be happy and get along*

Implementation Success

with similar results. In a major test of the cross-cultural generalizability of the three CF Styles, Shieh (1996) documented the intervention behaviors of six elementary school principals in Taiwan and observed the same differences in style and surprisingly similar anecdotal examples of perspectives and approaches to change leadership. Jehue (2000) found similar patterns in his study of military leader's CF Styles. Although they certainly do not represent all possibilities, these three CF Styles do have a basis in systematic studies in a number of settings and do offer a way to think more holistically about change leadership. Figure 6.3 is a brief summary of characteristics of each CF Style.

Research Findings: Relating Change Facilitator Style to Teacher Success in Implementing Innovations.   The relationship between principal CF Style and teacher success in implementation also has been studied. For the PTI study, the CBAM diagnostic dimensions of SoC, LoU, and IC provided very useful benchmarks for assessing the degree of implementation. In other words, the basic research question was, Is there a relationship between the principal's CF Style and how far and fast teachers move across the Implementation Bridge? Teachers who move to higher levels of use, with higher fidelity Configurations, and with reduction of Self and Task concerns and arousal of Impact concerns would be considered to have had more implementation success. They have moved further across the Implementation Bridge.

In the studies, the degree of implementation success has been compared with the intervention behaviors of their principals and the principals' CF Style. In most of the studies cited above, this comparison was made. In the original PTI Study a correlation of 0.74 was found between CF Style and teacher implementation success. In the other studies (for example, Schiller, 1991, 2002, 2003; Shieh, 1996; and Vandenberghe, 1988), similar patterns have been observed. As is described in Chapter 12, more recent studies have further documented these relationships.

The general finding has been that teachers with Initiator principals have the highest levels of implementation success. Teachers with Manager principals are successful, too, but not to the same extent as teachers in Initiator schools. Teachers with Responder principals are rated a distant third in terms of implementation success. One way to summarize these findings is to suggest that the Initiator principals "make it happen." They have the vision, passion, and push to help things move in the desired direction. They make decisions quickly and with consistency. Manager principals "help it happen." They see that things are well organized. They protect their teachers, but when implementation becomes an objective, it is accomplished efficiently. However, unlike the Initiators, they do not have the excitement and energy to keep doing more.

The conditions in schools led by Responder principals are quite different. These leaders "let it happen." Yes, they do listen to perceptions and concerns, but they seldom resolve issues with certainty. They continue to be open to new input and as a result do not bring closure, or else they will hear another piece of information and change their minds. Statistically, they are significantly less active in terms of the number of change-related interventions they make. The result for teachers is less implementation success and a tendency to have "Big W" SoC profiles (see Figure 4.4). Shieh (1996) observed that in the first months of implementation teachers in Responder schools tend to use more of the less desirable Configurations of the innovation, whereas teachers in Initiator schools tend to use more of the desirable Configurations.

Research Findings: Relationships of Principal Change Facilitator Style to Student Learning.   As interesting and useful as the CF Style idea might be, the bottom line question remains, Are there any relationships between CF Style and student outcomes? The first major study that addressed this question was done in 27 elementary schools in an urban school district in Connecticut (Hall, Negroni, & George, 2008). Principal CF Style was determined and fourth-grade students' test scores were analyzed for writing, editing, reading comprehension, and mathematics. The researchers found significant differences for three of the four subject areas. Students in schools with a principal who was seen to be an Initiator or a Manager had significantly higher test scores, with Initiator schools being highest in writing and reading. Students in schools with Manager CF Style principals scored highest in mathematics. Students in schools with Responder CF Style principals scored significantly lower for all subjects. The researcher's summary of the study findings is presented in Figure 6.4.

REFLECTION QUESTIONS

What do you make of the idea that the CF Style of the principal is related to teacher success in implementing change and also related to student learning? What is it that principals do that makes these differences? What are implications for you as a leader?

FIGURE 6.4   Relationships Between Principal's Change Facilitator Style and Student Test Scores: Findings from the First Study

1. Students in schools with "Manager" CF Style principals did significantly better on the fifth-grade math test than those in schools with either Initiator or Responder CF Style principals.
2. Students in schools with Initiator CF Style principals did significantly better on the fifth-grade reading comprehension test than those in schools with either Manager or Responder CF Style principals.
3. The predicted average Direct Assessment of Writing Scores, based on fourth-grade scores, was highest in Initiator-led schools, lower in Manager-led schools, and lowest in Responder-led schools. Overall, these differences were not statistically significant—that is, the estimated probability that differences of this size or larger could be observed using these sample sizes, and given the variance in scores, was not less than 5%. It is very close, however, at 6.2%. Pair-wise comparisons reveal there was a statistically significant difference between the student's scores in Initiator-led schools over the Responder-led schools.
4. Students in schools with Initiator CF Style principals did significantly better on the fifth-grade editing and revising test than those in schools led by Responder CF Style principals.
5. Also, students in schools with Manager CF Style principals had higher predicted 2006 math test scores than students in schools with Responder CF Style principals; however, this difference was not statistically significant.

Source: Hall, Negroni, & George (2008), p. 6.

IMPLICATIONS FOR SUPERVISORS OF LEADERS WITH DIFFERENT CF STYLES

Being successful and effective in working with different CF Style leaders can be a challenge. It also can be interesting and very rewarding. Each CF Style—Initiator, Manager, and Responder—brings with it certain advantages and disadvantages. Supervisors, coaches of leaders, and their followers will find that success in working with each CF Style leader requires different strategies.

SELECTING A PILOT/DEMONSTRATION SITE

Suppose there was a need to establish a demonstration site for an innovative program or some other new approach, such as a magnet school or a new manufacturing technology. Which CF Style would be best, and why? The Initiator would seem to be the logical choice. However, the idea will have to be presented and sold. If the Initiator sees how the new initiative will benefit his or her organization and its clients (teachers or customers), then there will be full support for implementing the pilot. However, if the Initiator is not convinced that there are benefits for clients and the organization, then it will be a hard sell, and quite likely little active support will be garnered for the initiative. The Initiator will ask, "How will *my unit* and *our* clients benefit?" The Manager will state, "*I* will need more resources to do this." One Manager who one of the authors has worked with will usually go further by stating an ultimatum based in the need for more resources: "If *I* don't get more resources, then *my* unit will have to stop what it is doing." The Responder will say, "Go ahead—*you* do it." (The italics have been inserted here to point out the differences in frame of reference for each CF Style.)

IMPLICATIONS FOR SUPERVISORS OF LEADERS WITH DIFFERENT CF STYLES   CONTINUED

SUPERVISION AND COACHING DIFFERENT CF STYLES

Supervisors who wish to differentiate their working with each of the leaders subordinate to them in the organization can use the CF Styles as a guide. The same can be done by coaches of leaders.

Responders will generally understand less and get less done, so closer supervision and more frequent contact will be necessary. In our experience, Responders often do not understand the deeper reasons and nuances. They tend to focus more on the surface and count on their friendly, nonthreatening style to carry the day. At the same time, they have the potential to be busy behind the scenes, spreading gossip and rumors with their staff and their peers.

Managers focus heavily on staying within the rules following all policies, and making sure the paperwork is done correctly. They also will press for more resources no matter what the issue or opportunity. Some are fun to coach, especially those who are interested in becoming more effective as leaders. Their efficiency and organization skills can be very important to implementation success and organization effectiveness.

Initiators are the ones who focus first on the needs of clients/students and are continually looking for programs and strategies that can make a positive difference. One of the consequences for their supervisors and coaches is that Initiators don't wait for you to come to them. They come to you! They will push for what they want for their unit. They also make their peers uncomfortable, since they will push and compete with them. As a result, one of the burdens for their supervisor is having to spend time in resolving conflicts and perceptions of favoritism. Problems also can develop when Initiators "forget" about a rule or procedure and just go ahead and do what they think will be best for their unit.

LEADERSHIP TEAM DIFFERENCES

The kind of dynamics inside leadership teams will vary by CF Style of the leader. In CBAM research a special role has been identified for what we call the Second CF, or consigliere. This person has a key role in change process success.

In the Initiator-led team, Second CFs do as many interventions as the leader does. The leaders and the Second CFs truly work as a horizontal team, with both working with the staff in complementary ways.

Contrary to what might be predicted, it is the Initiator-led team that is most collegial and collaborative. There is a shared agenda. Each member of the team will give the same answer to questions and will have the same priorities in working with others.

In the Manager CF Style team, the Second CF makes fewer interventions, such as one-legged interviews, and the Manager makes more. In fact, when compared to Initiators and Responders, the Managers make significantly more interventions. However, the total number of interventions across all members of the CF Team will be highest with the Initiator-led team. In addition, the relationship between the Manager leader and the consigliere is different from what has been observed with Initiators. It is much more of a supervisor–subordinate dynamic.

(continued)

The Responder CF Team is different again. There are significantly fewer interventions in support of the change process, and the Second CF does not have clear and ongoing support to facilitate implementation. The Responder also is significantly less active.

Each of these CF Teams requires different approaches to supervision and coaching. The Initiator-led team will keep on going. The Manager-led team will get the job done and tend to stop. And the Responder-led team will tend not to get organized and to remain unable to focus on facilitating implementation.

UNDERLYING DIMENSIONS AND MEASUREMENT OF CHANGE FACILITATOR STYLE

So far in your reading about CF Style the descriptions have been of a gestalt—that is, a holistic view of what leaders do. In this section we take the whole apart by identifying six underlying dimensions. Each dimension, individually, represents an important component of leadership. As you will see, the six dimensions can be combined to describe with more depth each of the CF Styles. In addition, a research instrument, *The Change Facilitator Style Questionnaire,* has been developed to measure each of these dimensions (Hall & George, 1999).

Six Dimensions of Change Facilitator Style

Researchers used a combination of data from observing principals led change efforts and asking teachers how they view the intervention actions of their principal to develop the six CF Style Dimensions (Hall & George, 1988, 1999; Vandenberghe, 1988). The full definitions of the six dimensions are presented in Appendix D. An abbreviated description of each dimension is presented in Figure 6.5.

Concern for People.   This cluster addresses the personal aspects of leadership and change. This grouping in many ways is addressing the Relationship dimension of the earlier leadership models described at the beginning of this chapter. As was emphasized in Chapter 4, there is a personal side to facilitating change processes. Different styles of leaders spend more or less time on each of these dimensions.

Social/Informal.   Some leaders spend a great deal of time chatting informally with staff, visitors to the school, colleagues, and district office personnel. The talk topics are not about work, or any specific change initiative; they are social and personable.

> The school is about as intimidating as it can get for a first-year teacher; it sits on a busy intersection and the numbers are staggering; there is a combined student body of approximately five thousand students. On the first day, like a scene out of a movie, I was the teacher with the briefcase stuffed full of papers and looking disheveled, trying to get someone in the enormous main office to help me out and get me going in the right direction.
>
> Like many of the new teachers who went through those gigantic doors, after a month of this type of impersonal hustle and bustle and wondering if anything I did made a difference, I seriously considered quitting.

FIGURE 6.5 Six Dimensions of Change Facilitator Style with Examples

I. CONCERN FOR PEOPLE

Social/Informal

- Sees the school as a family
- Begins staff meetings with celebrations
- Joins in attending ball game or concert
- Very sensitive to staff and student's individual needs
- Shows empathy through listening skills

Formal Meaningful

- Holds grade level/department meetings once each term to get feedback on successes and problems
- Links theory to action
- Listens before deciding
- Explains what is needed
- Provides needed resources without fanfare

II. ORGANIZATIONAL EFFICIENCY

Trust in Others

- Lets other take the lead
- Does not have to control everything
- Development of new rules is done slowly

Administrative Efficiency

- Schedules and procedures are established and clear
- Attends to day-to-day tasks
- Keeps policies, rules, and procedures at the forefront
- Paperwork gets done on time and correctly

III. STRATEGIC SENSE

Day to Day

- Focus is on now
- Today's problem is the one attended to
- Limited, or little, view of the future

Vision and Planning

- Long-term vision
- Depth of knowledge
- Anticipates possible future effects of today's interventions
- Maintains a systemic view

The difference was the leadership provided by Mrs. K. She was so good at stopping people in the hallways, sitting in on meetings, and having private discussions with you afterward and sitting down in the lounge to have coffee with us that I thought being principal was the easiest job on campus!

I distinctly remember one time having to stay late at school to finish some work and going across the street from campus to pick up some snacks. As I was waiting for the crosswalk light to change, Mrs. K. appeared right next to me, coffee and donuts in her hands as well. I readied my-self for any questions she might have about test scores, and such. Instead, her first question was "How's the parking situation going for you?" "Excuse me?" was the only reply I could muster. "Yeah, I know the lot fills up pretty quickly in the morning and finding parking on this busy in-tersection is nearly impossible. If you are having a hard time finding parking there is a little secret spot normally reserved for cafeteria employees that you can use." That was the first of many, many conversations that I had with her all over campus, and while she sometimes asked about what happened in the classroom, she understood that the more comfortable I felt outside of the classroom, the better I could perform inside the classroom. (Andrew Wang, reflecting on being a first-year teacher in the Los Angeles Unified School District, June 2009)

Formal Meaningful.   Having many one-legged interviews that are task related is important. Our studies document that in schools with more of these small "incident" interventions, teachers have more implementation success. This dimension doesn't always mean direct talk. For example, one principal overheard a teacher saying that she did not have enough micro-scopes to do a particular lesson. The next day five additional microscopes appeared on the teacher's desk. These are the types of interventions made by effective mentors and coaches. They offer brief tips and suggestions related to particular concerns of the moment of individ-uals and groups. The tips will be of the how-to-do-it type for those with Task concerns or the suggesting of an interesting article or Web site to those with Impact concerns.

Organizational Efficiency.   This second cluster of CF Style dimensions addresses the task or structure dimension of the traditional leadership models. The work has to be organized. Schedules, budgets, and paperwork have to be done.

Trust in Others.   Some leaders prefer to do all of the administrative tasks themselves. Others delegate to others. Different CF Style leaders balance these two ends of a continuum differently. Managers tend to hang on to most, if not all of the authority and responsibility. Initiators will delegate tasks and responsibilities "to those they trust" to get the job done. Responders and their staff are less clear about who has responsibility for any particular item: them or someone else.

Some principals expect teachers to take care of all the disciplines in their classrooms. They empower departments, grade-level teams, and committees to make decisions and imple-ment action steps. Other administrators hold all final decisions close to their vests.

Administrative Efficiency.   Some leaders see their primary task being to manage tasks such as reports, teacher evaluations, ordering supplies, and making schedules. These tasks are lower priority for others. Another indicator of this dimension is how clearly tasks and respon-sibilities are assigned. For example, are the staff clear about whom to go to obtain extra instructional supplies or to request a leave day?

Strategic Sense.   This third cluster focuses on the little decisions and issues that come up every day for leaders and the extent to which there is a vision and leadership with an eye to long-term goals.

Day to Day.   Some leaders are consumed with what is happening right now. The next issue that pops up is the one they deal with. They are not thinking much about the long term or how what they do now may affect what happens next week.

Vision and Planning.   Some leaders have in mind the long-term directions for what they want their organization to be like. They also have in mind the steps it will take to achieve the vision. As one teacher observed, "Ms. J's passion for education is felt by the high expectations she has set for herself, her staff, and the students." Another teacher in reflecting on her principal observed,

> She is always talking about doing more and improving what is already being done. When we were designated a *flagship school,* she took time out to celebrate our achievement as a school. But, the next day she was talking about how we could increase community partnerships and use the expertise of teachers and staff to create a professional development school. She is not content with settling on what is happening day to day—she is more concerned with a more comprehensive understanding of the direction the school is going. (Pam Johnson, June 2009)

Measuring Change Facilitator Style with the Change Facilitator Style Questionnaire

Each of the dimensions of CF Style can be thought about and rated separately. Just think about a scale from 0 to 10 for each dimension. The more a particular leader exhibits that dimension, the higher their score. There also is an instrument for doing this task with more reliability and validity, *The Change Facilitator Style Questionnaire* (CFSQ) (Hall & George, 1999), provided in Appendix E, along with its Scoring Device as Appendix F. Characteristic CFSQ profiles for each of the three Change Facilitator Styles have been established and are presented in Figure 6.6.

Pothole Warning

Do not be casual about use of the Change Facilitator Style Questionnaire, or followers as well as leaders will become threatened.

Pothole Repair

The CFSQ is a very useful instrument for self-assessment. It also can be useful for coaching leaders and as a valid measure in research studies. However, it can be uncomfortable for leaders, such as principals, and for those, such as teachers, who are asked to fill it out. All can see this as evaluation of a person, which can be very threatening.

The CFSQ profile for Manager principals is relatively flat and at the midlevel of each scale. Teachers see Manager principals as doing about the same amount of intervening relative to each of the six CFS dimensions. Initiator principals are scored high on the Social/Informal, Formal/Meaningful, Administrative Efficiency, and Vision and Planning dimensions. This profile fits with what would be expected from the earlier descriptions of Initiators, with the possible exception of being higher on the Social/Informal scale than might be expected. This finding from our research brought home an important point: Initiators have many one-legged interviews that not only are related to use of the change/innovation (Formal/Meaningful) but also deal with personal and general topics of discussion (Social/Informal). In other words, Initiators talk with teachers about how the change process is going and find time for social chat, too.

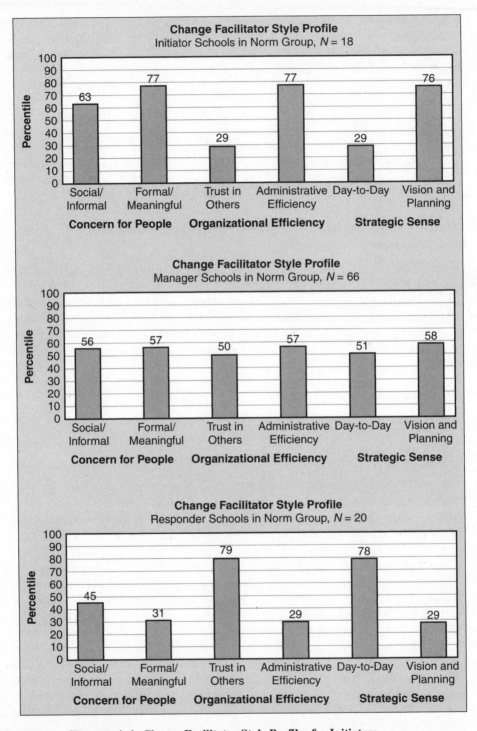

FIGURE 6.6   Characteristic Change Facilitator Style Profiles for Initiators, Managers, and Responders

The CFSQ profile for Responder principals is high on the dimensions of Trust in Others and Day to Day. Responders tend to focus neither on making the school run efficiently nor on engaging in long-term Vision and Planning. What is particularly interesting about this profile is the low score on Social/Informal. Based on our earlier description of the Responder CF Style, one would expect that a Responder would be rated highly on informal, nontask-related talk and chat, but this is not how they are seen by their teachers. In a research finding that might be related, we have found that Responder principals make fewer interventions related to a particular change process.

REFLECTION QUESTIONS

Use the six CF Style dimensions to assess a leader you know well. Rate from low to high how much the leader exhibits behaviors on each dimension. Once you have the CF Style profile, examine how closely it matches one of the characteristic profiles presented in Figure 6.6. How well does this profile match your impression of this leader?

■ ■ ■ ■ ■ ▬▬▬▬▬▬▬▬▬▬▬▬▬▬▬▬▬▬▬▬▬

VIGNETTE
PRINCIPAL SUCCESSION

One of the interesting applications of CF Styles is to envision different scenarios when there is a change of who is the leader. This analysis could be done from one or more perspectives. For example, if you have accepted the position of principal, you should be interested in finding out about the CF Style of your predecessor. You could also be interested in this analysis if you are a teacher in a school that is going through a turnover in principals, or if you are on the interview committee or in the district office with an assignment to advise on the selection of a new principal for a particular school.

The CF Styles can be used to understand the kind of leader the school needs next and to anticipate what some of the problems will be in the transition. Let's imagine what some of the transitions could be like. To do this we will use a combination of real cases and hypothetical examples.

WHEN AN INITIATOR FOLLOWS A RESPONDER

Frequently, an Initiator principal replaces a Responder. Consider the setting that the newly assigned Initiator will enter. To begin, Responder-led schools are characterized by the "Big W" concerns profile (see Figure 4.4). Teachers are not happy about their continually high Stage 3 Management concerns, which are reflected in the "tailing up" on Stage 6 Refocusing. They have some very strong ideas about how things ought to be. Remember too that a Responder principal does not make clear and final decisions. We also know that in a Responder school a small clique of teachers will have more control over what happens and that a large number of teachers will have little say in what occurs. In addition, each teacher tends to be strong and independent because the Responder's attitude is "I hire strong teachers who know more about teaching than I do." The result is that the teachers rarely agree on anything, ranging from which texts to use to where to place the coffee pot.

Administrators in the district office are delighted that a well-known Initiator principal has agreed to take over this school and "turn it around." This principal is known for having a strong focus on student success, and she insists that all the teachers work toward the betterment of the school: "My expectation is that they should lead, follow, or get the hell out of the way."

(continued)

VIGNETTE CONTINUED

Given your understanding of CF Style, what do you predict will happen in this situation? Will the transition go smoothly? What kinds of issues will be problematic? Will students be more or less successful? And what will the district office administrators do as the scenario unfolds?

In our case files are a number of examples of a transition from Responder to Initiator CF Style. One of the opening steps for Initiators is to study closely the achievement data of students and the records of the teachers. The Initiator arrives with a set of key themes, such as "treat students as you want to be treated," that she emphasizes repeatedly.

In our case study of the previous Responder principal, distribution of resources was unequal, with certain teachers getting more and some getting little. The newly arrived Initiator principal expects that resources will be distributed evenly and without favoritism. She also presses for teachers to use certain teaching practices and curriculum materials. All of the new principal's actions are intended to move things in the direction of her vision.

EARLY REACTIONS TO THE NEW PRINCIPAL

The reactions of teachers are aligned with how their influence has been affected and the degree of change that is expected of them. The clique of teachers that had more influence with the Responder principal are unhappy with the changes. In fact, some of them are complaining to the district administrators, and some even go directly to the school board. When asked, teachers who were not part of the influential clique but who are now being treated fairly express appreciation for the new principal, but they do not go out of their way to express their satisfaction to the district administrators or school board.

Typically, the administrators in the district office start to worry when they hear that things are not going well at the school. In this case, as with a number of similar transitions that we have observed, the district administrators maintained a hands-off stance, leaving the Initiator principal to sink or swim, on her own. One district administrator observed, "Well, I don't know if Teresa is going to make it." Ironically, this was the same administrator who placed Teresa in this situation. Rather than moving to address the concerns of the complaining teachers or to overtly encourage and support the new principal, the district administrators merely listened to the one-sided reports from the school. Fortunately, this vignette can have a happy ending. Two years later Teresa was acclaimed for having turned the school around.

Obviously there is more to this case that could be told. The purpose here was to briefly introduce the strategy of using CF Style concepts to examine transitions in school principals. In thinking about successions, it is important to consider the CF Style of the departing as well as the incoming leaders. It is also necessary to understand what the school has been like and what the new principal will expect it to become. Remember also that teachers, parents, district office administrators, and students may perceive and consider aspects of the principals' CF Style differently.

VIGNETTE CRITIQUE QUESTIONS

1. What do you see as being the critical characteristics of the Responder and the Initiator in this vignette? Was there a clear change in leadership style? How did the leaders differ in what they considered to be important? What should the district administrators have done?

2. What is the CF Style of your current principal/leader? Describe some of the things that you have learned to do to work effectively with this person. How do you think your role/work would change if a new principal/leader with a different CF Style were assigned to your school? Style?

IDEAS, IMPLICATIONS, AND REFLECTIONS ABOUT CHANGE FACILITATORS

Of course, the three CF Styles of Initiator, Manager, and Responder do not represent all the possibilities but rather certain basic types that differ in a number of important ways. The concepts and distinctions of CF Style along with the six CF dimensions can be used in a number of ways, some of which have been suggested above; others are summarized next.

Change Facilitator Style as a Heuristic

The concept of CF Style can serve as a heuristic, or a device that helps us think about what we should do in leading change processes. Using the CF Style concepts, we can ask ourselves questions such as these:

1. What kind of CF Style do I want to have?
2. In the successful change processes of which I have been a part, what was the CF Style of the leader?
3. When I interview for a new position, what characteristics will I look for in my new supervisor?

Working with Different Change Facilitator Styles

CF Styles also offer clues about why and how to be more influential with different leaders. Each leader by definition will be emphasizing particular aspects of the change process and elements of use of the innovation. They consider different factors when making decisions, and the amount of time that they need to make decisions varies considerably. Teachers and others who have determined the leader's style can have more influence. They also will be more accurate in predicting what the leader will decide. For example, when teachers would like their principal to make a decision in a particular direction, what they say to influence the decision making and when and how they say it will need to be adjusted to fit the principal's CF Style.

Working with Initiators.   For example, whatever the issue to be resolved, Initiators will want to have reasons and evidence that explain how the decision will affect student success and advance the school. They will expect teachers to have well-developed ideas and clear descriptions, supported by facts. Timing is important, since Initiators tend to think far ahead. They like to be able to anticipate what will work as well as what might go wrong. Providing them with information early in the process is key. Once they have heard what is being suggested, they may need to consult with others, but they will make a decision fairly quickly.

Working with Responders.   In contrast, Responders will be less interested in hearing specifics and more likely to encourage proceeding without careful thought or fully understanding all that may follow. In their effort to be encouraging, they frequently will agree to two or more initiatives that overlap and may actually compete. In other words, do not count on continuity of support and follow-through. One piece of good news is that Responders will allow and even encourage an array of change initiatives. Don't forget, however, that if what is being asked involves a major decision or may create controversy, Responders will be very slow to agree. They will want plenty of time for talk, which may seem like a way to avoid making a decision. A good approach when dealing with a Responder is to begin with casual social chat and then raise the general topic. An important side strategy would be to regularly and continually monitor other related decisions that the Responder is making.

Working with Managers.   When making a request or a suggestion to Manager leaders, remember that they will want to hear about the time, logistic, related policies, and cost implications. The structuring of work and scheduling are important considerations for them. They will immediately think about related rules and policies that might block what is proposed. Be prepared to know what resources will be needed and have suggestions about how your ideas can be managed. Managers can decide quite quickly if what is being asked is in line with initiatives that are already up and running. However, an entirely new proposal is likely to run into the dampening effect, which results from a combination of Managers' desire to follow the rules, intention to protect and maintain stability around current efforts, and the need to first study and ponder.

SUMMARY

In this chapter, the focus has been on characteristics of those who lead change processes. Three CF Styles have been proposed and confirmed through studies that documented the moment-to-moment and day-to-day intervention behaviors of principals. Findings from research have been used to illustrate and explain these different approaches to change leadership. One important point that was made early in this chapter was that *everyone* who is part of a change process has the opportunity, and some responsibility, to help lead. Also, attention must be given to distinguishing between facilitators' individual actions or behaviors and their overall style. As will be discussed in Chapter 8, the very same action by leaders with different CF Styles can be perceived and interpreted very differently by their followers. In other words, often what counts is not what you do but how others interpret what you do.

The style of change leadership makes a major difference in the implementation success of the followers. Being able to distinguish the different CF Styles has many implications, including their use by the followers, who need to work with leaders with different styles, as is illustrated in the vignette, and their use by the leaders themselves, who may want to analyze and reflect on their approach to change facilitation. In conclusion, it is crucial to remember that, since principals and other leaders, like students and teachers, are different, we should not treat them as if they are all the same.

DISCUSSION QUESTIONS

1. The research findings presented in this chapter describe a strong correlation between teacher success in implementation of educational innovations and the CF Style of the principal. Why do you think the correlation is so strong? What is it about the different CF Styles that makes for more, and less, implementation success?

2. In small groups, use specific behavior examples to analyze and discuss each of the six dimensions of CF Style of a leader you know, such as a principal, district superintendent, college president, dean, or department chair. You also could use a state or national leader, such as a

governor or U.S. president. Use examples of specific behaviors and actions as well, the six CF Style dimensions, and the general description of each CF Style to place this person at a specific point on the CF Style continuum presented in Figure 6.2.

3. Use the six CF Style dimensions and the CF Style continuum to assess your own CF Style and be ready to discuss it. Describe your behaviors during one change effort. In hindsight, what style were you using? What do you now know that you could have done differently?

4. Develop a chart or summary figure that identifies and describes actions and approaches that you should, and should not, take to positively influence (i.e., to get along with) supervisors, each of whom uses one of the three CF Styles.

5. One of the heuristic applications of CF Styles is to apply them to various succession scenarios. For example, what happens when a Responder follows an Initiator, or when a Responder follows a Responder? A number of succession patterns are possible. Pick one and predict what would happen in the organization with the professional staff, support staff, and change initiatives. Would change occur more quickly, more slowly, or at the same pace? Would the same change initiatives continue? How long would it take for effects of the new leader's style to be detected?

FIELDWORK ACTIVITIES

1. Ask two people to describe how they work to facilitate change. One of the people you interview should have a formal administrative position and be a designated leader. The other person should be one of the so-called followers. When interviewing the follower, keep in mind that at first the person is likely to say that he or she has no leadership role. But delve further by asking how he or she participates in planning meetings or helps other people who are engaged with the change process. Use the CF Style constructs to explain how change processes have worked in their setting.

2. Ask someone who has worked for a number of administrators to describe what it was like to interact with leaders with different CF Styles. Develop a report on the person's feelings and perceptions when he or she was engaged in change. You also should ask about the times when change was more and less successful.

3. The primary theme in this chapter has been that a critical factor in change process success is the CF Style of the leader. If you were to interview prospective leaders of a change effort, what kinds of questions would you ask? Develop a list of the questions, and explain how you would expect the answers to differ depending on the person's CF Style. You could also use this activity when you are being interviewed for a new position. After all, the leadership style of your prospective supervisor will make a difference in how you answer the interview questions and, if hired, how successful you can be.

CONDUCT A STUDY

CF Style can be used to study a number of important questions and directions for research. As illustrated in this chapter's vignette, the elements and issues encountered when there is leader succession is a very important area for research. There is a need to replicate the first study (Hall, Negroni, & George, 2008) to see if the significant relationships between CF Style and student outcomes hold. Their role in working with external change agents is another important topic.

CHAPTER 7

DESCRIBING WHAT CHANGE FACILITATORS DO
Interventions

Oh, my! I have just been called by the assistant superintendent to participate with a planning committee for introducing the new constructivist mathematics curriculum. I don't know whether to be thrilled or terrified!

—Mathematics department head, middle school

I am so pleased. Our school improvement team just finished writing a grant for $50,000 that will supply resource materials and equipment for our new science program.

—Assistant principal, high school

What can I do? My teachers have been to the fall series of three workshops and still don't understand how to operate the Students-Plus Tutoring process. It appears that one-to-one help is now needed.

—Elementary school counselor

Interdisciplinary curriculum development has required a significant amount of time and resources across these first three years, but it is well launched in our school, and we are preparing to report to the board about our efforts.

—Superintendent

You know, the staff in manufacturing really don't seem to get it. What can I do to help them "see" my vision for our new product that will surely make a great deal of money for our company?

—Design manager, auto accessories factory

For decades understanding of and attention to the process of leading change efforts have been lacking. In the public and professional minds, an assumption exists that change just happens. We are reminded of two theories articulated by Chin and Benne (1969):

1. The rational empirical approach to change postulated that a good program or process provided to good people would find its way into their practice. (The clue here is *good*.)
2. The power coercive approach maintained that a good program or policy delivered to good people through the offices of a power or authoritarian figure would certainly ensure change in practice. (The key here is *power* and its influence.)

Even today these two approaches tend to be employed by would-be change agents who assume that change will just happen if an attractive or needed innovation is presented (or mandated). What is typically overlooked by such would-be reformers is that most change implementers have full-time (or more!) jobs and don't have the opportunity to carefully and methodically design a self-changing approach. Particular difficulties arise if the innovation is one vastly unfamiliar to the persons who will implement it.

What we know from our own research and review of the literature on successful school change is that facilitators are needed in a major way to support implementers. The main purpose of this book is to help would-be change facilitators to understand a set of research-verified tools that can be used to develop the insights and skills needed to achieve successful change. Through our studies and firsthand experiences with facilitating change in schools, businesses, and other organizations, we have success stories. An important element of these successes has been the many actions of the leaders and other facilitators. These change facilitation actions will be the topic of this chapter.

FOCUS QUESTIONS

1. What do we mean by interventions?
2. Who delivers interventions?
3. Are interventions really necessary?
4. To support successful change efforts, what six basic kinds of interventions are needed?
5. What additional kinds of interventions may be considered by facilitators?
6. What are the sizes of interventions that researchers and practitioners use for studying and planning change?
7. How can an individual intervention be analyzed and studied?

INTERVENTION DEFINITION

We have used and will continue to use the term *intervention* with great regularity in this book. We know, as stated, how significant the work of facilitators is in the process of supporting change efforts. Facilitators provide the interventions that can increase the potential for the success of change or allow it to fail. Thus, we think it is important to understand this term as we use it in this chapter. Our explanation and definition follow; please bear with us.

GUIDING PRINCIPLES OF INTERVENTIONS

1. Successful implementation of new policies, programs, processes, practices, and even new personnel does not just happen. Assuming that the announcement of such changes is sufficient is tantamount to little or no implementation or, at best, very superficial implementation. Interventions both small and large make the difference.
2. Although principals and other leaders have been identified as change facilitators or significant suppliers of interventions, others also make many of these actions. Whoever will assume the role and responsibilities—whether they are teachers, parents, central office personnel, community members, or others—can and do provide change process-related interventions.
3. Many types of interventions must be provided to ensure the success of change efforts. Facilitators must acquaint themselves with and use their knowledge of interventions in planning, monitoring, and assisting their organization's efforts to change and improve.
4. Because change is accomplished at the individual level, facilitators will need to use diagnostic tools for shaping the interventions supplied to individuals as well as to remember to provide groups with the array of interventions necessary to ensure each implementer's success with change.
5. Interventions also need to be targeted toward the whole organization or system, while remembering to employ them across all persons in the system.
6. Since *learning* new information, skills, and behaviors is at the heart of any change project, facilitators would do well to keep this basic premise in mind as they consider, design, and deliver the interventions necessary for change process success.

If a central office curriculum coordinator brings microscopes to a teacher who is implementing a new life-science curriculum, this is an intervention to support the teacher's use of the change. If a university professor coaches three principals in developing instructional leadership, this is an intervention in behalf of the principals' new roles. If a principal conducts staff development for the faculty in cooperative learning techniques, the principal has provided an intervention to the staff. If the division chief sends notes or gives a party of appreciation for the company's staff in recognition of their efforts, that is an intervention. If two teachers talk about what they think of the innovation, that, too, is an intervention.

A deliverable for one of our earlier studies was developing a definition of the construct intervention. After extensive fieldwork and research team debate, we settled on the following:

> Any *action* or *event* that influences the individual(s) involved or expected to be involved in the process or the change process itself is an intervention. (Hall & Hord, 2006, pp. 185–187)

Notice the use of the terms *action* and *event*. An action is deemed to be planned and focused deliberately on an individual, group, or all users or prospective users of a new program or practice (see Figure 7.1). Such an action could be sending an article about the use of math manipulatives to all primary teachers who teach mathematics. Discussion in a staff meeting about how implementation is going is another intervention.

FIGURE 7.1   Definition of an Intervention

An Intervention is an

Action   or   Event

that is typically

Planned   or   Unplanned

and that influences individuals (either positively or negatively)
in the process of change.

An event, on the other hand, is something that occurs outside the deliberations and plans of the change process. Has this ever happened to your effort? Because we have observed that events do indeed influence the process of change, we have included them in our definition of intervention. Events that we have observed in our work include the following:

A blizzard that prevented all truckers from delivering necessary equipment for a district's new astronomy program

A fire in the intermediate service center's print shop that caused a 3-week delay in getting materials for the high school's drug-prevention initiative

A learning styles consultant's accident on a mountain trail that resulted in rescheduling campus-based facilitators' preparations and planning for the project

Another important element—whether it is an action or an event—is that an intervention's influence may be positive or negative. In the preceding examples of actions, the influence was intended to be positive, but the examples of events all suggest negative consequences. This does not mean that all actions are positive or that all events are negative. A refusal to approve funding for a how-to workshop (action) can be negative, whereas a flat tire that forces teachers to carpool (event) and thereby have the opportunity to share success stories could be positive.

Pothole Warning

Be very sensitive and observant to the unplanned events that will almost always creep into the change process. Beware that their influence can be negative—or not.

Pothole Repair

Keeping your ear to the ground and your hand on the pulse will be very helpful in forestalling unfortunate negative events that cause change projects to flounder. On the other hand, maintaining close watch as implementation unfolds can afford the possibility of identifying events that have a positive influence—these then should be capitalized upon and repeated for their continuing effect.

We have seen and recorded wide-ranging types and sizes of interventions—from quite simple and short-term actions to multiyear strategic plans. An example of a short-term intervention would be a one-legged interview, such as when a school improvement team member stops by to say hello to another teacher and then asks if she has any needs regarding the new technology. Another, more complex example is a change facilitator observing an implementer and providing feedback on his use of a new instructional Strategy. An intervention's simplicity or complexity may be analyzed, and this, as well as the various levels of interventions that constitute a typology of interventions that facilitators can consider in their work, are addressed later in this chapter.

REFLECTION QUESTIONS

Consider a change project with which you are familiar. Identify an action and an event that occurred during implementation. Who contributed the action and the event? What were the results of each action and event?

INTERVENTION DELIVERY

Who are the deliverers of interventions? The research and stories of successful school change are almost unanimous in identifying the principal as the primary catalyst and facilitator of site-based change. And yet, as we will discover in this chapter, the principal is not the only Source of interventions.

Also, it is easy to assume that principals and superintendents, because of their positions, are change facilitators. Although this is desirable, it is not always true. Frequently, they are a minimal source of change process-related interventions. Even when they are involved, almost inevitably, because of the multiple roles administrators have, others share in change facilitation (see Table 7.1).

Thus, based on our observations, we suggest that innovation-related interventions and change facilitation support and assistance may be delivered by any person who assumes the role and responsibilities of the change facilitator (whether implicitly or explicitly). In other words, there are many possible and actual sources of change process-related interventions.

One important implication is that many change process participants, including implementers, do not realize that they take actions that influence an individual, a group, or perhaps the entire change process. Another implication is that many people can be involved in the delivery of planned interventions. One significant result is that the burden of support and assistance to the users and nonusers is shared. This is important in view of the limited time that people typically have to invest in facilitating change. Sharing the responsibilities

TABLE 7.1 Sources of Interventions

CAMPUS	DISTRICT	COMMUNITY	STATE
Principals	Superintendent	Parents	Policymakers
Key teachers	Curriculum coordinators	Business representatives	State board/ superintendent
Counselor	Instructional supervisors		
Students		Legislators	

of the facilitating role means also that the role is not necessarily positional but becomes operationally defined by what is done and by whom, which is the focus of the discussion that follows.

REFLECTION QUESTIONS

Think back to your involvement in a change effort. Recall any and all individuals who supplied help and assistance in the implementation of the change. What roles did these individuals represent? Were they administrators? Teachers? Coaches? Parents? Others?

SIX FUNCTIONS OF INTERVENTIONS

Many organizations, leaders, and consultants have been committed to implementation of various changes and improvements. Considerable time and attention are given to the matter of implementing planned change. Although planning activities for change seem generally to receive great attention, facilitating their implementation frequently falls between the cracks. Up-front planning can be very well thought out, but often there is an implicit assumption that change is an event. This can be seen when the plan for implementation has limited resources and is expected to be accomplished in a relatively short time period.

Focusing on implementation is critical for all organizations and especially for school success in implementing today's complex innovations and comprehensive reform efforts. To respond to this issue, earlier the staff of the Southwest Educational Development Laboratory (SEDL) undertook a broad review of the leadership and change facilitation literature to identify relevant research-based concepts and information that could support the development of effective facilitative leaders for school improvement projects. To help these busy practitioners get to the center of change facilitation work, this wide-ranging review of the literature focused on the actions and behaviors of leaders who were facilitating change (Hord, 1992a)—in other words, on interventions. What could be more important, the staff asked, than assisting potential facilitators in understanding the demands of the role and the interventions required?

The literature review resulted in identifying these interventions, which were organized into six types of *Functions* (see Figure 7.2). A major source of this information came from earlier CBAM research, specifically the Principal/Teacher Interaction (PTI) Study reported by Hord and Huling-Austin (1986) and the conceptualization of Game Plan Components in an Intervention Taxonomy done by Hall and Hord (1984). These six Functions were deemed necessary for making change happen, and they constituted the job description of the change facilitator, whether they were assigned to local schools and districts or to state departments of education and other organizations. The ultimate purpose is to think about the importance of different types and sizes of interventions that are necessary to realize successful change in organizations. These six Functions have been continuously reviewed and revised through ongoing literature reviews, especially the research on successful change (Hord, Rutherford, Huling-Austin, & Hall, 2004). The introduction of these six Functions, described next, is designed for students early in their study of the change process. More detailed descriptions follow thereafter.

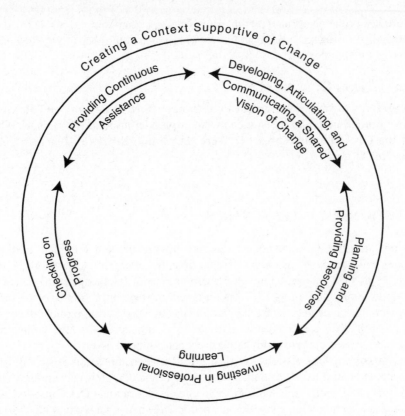

FIGURE 7.2   Six Functions of Interventions

Function I: Developing, Articulating, and Communicating a Shared Vision of the Intended Change

A first step in moving toward a changed and improved future is the development of a shared dream or vision of what will be—that is, a vision of the future that increases student outcomes. The goal of increased student outcomes results from specific changes or innovations that are selected for adoption and implementation. Many change efforts fail because the participants do not share mental images or pictures of what classroom and/or school practice will look like when an identified change is implemented to a high quality. Picturing the change in operation provides the target for beginning the change journey. A part of this process can be creating an Innovation Configuration (IC) Map of the change—a useful way of defining what the change/innovation will look like when it is actually and actively in operation in its intended setting (see Chapter 3).

The elements of the shared vision of change must be as clearly defined as possible, and facilitators must continuously communicate this vision to enable implementers to move toward high-quality implementation. When implementers have a shared vision, facilitators can be consistent in supporting individuals and groups.

Specific facilitator interventions for developing a shared change vision could include but are not limited to engaging the school staff and community in identifying its beliefs and values regarding the purposes of the school, determining areas of the school program in need of change and improvement, selecting solutions to address the areas in need, and collectively developing clear mental images of the solution (i.e., the vision of change) when it is in operation in the school or classrooms.

The shared vision can be communicated in multiple settings: on the school's Web site, in school and district newsletters, at school board and other community meetings, at the local coffee shop, and even on the golf course. The idea is to continually remind all constituents, in various ways, of the vision and where the school is in relationship to realizing it. Related is the understanding that attention to the vision must be provided throughout the process of change in order to capture and capitalize on (or diminish) evolving changes in the vision.

For further material on vision and on the six Functions of basic interventions, see the Additional Readings/Resources at the end of this chapter.

Function II: Planning and Providing Resources

When an initial vision for change has been established (the vision can certainly evolve and change as the school staff experiences, learns, and gains more expertise), planning for its realization is both possible and necessary. All logistical factors and resource allocations, along with policy implications, must be considered. Although it seems obvious, the planning and provision of resources represent an important means by which implementers are enabled to initiate implementation and sustain the change process. We have observed change efforts that lacked necessary resources, which forestalled the expected beginning of the change process and doomed the entire effort.

We frequently observe school district and other organizations that have well-articulated policies for selecting innovations. What we find missing is the equally important set of policies that address how implementation is to be supported and achieved.

Planning is not a one-time event. Like a holiday trip, destinations sometimes change, and unexpected additions frequently may be made for increased effectiveness and/or satisfaction. Thus, although a plan is essential for understanding where the change journey begins, it should never be considered to be cast in concrete. Likewise, the resource requirements for a change are altered across time as implementers become more expert in the use of an innovation and as the Configuration of use may make differing demands. Not to be forgotten is the regular depletion of program materials and equipment and the need for updating supplies to teachers and students.

Other types of resources also require planning. One of the most important, and most typically lacking is time: time for planning, time for professional development, time for sharing, and projecting the time (years) it will take to have high levels of use. Also important, of course, is time for facilitators to do *their* work. School administrators would do well to plan dedicated time for one or more skilled facilitators to coach and address Stages of Concern (SoC) and Levels of Use (LoU) III Mechanical Use. Scheduling time for implementers to meet to discuss successes and share solutions to problems has proven to be valuable.

Other specific actions of facilitators related to this Function include developing policies related to implementation (if they are not already in place), establishing rules and guidelines by which the implementation will be monitored, staffing new roles and/or realigning existing ones, scheduling meetings and other regular and nonregular events, seeking and acquiring materials and equipment, providing space, and accessing funds needed for the new program or practice.

Function III: Investing in Professional Learning

Change means developing new understandings and doing things in new ways. If faculty are to use new curricular programs or instructional practices, they must learn how to do that. Thus, *learning* is the basis of and the corollary to change (see Change Principle 1, Chapter 1). Formal training and other forms of staff and personal development, then, are essential to prepare implementers for the change. Also, when change is viewed as a process, learning opportunities for implementers should be ongoing as they develop more expertise in using the innovation. All too frequently, training workshops are scheduled only at the beginning of a change process. We know that Task concerns do not become intense until after use begins. Therefore, SoC can be used to design and shape the development and learning sessions in the pre-implementation period of preparation as well as during implementation, when implementers are changing from novices to mature users of the new practices (as discussed in Chapter 4). Note also that different levels of understanding and different learning are characteristic of peoples' knowledge at each LoU (see Chapter 5).

Leaders of the change effort will need to consider the following interventions, and others, in the learning and development category: scheduling training and development sessions across time as the implementers move from novice toward expert, identifying and contracting with trainers and other consultants (internal and external), providing information about the change, teaching the skills required of the innovation, developing positive attitudes about use of the new program, holding workshops, modeling and demonstrating innovation use, and clarifying misconceptions about the program or practice. At this point the training is characterized as formal—that is, it is provided as large-group instruction. Professional learning interventions at the individual or small-group level are found in Function V.

It is important that training and development are concerns-based and focused on the vision for the change. When this occurs, implementers gain the information and learn the skills necessary for the new way of behaving in the classroom and school. Too often, professional development has been vague and off target. With a focus on the staff's concerns about its new program and practices, and on the vision of what the change will look like in operation, investing in professional learning will pay large dividends.

Function IV: Checking on Progress

Because change does not happen overnight, the process must be continuously assessed and monitored. Even though a clear articulation of the change has been expressed and material and human resources have been provided, the change journey is not without its bumps and detours. A significant set of facilitator interventions focuses on keeping a hand on the pulse of change. One-legged interviews are an excellent way to check with implementers to identify emerging needs, clarify questions, and solve small problems. Not only does this enable the facilitator to assess progress; it also signifies continuing interest to the implementers and that their efforts are worthy of notice and support.

Decision makers and regulatory agencies have always known that what is measured or monitored is given more attention. A change effort will be given more attention if facilitators continual check on how implementation is going.

More often than not, the change effort is lost when the leadership team, or whatever the facilitating team is called, fails to routinely check the progress of each implementer. Important checking actions include gathering data about the implementers' needs; collecting information about the knowledge and skills of the implementers; collecting feedback at the end of workshops and providing feedback on the feedback; at regular intervals systematically measuring, analyzing, and interpreting SoC, LoU, and IC; and talking informally with users about their progress. It is important that data collected about implementation are analyzed, carefully interpreted, and used to guide subsequent interventions.

Function V: Providing Continuous Assistance

Assisting is directly coupled to assessing, as discussed earlier. When needs or problems are identified, a response is required to support implementation. Assistance may take the form of supplying additional materials, providing formal or informal learning activities, teaming with the implementer to demonstrate refinement of practice, and coaching. It makes sense to assess progress in order to identify needs and then to provide assistance to respond to the needs. This coupling of *assessing* and *assisting* is labeled *coaching, consulting,* or *follow-up* and typically occurs with individuals or very small groups of implementers.

These are crucial behaviors by facilitators. Other assisting actions of facilitators include stopping by to greet implementers and simply asking "How's it going?" Additional actions include responding to individual's questions and confusions, encouraging individuals in their use of the innovation, assisting single and small-group implementers in problem solving, providing follow-up and technical assistance, conducting quick conversations about the implementers' use and reinforcing what they are doing, and celebrating successes both small and large, publicly and privately.

The importance of the coaching role should not be underemphasized. We have observed repeatedly that when an expert coach, such as a master teacher, has assigned time (several days each week) to coach implementers, Task concerns (i.e., Stage 3 Management) do not become intense. In other words, during the first year of implementation the typical wave motion of high Task concerns does not occur.

Function VI: Creating a Context Supportive of Change

Increased attention is currently being paid to the context, climate, and/or culture of the school and district and how these factors influence the workplace and, subsequently, how professionals' respond to change initiatives. For example, Boyd (1992b), in a review of the literature on context that supports or inhibits change, defined two components of context. One is the *physical,* or nonorganic, aspects of an organization: its building facilities, schedules, policies, and the like. The second component is the *people* element: the beliefs and values held by the members and the norms that guide their behavior, relationships, attitudes, and so on. Although the context is identified by its two parts, the parts are interactive and influence each other. For example, a small faculty in a small facility (but one with an available meeting space) will find it much easier to come together to interact and build trust than would a much larger faculty spread over multiple buildings. A supportive context decreases the isolation of the staff, provides for the continuing increase of its capabilities, nurtures positive relationships among all the staff, students, and parents/community members, and urges the unceasing quest for increased effectiveness so that students benefit. (For further discussion of the characteristics of a supportive context for change, see Chapter 2.)

In such a context the participants value change as a means for improving their effectiveness and seek changes in order to improve their practice. Boyd (1992a) reports that school leaders can take actions, such as the following, to create this context:

1. *Shaping the structural features of the context* by manipulating schedules and structures (such as faculty meetings) so that people can come together and share improvement ideas, by allocating resources to support the improvement effort, and by developing policies for enhancing staff capacity
2. *Modeling* the behaviors and norms desired of the staff by interacting and cooperating in a significant way with all staff, by working with focus and commitment, and by being highly visible in the daily routines that they hope the staff will emulate
3. *Teaching and coaching* by reading, studying, and subsequently sharing materials that will nurture and develop the staff's expertise, by attending professional development activities with the staff, and by attending conferences and sharing substance with the staff
4. *Addressing conflict* by facing it rather than avoiding it, and thus using conflict as a vehicle to resolve disputes and build unity
5. *Selecting, rewarding, and censuring staff* by recognizing their work publicly and privately, by inviting the staff to share their efforts and experiences related to improvement goals, and by insisting that staff commit to school goals through the selection and termination processes

In summary, the six types of basic interventions or Functions have been widely used as a framework for developing the knowledge and skills that facilitators need to plan for change, monitor its progress, and evaluate its outcomes in terms of degree of classroom implementation.

REFLECTION QUESTIONS

Have your experiences with change projects contained these six Functions? If any were omitted, did this omission have any effect on results? If so, how?

IMPLICATIONS FOR LEADERS FACILITATING CHANGE

The six Functions of interventions provide a practical framework to facilitators for supporting and guiding change. These are the "sacred six" kinds of actions demanded for the success of change projects.

An interesting way of generating actions or specific interventions for these Functions is in employing the IC Map as a guide. Function I is the articulation of a shared vision of the intended change when it is implemented in a high-quality way. The IC Map is the written product that represents the creation of a shared vision of the change. When this IC Map is completed, it can be used for designing the Function II interventions: Planning and Providing Resources. The map indicates the desired outcomes—what actions are taking place in the innovation's setting—and is the point of reference for making an action plan to reach those desired outcomes. It can also be referenced to determine fiscal and human resources needed to reach the desired outcomes, or the vision of the change.

IMPLICATIONS FOR LEADERS FACILITATING CHANGE   CONTINUED

Referring to the IC Map provides clarity for identifying professional development for staff (Function III) needed to reach the actions delineated on the map. Professional developers use the map to plan training and development for participants. But that is not the end of the change process, though many seem to believe if initial training is provided that the process is complete—which is not true.

The map is used for Function IV, Checking on Progress. The facilitator uses the map as an instrument to ascertain where each individual is in the change effort, so that Function V, Providing Continuous Assistance, may be planned appropriately to support individuals in moving closer to the ideal variation of each component on the map.

An IC Map may not directly address Function VI, Creating a Context Supportive of Change. But a map of such a context for change could be produced to guide the facilitator in designing interventions to enable the creation of a more supportive context in the organization.

ADDITIONAL KINDS OF INTERVENTIONS

Four of the six basic intervention types discussed—planning and providing resources (developing supportive organizational arrangements), investing in professional learning (training), checking on progress (Monitoring and Evaluation), and Providing Continuous Assistance (Providing Consultation and Reinforcement)—accounted for the majority of interventions identified in earlier CBAM studies; the original CBAM names are shown in parentheses (Hall & Hord, 1984, 1987; Hord & Huling-Austin, 1986; Hord et al., 2004). Two of the six categories of interventions—developing a shared vision of the change and creating a context for change—were identified by Hord (1992a).

The CBAM studies revealed two additional Game Plan Components that are less frequently given attention but are quite important in change efforts, especially for larger systems: communicating externally and disseminating information. We examine the importance of these interventions next.

Communicating Externally

An important but often neglected set of interventions are those actions taken to keep individuals and groups external to the implementation site informed about what is happening. To gain their support or approval, these groups need to be informed by the on-site participants. One of the quotes at the beginning of this chapter reports that the change effort on interdisciplinary curriculum is going well and that a report on progress will be made to the board. It is easy to understand the politically and economically astute reasons for communicating externally to such an influential group, but too often too little is done, or it is done too late.

Activities related to this category of interventions include describing the change, its purpose and its benefits to those outside the school, not only having but keeping up to date a web site, making presentations at various district and community meetings, keeping the external members of the site council and the PTO/PTA informed about progress and setbacks, informing all possible constituents about progress, and developing a campaign to gain the support of the public and other relevant groups.

Disseminating Information

Efforts to share information about the new program or practice and to let others know of its value and positive impact, with the intention of persuading them to adopt the program, are dissemination interventions. These interventions are important first steps in "going to scale." In broadcasting the virtues of the innovation, broader support and influence may be gained as well, but in this category the primary intent is to inform prospective adopters from other sites.

To accomplish the purpose of this category, the facilitators engage in various activities, including e-mailing descriptive information to external persons, colleagues, friends, and others who might be interested; making presentations at regional and national meetings; encouraging others to adopt the innovation by reporting its benefits; making large-group presentations about the innovation to potential adopters; providing free sample materials; and training expert colleagues to represent the innovation.

Note that it is not necessary to do disseminating interventions in order to have change success at the home site. As a matter of fact, spending too much time on disseminating, especially early in implementation, can be a distraction and draw needed energy and resources away from the project. Early dissemination also runs the risk of appearing premature, since everything may not have been worked out at the home site. Four or 5 years into a change process can be an excellent time to begin disseminating actions, for at this point those actions can serve to reward and expand the perspectives of successful implementers while increasing visibility for all.

In the early work, these CBAM intervention classifications were labeled *Game Plan Components* and were part of a system that provided for further detailed and enriched planning and analysis of a change endeavor. The additional concept of sizes or levels of interventions, also were identified in the Intervention Taxonomy (Hall & Hord, 1984). Brief descriptions of this part of the framework are presented next. Although these were developed for research purposes, many experienced change facilitators have found them to be instructive and useful.

REFLECTIVE QUESTIONS

Imagine that you are assigned the task of communicating externally about your change effort. Who would you target for this purpose? What might your talking points be? How would you know if you have been successful?

The following vignette returns to the basic six Functions of interventions.

■ ■ ■ ■ ■

VIGNETTE

IMPLEMENTING A NEW CAR

Perhaps a simple story of the integration of a new product into everyday life will be helpful in illustrating what so frequently happens when something new is introduced to individuals.

In 1989, Mrs. H challenged her husband's practice of securing two heavy but speedy, gas-demanding Oldsmobiles for the family by researching and purchasing a new four-door Honda Civic hatchback. This car, silver in color, had a standard transmission, heat, air conditioning, and windshield wipers, and that was it—no radio, no frills. Fortunately for Mrs. H, this car proved abundantly successful, until after 13 years and nearly no visits to the mechanic except for the recommended periodic check-ups, the Honda service technician proclaimed that, at 195,000 miles, "Silver Belle" was "terminal."

Not surprised, although she had planned to run this car to 350,000 miles (a record in effect at this dealership), Mrs. H presented herself at the Honda showroom. Now note the parallels between this personal experience of change—buying a new car—and the steps in the six basic interventions recommended for any change process:

CREATE A CONTEXT SUPPORTIVE OF CHANGE

The Honda showroom was filled with shiny autos, festive balloons, and coffee and cookies for potential customers. A charming and not unattractive young salesman, Jeff, offered to help Mrs. H review the auto possibilities.

DEVELOP A SHARED VISION

Jeff was quite insightful in playing to Mrs. H's concerns for information and her growing interest in a "fine, new car." He was descriptive and persuasive in developing the mental images in the prospective buyer's mind of sailing along the highways in a handsome and upscale new car.

PLAN AND PROVIDE RESOURCES

When Mrs. H decided to make a purchase, Jeff planned the process, developed a contract, and queried Mrs. H about her resources to pay for the car. Although her Personal concerns erupted over the prospects of writing such a large check, Jeff assured her that she was doing the right thing, thus decreasing these concerns. Further, he asked her to give him 30 minutes when she picked up the car the next day.

INVEST IN LEARNING

When Mrs. H arrived the next day, Jeff sat behind the wheel, with Mrs. H leaning in the car window, as he recited his litany: This button does this, that one does that, the lever on the left is for this, this knob controls that, and so on. At the conclusion, he handed Mrs. H the keys, told her to have fun, and thanked her for her business.

At this point, Mrs. H's management concerns escalated, and she left the dealership parking lot with some trepidation (albeit excitement also) but successfully navigated the traffic, hills, and curves to her home.

CHECK ON PROGRESS

To this day, nearly 2 years later, Mrs. H does not know how to play a CD in the car (although she keeps a supply of them ready just in case). When does she think about using the CD player? When she is sailing down the freeway, which is not a good time to refer to the user's manual. Finally realizing that this was an unacceptable situation, she brought the manual into the kitchen so that she could study it.

(continued)

PROVIDE CONTINUOUS ASSISTANCE

"You goose," Mrs. H said to herself, "this is not the appropriate place to study the car manual—you should be in the car." She also was still not clear about how to tune the radio. Further, certain buttons and thingamajigs on the dashboard were befuddling.

The lesson of this not-untrue fable is that the training in use of the car that the change facilitator/ salesperson provided was perfunctory, with no hands-on experience, no practice, and no feedback. Further, he did no checking into Mrs. H's use of the car. The lack of personalized training, with the absence of Checking Progress, followed by no follow-up, resulted in Mrs. H being a very low-quality user of her car.

Mrs. H and her car provide an excellent example of what happens far too often to teachers in classrooms. They become interested in new programs after learning how they work in similar places and developing a vision of how they can contribute effectively to their work so that students benefit. Many times adequate resources are provided, although this is not always the case. Staff development in the new program/practice is provided at the beginning in very ineffective ways (as it was for Mrs. H). Almost without exception, poor training is followed by an absence of the continuous help and assistance that can ensure that high-quality (rather than perfunctory) use results in classrooms and contributes to students' growth, learning, and success.

VIGNETTE CRITIQUE QUESTIONS

1. Have you had an experience similar to Mrs. H's with a new product (such as a new computer, microwave oven, or cell phone), when you did not receive proper support? Reflect on your experience and consider what might have been done to make your implementation of the new product more successful.

2. It would appear that sales personnel, school administrators, and others who are interested in changing their public's products or practices assume a great deal about their clients' capacity with those innovations. How could you help Jeff, the car salesperson, or a school or district administrator understand the real needs of clients for supportive and appropriate interventions?

3. Why would we use a story about purchasing a car in a chapter on interventions? How does it relate to what happens all too frequently when new programs and practices are introduced in schools and classrooms?

SIZES OF INTERVENTIONS

Game Plan Components constitute one size of interventions, but we have also identified other sizes of interventions that are distinguished by their relative duration and the degree to which they affect few or many people. In classifying by these two factors, policy-level interventions are identified as the most comprehensive of the interventions. Strategies, Tactics, and Incidents are additional interventions that can be distinguished by size (see Figure 7.3).

Policies

Since they affect the whole organization/system and exist typically for an extended amount of time (years), the policies of an organization must be taken into account when planning for change or when studying a planned change project. Policies that have long been in place as

FIGURE 7.3   The Relative Size of Interventions

Policies: Decisions that affect the whole organization for an extended period
Game Plan Components: Major functional groupings of interventions
Strategies: Interventions that operationalize the Game Plan Components into actions
Tactics: Sets of small actions that comprise the Strategies
Incidents: Brief in-time actions that focus on one or a few users or nonusers, and that may or may not add up to Tactics

---

well as new ones can affect a change initiative. For example, a long-standing policy could include contract specifications that restrict staff development to the school day. This then becomes an intervention that affects having after-school sessions to support implementation of a new program. Or there may be a policy that prohibits staff development during the school day, thus requiring its scheduling for after the formal school hours, with stipends being paid to the teachers who participate. Such overarching policies can have significant and far-reaching influence on a change process. Facilitators ignore them at their risk.

Game Plan Components

Previously in this chapter, this large clustering of interventions was referred to as "Functions." Our original thinking was to use the metaphor of the coach who prepares an overall plan ahead of the game. Just as with a coach, our assumption is that as the game (of change) unfolds, leaders will need to make adjustments in the Intervention Game Plan. We have changed the name to "Functions" to place more emphasis on the like purpose of each intervention grouping. With either term, *Functions* or *Game Plan Components,* the message is to be sure to have planned interventions within each grouping. Game Plan Components, aka Functions, can be a major change process planning device for clustering interventions into meaningful and functional groupings that provide an overall organizing framework.

Strategies

Strategies are an accumulation of smaller interventions that over time accomplish specific change process objectives. They can be thought of as the sets of interventions that operationalize the Game Plan Components through their impact on a large number of the implementers. For example, under the Game Plan Component of Monitoring and Evaluation (aka Checking Progress), the Strategy of one principal, who was closely guiding and supporting change in his school, was to collect every Friday samples of students' work. This Strategy led to another Strategy, Providing Consultation and Reinforcement (Providing Assistance), as the principal led the staff in reviewing the students' work every other week. These Strategies mutually informed the teachers about additional possibilities for student work and reinforced and/or encouraged various teachers and students in their use of the innovation.

Tactics

This intervention is defined as a set of small, interrelated actions. A daylong workshop would be a Tactic that is part of the Strategy of "Designing and Providing Training" sessions across the first year of implementation. The Strategy is, in turn, part of the Game Plan Component of Training.

Other examples of tactics are visiting each implementer in his or her classroom over a three-day period to solicit concerns about training sessions for the new computers and scheduling a consultant to be in the school for a week to provide technical assistance to any teacher who indicates interest.

Incidents

We have learned with certainty how significant the small and more individualized interventions known as Incidents are. They are short in duration, focus typically on one or just a few implementers, and most occur in informally. This is not to say that they are unplanned, for they are so powerful that they should be on the mind of every facilitator. It is in these little day-to-day, moment-to-moment actions (which frequently take the form of the one-legged interview described in Chapter 4) that the change effort is most frequently won or, unfortunately, lost. We have observed repeatedly in schools and other types of organizations that where there are significantly more Incident interventions, there is significantly greater implementation success due to this personalized help and support. Opportunities are many for enacting Incident interventions, such as the following:

- When meeting a user or nonuser in the hallway, the facilitator can offer comments to support his or her hard work with the innovation or to increase his or her interest in learning about it.
- At the staff mailbox, the facilitator can share requested information with the person who is early into use of a new program.
- Crossing the parking lot to go home, the facilitator can inquire about concerns or whether the innovation equipment that was provided the day before is working.
- In the cafeteria line, the facilitator can provide a brochure about professional development sessions.

The effective facilitator uses these small interactions to probe about SoC, LoU, and/or IC and provides customized encouragement and assistance. If the change process planners or policymakers think only of the Tactic of workshops as the key interventions for a change effort, the implementers will be shortchanged. Incident interventions are the building blocks that make Tactics, which combine to make Strategies, that in combination come to represent each Game Plan Component. It is in these one-to-one interventions that individuals and small groups have many of their more idiosyncratic—yet vastly important—concerns attended to. As the title of the classic song says, "Little things mean a lot."

Pothole Warning

So, you have assumed that giving the change effort participants the guide and materials, plus sending them to a day-and-a-half large group learning session has prepared them to adopt and implement the new curriculum. And you now are surprised when you visit classrooms to find the new materials stashed at the bottom of shelves or unopened on the back-of-the-room worktable. Alas!

Pothole Repair

Recruit several teacher leaders, provide them a crash course in facilitating change, and engage them in conducting one-legged interviews to learn where the staff are in terms of implementation. Identify those who have managed to begin implementation and invite their assistance in helping buddy teachers to get started. Then reserve time with your teacher leaders to plan a set of Incident- and Tactic-level interventions to support the staff in learning how to use the new curriculum and to begin its use. You might also re-read the previous section on the six Game Plan Components/Functions. Which have not been emphasized enough?

The Types and Details of Incident Interventions

In a bit more detail, Incidents may be further described as one of five types: Isolated, Simple, Chain, Repeated, and Complex.

Isolated Incident.   This singular action is distanced in time, space, and purpose from any others. It is given little time and generally is addressed to a single individual. The key is that Isolated Incidents do not accumulate or become related to any other interventions. An example is requesting a teacher to respond to a request from a parent for information on language manipulatives.

Simple Incident.   Although this single-action intervention is typically short and aimed at one or only a few individuals, it is linked in its purpose to other interventions. For example, when a facilitator stops by to check on the two chemistry teachers to check on their concerns, this is an example of a Simple Incident. Peer faculty could also provide this same intervention to their colleagues on a one-to-one basis. An innovation-related announcement about an upcoming workshop made in a staff meeting would also be a Simple Incident intervention.

Chain Incident.   As suggested by its name, this is a series of short Incidents provided to multiple targeted individuals by the same person and for the same purpose. A facilitator dropping by to remind each teacher of the afternoon's workshop in the cafeteria is an example of a Chain Incident.

Repeated Incident.   Unlike the Chain Incident, which delivers the same action to multiple audiences, the Repeated Incident delivers the same action to the same target multiple times. The central office's director of school improvement reminding the assistant principal three times to complete the implementation report for the superintendent is such a Repeated Incident.

Complex Incident.   This type of Incident is composed of a set of Related Incident actions that occur within a short period. An example in the definition section of this chapter is the feedback conference with a teacher held following an observation. This Complex Intervention could also include the development of a growth plan for supporting the teacher and a number of related topics, such as scheduling a follow-up focused observation. A staff meeting and an all-day workshop might be classified as Complex Incidents.

Combing All Interventions. The sum of all these intervention sizes, levels, Functions, and components should represent a comprehensive set of actions that are undertaken to provide nonusers and users with what they need to successfully implement an innovation. Together they represent the Intervention Game Plan as it was planned, and in the end as it was carried out.

REFLECTION QUESTIONS

Have you considered how policies at the state, district or school level can impact implementation? Have you had the experience of ignoring a policy that later on resulted in a problem for the change effort? How could this have been avoided? What do you do now?

THE ANATOMY OF INTERVENTIONS

An even more specific analysis of interventions can be done. The framework for this was developed by researchers in order to quantify the internal elements of XXXXXX. Since this framework is a way to examine the internal parts of interventions, we call it the Anatomy of Interventions (Hall & Hord, 1987). This is a framework for analysis of the Source, Target, Function, Medium, Flow, and Location of each intervention (see Figure 7.4).

Such an analysis and coding of interventions across time make it possible to ascertain who is providing intervention actions to whom, for what purpose, how, and when. Thus, redundancies and gaps may be identified and corrections taken so that all persons involved receive the supportive interventions that are needed. This type of analysis also becomes documentation of who is doing more and of what types of interventions. These data are what have made it possible for us to report findings such as "There are significantly more interventions in Initiator CF Style schools."

Source

The Source of an intervention is the person who is initiating the action. Typically, this will be an administrator or other lead facilitator who has determined the need for the intervention and designed it to respond to that need. However, the Source could be any campus or district person

FIGURE 7.4   Internal Elements of Incident Interventions

Source: Person(s) providing the action
Target: Person(s) receiving the action
Function: Purpose of the action
Medium: Means by which the intervention is delivered (telephone, face to face, etc.)
Flow: Directionality of the intervention action (one-way, interactive, etc.)
Location: Where the action took place

who makes a change process–related action. Teachers, as well as persons more external to the implementation site, do initiate actions. However, in our studies, it is clear that principals and others in a leadership role are the most frequent sources of interventions.

Target

The person (or persons) who receives the action is the Target. The Target may be a single individual with particular concerns or many persons (such as participants in a workshop). If hundreds of persons are targeted, the intervention will obviously be less personalized. The Diagnostic Dimensions—SoC, LoU, IC—provide data useful in designing interventions that will be relevant and effective for each Target.

Function

Function is the purpose of the action. Interestingly, an intervention can have multiple Functions. In analyzing interventions, it is frequently difficult to identify a single purpose to any one action. On the other hand, it's quite useful for Functions to be multipurposeful. For instance, it is easy to imagine that when a facilitator (particularly a principal) drops by a classroom to ask the teacher how the new instructional Strategy is working, the teacher feel supported and also somewhat pressured to be using and improving use of the Strategy. The visit signals that the principal considers the new practice important (pressure) and is also interested in supplying help (support). The same intervention also provides the principal with information about how the innovation is going.

Source, Target, and Function can provide the facilitator with important information about who is being attended to in a change effort, by whom, and for what purpose. Redundancies (which do not occur very often) and gaps in the provision of intervention actions may be revealed by analyzing these subparts of interventions. For research purposes, these three subparts—along with medium, flow, and location—may be coded using a set of carefully defined codes and coding rules. (See Hall and Hord [1987] for additional information.)

REFLECTION QUESTIONS

When might you use the Anatomy of Interventions in a change project? How would you apply this tool in your project?

SUMMARY

The concepts, Strategies, and tools described in this chapter were created and designed with change facilitators in mind (whether they be school principals, district supervisors, key teachers, or others in the private sector). Typically, interventions are made without prior thought. Our intent in this chapter has been to focus on the concept of interventions, to introduce a number of ways that interventions can be considered, classified, and assessed, and to stimulate increased consideration of being aware of the role of interventions in implementing change.

It is absolutely clear that in those change processes with statistically significantly more innovation-related Incident interventions, teachers have greater implementation success. It is also clear that in schools where coherence in Incident interventions accumulates to form Tactics and ultimately Strategies, change is more successful. And, if interventions focus on LoU V Integration (see Chapter 5), a more collaborative culture (i.e., a professional learning community [PLC]) and greater sharing of a vision result. Strategies will be needed to promote collaboration if that element of culture is desired in the workplace.

Interventions take time and thought. Without them, members of the organization work in isolation and innocence in terms of use of the innovation. As we admonish in our workshops, "Change facilitators, *do* something."

DISCUSSION QUESTIONS

1. What preparation relative to interventions should be provided to a person who will serve as a change facilitator? Would your prescription be different if the facilitator was based at the school, district, or state level?

2. What length of time should be allotted for implementing a transformational change such as changing from a teacher-centered to a learner-centered or constructivist-based approach? Which Functions (Game Plan Components) will need to have the most Strategies? How much time will be needed to fully implement this change?

3. How might the song title "Little Things Mean a Lot" apply to the various types of interventions?

4. How might a campus-based practitioner, a state policymaker, or a researcher employ the information on interventions in this chapter?

5. Which of this chapter's intervention concepts are most applicable to the corporate world or private sector?

FIELDWORK ACTIVITIES

1. Obtain the implementation plans for a change effort for two schools or other organizations. Which basic types of interventions are included, and which are absent in each case? On this basis, compare, predict, and explain the degree of implementation success that is likely to be gained in each organization.

2. Develop a plan for making a presentation to the school board using the six basic types of interventions as a framework to explain the attention and resources needed to further a change process.

3. Develop a plan of interventions to be supplied to a school, or business, whose staff will be implementing a complex innovation. Be as thorough and comprehensive as possible, identifying key Strategies within each Game Plan Component/Function and examples of relevant Incidents.

CONDUCT A STUDY

1. For one month, document all the interventions provided for implementation in one organization. Use the Anatomy of Interventions to analyze the interventions in terms of their Source, Target, and Function. Share the results with the implementation facilitators. Then record their subsequent interventions to ascertain if they are acting in ways related to the study results.

2. Collect baseline data on the extent of implementation in two settings. Document the interventions provided to both settings for 4 to 6 weeks. Analyze each setting's interventions in terms of Functions, Strategies, and Tactics. How does each Intervention Game Plan seem to relate to the extent of implementation? What would you recommend be done to increase implementation success?

ADDITIONAL READINGS/RESOURCES

Folkman, J. (2006). *The power of feedback: 35 principles for turning feedback from others into personal and professional change.* Hoboken , NJ: Wiley.

Gawande, A. (2007). *Better: A surgeon's notes on performance.* New York: Picador.

Hargreaves, A., & Shirley, D. (2009). *The fourth way.* Thousand Oaks, CA: Corwin Press.

Professional development focused on developing the knowledge base and skills of facilitators related to the six Intervention Functions is available as a three-day institute. For information about *Leadership for Changing Schools,* contact Southwest Educational Development Laboratory, (800) 476–6861.

A leader's guide, videotapes, audiotapes, and copy for handouts and transparencies from the *Leadership for Changing Schools* institute is available as a stand-alone set of materials and activities. For information, contact, Southwest Educational Development Laboratory (800) 476–6861.

CHAPTER 8

THE CONSTRUCTION OF UNDERSTANDING
Intervention Mushrooms

District A: Following the second round of restructuring and downsizing of the district central office, the superintendent announces that it's all done and that everyone should get to work and do what is best for the district. The typical employee response is "Why should I believe you now?"

District B—Teacher from School R: "I was so surprised last week when my principal stopped me in the hallway to ask about what I was doing with the new computers. He never asks me anything about what I am doing in the classroom. I wonder what he was after?"

District B—Teacher from School I: "I don't see anything unusual about that. My principal is always stopping by and asking me about what I am doing. Sometimes he makes really interesting suggestions."

District B—Teacher from School M: "My principal stops by sometimes, but she only wants to see if I have enough supplies."

District C—First teacher: "Wasn't that neat—what the superintendent said in her talk with our school faculty? She really cares about us and what we teach our students."

District C— Second teacher: "Yes, it is the same points that she made at the district-wide meeting in the beginning of year. Best teaching practices and student success are important priorities for her."

District C—Third teacher: "Yes, it is so great to be in this school district."

The critical point that will be made repeatedly in this chapter is that it is not what you do that counts but how other people perceive and interpret what you do. As the preceding quotes illustrate, participants in a change process develop a wide range of impressions and interpretations about what the change effort is about and what different Change Facilitators (CFs) intend. Just because the leaders of a change effort are well intentioned does not mean that the participants will see them that way. Each participant individually, and each group of participants collectively, will construct their own understandings about what was intended and what it all means. Regardless of what was intended, participant interpretations will have an effect on implementing change. In other words, the construction of understanding is a second very different major category of interventions.

FOCUS QUESTIONS

1. How is the interpretivist perspective different from the more traditional behaviorist perspective?
2. What is an Intervention Mushroom?
3. What are distinguishing characteristics of nutritious and poisonous Intervention Mushrooms?
4. Describe the dynamics of individual and social construction of Intervention Mushrooms.
5. What are keys to predicting and detecting Intervention Mushrooms?
6. How is group construction of understanding affected by different CF Styles and Stages of Concern (SoC)?

A shift in perspective is important to understanding the kind of interventions that will be introduced in this chapter. In all of the preceding chapters the assumption was implicit that leaders led the change efforts. An innovation was identified, implementers were engaged, and CFs and others were making interventions. In many ways the thinking was that a change process can be successful if all the right steps are taken. The construct introduced in this chapter challenges that assumption. The leaders and facilitators do not control all that happens; there is another form of influence.

The key to understanding the ideas presented in this chapter is to make a shift in thinking. Instead of thinking only about the intentions behind the interventions that are made, thought has to be given to how the targets of those actions interpret what is being done to them. After reviewing an earlier version of the manuscript for this chapter, Carolee Hayes, formerly the Director of Staff Development for the Douglas County School District in Colorado, observed:

> This chapter represents a major shift in the book. Up to this point, the authors have taken a fairly left-brained approach to making sense of change. In this chapter, the reader will sense a shift to considering the uncontrollable, unpredictable factors in change and is drawn into a process of integrating the controllable, predictable factors with those that are controlled only by individual and shared interpretations. (personal communication, 2005)

INTRODUCING MUSHROOMS: A UNIQUE FORM OF INTERVENTION

In Chapter 7 attention was given to discussing the different forms, sizes, and functions of interventions. In all those descriptions and analyses, the assumption was that CFs and others *initiated* the interventions—in other words, they sponsored the actions that were taken. In this

FIGURE 8.1   Intervention Mushrooms Come in a Variety of Shapes and Sizes

chapter, we will describe a different form of change process intervention that is *unsponsored.* In fact, the sources of interventions have little control over this type of intervention that we call Mushrooms (see Figure 8.1).

The metaphor of Mushrooms is particularly salient for describing this special class of interventions. Just as mushroom plants can be nutritious or poisonous, so can Intervention Mushrooms. Some help advance the change process, whereas others erode it. Just as mushroom plants come in many colors and shapes, Intervention Mushrooms in a change process take different forms. There may be none, one, or a great variety. Just as mushroom plants grow in the dark and are fed "manure," Intervention Mushrooms grow in the shadows of a change process and are fed by the actions of the CFs and other participants. Just as it takes an expert to identify and pick the nutritious mushroom plants, some CFs are much more skilled at detecting and sorting Intervention Mushrooms, taking advantage of the nutritious Mushrooms, and discouraging the growth of poisonous ones.

Two Ways of Knowing: Objectivist and Interpretivist

Before further explaining the construct of Intervention Mushrooms, it will be useful to review briefly two research traditions that have been very influential during the past 50 years. Each of these traditions has made significant contributions to our understanding of the change process. As is true in most fields, each of these traditions has a history of disagreement and competition among proponents. Interestingly, each tradition can be complementary of the other. In this chapter, these two research traditions will be used in combination to better explain and illustrate the concept and dynamics of Intervention Mushrooms.

The Objectivist Perspective of Change.   From the 1950s to late in the 1980s, the dominant way of thinking about learning was labeled *behaviorism.* The focus in this approach was on observable behaviors. For example, classroom teachers were expected to describe student learning in terms of what the students could *do,* not what they "understood." Curriculum developers and teachers were trained and required to describe student learning using "behavioral objectives." The design of the research was influenced by the behaviorist perspective as well. Researchers focused on describing and counting the observable behaviors of teachers, such as the quantity of questions asked and the frequency of giving management directions. All were admonished to never ever use the word *understand* because one cannot *see* "understanding." Instead, they were to deal only with what could be observed.

Since the primary emphasis in behaviorist research and practice was on being absolutely objective about what one did, the term *objectivist* was applied to this approach. The goal was to remove the biases and perspectives of the observers (e.g., teachers and researchers) by describing events in terms of cold, hard facts or, in other words, objective descriptions of observed behaviors. This perspective dominated research on organizations throughout the 20th century.

The Interpretivist Perspective of Change.   As Kuhn (1970) so eloquently proposed, there comes a time in the study of any field of science when the regular way of thinking and working (i.e., the established paradigm) is challenged by a new model (i.e., a competing paradigm). When the established paradigm fails to predict some aspects of a phenomenon, a new, competing paradigm is proposed. Such a revolution in the study of organizations and in education research and theory has been represented by the recent movement toward *constructivism*, which emphasizes how the learner develops, or "constructs," his or her own "understanding," or "interpretation," of reality. *Interpretivists* strive to analyze how understanding is developed by studying the way people interpret and give meaning to events (e.g., by examining quotes like those at the beginning of this chapter). Rather than simply dealing with observable behaviors, the interpretivist paradigm stresses unearthing and describing the interpretations and meaning that people attach to an action, event, or concept.

> *Pothole Warning*
>
> *Do not assume that everything about change is rational.*
>
> *Pothole Repair*
>
> *As is suggested by introducing the interpretivist perspective, much about change is not subject to logical thinking and control. Intervention Mushrooms are not under the control of the leaders and CFs but are critical to change success.*

INTERVENTION MUSHROOMS ARE CONSTRUCTED

So what does this discussion of paradigms, behaviorism, and interpretivism mean for understanding the change process? Combining elements of the objectivist and interpretivist paradigms is very useful for explaining a very important but little understood component of change process dynamics: Intervention Mushrooms. To be sure, change processes are affected by the behaviors (aka interventions) of the CFs. But another category (dare we say species) of interventions grows out of the participant's interpretations of what the actions of the CFs and others mean.

FIGURE 8.2   Initial Growth of an Intervention Mushroom

Action 1: In a hallway conversation with Bill, Sarah complains about having to attend a workshop. "Why do I have to go to that?"

Action 2: Subsequently in the lunchroom, Sarah complains to a friendly colleague (Judy), who does not want to attend the workshop either. "I don't have time for this."

Action 3: In the parking lot after school, Sarah and Judy again complain and plan to talk to their department chair.

Action 4: The next day during planning period, Sarah catches the department chair and complains about having to attend the workshop. "They are always demanding that we do these, and—you know—we never learn anything new."

Action 5: The department chair talks with the principal about the complaint.

Theme: (Some) Teachers are complaining about having to attend the workshop.

There are observable behaviors associated with Intervention Mushrooms. For example, a teacher complains about having to go to a workshop. Both the teacher's complaint and the workshop are observable and describable change process–related actions, or interventions. Holding the workshop is a CF–initiated intervention. But what about the teacher's complaint? It fits the definition of an intervention introduced in Chapter 7 in that it is an action or event that can influence the change process. However, it has the potential to become more. Depending on how the complaint was stated and what the teacher does next, the complaint could be forgotten or start to grow into an Intervention Mushroom. If nothing more is heard, then the teacher's complaint disappears as an Isolated Incident. However, as is illustrated in Figure 8.2, if the teacher complains repeatedly and involves others, then a *theme* of "teachers complaining about having to attend the workshop" develops. This theme is constructed across the individual actions.

Recognizing the Theme of an Intervention Mushroom

The very first challenge with Intervention Mushrooms is for CFs and other leaders to recognize that a theme is being constructed. If they only see the individual actions, then it is likely that the theme will continue to grow. An early step is to understand more about the reason for the interpretation that the teacher has given to the announcement that there will be a workshop. A number of plausible interpretations can be imagined. For example, does the teacher see the workshop as useless in terms of content because she already knows the subject? Or is there a scheduling conflict because the teacher is committed to make an exploratory visit to a site where the innovation is in use? Or is she concerned that her lack of knowledge might be exposed and that she could be embarrassed? Depending on the reason for the teacher's complaint, not wanting to attend the workshop could have very different implications for that teacher, other teachers, and the success of the change process. Note that we have not talked about the leader's reasons for offering the workshop; instead we are focusing on the participant's view.

This is why the interpretivist perspective is so important to understanding the change process. Carolee Hayes has summarized nicely:

> The metaphor of mushrooms provides an image of fungi creeping into a system without any nurturing or intention on the part of the leadership. That is a powerful image, one which all leaders have experienced when best efforts become interpreted as something otherwise. It reminds us that being right or well intentioned is only one perception of a situation. (personal communication)

REFLECTION QUESTION

What are some examples of Intervention Mushroom themes you have seen constructed in your work setting?

■ ■ ■ ■ ■ ▬▬▬▬▬▬▬▬▬▬▬▬▬▬▬▬▬▬▬▬▬▬▬▬▬▬▬

VIGNETTE

GROWING A NUTRITIOUS MUSHROOM

Poisonous Mushrooms are easy to find. We all have experienced them, and in many cases have helped to grow them. Nutritious Mushrooms are less well understood and rarely celebrated. There is something about the compulsive nature of educators that makes them overlook or discount the positive aspects of their work. Therefore, we decided to present a short story about one Nutritious Mushroom. Table 8.1 is a map of this Mushroom.

This nutritious Mushroom, which we shall call "enthusiasm for teaching and learning science," grew in one elementary school as a new science curriculum was being implemented. This innovation contained the usual elements: manipulative materials, living organisms, cooperative groups, no textbook, and field trips. All teachers had been given released days to participate in a series of all-day training workshops. The workshops had been designed to be Concerns-Based by regularly assessing SoC and adjusting each day's sessions accordingly.

Across the district, teachers in most schools were implementing the new approach and had the predictable array of Stage 3 Management concerns, such as, "The daphnia are dying" and "The crickets escaped!" A few schools experienced Negative Mushrooms about all the work, the mess, and the uncontrollable students.

In one school, however, we found no Negative Mushrooms. In reviewing the data, it was clear that the principal in this school was an Initiator. He was very supportive of the new approach to teaching science. He advocated for the new curriculum and did the little things that signaled he was willing to help. He had attended the orientation provided by the district and closely monitored how implementation was going for teachers, students, and parents. He made sure teachers had the necessary materials and that schedules were supportive, and he expected all teachers to attend the training workshops. He regularly visited classrooms when science was being taught.

As implementation unfolded, teachers were discovering that their students liked the new approach and were asking to have science classes every day. Parents began commenting about their children's enthusiasm for science. The district office science coordinators also were pleased with how implementation was progressing in this school. We researchers were intrigued that the SoC Questionnaire (SoCQ) profiles were low on Stage 1 Informational, Stage 2 Personal, and Stage 3 Management concerns. Further, there was an arousal of Stage 4 Consequence concerns. All these actions and indicators document the spontaneous birth and growth of a Nutritious Mushroom. Everyone was talking positively about what was occurring around use of the new approach.

When we pointed out this Nutritious Mushroom to the principal, he said that it had been part of his plan all along. As the researchers, however, we had a different hypothesis: The principal actions and early implementation success by teachers resulted in few Stage 3 Management concerns. The principal reinforced and nurtured the growth of a Positive Mushroom by providing the needed materials. He made every effort to reduce the potential arousal of Task concerns and experiences that could lead to the growth of a Poisonous Mushrooms. In summary, either way this Nutritious Mushroom is diagrammed—through accident or proactive principal leadership—the clear consequence was dynamic and positive schoolwide implementation success.

(continued)

TABLE 8.1   Mapping a Mushroom Intervention: Principal Changes Meeting Process

SEQUENCE OF EVENTS	INDIVIDUAL ACTIONS	PARTICIPANT INTERPRETATIONS	CHANGE FACILITATOR'S ISOLATED RESPONSES	ACCUMULATING EFFECT(S)
0	Principal changes meeting process.	Some notice, some don't, some are surprised.	Principal explains the change.	None observed
1	Teachers talk with each other about the change.	Some see it as no big deal; some think it means something.	—	Some energy going into examination of what the change means
2	More teacher dialogue occurs.	"The principal is looking for another position."	—	More energy going into constructing shared interpretation
3	Superintendent makes an unannounced visit.	"The principal is being checked out."	—	Increasing talk and distraction
4	Principal says to the secretary, "I am ready for a change."	"The principal *is* looking/leaving!"	—	More support for the Mushroom and less work activity
5	Principal closes the door to take phone call.	"The principal has a call about the new position."	—	More support for the Mushroom and less attention to teaching and learning

Constructed Theme

"The Principal is Leaving."

Change Facilitator's Responses to the Total Mushroom

None

Accumulated Effect(s)

Time and energy being drawn away from teaching and leaning

■ ■ ■ ■ ■

VIGNETTE CONTINUED

VIGNETTE CRITIQUE QUESTIONS

1. What do you see as the kind of actions that contributed to the construction of this Nutritious Mushroom?
2. What type of action would lead to the death of this Mushroom? How long would it take to kill it?
3. In this case, the principal claimed that the Nutritious Mushroom had been part of his plan from the very beginning. Do you think this was true?
4. What was the principal's role in the continued growth of this Nutritious Mushroom? How did the teachers contribute? Did the students also have a role?

THE LIFE CYCLE OF INTERVENTION MUSHROOMS

Intervention Mushrooms are constructed out of the interpretations that each person makes of the unfolding actions and events in a change process. People look for ways to make sense of and to explain what is happening to them and around them, especially during a time of change. Each participant develops his or her own interpretation and understanding based on past experiences and what others say, as well as on the themes and patterns that are characteristic of his or her organization. Over time a theme is constructed and used to provide meaning for subsequent actions.

The Birth of a Mushroom

Typically Intervention Mushrooms begin in response to a single action or event. For example, something as simple as the superintendent's statement at a school board meeting that a curriculum director from the district office will be reporting on a new initiative at the next meeting could trigger the growth of an Intervention Mushroom or no reaction at all. If one or more persons thinks further, then "germination" may begin. For example, one principal who heard the superintendent's comment develops an "educated guess," based on extrapolations from past experience, that "a big change is coming." The principal's interpretation is his or her own (i.e., an individual construction) until he or she says to another principal, "Guess what I heard at the board meeting last night?" Then *social construction* begins. There is a high probability that this Intervention Mushroom will grow quickly with the theme being "The superintendent has another big change coming."

Consider another example of the birth of an Intervention Mushroom: If the principal always runs a staff meeting in a certain way, the staff comes to expect that this is the regular pattern. But if one day the principal changes the way the meeting is run—such as sitting at a different location or changing the sequence of agenda items—it may be seen as a sign of something. At first, what the "something" is will be uncertain. If the principal explains why the change occurred, this additional intervention will alter the potential for teachers to grow their own interpretations. If no explanation is offered as the meeting unfolds, some staff members will begin to develop their own explanations, or hypotheses, about what the change means.

Regardless of whether the principal explains the reason for the change or some staff members develop their own explanations, it is likely that some will exchange interpretations following the meeting. Then there will be gradual development of a shared interpretation of what the change means.

The shared interpretation becomes the Constructed Theme of the Intervention Mushroom. In the example here, which is mapped in Table 8.2, one teacher thinks that the principal just forgot to do the usual routine. Another teacher thinks that the principal is using some new techniques that she picked up at a principals' conference last week. Two others believe that the change means that the principal is looking for a new job and is practicing a different leadership style. No one knows for sure what the principal is doing, but all have an individual interpretation to share and advocate. Arising out of the discussions comes a consensus that the principal is looking for another job: "She has been here for five years; it's time." An Intervention Mushroom is born.

The Growth of a Mushroom

Intervention Mushrooms can grow rapidly or very slowly. In some cases they don't grow; they just fade away. Over the next 2 days several new actions contributed to the growth of the principal-is-leaving Mushroom. One teacher overheard the principal say to the assistant principal that she really is ready for a change. The teacher did not hear all of the conversation but is certain about what she did hear. Another teacher, who had been at the administration building to pick up a book, heard about an opening for a principal "downtown." Both of these individual events are shared and interpreted by all as further confirmation of the-principal-is-leaving Mushroom. Interpretation of new actions and events are shared. The Mushroom is growing and beginning to take on a life of its own. Note that the mapping of this Mushroom in Table 8.2 contains no principal responses since she is unaware of the individual actions and the theme.

The Maturing of a Mushroom

Many Mushrooms become well established and live on with occasional new actions to support them. The principal-is-leaving Mushroom reaches maturity quickly. Over the next several weeks, other actions and events occur that—if the Mushroom did not exist—either would not have been noticed or would have been interpreted differently. However, with a rapidly growing Mushroom, many otherwise innocuous actions can be interpreted as support for the Mushroom theme and contribute to its continued and quick growth. For example, the superintendent's unannounced visit to the school and closed-door meeting with the principal further feeds the principal-is-looking Mushroom. Teachers begin comparing the frequency of principal visits to the lounge with memories of her past behavior: "She is not in the lounge as much now." Something as simple as the principal closing the door to take a phone call adds further support to the Mushroom. Events and actions, many of which may in fact have nothing in common, are thus interpreted as being part of an overall pattern and theme.

As can be seen in this very simple example, it is quite easy for a Mushroom to get started and for its growth not only to be assisted but to race ahead without any of the CFs being aware that it is happening. In this case there was no recognition of the Constructed Theme and no Response taken against the theme. There was an Accumulated Effect, however: Time and energy were drawn away from teaching and learning.

TABLE 8.2   Positive Mushroom for Teaching and Learning Science

SEQUENCE OF EVENTS	INDIVIDUAL ACTIONS	PARTICIPANT INTERPRETATIONS	CHANGE FACILITATOR'S RESPONSES	ACCUMULATING EFFECT(S)
0				
1	First workshop day before implementation	Maybe I can do this.	Reduced Task concerns at the beginning	We are ready to start teaching this.
2	District coordinators show their support.	We are being supported to do this.	Principal expresses support all the time.	It takes time and there is a lot of stuff, but it seems to be working.
3	Second workshop day halfway through the year	Now I know what to do with the next lessons and materials.	Principal expresses support all the time.	
4	Teacher needs extra materials.		Principals hears and provides materials.	We are succeeding.
5	Kids like science.	I need to keep trying.	Kids tell me they like science.	
6	Teachers talk with each other positively.	We are having successes.	Keep it going!	Others see school succeeding with new approach.
7	Parents are telling teachers and principal that their kids like science.	Everyone is liking science.	Our school is a winner.	

Constructed Theme

Enthusiasm for teaching and learning science

Change Facilitator's Responses to the Total Mushroom

Continuing

Accumulated Effect(s)

All teachers teaching and all kids receiving science

Pothole Warning

Do not argue with the accuracy or correctness of an Intervention Mushroom Constructed Theme.

Pothole Repair

Those who have constructed the theme believe that it represents reality as they see it. In most instances, arguing with the validity of a theme will reinforce its construction.

An important implication of Intervention Mushrooms is that the truth of the theme is not easily questioned. For most, the constructed interpretation of the meaning for the actions is accepted as valid. With the case just described, whether or not the principal really is leaving is irrelevant to the ways that the principal-is-leaving Mushroom is an intervention affecting the change process.

REFLECTION QUESTIONS

Think about an Intervention Mushroom that you have witnessed. What was the Constructed Theme? What were some of the actions and interpretations that contributed to its construction? Did anyone address relative truth of the Constructed Theme?

IMPLICATIONS FOR LEADERS FACILITATING CHANGE

Change efforts can be won, and lost, based on the array of Intervention Mushrooms that are in place at the beginning and that grow as the implementation process unfolds. Too many poisonous Mushrooms can kill a change process before it even begins. A very difficult challenge for CFs is to detect and map the array of Mushrooms at the beginning.

For example, if Self concerns are very high, there is a high probability that Poisonous Mushrooms are already growing. If there are Impact concerns, then Positive Mushrooms should be in place. When Positive Mushrooms are in place before introduction of the innovation, the likelihood of the change process being given open and fair consideration is increased. If Task concerns have been high for a long time, the possibility is strong that the new initiative will be seen as "too much work."

One of the biggest challenges for leaders, internal CFs, and especially external CFs is to understand enough about the setting so that the birth of Mushrooms can be anticipated. This is a special skill. One of the problems for the change leaders is that members of the organization will not always tell them what they are thinking and sharing with each other, especially if it is negative.

In one situation, one of the authors was in a major administrative position, and none of his direct reports would tell him what they were talking about with each other. Based on little tidbits that were dropped and given some policy and leader changes that were taking place higher up in the organization, it seemed likely that at least one poisonous Mushroom was growing. For example, frequent off-campus lunch meetings that were never referenced in open meetings were discovered. Without going into all the details, with time it became clear that the prediction was correct: A Toxic Mushroom was being constructed. The problem in these situations is that if there is no way of knowing a

IMPLICATIONS FOR LEADERS FACILITATING CHANGE   CONTINUED

Mushroom is growing, it is very difficult to address its themes. CFs must develop and continually refine their skills at Mushroom detection. In many situations detection is based on having been there before and/or making educated guesses using the constructs and reasoning that have been outlined in this chapter.

KEYS TO THE CONSTRUCTION OF INTERVENTION MUSHROOMS

There are several ways to analyze Mushrooms. Some of the techniques can be used to anticipate the growth of new Mushrooms, and other approaches can help to explain those that already exist. Most of the constructs introduced in previous chapters are very powerful tools for understanding the different ways that Mushrooms can start as well as the dynamics of their growth. Here, the constructs of Levels of Use (LoU), SoC, and CF Styles are used to illustrate how Mushrooms are constructed and why they turn out to be nutritious or poisonous.

Stages of Concern as a Source of Mushrooms

SoC are a powerful catalyst for the development of Mushrooms. The perceptions and feelings that one has in relation to a change process are constantly in flux, and there is high sensitivity to everything related to the instability of change. Therefore, it is important not only to be assessing SoC for use in planning interventions but also to use SoC assessments to recognize developing Mushrooms and to anticipate the potential for others to grow. Here again, the Mushrooms that are constructed can be either nutritious or poisonous and can be limited to one individual or shared by a group.

Personal Concerns: A Significant Source of Negative Mushrooms.   Stage 2 Personal concerns represent a particularly sensitive time for individuals and groups. When Personal concerns are high, the antennae are up and looking for anything and everything that might represent a threat to the person, real or imagined. By definition an individual with high Personal concerns is interpreting actions and events chiefly in terms of what they might mean for him or her. The individual is not as concerned about what the change might mean for students or others; the concerns are centered on implications for oneself. Note that the real intentions of the CF are not at issue here but rather how someone with high Stage 2 Personal concerns *perceives* and *interprets* actions and events.

Persons with high Stage 2 Personal concerns can easily interpret whatever occurs as an attempt to undercut or attack them. If this happens only once, there is no Mushroom. However, if over a few days or weeks the person perceives several events as suspicious, a poisonous individual Mushroom of insecurity and resistance will start to germinate: "The principal doesn't care what *I* think. He has his mind made up already." "I can't do this. I am just going to close my door and hope that nobody will see that I am not doing it." "You know the superintendent is all politics. She doesn't care at all about kids."

When two or more individuals who are growing such Insecurity Mushrooms talk to each other, the social construction process works overtime. "You are right. The superintendent doesn't care at all what we think or how hard we have to work." "Why, the last time we did this, do you remember how she went on and on about this being such a good thing? It turned out to be an absolute disaster." At this point the individual Insecurity Mushrooms have combined into one that is shared and is ready for rapid growth through continued group construction. If an SoC profile were made, it would show high Stage 2 Personal concerns as well as a "tailing up" on Stage 6 Refocusing concerns. With this sort of concerns profile, the "here-we-go-again-I-don't-buy-this-one-either" Mushroom can grow faster and taller than Jack's beanstalk.

Intervening on Insecurity Mushrooms.   There are many wrong ways for leaders to respond to Insecurity Mushrooms. One very risky approach would be to say such things as "This really is different" or "Trust me. It will work well." "Trust-me" interventions usually accelerate the rate of growth of already rapidly expanding Poisonous Mushrooms: "Sure, I should trust him. He doesn't have to do it. What does he know?" Another intervention that must only be used if carefully thought out is to put something in writing. Persons who have high Stage 2 Personal concerns and are cultivating a shared Insecurity Mushroom will be able to come up with interpretations of a written document that were never intended, or even imagined, by the author. No matter how well a document is written, it can be perceived by those with high Stage 2 Personal concerns as further proof of the theme of the Toxic Mushroom. "See, I told you so. She has no interest in what we think. She already has made the decision."

One potentially effective intervention would be to speak individually with people with high Stage 2 Personal concerns and present a positive, straightforward stance of interest in and support for them. Offering reassurances that the change process will work out well is useful. It is especially important for the leaders of the change process to constantly and continually act positively with such individuals. They also need to carefully monitor their own statements and actions for any that could be interpreted as negative or in some way doubtful of the chances of success. Those with supertuned Personal concerns antennae will pick up on any hints of doubt or uncertainty within the leaders.

Impact Concerns: A Significant Source of Positive Mushrooms.   Frequently overlooked in change processes are those people with various forms of Impact concerns. These are the people who have some combination of high concerns at Stage 4 Consequence, Stage 5 Collaboration, and Stage 6 Refocusing. All are concerned about the impact of the change on clients, especially students. Impact-concerned people are positive and enthusiastic and talk to each other about the strengths and successes they are experiencing in using the innovation. These are the people who naturally grow Positive Mushrooms within themselves and through dialogue with others.

The research and concepts related to organizational culture, such as those that were introduced in Chapter 2, are important to keep in mind in relation to the growth of Positive Mushrooms. A Professional Learning Community (PLC) is a culture of positive norms and Positive Mushroom themes. When talking to each other about teaching and student learning, teachers are growing a Positive Mushroom related to teacher collegiality with a shared focus on student learning.

Interestingly, Positive Mushrooms are quickly claimed by the CFs: "I know that we are collegial in this school. I have been doing a number of things to help this happen." From a practical point of view, who gets credit for Positive Mushrooms is of little consequence. However, researchers as well as CFs need to understand when and how Positive Mushrooms develop, since by definition Mushrooms are not knowingly created by CFs. All Mushrooms begin their growth "in the dark"; it is the more finely attuned CF who detects the beginning of a Positive Mushroom and actively intervenes to nurture its further growth.

Levels of Use as a Rubric for Developing Understanding of Mushrooms

LoU was introduced in Chapter 5 as a way to describe and understand a person's gradual development of skills and expertise in using a change/innovation. In that chapter, LoU was described in purely objectivist terminology. Very strong emphasis was placed on the fact that LoU is a behavioral Diagnostic Dimension. Further, LoU was defined in operational terms, and the LoU chart (see Appendix C) is composed of behavioral descriptions and indicators that are characteristic of each level. The method of assessing LoU is a special focused interview procedure that is based purely on soliciting and coding examples of the interviewee's innovation-related behaviors. Obviously development of the LoU construct and its measurement relied heavily on the objectivist research tradition.

Levels of Use from a Constructivist Perspective.   LoU also can be viewed and described in a constructivist tradition. Notice in particular the Knowledge Category in the operational definitions of LoU in Appendix C. If cognitive theory were applied to the LoU descriptions, the Knowledge column of this table would be seen as presenting snapshots of gradually increasing sophistication and complexity of "understanding" about how to use the innovation. Each Knowledge level represents a major step in the transition from nonuser to novice to expert. At the lowest levels, the schemas are very simplistic and incomplete. As one moves to higher LoU they become more complex and multifaceted. In other words, although the early development and studies of LoU were based in the behaviorist paradigm, LoU can be explained in terms of the constructivist paradigm as well.

LoU-Based Mushrooms.   LoU can be a very useful tool for predicting and understanding Mushrooms. First of all, the types of Mushrooms that an individual constructs will be different depending on the person's level of understanding (i.e., his or her Knowledge Category rating). As obvious as this may seem, we frequently fail to recognize that there could be a number of Potential Mushrooms growing in relation to a person's level of knowledge and understanding about what the innovation is and how it can be used. For example, a person at LoU I Orientation may have such limited knowledge that even when the innovation is described in minute detail, he or she cannot make the link back to how the change would work in his or her situation. As a result, the person might reject the innovation because it is perceived as being too complex, confusing, and unrelated to the immediate problem/need.

This episode could be the beginning step in the growth of a Poisonous Mushroom. "That innovation won't work in my classroom." The Mushroom could disappear if the next facilitator intervention helps the person develop a clearer connection between his or her current understanding of the innovation and his or her needs. However, if the subsequent interventions are also detailed and intricate, they could reinforce the developing perception that this innovation is too complex and not relevant (see "Perceived Attributes of the Innovation" in Chapter 10.) Then an individual Mushroom of resistance to the innovation could begin growing.

The same intervention of providing minute detail about the innovation could easily lead to growth of a Positive Mushroom for a person who is at LoU IVB Refinement. He or she already has a full understanding of how the innovation works in the classroom and how it can be fine-tuned for special needs. If this person were to meet and plan with another LoU IVB individual, they both could develop an interest in taking something new back to their classrooms. If these decisions were to happen several times and with several other teachers, a Positive Mushroom related to collegiality and collaboration could begin growing. In this case, the movement toward LoU V Integration would be clearly indicated.

Pothole Warning
Leaders and other CFs are not able to detect some Mushrooms.

Pothole Repair
Instead, leaders must rely on knowledge from past experiences and key constructs such as LoU and SoC. They also must listen carefully and continually for the potential emergence or existence of some Mushrooms.

Change Facilitator Style and Mushrooms

Another frame to use in examining the growth of Mushrooms is the CF Style of the leader(s). The literature contains a long-running debate about the relationship of leader behaviors to style and whether a leader can easily change his or her style. Our studies and those of our colleagues, as summarized in Chapter 6, lead us to conclude that leaders cannot easily or automatically change their overall style. Ideally, they will adapt or adjust their behaviors from situation to situation, but they do not readily change their overall style. Therefore, one source of continuity and predictability is the CF Style of the leader. Whether he or she is an Initiator, Manager, Responder, or something else, that style represents a pattern within which individual actions can be understood.

One of the generalized activities in which participants in a change process engage is constructing a shared description of the styles of the various leaders. The individual actions of the leader are interpreted within the constructed context of his or her overall style. As one veteran teacher said to a first-year teacher after the principal had growled at her, "Oh, don't worry about that. That is the way he always is. He doesn't mean anything by it." The principal had made a comment that by itself could be interpreted as demeaning of the new teacher. However, when it was interpreted by the veteran in the context of that principal's style, the meaning was mollified. *Once again, it isn't only what you do; it is how others interpret what you do.*

Different Change Facilitator Styles Have Different Meanings.   An interesting example of the importance of understanding style is how the same action can have very different meanings depending on who does it. In other words, the same action done by leaders with different CF styles will have very different meanings for their followers.

Consider a simple CF action, a one-legged interview in the hallway, as the principal stops and says to a teacher, "How's it going with your use of the new computers?" This is a Simple Incident intervention that could be coded, using the objectivist paradigm outlined in Chapters 7, by Source (the principal), Target (a teacher), Location (the hallway), and so forth. If a number of these types of interventions were recorded, a quantitative analysis could be done, and different principals could be compared in terms of the frequencies of occurrence of different types of interventions and the difference that these made on teacher success in implementation. This is exactly what was done in the original Principal/Teacher Interaction Study and the subsequent studies that confirmed the three different CF Styles.

An analysis of the same one-legged interview using the interpretivist paradigm would be different. Instead of coding and counting the parts of the action, the analysis would focus on the interpretation of the action that a teacher constructs. In other words, what does the intervention mean to the teacher who receives it? Our hypothesis is that it will depend on the CF Style of the principal.

Initiator Change Facilitator Style: The Meaning Within a Question.   An Initiator principal meets a teacher in the hallway and asks, "How's it going with your use of the new computers?" What goes through the mind of the teacher? First, the teacher will place this individual action in the context of the CF Style of the principal. Given that this is an Initiator principal, the teacher will know that the principal is expecting several things of the teacher, including (a) the teacher *is* using the computers, (b) descriptive information about what is happening with students, and (c) identification of any need or problem. Further, the teacher knows that if something needs to be done to support the teacher, the principal will see that it is done. Based on this interpretation, the teacher goes ahead and describes some "neat" things that are happening with students, which leads to a short dialogue and ends with a commitment by the principal to stop by to see the sixth-period class in action.

Manager Change Facilitator Style: The Meaning Within a Question.   If a Manager CF Style principal met a teacher in the hallway and asked, "How's it going with your use of the new computers?" the teacher's interpretive processing would be different. The teacher would understand that this principal is interested in knowing whether (a) there are any logistical or mechanical problems, (b) the schedule is working, and (c) there are enough supplies. Of course the principal is interested also in how the students are doing in a general sense. So the teacher responds that having some additional chairs or printer cartridges would help. The dialogue continues with discussion of the need for additional rules about student uses of computers outside of class time.

Responder Change Facilitator Style: The Meaning Within a Question.   Interpretation of the same opening statement from a Responder principal would differ from that of either the Initiator or Manager principal. If a Responder principal stopped the teacher and asked, "How's it going with your use of the new computers?" the teacher's first reaction would be to mask surprise and to try to recover from the shock of being asked at all, since the normal style of the Responder principal is to chat in general about school topics or about some current issue in the community or in professional sports, not about what has been going on in the classroom. The typical Response of the teacher would be to offer some generalities, such as

"Things are going well," and see what the principal says next. The point here, as throughout this chapter, is not to present intricate depictions of the actions and interpretations of principals and teachers. Instead, the purpose is to use brief anecdotes to illustrate the Mushroom concept and to ask you to shift the way that you think about an important aspect of the change process. Rather than thinking solely in terms of what the CFs do, consideration needs to be given to the interpretations that the participants ascribe to the actions. Again, it is not only what you do but the meaning that others assign to what you do that counts. Further, there are both individual and group-constructed interpretations as well as interpretations of isolated events and of perceived patterns drawn across a number of events and experiences, all of which can result in Nutritious and/or Poisonous Mushrooms.

REFLECTION QUESTION

In your experience, what events and factors have contributed to the construction of (a) a Positive Intervention Mushroom and (b) a Negative Intervention Mushroom?

DETECTING, ERADICATING, AND/OR FACILITATING THE GROWTH OF MUSHROOMS

As we stated at the beginning of this chapter, Mushrooms tend to grow in the dark. Still, their presence may be detected at any point in their growth, and responding interventions can occur. Once they are detected, deliberate efforts can be taken to nurture Positive Mushrooms and to weed out the toxic ones. However, efforts to eradicate Poisonous Mushrooms are not easy or always successful.

Influencing growth and death of Intervention Mushrooms requires recognizing their totality. Targeting individual actions in isolation will only lead to more rapid growth, especially of Poisonous Mushrooms. Unfortunately, leaders do not always see the overall pattern and theme of individual actions that aggregate to make a Mushroom.

It is critical for leaders and other CFs to become skilled at Mushroom detection. They must continually be looking for positive themes arising out of individual actions and strive to support their further growth. On the other side, they must be constantly tuned to the potential for germination of Negative Mushrooms as they start to grow in the dark and at the edges of change processes. When a Negative Mushroom is detected, effort must be directed toward destroying its Constructed theme, rather than responding independently to individual actions.

Keys to Detecting Mushrooms

The first key to detecting Intervention Mushrooms is to be continually looking for patterns in people's actions that might hint of a theme under construction. As obvious as this recommendation may appear, it is not easy to do. In our experiences as coaches and researchers, we have regularly observed leaders and CFs who did not see the overall patterns. Instead, they tend to react to individual actions as if each were occurring in isolation. They do not see that there is a theme accumulating across the individual actions that *together* are affecting the change process.

A second key to Mushroom detection is to keep in mind constructs about change introduced in previous chapters. Each of these constructs can be used to anticipate possible Mushroom germination. For example, it is easy to predict for staff having year-long unresolved Stage 3 Management concerns. If not resolved, increasing frustration and dissatisfaction will arise and will be indicated by "tailing up" on Stage 6 Refocusing concerns. This is a fertile condition for birth of a Poisonous Mushroom, such as "The darn thing doesn't work, and everything is a mess." Leaders and other CFs must be continually thinking about the potential for Mushrooms in relation to all that they are hearing and seeing as a change process unfolds.

Positive Mushroom Growth Can Be Encouraged

Don't forget that Mushrooms can be nutritious and a significant indicator of change success. More Positive Mushrooms indicate more success with the innovation and/or the change process. For example, teachers excitedly and continuously chatting with other teachers about the helpful things that parents are doing in classrooms is a Positive Mushroom that should be nurtured. Taking advantage of Positive Mushrooms should be a straightforward process, assuming that the different individual actions are seen in the context of the larger pattern of each Mushroom's Constructed Theme.

Intervening on Positive Mushrooms.   A frequently observed problem is that CFs spend little or no time attending to Positive Mushrooms. In fact, they often fail to see their Constructed Themes. They may react to individual statements of enthusiasm but are slow to see the whole theme. For example, more deliberate effort need to be made to recognize and support the Impact-concerned people and the Positive Mushrooms that they generate. Facilitators tend to be compulsive about attending to the persons with Self and Task concerns while failing to realize that people with Impact concerns like attention, too.

Frequently, all that is needed is to take the time to offer a compliment or a word of encouragement. Visiting a classroom and observing the innovation in use can be very supportive of the further growth of Positive Mushrooms. The facilitator can compliment the individual and then share anecdotes about success with others. Another effective approach is to point out the existence of a Positive Mushroom. Once it has been identified, claim it as a strategy that all can nourish.

Mushroom Detection by Change Facilitator Style

Leaders and other CFs vary in their skill to detect, understand, and deal with Intervention Mushrooms. Some continually respond to the Individual Actions, and even when the Constructed Theme is pointed out they fail to attack the whole. Others are highly skilled at early detection of emerging Mushrooms and even anticipate the potential for certain ones to develop. Sometimes leaders and other facilitators unwittingly contribute to the growth of a Mushroom. For example, a principal not attending a staff meeting may receive little attention. However, by the time the principal misses three meetings in a row and no explanation is provided, a toxic Mushroom will likely be germinating.

Initiator Change Facilitator Style Leaders Are Early Detectors.   Initiator CF Style leaders are good at Mushroom detection and disposal. They detect Positive Mushrooms almost as soon as they germinate. They take advantage of Nutritious Mushrooms by supporting and nourishing their further growth. They also are quick to claim Positive Mushrooms as something they caused to happen. Initiators cheer on individuals and teams to keep going. They will encourage spread of a theme by linking Impact-concerned people with those who have Task and Self concerns. They will provide extra resources or offer a special award to keep a Positive Mushroom growing. They may make a special point to acknowledge a Positive Mushroom in a staff meeting and recruit others to do things that contribute to its development. On the other hand, Initiators are telepathic about sensing the emergence of Poisonous Mushrooms and quick to take actions to kill them, neutralize their toxicity, or turn them into Nutritious Mushrooms. In both cases, Initiators do not waste time on Individual Actions; they see the overall pattern, anticipate what is likely to happen next, and go right at the Constructed Theme.

Responder Change Facilitator Style: Respond to Some of the Individual Actions. Responders tend not to see the overall Mushroom pattern and theme, which means that when they do react, they tend to respond to some of the Individual Actions of the Mushroom instead of its Constructed Theme. The result is a lot of flitting around from complaint to complaint in response to what was heard last. This approach reduces continuity and contributes to the growth of existing Negative Mushrooms and often fosters the development of new ones. Very few Positive Mushrooms seem to be growing in Responder-led organizations, while Negative Mushrooms thrive.

Manager Change Facilitator Style: Keep Things Evened Out.   Managers, as would be expected, focus on the potential growth of Mushrooms related to resources, logistics, and following all the rules and procedures. They are so efficient that, if it is within their control, Negative Mushrooms related to these issues will not grow. Although we do not have research related to the type and distribution of Mushrooms by CF Style of the leader, a working hypothesis is that there are fewer Mushrooms of either type with Manager CF Style leaders. Everyone is treated equally, resources are organized, external pressures are dampened, and rules and procedures are clear. Also, less proactive energy is likely to be directed toward the growth of Positive Mushrooms.

> ### Pothole Warning
> *Some Intervention Mushrooms cannot be eliminated; they keep coming back.*

> ### Pothole Repair
> *Some Mushrooms won't die; they have to be tolerated along with occasional actions to keep them from flourishing. An important consideration is to reflect on how much effort to invest in restricting the growth of difficult-to-kill Poisonous Mushrooms. Too much time spent in this effort is time not spent on facilitating further implementation*

EVERGREEN MUSHROOMS

Some Mushrooms simply will not go away. No matter what is tried, they just keep coming back. We call them Evergreen Mushrooms. One example of an Evergreen Mushroom that we have experienced several times is the two-against-one Mushroom that grows in offices staffed by three secretaries, and another occurs when there are three or more department chairs or team leaders. Using the secretary example to elaborate keeps the illustration of Evergreen Mushrooms relatively simple. A natural occurrence, due to the intensity of the work and the extensive time in the same work environment, will be on occasion for two of the secretaries to become upset with the third. The two start having whispered conversations and leave out the third. After a while, work tasks are dropped or a key piece of information is not communicated due to the unwillingness to talk with each other. An initial attempt to stop the growth of the Mushroom is for the leader to talk to each secretary individually and asks what can be done to resolve the issue. This seems to take care of the problem. The three return to working as a team.

However, within months, again two of the secretaries will be at odds with the third!? It may be a different two, but the same scenario starts to unfold. Communications are dropped, and certain tasks are not done. The Response to the theme this time could be to take all three to lunch and talk through the problem. Perhaps some tasks are restructured or schedules are changed. Following this Response to the Constructed Theme, the three go back to being a team—for a while. However, no matter what interventions have been tried, in time this Evergreen Mushroom returns. Some Mushrooms cannot be killed; they just have to be tolerated.

Many other Evergreen Mushrooms could be discussed, such as the annual panic to create the revised strategic improvement plans, the trauma surrounding yearly evaluations, and the disbelief over administering standardized achievement tests to all students at a time of year that means by the time the results are returned they are of little use. These examples won't be mapped out here, but the key point to remember is that part of the wisdom of leading and facilitating change is to recognize when something is not likely to go away. Some parts of the change process, such as Evergreen Mushrooms, need to be understood and then worked around.

GUIDING PRINCIPLES FOR MUSHROOM INTERVENTIONS

1. Mushrooms grow out of interpretations of actions and events as a change process unfolds.
2. A Mushroom may be constructed by an individual or socially constructed by a group.
3. A critical aspect of understanding a Mushroom is to be able to see the overall pattern of actions that have contributed to growth of its Constructed Theme.
4. Mushrooms may be nutritious or poisonous to a change process.
5. In most cases, intervening in response to Individual Actions will not kill a Poisonous Mushroom but instead will contribute to its further growth.
6. Contrary to what one might predict, both Positive and Negative Mushrooms can be constructed by people at each SoC and LoU.
7. An important CF skill is to keep one's antennae tuned for actions that could be the germination of Negative and Positive Mushrooms.
8. To sustain or kill a Mushroom, interventions must be aimed at its Constructed Theme.

As a check on your understanding, review the Guiding Principles for reminders of how to recognize and attempt to influence the growth of Intervention Mushrooms.

Sometimes Doing Nothing Is Best

The majority of discussion up to this point has assumed that leaders and other CFs can do things to accelerate growth or reduce Intervention Mushrooms. However, with some Mushrooms no action is best; any action taken just adds to Mushroom growth. For example, a politician may make one small comment, such as "The police acted stupidly." The media and the mayor's political opponents then take the statement out of context and for days add their interpretations of its meaning, thereby growing a Mushroom. In an attempt to kill the Mushroom, the mayor says, "That is not what I said." This response just adds fertilizer. The next day he offers an expanded apology and then invites the chief of police to lunch. Those growing the Negative Mushroom quickly label the apology as "incomplete" and the meeting as the "Lunch Summit." In this case, as well as with others, there are times when the best response is to do nothing and hope that with time the Mushroom will wither.

REFLECTION QUESTIONS

How good are you at detecting Mushrooms? What have you done to encourage the growth of a Mushroom? Have you ever tried to kill one? What happened?

SUMMARY

The success of any change effort is dependent not only on what the CFs do but also on how the participants individually and collectively interpret and construct meaning for these actions and events. All participants in a change process are looking for ways to explain and simplify what is happening. Today's innovations are complex and sophisticated; failing to plan for and effectively facilitate the process adds to the uncertainty and extends the time it takes to move across the Implementation Bridge. The individual and social construction of Mushrooms serves as a very useful strategy for making sense. Whether the resultant Mushrooms are poisonous or nutritious depends on many factors.

Success in facilitating change also depends heavily on one's ability to detect Mushrooms early in their genesis. More successful CFs are skilled at early detection. They are quick to see the overall pattern and themes of both Positive and Negative Mushrooms, and they then take actions that are aimed at their totality, rather than just addressing some of the Individual Actions.

In the ideal setting, the most effective CFs are both objectivist and interpretivist. They observe behaviors, and they assess how things are going. They use these diagnostic data to anticipate likely interpretations that could be made, and they listen for individual and social construction of meaning. They check for understanding and map the overall pattern of Individual Actions that may combine and become a Mushroom. By keeping the big picture in mind, they are better able to respond to Individual Actions and events as they unfold. They then are prepared to sense the emergence of a Constructed Theme. With this approach, Mushrooms grow for a shorter period in the dark, and more of them can be put to positive use as the change process continues to unfold.

DISCUSSION QUESTIONS

1. Describe and analyze a nutritious Mushroom that you have seen in your organization. What name would you give it? What was done to sustain it?

2. Describe and analyze a Poisonous Mushroom that you have seen in your organization. What name would you give it? What was done to kill it? What was done to sustain it?

3. What are some critical means for detecting Mushrooms? What skills will help CFs detect Nutritious and Poisonous Mushrooms?

4. What are important ideas to keep in mind when intervening on Positive and Negative Mushrooms?

5. For each SoC, predict likely Positive and Negative Mushrooms for a staff that has high concerns at that stage.

6. Describe experiences you have had or observed about the construction of Mushrooms with leaders using different CF Styles. Did they react to individual Incidents or to the totality of Mushrooms?

FIELDWORK ACTIVITIES

1. Interview a CF about the degree to which he or she is sensitive to and watches for overall patterns in a change process. See if this person can describe examples of Positive and Negative Mushrooms he or she has experienced. What did he or she do to support or discourage the growth of particular Mushrooms? As was done in Table 8.2, develop a map for one of these Mushrooms to share in class. Estimate the person's CF Style and consider whether that style is related to his or her perception and handling of Mushrooms.

2. Follow the national news for several weeks and look for the growth of Mushrooms. Identify and map the growth of one such Mushroom. List some of the Individual Actions. What is the Constructed Theme? After studying your Mushroom map as a change process consultant, what would you advise the person(s) do now?

CONDUCT A STUDY

Our understanding of Intervention Mushrooms is much more limited than for many of the other constructs introduced in this book. To understand more, systematic studies of the construction of Nutritious and Poisonous Mushrooms are needed. Better procedures for identification would be of help in research and in training change leaders in Mushroom detection. We also need many more examples of interventions targeted at Constructed Themes. Since Mushrooms are individual and social constructions, it is likely that more of the studies will use qualitative methods.

A working hypothesis, based on clinical experience with change processes, is that Initiators are quite good at detecting Mushrooms. Assuming this is the case, how do they do it? What are their clues? In several cases, we have observed that Initiators anticipate the birth of Mushrooms. What do they look for, and what frames of analysis are they employing?

Alternatively, it appears that organizations led by Responders have more Poisonous Mushrooms. If so, why is this the case? What could be done to reduce the potential for the occurrence of Poisonous Mushrooms? What drives their construction, especially when they hurt individuals and the organization as a whole?

ADDITIONAL READINGS

Bolman, L. G., & Deal, T. E. (2008). Part V: The Symbolic Frame. *Reframing organizations: artistry, choice, and leadership*. San Francisco, CA: Jossey-Bass.

Smircich, L. (1983). Organizations as shared meanings. In L. Pondy, P. Frost, G. Morgan, & T. Dandridge (Eds.). *Organizational symbolism* (pp. 55–65). Greenwich, CT: JAI.

DIFFERENT PERSPECTIVES FOR UNDERSTANDING THE BIG PICTURE OF CHANGE

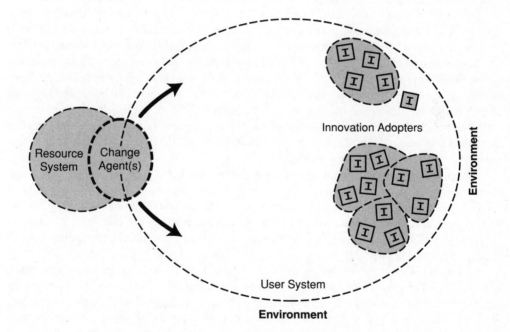

Innovation Adopters

Resource System

Change Agent(s)

User System

Environment

Environment

PART IV ORGANIZING FRAMEWORK

The graphic for this part has more open space than those for the earlier parts. There are two reasons for this: (1) The previous chapters focused in on the details of the innovation(s), the view of implementers, and the different styles and actions of the leaders, and (2) the next three chapters present more macro-system, large-scale views of how change works. These more macro perspectives are three of the classic change perspectives. Many of the key ideas will be familiar to you. Anyone studying and learning about change needs to be conversant with each of these perspectives.

CHAPTERS 9, 10, AND 11

Change can be viewed from many vantage points. For example, the end-users (teachers, staff, and assembly-line workers) who are expected to implement change have one view. They are close to the daily action and details of implementation. Leaders (executives and middle mangers such as superintendents and principals) and policymakers will be aware of some of the details of implementation at the individual level but have a broader view of what is happening across the whole organization or social system. Students and customers have still another view. Researchers and those who have developed models and theories have used one or more of these views as a frame of reference to describe and explain how change works. Each perspective emphasizes certain aspects and has reduced attention on other aspects. Each provides very useful constructs and tools for understanding, facilitating, and studying change.

A long and rich history of the study of change has resulted in several very different perspectives becoming mainstays. Each of these has its own particular emphasis and view. Three of these perspectives with particularly useful constructs for those who are interested in facilitating change are described in Chapters 9, 10, and 11. Each of these perspectives is well established in the literature and widely applied. These perspectives make sense, and each has more than 50 years of related research. At the same time, they represent extremely different views and ways of thinking about change.

Even when the same phenomenon is being addressed, it will have a perspective-specific interpretation or twist. The vocabulary used with each perspective is unique and has been carefully chosen to symbolize what is seen as most important within that view. The factors that are central to each perspective are unique, too. Although they are different in focus and construct definition, each perspective offers many useful suggestions for understanding, facilitating, and studying change.

Chapter 9 will introduce the systems perspective, which is based in having a large-scale, holistic view. The systems perspective begins by including all factors inside and outside the organization that in any way might be related to a particular change effort. A second important element in the systems view is interactions. Rather than seeing the whole as static, in the systems perspective all the elements and pieces are seen as composing subsystems that are, at least to some extent, interconnected and dynamic. When something happens in one part of the system, it affects other parts. Leaders who can think *systemically* are much more effective in leading change efforts.

Chapter 10 will introduce another long-established, extensively researched, and widely used perspective, Diffusion. In this perspective the central theme is communication. Keeping track of who talks to whom and the lines of communication are important Diffusion constructs. Characteristics of individual innovation adopters have been examined and categorized according to how quickly they adopt an innovation. Another important component of the Diffusion perspective is description of the innovation in terms of how it is perceived by adopters. In the Diffusion perspective, an important role is that of the change agent who introduces the innovation to members of the user system.

Organization Development (OD) will be introduced in Chapter 11. This perspective emphasizes a different set of constructs. One focus is the process skills that various groups/teams and the whole organization possess or may need to develop. Process skills for problem solving, decision making, and communicating are seen as essential for change success. Each individual also should develop a set of process skills in order to help the various groups/teams succeed. The OD perspective is guided by an external process consultant. A key assumption is that an organization that has well-developed process skills can better handle change.

Each of these perspectives has a rich history of research and application in business, government, schools, and developing countries. Each offers a number of constructs and tools that can help everyone to better understand, more effectively facilitate, and systematically study change.

CHAPTER 9

SYSTEMS THINKING
Interconnections of Parts That Make a Whole

*Now that we've aligned our curriculum and instruction with assessment
and the state's standards, we've seen positive gains in our students'
achievement test scores.*

—Elementary school principal

*Well, what we have not yet done a good job of is coordinating and aligning our
advertising protocols with the legal department's recommendations.*

—Manager of a large chain of stores

*Our board of directors is working on budget reallocation in order to provide
training resources that support the corporation's work across all elements of
management, the production line, and the payroll office.*

—CEO of a small manufacturing company

*My child's school sent a letter to us explaining how the school is addressing
our state's new curriculum standards, and how the administrators and teachers
are learning to redesign their work with children to accommodate that. I don't
quite understand all this, but I'm going to a meeting to learn how families can
be part of this activity.*

—Parent of a middle school student

*Sales are going well, but the increasing cost of fuel, along with the shortage
of plywood (due to the hurricanes) and not enough carpenters, could hurt
things over the next six months.*

—Real estate agent

For a very long time a major goal of educators and the public has been school change and
improvement to more effectively support students in their successful learning. Various
approaches and strategies have been initiated but have not achieved broad-scale change.
Examining these efforts has engaged the attention of numerous researchers and writers. For
example, in 1992, Sashkin and Egermeier conducted an analysis of the history of policy
approaches to school change and identified four strategies. The first was the "fix the parts"

approach that involved introducing and adopting specific innovations such as curricular programs and instructional practices. This approach was viewed as an exchange of new products (curriculum) or processes (instruction) for old.

Sashkin and Egermeier termed the second approach "fix the people." In this approach, training and development were provided to educational personnel to change their practices/behaviors, attitudes, values, and beliefs. In the third approach—"fix the school"—the school (rather than programs or people) was seen as the unit to change. A school improvement team would guide the school in needs analysis, solution identification, and plans for change. This approach was widely used throughout the 1990s and continues to be popular.

After analyzing these three approaches, Sashkin and Egermeier concluded that successful change had not been achieved but that a fourth approach, which they called "fix the system," could do it. This meant giving attention to all parts of the system simultaneously, since changing one part of the system influences other parts. These four approaches range in scope or magnitude from targeting selected parts in isolation, to more recent holistic efforts. It is this whole system view that is the focus of this chapter.

FOCUS QUESTIONS

1. What is meant by systems thinking and using a systems approach" for implementing change?
2. How are the critical pieces or parts of a system identified?
3. What is the value of a systems approach? Why consider working systemically?
4. How can the systems approach be applied to implementing change in education?

FAMILIAR NAMES IN SYSTEMS THINKING

Systemic change (not systematic change), *systems thinking, working systemically,* and a host of other similar labels have been bandied about for several decades. These labels have been sprinkled across the conversations of educators at the campus and district office levels. When asked what they mean in their use of such a term, many leaders tend to look askance, frown quizzically, and appear unable to provide a coherent response. Such reactions to the use of relatively new terms is not unusual. It seems that the nature of many executives and policymakers is to hear a new idea, refer to it before fully learning about and understanding it, and then try to use it as an uninformed novice.

A useful beginning point for examining systems thinking and theory is *Designing Social Systems in a Changing World* by Bela H. Banathy (1996). Throughout his career Banathy examined systems and was a student of the works of others. Banathy suggested that "people . . . cannot give direction to their lives, they cannot forge their destiny, they cannot take charge of their future unless they also develop competence to take part directly and authentically in the design of the systems in which they live and work, and reclaim their right to do so" (p. vii).

Banathy further maintained that "this kind of empowerment when learned and exercised by families, groups, organizations, and social and societal systems of all kinds, is the only hope we have to give direction to our evolution, to create a democracy that truly represents the aspiration and will of people, and to create a society about which all of us can feel good" (1996, p. vii). Banathy expressed a grand challenge and a powerful goal.

Banathy's early work was followed much later by Peter Senge (1990), who used systems thinking to articulate how organizations should be created and operate. Senge's *The Fifth Discipline* found its way from the corporate world to school trustees' boardrooms and served as a wake-up call for educators who were considering how best to design their systems for improved student outcomes.

Another volume that has been most helpful in understanding the complexity and interdependence of the parts of systems is *Systemic Change: Touchstones for the Future School*, edited by Patrick Jenlink (1995). Jenlink brought together the intellect, expertise, and advice of a score of writers to help us "get a handle" on systems in education.

Whereas Banathy first penned a book in 1973 about a systems view of education and others like Jenlink have followed, the current work of researchers, administrators, and field practitioners in regional educational development laboratories and in higher education offer informative illustrations about the use of systems thinking in today's organizations. This chapter will briefly sketch what is known about systems from the literature and look intimately at applications in the field: how systems thinking is being used to define work, test its efficacy in practice, and make adaptations based on new learnings.

REFLECTION QUESTIONS

Banathy stated, "people . . . cannot give direction to their lives . . . unless they also develop competence to take part directly and authentically in the design of the systems in which they live and work." What is your reaction to this statement? What do you think influences your reaction?

GUIDING PRINCIPLES OF SYSTEMIC WORK

1. All parts or components of an organization or system must be given attention when attempting systems work.
2. Any organization or system is made up of subsystems or components; these can be and should be identified.
3. Most systems are organized in levels; these should be recognized as should the individuals within them.
4. For work in any system, certain competencies are required; these should be identified and developed in the relevant individuals.
5. In systemic reform, as in any reform, certain actions and conditions facilitate and others impede; the wise leader will plan for systems work with these in mind and watch for new "arrivals."
6. Systems work is not without its shortcomings; be aware and plan accordingly.
7. Doing systems work is like juggling: Keep all plates in the air at the same time, and keep your eye on each of them.

GOING DEEPER TO EXAMINE A SYSTEMS VIEW

In early work, Peter Checkland (1981) defined *human activity systems* as a "collection of structured sets of activities that make up the system, coupled with a collection of activities concerned with processing information, making plans, performing, monitoring performance . . . that express purposeful human activity that could be found in the real world" (cited in Banathy, 1996, p. 14). Similarly, Ackoff and Emery (1972) characterized social systems as purposeful systems whose members intentionally and collectively formulate objectives. These social organizations are such that the state of the parts can be assessed only by reference to the state of the whole system. Further, change in one part of the system is influenced by changes in the system as a whole.

Argyris and Schon (1978) maintained that a social group is an organization when it designs decision-making procedures for the collectivity, giving to individuals the authority to act for the collective group and setting boundaries. Laszlo (1972) suggested that social systems are guided by values; thus, social systems are not concerned with physical needs but with values that depend on the beliefs and values that members have.

In 1995, Banathy explained a systems view of education. He noted that a systems view makes it possible to examine and describe the system and its setting, and also its components and parts. The systems view is a way of thinking that allows understanding and description of

- The qualities or descriptors of the amalgamated educational system operating at numerous interconnected levels (organizational, administrative, instructional)
- The relationships and interdependencies of the systems in operation at the levels
- The purposes and parameters of educational systems
- The relationships and activities that are undertaken between the systems and their environment
- The dynamics of the actions and relationships and designs of connectivity among the parts of the systems
- The characteristics of the whole system and the qualities that characterize various levels of the system as a result of systemic interaction and synthesis
- The behaviors and system changes and their environments that occur over time (p. 12)

Pothole Warning
The preceding statements seem destined to make understanding change difficult; there are so many of them, and each is so complex.

Pothole Repair
To develop deeper understanding, check out the statements that follow.

Perhaps a briefer and crisper articulation of systemic change offered by Jenlink, Reigeluth, Carr, and Nelson (1996) is helpful: Systemic change is an approach that

[r]ecognizes the interrelationships and interdependencies among the parts of the educational system, with the consequence that desired changes in one part of the system are accompanied by changes in other parts that are necessary to reach an idealized vision of the whole, and

[r]ecognizes the interrelationships and interdependencies between the educational system and its community, including parents, employers, social service agencies, religious organizations, and much more, with the consequence that all stakeholders are given active ownership of the change effort. (p. 2)

Obviously, a systems view examines the whole and its relationships to its parts or subsystems. One could ask, What are these parts?

COMPONENTS OF THE EDUCATIONAL SYSTEM

The components or parts of the education system have been hinted at by several authors cited previously. Other researchers and writers have further expanded identification of the parts or subsystems of an education system, specifically in the reform context.

IMPLICATIONS FOR LEADERS FACILITATING CHANGE

When working in any organization, leaders must understand their system, its parts, and its people. Typically, leaders tend to work more with one part of the system and give limited consideration to its connectedness to other parts and the mutual influence they may have—and then are surprised when things don't work as they had anticipated. The major message for leaders planning for systemic work is that it is imperative to take into account the various subsystems and the system as a whole system plus the external factors that impinge on it. Also, as noted, attention must be directed to the interconnectedness of the subsystems. If the parts are not interconnected, or are loosely coupled, then work must be initiated to enable interconnectedness and interrelationships to develop, for a loosely coupled organization will flounder. The challenge here is to see the interconnectedness between all the subsystems and the whole, not just some of the parts.

Similarly, acknowledging and attending to all people in the system is required. A culture of collaboration and interdependence is helpful (see Chapter 2). This means that people at all levels of the system (executive, administrative, instructional if this is a school, sales or marketing or advertising if it is a business, support staff such as secretaries and custodian, etc.) must be involved. There are tools for planning and implementing systems change, and these tools can be found in Part III of this book.

Systemic change, like any change, will not happen without consistent planning for implementation, taking action, and monitoring the results so that successive actions may be designed and taken. Short-term and long-range strategies will be necessary (see Chapter 7) and applied to a systemic effort. A primary strategic action by leaders must be an articulation of the vision for change that leaves some space for others in the system to add to and shape or contribute to the vision. To fail to develop a shared vision and a plan for its articulation across the system dooms the reform work to an early death.

Components of Systems in Change

Anderson (1993) identified the components of a system in change as vision, public and political support, networking and partnerships, teaching and learning changes, administrative roles and responsibilities, and policy alignment. Danek, Calbert, and Chubin (1994) stated that the essential components of systems reform are national standards for content, skills, and attitudes; learning, teaching, and assessing standards; ambitious learning expectations and outcomes for all students connected to a rigorous academic core program; examination of policies, practices, and behaviors, and their modification to remove barriers and achieve the standards; broad-based involvement in designing an action plan with autonomy in implementing the plan; outcomes that measure systemic change; a system for monitoring and evaluating progress and adjusting programs accordingly; and a timeline for delivering the outcomes.

Characteristics of Systemic Policy

Clune (1993) reported five characteristics of systemic policy: research-based goals in education practice and organization; models of new practice and knowledge; centralized/decentralized change process; regular assessment of inputs, outcomes, and process; and a coherent, sustained change-oriented political process. In the same year, the National Science Foundation noted the requirements of systemic reform: changes in financing, governance, management, content, and conduct of education (teacher preparation and enhancement, curricula and instruction, assessments), and all students learning science and math in a diverse educational system.

Elements of Systemic Reform

Smith and O'Day (1991) articulated three major elements for systemic reform. First was unifying the vision and goals of what schools should be like; second, establishing a coherent system of instructional guidance (knowledge, skills, capacities, curriculum, materials, professional development, accountability assessment) aligned with goals; and third, restructuring the governance system (state develops outcomes and accountability, schools determine means to achieve outcomes). An examination of Table 9.1 reveals wide disparity across the elements of attention in systemic change or reform, suggesting wide variance in what researchers and writers deemed important as components of the system.

REFLECTION QUESTIONS

Study Table 9.1 in order to organize the information shared in the sections on components, characteristics, and elements of systemic work. What, if any, items surprise you? Are there factors that you expected to find there that are absent?

TABLE 9.1 Components of Educational Systems

	ANDERSON (1993)	DANEK, CALBERT, & CHUBIN (1994)	CLUNE (1993)	NATIONAL SCIENCE FOUNDATION (1993)	SMITH & O'DAY (1991)
Vision	✓				✓
Public/political support	✓		✓		
Networking/partnerships	✓				
Teaching–learning changes	✓	✓		✓	✓
Administrative roles/responsibilities	✓			✓	
Policy alignment	✓	✓			
National content standards		✓			
Ambitious student learning outcomes		✓	✓	✓	
Action plan/implementation		✓			
Systemic change outcomes		✓	✓		
Monitoring/evaluating/adjusting		✓	✓	✓	
Timeline for outcomes		✓			
New models of practice			✓		✓
Centralized/decentralized change process			✓		
Finance				✓	✓
Governance				✓	
Teacher preparation				✓	
Curriculum					✓
Materials					✓
Professional development					✓
Accountability/assessment					✓

WORKING SYSTEMICALLY IN SCHOOLS

In the late 1990s, as frustration grew over the single-shot, hit-and-run approaches to educational change and improvement, systemic change or systemic reform became more frequently considered as an alternative. Staff at one of the nation's regional educational laboratories, Southwest Educational Development Laboratory (SEDL), reviewed the literature and developed a scope of transformation work employing a systems approach. The goal of this work was to transform low-performing schools into high-performing learning communities, with the work centering at both the district and school levels. This project's review and synthesis of the literature revealed three major parts of education systems that required reform and were incorporated into the laboratory's model: components, levels, and competencies (Stiegel-bauer, Tobia, Thompson, and Sturges (2004).

Components

In systems thinking all parts or components (aka subsystems) of the system are inextricably linked. Support or pressure on one part exerts influence on others. This model gives attention to thinking and working across all the components that are listed here:

Standards: What students are expected to learn and be able to do

Curriculum and instruction: What is taught and how it is taught

Assessment: Testing to discover what students have learned

Policy and governance: Rules and procedures to be followed

Professional staffing: Recruiting and retaining high-quality personnel, professional development, and appraisal

Resources: Staffing, time, budget, facilities, equipment, and materials

Family and community: Support systems outside the district, including social service agencies

Again, keep in mind the interconnectedness of these many parts; none function in isolation of the others. Quite obviously, curriculum and instruction are, or should be, tied directly to standards. Assessment must be closely related to the standards; thus, standards, curriculum and instruction, and assessment are aligned. Professional development must focus on the standards and on curriculum and instruction so that the staff is prepared to effectively teach what students need to know and do. Resources must be allocated with the aforementioned components for all to function well. In working systemically—that is, *paying attention to all the parts*—all subsystems must be considered in the planning and implementation of new practices.

Levels

In addition to the components, working systemically requires all organization levels of the system—state, district, school, and classroom—be given attention. These levels can be thought of as concentric circles, each providing expectations and demands that influence student achievement. The federal and state governments create policies and regulations that districts must implement; districts set rules and procedures to which all schools must adhere; schools provide the structures and immediate facilities in which classrooms operate; and all these impinge on classrooms and the teaching and learning that occur. In reform efforts, all levels of the system of public education must be kept in mind. A third part of the system focuses on competencies to be mastered by individuals involved in the effort.

Pothole Warning

Ah, all this information is like slugging along in soft sand and then hitting a hole. It all sounds quite befuddling.

Pothole Repair

Fear not. Clarification is next on the agenda. The competencies detail will be helpful and may well enable you to imagine mental pictures of what is happening in systemic work.

Competencies

In addition to components of the system and levels of the system that require attention, competencies for successful systemic work are needed and have been identified by Cowan, Joyner, and Beckwith (2008):

> *Creating coherence.* Creating coherence is making certain that the different parts of the system reflect the beliefs and values held by the organization and that they function together to accomplish the goals of the system. This approach ensures a shared understanding of the extent to which curriculum, instruction, and assessment are aligned to state standards and involves a coordinated effort to avoid competing priorities. Stakeholders at all levels engage in collaborative and purposeful work to improve teaching and learning— essential for creating a coherent instructional focus.
>
> *Collecting, interpreting, and using data.* Collecting, interpreting, and using data supports leaders in identifying underlying factors contributing to core issues and problems that need to be addressed. It entails collecting data from multiple sources, organizing the data in formats that help staff interpret and draw conclusions, and using information from the data to take appropriate action. It is essential to making sound decisions about improving schools and districts, and demands developing the capacities of school and district staff to collect, interpret, and use data effectively.
>
> *Ensuring continuous professional learning.* This competency ensures that all staff continuously develop their knowledge and skills that are most effective for helping students meet challenging standards. Further, it increases the probability that staff will become ever more effective in enabling all students to become successful learners. In these systems, principals participate directly in professional development sessions with staff in planning, conducting, implementing, and evaluating the effort. This process is long term and integrated into daily practice.
>
> *Building relationships.* District and school leaders create structures and processes that promote collaboration and collegiality so that all educators share their knowledge, ideas, and strategies. Mutual respect and trust are essential to building these professional relationships. In this environment, school, district, family, and community leaders work to define a common vision for improving schools. Time and settings to encourage positive interactions among all stakeholders must be provided to support such relationships and their outcomes to develop.
>
> *Responding to changing conditions.* Adapting to myriad demographic, societal, economic, and political changes is a reality in today's schools and districts. Changes that districts and schools typically confront include leadership transitions, resource allocation, availability of quality teaching staff, state and local politics, and state and national policy. Staffs are better equipped to face these pressures when the members are knowledgeable of appropriate solutions and the schools and districts promote continuous learning for adults as well as students. (pp. 9–13)

The Cube

Figure 9.1 graphically portrays the cube that contains the levels, components, and competencies of the SEDL's working systemically model. These three dimensions of the model are the

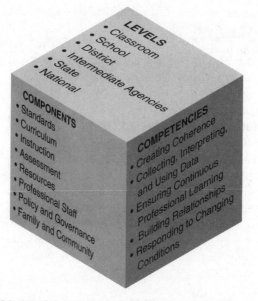

FIGURE 9.1   The Cube Model of the Working Systemically Approach

focus of attention for work planned and carried out through district and school leadership teams. These teams have overlapping members. Early in the project, SEDL staff guided and directed work in the field sites with the district and schools teams, giving their attention to the levels of the larger system and their interrelationships. The SEDL staff planned for the sites' learning of the components that must be addressed in order to improve student achievement. Particular attention was given to the alignment of standards, curriculum, instruction, and assessment, along with coordinated professional development.

The competencies received much attention from the SEDL site staff who led the district and schools in identifying root causes that could explain the areas of student achievement data that were of concern. Building the capacity of site educators was always the objective. This was done through well-organized staff-development sessions as well as through follow-up coaching and assistance. Multiple phone calls and e-mails supported the efforts between the twice-monthly visits by SEDL staff. When the teams were ready to provide more leadership, SEDL staff stepped back into a facilitating and supporting role.

Competencies from Other Writers

Other writers have addressed competencies needed for systemic work. For example, Floden, Goertz, and O'Day (1995) described strategies that are needed for capacity building in systemic reform. These are enhancing teacher capacity; providing vision and leadership; changing the organization or governance of schools; providing guidance on curricular content and instruction; establishing evaluation or accountability mechanisms; providing resources; and facilitating access to outside sources of support. These competencies resonate with some of those mentioned earlier by Stiegelbauer and colleagues. At the state level, Timar and Kirp (1989) noted the roles, and thus the capacities or competencies, required of state-level personnel. These are to establish professional standards and expectations, provide support, and nurture organizational characteristics that foster excellence.

EFFECTS OF WORKING SYSTEMICALLY

The SEDL staff used its cube model to conduct field work (as described) in 16 districts in the five-state region served by SEDL (Arkansas, Louisiana, New Mexico, Oklahoma, and Texas). It has fine-tuned the model and developed more specificity and a sharper focus, particularly in the competencies needed by school and district leadership to do the work. SEDL staff members also have seen progress in field site participants' knowledge and understanding of systemic work, as measured by the Working Systemically Survey (created by SEDL's research team) and through semi-annual interviews conducted by the research team that followed the effort.

Outcomes for Educators

The survey and interview data suggest that educators (administrators and teachers) perceive that alignment of curriculum, instruction, and assessment has improved over time. Alignment of these important components of the system is essential for systemic work. The data also indicate positive changes in alignment between instruction and assessment, curriculum and standards, and vertical alignment. The educators also perceive that leaders' capacities to promote alignment in the district and schools has increased over time. Further, the educators indicate that describing and setting expectations, monitoring, classroom involvement, and understanding data and alignment are the top roles for leaders at the school and district levels. Responses to questions examining leadership roles suggested that leadership around alignment improved somewhat from the previous year. If some positive changes have been noted in educators' capacities and actions, what about student change?

REFLECTION QUESTIONS

If you have been involved change initiatives, to what extent was systemic thinking included? Did you observe leadership that addressed the various components/ parts/subsystems and results such as those reported above? Were some of the subsystems given too much or too little attention?

Results for Students

Student results in 13 of 16 SEDL schools were examined for the 2004 year-end report (Bond-Huie, Buttram, Deviney, Murphy, & Ramos, 2004). Student results in one or more grade levels showed decreases in the percentage of students categorized at the lowest performance categories. Out of 21 sets of test results in one of SEDL's states, 15 sets of results suggested a decrease of greater than 5% in the percentage of students categorized at the lowest performance levels on the state exam. Although there are positive trends in the data, three sets of test results indicated an increase in the percentage of students who were categorized at the lowest performance levels as defined by the state. SEDL has adjusted its approach so that its current work launches the model at the school unit, subsequently expanding participation across the district.

FACILITATORS AND BARRIERS TO WORKING SYSTEMICALLY: A CASE FROM ANOTHER COUNTRY

At the same time that SEDL was working systemically in south-central United States, a large-scale systemic reform effort was underway in Mexico. The Instituto Tecnológico y de Estudios Superiores de Monterrey (ITESM), more familiarly known in the United States as the Monterrey Institute of Technology, had undertaken a major effort to transform the teaching–learning paradigm across its entire higher education institution of 33 campuses spread across Mexico. ITESM is among the first institutions of higher education to recognize the need for incorporating new learning approaches into classroom instruction throughout an entire multicampus system.

The mandated change resulted from a broad study conducted by the highest level of the university system to determine if the university was preparing its graduates for success in the 21st-century knowledge-based, global economy. It was learned that many graduates were lacking in nine key attributes necessary for today's high-performance jobs: leadership, teamwork, problem solving, time management, self-management, adaptability, analytical thinking, global consciousness, and basic communication skills. After considering this report, and further study of the university's classroom environments and pedagogical approaches, a new vision of the teaching–learning process for the university's classrooms was developed and prepared for launching. As can be imagined, a careful attempt was made to balance academic freedom and academic performance expectations—a journey into uncharted territory.

A top-down mandated strategy (note that in Chapter 1, Change Principle 9 indicates that mandated change can work) was employed that involved multiple aspects of support and assistance for faculty and administrators. Several years of intensive professional development were provided to enable faculty to use a more constructivist and technology-based approach to teaching and learning. The professional development focused on multiple levels of the university's system: executive, administrative, faculty, and support personnel. It impacted resources and policy and resulted in new ways of delivering professional development electronically. New capacities were developed throughout the staff to accommodate the implementation of the new model. So, what success was accomplished?

Facilitators of the Change

A study of one ITESM campus was undertaken to understand better how the change process was facilitated and what barriers hindered its progress (Gonzalez, Resta, & De Hoyos, 2005). The facilitators depicted in Figure 9.2 are a mix of people who provided interventions

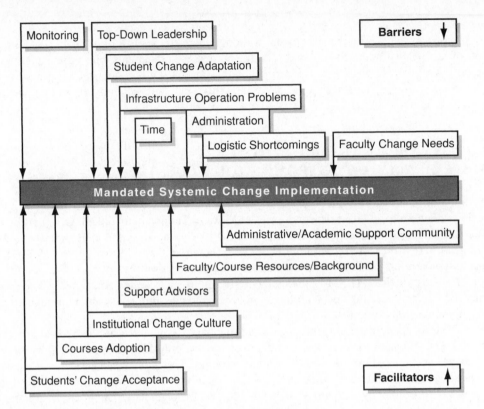

FIGURE 9.2   Facilitators and Barriers of the Systemic Process

Source: C. E. Gonzalez, P. E. Resta, and M. L. De Hoyos. Paper submitted for presentation at the annual meeting of the American Educational Research Association, 2005. Reprinted by permission of Carlos Enrique Gonzalez.

(support advisors and administrative and academic support) and conditions present in the university setting. Their brief descriptions follow:

Students' acceptance of change: ITESM students' participation and acceptance of the change that included the use of technology aided the change process.

Adoption/adaptation of courses: The faculty had system-level, high-quality courses available for their adoption, or they could adapt existing courses for their use.

Institutional change culture: ITESM philosophy and values-based culture promoted innovation, change, and an entrepreneurial spirit.

Ongoing support and training: Support was provided by pedagogical and technological advisors from ITESM Learning Technology Centers.

Faculty academic background: Faculty members' individual academic discipline, years of teaching experience, and pedagogical skills supported the change process.

Professional Learning Community: Collegiate work in ITESM systemwide academies and local academic departments, and the appropriate organizational structure of the institution, enabled the change effort to make progress.

These strategic interventions were identified through a five-stage process. First, administrators were asked to generate a listing of interventions that they had done that they believed were helpful to the change effort. Second, faculty were invited to identify actions that administrators had taken to facilitate the process. Third, the lists of both the administrators and faculty were submitted to factor analysis. The results were then field-tested in the fourth step. These results were further analyzed in the fifth step and produced the six facilitating factors (described above) and the eight barriers, which will be described next.

Keep in mind that this was a nationwide systemic effort and that the facilitators (i.e., strategies identified in Figure 9.2) were present across all campuses of the ITESM system. Support for implementation was provided at all levels of the system (executive, administrative, and instructional). The resources and policies at all campuses were coordinated to focus systemically across the entire university on curriculum and instructional processes and on professional development to support the change to a new teaching–learning model.

REFLECTION QUESTIONS

It was quite exciting to learn about this large-scale change effort across a large university system and to learn how it evolved. What is your take on the approach that was used by the executive level of the university system? How would this type of systemic change effort unfold across your state?

Barriers to the Change Process

Any change effort will be challenging. In the ITESM initiative eight barriers were identified:

Monitor implementation: This factor cited the lack of institutional evaluation of the implementation of the project and lack of classroom monitoring to improve.

Top-down leadership: ITESM's centralized decision-making process promotes upper-level decisions to the exclusion of a bottom-up effort.

Students' adaptation to change: There was a lack of students collaboratively developing new learning habits and adaptation to the work, and students showed apathy toward ITESM's new teaching–learning process (interestingly, students' acceptance appears to be both a facilitator and, when it is absent, a hindrance—easy enough to understand).

Infrastructure operational problems: This involved proper operation of technological platforms, computational servers, operational failures, and general maintenance of the infrastructure.

Time: This complaint is a typical one. In this case, the problem was lack of time for continuous improvement of courses and interaction with students, lack of time needed to fully understand the new approach, and lack of time to become involved in the change process and for feedback during the implementation process.

Administrative alignment and support: Academic units and administrative staff had different goals, and alignment of administrative processes with the change was somewhat lacking. In addition, academic administrators' understanding of the change was an issue.

Support shortcomings: Cited were support deficiencies during the implementation process as well as lack of support from technological and pedagogical advisors. (Here again is a contradiction of a factor that was a facilitator to some and a barrier to others, most likely stemming from participants' own personal experience with the change process.)

Faculty issues: Faculty skepticism arose about the effectiveness of the new approach, which required use of didactic methods in redesigned courses.

These barriers clearly reflect the systemic nature of change initiatives. There are no surprises in this list. All are regularly identified in change efforts. In hindsight, the ITESM effort could have thought more about working systemically so that all of the subsystems were kept in mind simultaneously.

For example, time is typically an implementation issue, and it seems reasonable that the executive and administrative layers of ITESM could have provided resources and developed policies to make time available at all campuses. In addition, policies could have addressed administrative alignment and support. More professional development for administrators would have clarified their understanding of the change so that monitoring implementation would occur more comprehensively and systemically.

The sheer scope or magnitude of conducting such a far-reaching change across 33 campuses of a very large university system challenges the intellect. What is useful here is the identification of what worked systemically to encourage implementation and the identification of factors that need to be addressed more directly in order for implementation to make additional progress across the entire system. Further, these findings represent useful ideas for the consideration and study by others who anticipate attempting large-scale systemic change efforts.

LIMITATIONS OF WORKING SYSTEMICALLY

If the definition and the expansive lists of components required for using a systemic approach to educational reform sound daunting, they are. Fullan (1993) identified two limitations of the systemic approach. First is that individuals and groups greatly underestimate the complexity of how systems operate and the daily dynamics that ensue, requiring large amounts of attention, energy, and resources. Second, it is not clear if the systemic approach or process can be extended to new situations. What is needed, Fullan suggested, is a new paradigm more in tune with the realities of systems and their dynamic complexity.

At this point, the reader may be haunted by the early work of Karl Weick (1976), who introduced the concept of *loose coupling*. Weick explained that in viewing an organization as a system, some elements will be tightly coupled, such as budgeting and spending. Other areas may have limited linkages, such as a nonspecific policy about how employees dress (i.e., loose coupling). Weick explained that the connections, links, or interdependence between any two entities will have a degree of coupling. More tightly coupled individuals, groups, and events will respond to each other. Also, the degree of coupling between two parts of a system depends on the amount of activity or strength of the variables or elements that the two share. If the two have few variables in common or share weak variables, they will be loosely coupled and more independent of each other.

For example, if budget decision-making is closely held by the principal and not shared with teachers, then teachers and the principal can be assessed as being loosely coupled with regard to the budget. At the same time, if the principal is closely associated with teachers in instructional planning, then they are considered to be tightly coupled instructionally. Weick says, "Loose coupling simply connotes things, any things, that may be tied together either weakly or infrequently or slowly or with minimal interdependence" (1976, p. 5).

Pothole Warning

Although interconnectedness and interrelationships are required for successful systems work, be careful in making casual assumptions about the degree of interconnectedness and tight coupling of the system's parts.

Pothole Repair

As noted, some parts of the system will have tight coupling, and others will be loosely connected. Charting where connections are tight and loose along with continuous observation and monitoring so that adjustments may be made are wise strategies to consider.

Clearly, if the parts of a system are loosely coupled, developing change process–related integration and coordination will require more effort. However, Weick (1976) noted that if there are rules, regulations, or prerequisites for how the subparts of the system will interact and relate to each other, then the longer the list, the tighter the coupling. One might be reminded of the introduction of site-based management in the late 1980s. Schools were given unbridled authority to act, and soon in many districts the flotilla of schools was meandering in all directions and floundering on the shoals. For this, and other reasons, efforts have been made in many districts to tighten the coupling so that the district operation is better aligned with the schools and the system at large functions coherently. For systemic change to work, the components of the system must have sufficiently tight coupling so as to work with maximum interdependence. The following vignette illustrates some of these points.

■ ■ ■ ■ ■ ▬▬▬▬▬▬▬▬▬▬▬▬▬▬▬▬▬▬▬▬▬

VIGNETTE
THE HUNTER HILL SCHOOL DISTRICT

Hunter Hill, a small rural district with 1,100 K–12 students (a K–2 primary school, a grades 3–5 intermediate school, a grades 6–8 middle school, and a grades 9–12 high school) began a school improvement (SI) process 18 months ago. The four schools, with their school-improvement councils, provided the energy to respond to the superintendent's suggestion that they examine their data and plan for improvement. Professional development for the councils was provided by an intermediate service agency.

The councils did a substantial amount of work and seemed to be successful in guiding the schools in self-study and analysis. At the end of the fall semester, each of the schools had developed a campus action plan that emphasized its need for improvement—which, as it developed, was a need for attention to writing achievement of the students at all the schools.

(continued)

V I G N E T T E   CONTINUED

Each of the schools selected its own writing program. As the primary school's council said, "Our colleagues in the next county found this to be a fun program for the kids." The intermediate school's principal announced that his school had studied the state's curriculum standards and selected a program that was quite congruent with the standards. The middle school principal shared that she didn't think the students were so poor in writing and that she had decided to continue using the old textbooks for writing instruction. The high school principal, considered to be a "strange duck," was working on his superintendent's certification at a nearby university and solicited help from the university faculty; as a result, his school's faculty members studied several writing programs, compared them to the students' needs and to the standards explicated by the state department for the state's students, and selected what they thought was the best all-around fit.

As the spring semester spun by, the superintendent met with the four principals as a group to check on progress with their improvement work. She inquired about the professional development in which the faculties had engaged and what formative assessments were revealing about the students' learning in writing. Two of the principals reported that their teachers had not needed professional development as they (the principals) were sure that their teachers knew how to teach writing.

The intermediate school principal had exhausted his professional development monies and asked for additional funds to release teachers for studying their latest assessments of students and to gain additional skills in delivering the last quarter of the semester's curriculum and its appropriate instructional strategies. He further requested that the school-improvement councils and the school board look into the district's policies governing professional development for the teachers. "Teachers cannot use the new writing program without having long-term, in-depth learning of the new curriculum and its associated instructional strategies, with follow-up to help them really gain deep content and skills needed to use the new program."

Although the primary and middle school principals looked puzzled, the high school principal chimed in with his concerns. "I'm wondering, even if we are giving attention to the state standards for writing at our schools (at this point, the two principals looked even more puzzled and disturbed), I wonder if our curriculum is well articulated vertically across the four schools, so that when students reach high school they have not been subjected to gaps or overlaps in the skills needed for being successful writers. And, I worry about our assessments being aligned with the standards—and whether professional development is focusing accurately on helping the teachers develop the skills they need to teach the students so they do well on the state achievement tests and are skillful writers as well."

At this juncture, uneasy looks were exchanged all around. The district and campus administrators collectively found themselves in an uncomfortable position. The superintendent suggested, as it was quite late in the afternoon, that they meet again in 2 days to further discuss their concerns and take stock of where they were in their school improvement process. She also suggested that they bring as many of their school-improvement council members as could attend on short notice.

ANALYSIS

At their meeting, the superintendent led the group in identifying and listing all the aspects of the district's system that influenced the schools' efforts to improve student writing. During their discussion and identification of the factors of the system, it became clear that everyone had failed to understand the interconnectedness and interrelationships of the various parts of the district as a system. They noted that each school had selected a different curriculum without consideration of how the curricula fit and flowed from one level of school to the next. Nor had all the schools selected their programs with attention to the competencies that all students would need to accomplish, as reflected by the standards.

■ ■ ■ ■ ■ ▬▬▬▬▬▬▬▬▬▬▬▬▬▬▬▬▬▬▬▬▬▬▬▬▬▬

V I G N E T T E   CONTINUED

Resources had not been appropriately allocated for the introduction and implementation of new programs. Neither principals nor faculties knew the programs well, since professional development had not been properly considered. Giving the schools the authority and latitude to select their own programs had been a good idea, but there had been no selection criteria established to guide the district's schools in their choices of programs. One of the principals had mentioned policies, and the group agreed that a districtwide committee needed to look into the policies that provided guidance to all aspects of the schools' efforts for improvement: resource allocation; time for professional development and funds to support consultants if needed; guidance for curriculum selection or development; a means to align the district's curriculum, instruction, and assessment with professional development; and a well-articulated governance structure so that issues and concerns about the district's school-improvement processes could be addressed quickly and fruitfully.

In short, the district and campus personnel had not viewed the district as a system with their schools as part of the system but had taken free rein so that each school became its own isolated, independent entity. In other words, although tightly coupled around the state standards, district budgets, and line authority, decisions for curriculum selection were left to each school (i.e., loosely coupled).

NEXT STEPS

Since the state's achievement tests had been administered and test scores just delivered, the superintendent shared test data with the group and led a review of the data, beginning with the writing scores. Interestingly, the two schools that had selected their writing programs based on the writing programs' relationship to the state writing standards had small but positive gains in student writing. They were not large enough to be totally satisfying, but they did signal the value of paying attention to the competencies deemed by the state as important for students to know and achieve.

It was clear to the school councils what was needed for making a comprehensive and concerted effort in addressing increased student achievement: more communication across all the schools and district office as well as consensus as a whole system in decision making for tighter coupling and improved alignment. A number of committees were formed that would work during the summer. One group would work with the district's business manager to examine funding and to ascertain if some shifts might be made in allocations in order to provide more materials and professional development for teachers. This group had a representative from each of the district's schools. Another group whose members crossed all four of the schools would convene with the district's director of instruction and make a plan for developing curriculum that was aligned with the state standards and also to align assessments.

A third group would meet with several school board members to explore policies that were not favorable to the execution of school change and improvement and would make recommendations for additions, deletions, and changes in policies and their decision-making process. This group also included representatives from each school. The fourth group would solicit involvement of parents from each of the four schools to discuss how they might be supportive of the schools in their improvement efforts as well as of a school-year opening event for the district that would bring together district personnel, all schools, parents, teachers, and students.

The plan was to investigate all aspects of the district education system that affected the learning of the professionals in the schools as well as their students. In addition, the plan was to investigate the relationships that the parts had to each other and how those relationships might be made more effective, efficient, and productive.

(continued)

■ ■ ■ ■ ■

VIGNETTE CONTINUED

ONE YEAR LATER

Several of the committees addressed their work with confidence and zeal, and when they didn't know what to do, they called their regional educational laboratory for advice and counsel. When committees seemed to falter or grow dispirited, the superintendent made herself an honorary member of each committee, providing attention to progress and celebrating small successes. This worked very well until the district hit a budget snag and faced a shortfall that needed immediate attention. The end-of-year state achievement tests were administered with high hopes for the results. The two schools that had gained increases the first year continued to gain the second year. The primary school principal had critical surgery soon after the Christmas season, and this school seemed not to regain its energy. The middle school suffered the loss of its band director in an automobile accident, causing an interruption in the instructional program, but revived enough to show small gains on the tests. At the close of the school year, the superintendent announced that she was accepting a position in a larger district in the northern part of the state. All the schools and community wondered, What will happen now?

VIGNETTE CRITIQUE QUESTIONS

1. What systems factors contributed to the success or failure of Hunter Hill's change effort?
2. From a systems perspective, what advice would you give to the district office planners or to the community supporters of this district?
3. This district's parts seemed not to be able to see beyond the shadow of their own role or school setting. If you had been superintendent, what might you have done in this narrative to change this situation?

SUMMARY

Systems work, systems thinking, and *systemic change and reform* are terms that have been used for some years but seem only fairly recently to have concrete definition. The ideas have been in the literature for decades, but this perspective has only recently been espoused for application in schools and school districts. In implementing change, it seems reasonable to consider all the parts of the system even when attempting to change only one or two elements. Theorists and practitioners have regularly pointed out the fallacy of not engaging in thinking about the entire system. Common sense suggests that punching on one part of the system will cause something to pop up in another part. Thus, in today's climate of addressing the challenge of organizational improvement, most especially school districts, attention to all parts of the system seems highly realistic. Interconnectedness and interrelationships must prosper for the system to operate effectively and efficiently. But this approach is no panacea as the citations in this text point out: There are multiple parts to any organization, and the systems approach requires consideration of all. "Complexity in a system occurs from the interaction of system variables over time . . . [and] complexity is complex, meaning that it is difficult if not impossible for humans, given their cognitive processing limitations, to comprehend—predict—phenomena under this condition" (Schneider & Somers, 2006), noted previously in the "Limitations of Working Systemically" section in this chapter. As with other approaches in systems thinking, monitoring the process is of high importance in order to make corrections when data deem it necessary. And there are limitations to this approach in education and other organizational reforms. Guiding and managing such efforts will require leaders who can take the balcony view (watching all elements of the system), who are conceptually and intellectually capable at a high level, who are quick witted and have the energy to act on short notice, and, above all, who continually care about the organization and its individuals. Those who would consider systems work will be advised to know as much about it as the literature makes possible.

REFLECTION QUESTIONS

What is the most compelling idea that you found in this chapter? Why did it grab your attention, or confirm your values or beliefs, or cause you to disagree strongly?

DISCUSSION QUESTIONS

1. Why would you want a school's administrators to think about their school's change efforts systemically?

2. What difference would it make to a district's or a state's change efforts if the effort were planned and executed with systems thinking?

3. Identify and discuss the key characteristics of highly effective leaders involved in systems work.

4. List and explain strategies that should be provided for a systemic reform to be successful.

5. For systems reform, hypothesize factors that could be considered to engage the participants in developing systems thinking.

FIELDWORK ACTIVITIES

1. Do you know an organization that operates in a systemic way? If so, describe it. If not, what topics would you use to study an organization to ascertain if it operated systemically?

2. Assume that an executive or superintendent asked you to identify any of her administrators who engage in systemic thinking. What characteristics would you look for?

3. Find a district, a school, a business, or another organization that has accomplished major change through a systems approach. Query the staff to learn (a) how it started, (b) who initiated the effort, (c) what parts of the system were key, and (d) how the staff knows it was successful or not successful.

CONDUCT A STUDY

1. Identify tools and interventions that are typically found in noncomprehensive or nonsystemic change. Apply these tools to the planning and implementation of a systemic effort. Observe and document the results, and compare them to results gained in nonsystemic change. Derive conclusions about the utility of using these tools and interventions in systemic processes.

2. What is the array of skills and knowledge that the facilitators of systemic change initiatives require? Design a descriptive study that will identify the skills, knowledge base, and qualities/characteristics of effective facilitators of systemic change.

ADDITIONAL READINGS/RESOURCES

Jenlink, P. M., Reigeluth, C. M., Carr, A. A., & Nelson, L. M. (1998). Guidelines for facilitating systemic change in school districts. *Systems Research and Behavioral Science,* 15, 217–233.

> This how-to-do-it monograph describes the characteristics and elements of a systemic change guidance system that builds on the principles of process facilitation and systems design. It examines the integral values or beliefs related to facilitation and systemic change, the types of events and activities typically needed, the processes that form the guidance system, and how to create the guidance system.

Joseph, R., Jenlink, P. M., Reigeluth, C. M., Carr-Chelman, A. A., & Nelson, L. M. (2002). Banathy's influence on the guidance system for transforming education. *World Futures, 58,* 379–394.

> This publication is a tribute to the work of Bela H. Banathy. The article identifies how Banathy has influenced the authors' work on systemic change in education, the crux of which is found in systems design. Systems design is a process that engages stakeholders in conversations about their visions, ideals, values, and aspirations with the goal of creating their ideal educational system. The authors identify the process values and the process activities that drive Banathy's theoretical framework and compare these to the values and activities that they have developed in their guidance system. The intention of the article, as noted in the title, is to demonstrate the extent to which Banathy's work has influenced the development of a guidance system for facilitating systemic change in public school districts.

CHAPTER 10

DIFFUSION
Communication and Change Agents

Scene One

This is really a neat new approach. I really get a thrill out of trying something new.
—Jim

I think I will wait for a while. It would be a big risk for me to try it and have it not work out.
—Mary

Greg says it really works well. That's good enough for me.
—José

That person from the university extension office seems to know what she is talking about. I understand what she is saying about why this is a better way.
—Greg

Scene Two

Two professors meet at an international conference and learn about a new research method. They return to their own home universities and introduce the method to their students.

If one approach to understanding change were to be selected as the grandparent of change models, the likely winner would be the Diffusion Perspective. The groundwork for this perspective was established early in the 20th century. Now, there are more than a hundred years of accumulated research findings and widespread applications of the many Diffusion constructs. One of the earliest contributors was French sociologist Gabriel Tarde (1903). As he reflected on change, one of his wonderments had to do with why so few innovations were actually used out of the hundreds that were conceived. Through his studies and writings he introduced many of the concepts that are still foundational to the Diffusion Perspective.

Ryan and Gross (1943) carried out a second seminal set of Diffusion studies. They examined the rate of adoption of hybrid corn seed in two communities in rural Iowa. Before the 1930s, the source of corn seed available to farmers was the ears of corn that had been stored over the winter in a specially designed crib or shed. Researchers at Iowa State University (ISU) had been developing hybrid corn seed specifically grown to include various plant characteristics such as disease resistance, consistent height, and a standard number of ears per stalk. In 1928, hybrid corn seed became available to farmers through the ISU Agricultural Extension Service and seed companies.

Hybrid corn seed at that time was an innovation. It also represented a new cost for farmers. Instead of using the seed available, for free, in the crib from last year's crop, farmers had to buy hybrid corn seed. As would be expected, some farmers made the decision to adopt hybrid corn seed quickly while others delayed for years. In the early 1940s, Ryan and Gross reviewed the history of the adoptions in two communities by interviewing well over three hundred farmers. Based on analyses of these interviews they proposed many of the key Diffusion constructs that are used to this day.

Since then, the research methods, study findings, and related constructs have been used to study a wide range of innovations and adopters. The characteristics of physicians and their rate of adoption of new pharmaceuticals have been studied. The adoptions of boiling water and steel-tipped plows by rural villagers have been studied, as has been the spread of disease such as AIDS. Diffusion constructs are regularly included in the training of sales representatives and applied to the introduction of new products and services.

Two key components of the Diffusion Perspective that will be reflected in the examples presented in this chapter are thinking about change as it takes place inside of *social systems* and the act of *communication*. In the Diffusion Perspective, information about a new idea becomes distributed throughout a social system by people talking to people. For example, farmers are members of their community, which is a social system. Any single farmer talks to some farmers a lot and to others very little or not at all. Their learning about and deciding to take on a new idea, such as hybrid corn seed, unfolds through communication.

Another important construct in the Diffusion Perspective is *adoption*. Rather than change being seen as an exploration and implementation process, as in Change Principle 2 (Chapter 1), in the Diffusion Perspective the emphasis is on each individual making an *adoption decision*. Third World villagers either boil water or they do not. Physicians either prescribe a new drug or they do not. Individual consumers decide to purchase a hybrid car or a flat-screen TV, or not. They work their way through a decision-making process. In the end they either adopt the new idea or continue with their traditional practice.

The leading scholar for the Diffusion Perspective remains Everett Rogers. For nearly 50 years he contributed as a researcher, educator, and leading spokesperson for the Diffusion Perspective. His classic book, *Diffusion of Innovations* (2003), is a very informative and useful resource. Key constructs from the Diffusion Perspective will be introduced in this chapter along with illustrations of how they can be used to implement change.

FOCUS QUESTIONS

1. How do characteristics of adopters affect their decision to adopt?
2. What methods are used to understand the innovation communication process?

3. What is it about some adopters that make them so influential with those who have not yet adopted a new idea?
4. How is the innovation defined in the Diffusion Perspective?
5. What is the role of the change agent?
6. What does the construct of critical mass have to do with change?

COMMUNICATION WITHIN THE LINES AND NETWORKS?

Many of the findings from Diffusion research are obvious and interesting. Once stated, the immediate reaction can be "Well, of course, but I had not labeled it." No matter how obvious the findings may seem, they can be useful and often are overlooked. In some ways, the findings from studies related to lines of communication are like this. They seem to be more obvious in hindsight than appreciated as a change process is unfolding. One basic finding is that communication about the innovation occurs along the established lines, or channels, of communication.

Components of Interpersonal Communication

Interpersonal sharing of information about an innovation is core to understanding change from the Diffusion Perspective. In a social system the spread of adoptions is mainly driven by people communicating with others. Keep in mind that in a social system the distances may be large and therefore the spread of information across the system will not be even. Face-to-face communication requires proximity, but distance is not a factor with electronic communication. Corporate and professional social systems are spread across states and nations that have near instantaneous communication. Still, the type and layout of the lines of communication can enhance or inhibit the transmittal of information.

A wonderful illustration of the role of communication lines can be seen in a study by House, Steele, & Kerins (1971). In 1963, the state of Illinois established a grant program that provided state funds to school districts for gifted and talented student activities. The program was voluntary, but if school districts applied they received funding. Each year, House et al. plotted the statewide distribution of school districts that received the grants (see Figure 10.1). This plot graphically illustrates two key points from the Diffusion Perspective.

First, the researchers found that there were more adoptions in those parts of the state with larger cities and where there were universities. (A criterion for receiving the grant was to partner with a university.) Do not miss the key point with this generalization. Yes, there are more schools and districts in cities. From the Diffusion Perspective the generalization is this: Where there are more people, there will be more and earlier adoptions, since there is greater likelihood of adopters exchanging information about the innovation and perhaps seeing it in use.

The second finding, which is so well represented in Figure 10.1, is that adoption of innovations occurs along the lines of communication. The lines of communication in this case are the U.S. highways. In the 1960s, the network of U.S. highways was the main travel pattern within the state. Early adoptions of the gifted and talented grants occurred mainly along these highways. For adoption of innovations in other settings, think of the U.S. highways as a metaphor for the lines of communication. In other systems the lines of communication would not be highways per se, but the equivalent could be the regularly traveled corridors in a school

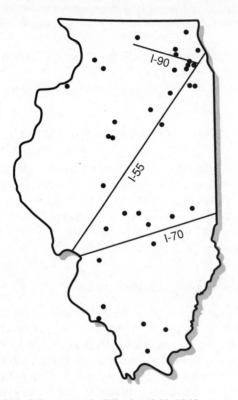

FIGURE 10.1   Spread of Gifted Programs in Illinois, 1964–1965

Source: Based on E. R. House, J. Steele, & C. T. Kerins, *The gifted classroom.* Urbana, IL: Center for Instructional Research and Curriculum Evaluation, University of Illinois, 1971.

or office building. They also could be the regularly traveled streets between headquarters and a satellite office. People who are in the loop are likely to receive more and earlier information than will those who are more isolated.

Pothole Warning

Do not assume that communication is always one way and in a straight line and accurate.

Pothole Repair

Communication is often multidirectional with one person sharing with several others. Also, the content of communication can be distorted when passed along, so repeating the original content and checking for distortions are important steps.

Understanding Communication Networks.   Another useful tool for understanding communication about an innovation is to analyze the social networks. Whether the system is a geographic region, a community, or a school, some people will be more closely connected to others, and some will have little or no connection with many others. Diffusion researchers will

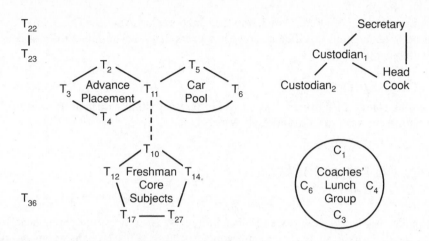

FIGURE 10.2   Social Networks in One High School

make charts of the connections each person has with others. They will identify the different cliques as well as the individuals who are more isolated socially. An example of this charting is presented in Figure 10.2. The data for this type of sociogram can be obtained by observing and asking about who talks to whom. Which people eat lunch together? Which departments/grade levels are more cohesive? Who never attends meetings? Who seems to be most aware of what is going on across the whole system? Who plays on the softball or bowling team or is part of the quilting group? Whose Twitter tweets or Facebook pages are monitored and talked about the most? Charting the interpersonal networks is very useful for understanding to whom information about the innovation will spread more quickly and who will have less opportunity to learn about the change. People with more connections to others will be in a better position to learn more and learn it earlier than those with fewer networks. The same people will be able to tell others and share more information because they have more contacts.

Implications of Communication Networks for Facilitating Change.   Failure to attend to the lines or channels of communication is regularly observed in change efforts. Instead of thinking of a state as the social system, as was the case in Figure 10.2, think about the geography of a school campus. What are the lines of communication in this case? If an innovation is to be introduced through a pilot or demonstration site, which classroom should be selected? Do not select a classroom that is far off the highway that prospective adopters travel daily. Instead of having the pilot done in a remote portable classroom, select a classroom that is on the direct route to the staff parking lot or on the way to the office or the staff lounge.

Once a sociogram has been developed, use it. From the Diffusion Perspective, working with T36 (in Figure 10.2) makes no sense. Apparently, this teacher does not associate with any others. Therefore, he or she will have little communication with others about the innovation. The most obvious candidate to persuade to become involved early is T11. This person is interconnected with three groups. Whatever T11 says and does has the potential of being shared with 10 colleagues. If T11 likes the innovation, then a number of other prospective adopters are likely to hear about it. The corollary is also true. If T11 does not like the innovation, a number of other prospective adopters are likely to hear about that. Also, the Coaches' Lunch Group will need to be targeted specifically, since it appears that it has minimal lines of communication with other groups.

REFLECTION QUESTION

Take another look at Figure 10.2. Who would be the primary target for communication within the support staff clique? Why?

COMMUNICATION OF INNOVATIONS: WHO IS DOING WHAT?

In the Diffusion Perspective, change is seen first and foremost as a process of communication. Initially, a new idea is introduced to a few members of a social system. Through various means of communication, word of the new idea is passed to other members. Over time, most members become aware of the innovation and may adopt it. Understanding communication processes is a core component of the Diffusion Perspective. Knowing who is talking with whom and what is being said about the innovation are important. Identifying the paths along which information is communicated and charting the interpersonal linkages are other important tools. Keep in mind that the medium that is used can include more than talk. Radio, print, television, e-mail, the Web, and texting are important sources for learning about an innovation.

Communication Elements: Sources, Targets, and Media

An often overlooked, and certainly underappreciated, element of change is the talk that occurs among the various members of a social system. The Diffusion Perspective highlights the importance of these actions. Consider each of the following quite typical interactions:

> In a regional sales meeting, the manager tells the sales representatives about a new product line that will soon be available.
>
> Two teachers talk about how things are going with their students' efforts to incorporate digital photos into their reports.
>
> A farmer goes to the Web to find information about the best interval to use between each planting. The farmer then shares the information with a neighbor by e-mail.
>
> A teacher Tweets.

When reminded that change entails communication, it is easy to see how each of these actions would be especially important to the adoption of an innovation. In any change effort hundreds of these types of interactions take place. At a minimum, change leaders and researchers need to be fully aware that there is a lot of talk taking place.

Sometimes it can be useful to develop a record and count of the various communications that are taking place. A simple, but useful, coding system for doing this is presented in Table 10.1. As is described in Chapter 7, this basic coding system has been used to count and categorize interventions in several year-long studies.

TABLE 10.1 Codes for Use in Analyzing One-on-One Communications in a School

I. SOURCE	II. TARGET	III. MEDIA	IV. PURPOSE
IA. Principal	IIA. Principal	IIIA. Face to face	IVA. Provide information
IB. Assistant Principal	IIB. Assistant Principal	IIIB. Phone	
IC. Department Chair	IIC. Department Chair	IIIC. Cell phone	IVB. Seek information
English	English	Twitter	
Social Studies	Social Studies	IIID. E-mail	IVC. Non-innovation related
Science	Science	Web	
Math	Math	IIIE. Print	
ID. Teacher	IID. Teacher	IIIG. Other	
Mary	Mary		
Alice	Alice		
Rosetta	Rosetta		
IE. Secretary	IIE. Secretary		
IF. Technology	IIF. Technology		
Web	Web		
E-mail	E-mail		
IG. Other	IIG. Other		

Sources of Communication.   Communication begins with someone initiating action. In an organization setting, it can be fairly easy to find out who said something. This set of codes could be adjusted and expanded to name who initiated communication actions in a single school, or any other type of organization. Obtaining information about all the sources of action across several schools, a school district, or a state would be increasingly difficult. But the same approach to coding would work. If a careful record is kept for 1 or 2 weeks, or for months, the frequency count would be informative. These data would provide direct evidence about who is initiating the most communication, as well as who may not be communicating with anyone.

Targets of Communication.   The list of codes that is developed for *Sources* generally will work for *Targets*. The Source initiates communication with a Target. The Target is the recipient of the communication. Knowing the frequency with which each person is targeted provides an indication of how well informed he or she may be. Note that technology (e.g., e-mail and the Web) can be listed as a Source, a Target, and Media.

Media in Communication.   Another useful set of codes addresses the form that was used to make the communication. In most change efforts, face-to-face interactions will be frequent. However, other Media forms are increasingly being used. Especially e-mail, the Web, cell phones, and text messaging.

Purpose of Communication.   The last column in the Communication Coding System in Table 10.1 addresses the purpose or intention of the communication. The purpose is defined in relation to the Source of the communication action. What did the Source intend with each communication action? The Target may have a purpose, too. Another column could be established to document the Target's perception of the action. One of the important cautions to keep in mind relative to the purpose is that setting a certain intention does not guarantee that the desired result followed. All too often what is intended in a particular communication is not what is heard by the Target. As is described in Chapter 8, miscommunication can have serious consequences for a change effort.

Coding Communication Actions in General.   The list of codes in Table 10.1 easily can be expanded to track communications within a particular setting, such as a school. The names of individuals could be listed, the purposes could be more detailed, and other forms of Media could be named. The same approach could be used to code interactions in any type of organization or other social system. Other categories of codes could be added, such as whether the interaction is two way or one way or is concurrent or delayed. A simple form could be devised to code each interaction, or the key ones could be noted in a personal digital assistant (PDA). If a PDA were used, it would be easy to keep track of the date when each interaction occurred. Sometimes being able to review when a certain communication took place is important information.

Implications of Coding Communications for Facilitating Change.   As obvious as each of the findings from Diffusion research may be, it is surprising how frequently findings are ignored when change is being implemented. In some cases, actions are taken that are exactly opposite what the coding of actions should suggest. For example, keeping track of the most active sources of communication provides clues as to whom to target to help with sharing additional information. Asking someone who does not initiate many communication actions to tell others about the innovation is not likely to result in information being spread rapidly.

REFLECTION QUESTIONS

Pick a change effort during which you were an active communicator. Which Targets did you communicate with most frequently? Why did you emphasize these particular Targets?

IMPLICATIONS FOR LEADERS FACILITATING CHANGE

1. Keep in mind that communication is never done. Making on announcement in a staff meeting or sending everyone an e-mail does not mean that everyone "received" the message. It is very important to repeat messages and to use a variety of Media to say the same thing. Off-site opportunities to communicate are important, too. Carpools, meetings at the district office or headquarters, and train and plane time are important opportunities during which to share information.

IMPLICATIONS FOR LEADERS FACILITATING CHANGE   CONTINUED

2. The metaphor of the U.S. highway system representing the lines of communication can easily be applied in organizational settings. Teachers, or other employees, travel certain routes as they come in from the parking lot, as they pick up mail, and as they go to the cafeteria. Amazingly, many change efforts do not take advantage of this phenomenon. Use it! Set up the demonstration classroom, the innovation exhibit, examples of kids w ork along the lines of communication. Be visible and introduce information by deliberately inserting it into these channels.

3. The importance of Opinion Leadership and Opinion Leaders cannot be underestimated. One of the early activities in any change effort is for the change agent(s) to identify the Opinion Leaders. These individuals need to be courted and sold on the importance of the innovation. If they adopt the new idea, then others will follow. If they resist, others will follow their lead.

4. If the Adopter Category studies are accepted, then early in a change effort there is little reason to engage with the Late Majority and Laggards. However, there are some exceptions. For example, if an individual with many of the characteristics of a laggard is a leader of a key unit, then that person must be courted. With that person's understanding and support, the rate of adoption will be much faster.

5. An external change agent needs to build linkages with the Opinion Leader(s). There is a personal side to this process, which may mean talking about hobbies, playing golf, or joining in some other, more social, activities. Most change agents are not seen as all business.

6. Be alert to the interpersonal connections. Sociograms become a very useful tool for charting relationships. Members of one group will have similar levels of knowledge about the innovation. Knowing which individuals participate in multiple groups is important, since they can pass information across groups.

CHARACTERISTICS OF ADOPTERS

Probably the most widely studied and shared ideas from Diffusion research are those related to the characteristics of adopters. An early research question for Diffusion researchers was this: Why do some people adopt an innovation quickly and others take longer? Even when there are obvious advantages, some people take longer to make the adoption decision. Literally thousands of studies have examined the characteristics of adopters. A major part of the Ryan and Gross (1943) study of farmers adopting hybrid corn seed addressed this question. Many studies have been done in Third World countries as various technological innovations have been introduced. Out of all the studies a general set of Adopter Categories has been agreed upon, and extensive descriptions of the characteristics of each have been established. Use of these categories is widespread in business and technology transfer. However, keep in mind that each of these categories is a composite and that real people will vary from these archetypes.

Five Adopter Categories

A number of variations on the names and number of categories of adopters have been proposed. Today use of five categories is widespread: Innovators, Early Adopters, Early Majority, Late Majority, and Laggards. Curiously, these categories and their associated characteristics tend to hold up across innovations and cultures.

Innovators Are Excited about Trying Something New.   The very first people to adopt an innovation are the *Innovators*. Rogers (2003) calls them "venturesome." They enjoy change for the sake of change. They are always looking for new ideas and are ready to try them. Innovators tend to be more cosmopolitan and have more extensive networks. In schools, these are the teachers who are very active in their profession regionally and perhaps nationally. Through their more extensive networks, they are likely to hear about new ideas first and bring them back to the local setting. In business and agriculture, the Innovators tend to be more wealthy. Their companies have larger budgets, and the farms have more acreage. This means that trying a new idea on a few acres doesn't equate to "betting the whole farm." There is less risk if an adoption fails. Innovators also tend to see themselves as having control over their destiny (internality), rather than being the victim of circumstances (externality).

Early Adopters Think Before Adopting.   *Early Adopters* adopt new ideas quite quickly but only after reasoned consideration. They are respected locally and tend to have been in place for an extended time. Their focus is local, and they are seen by their colleagues as solid, sensible decision makers. Once they adopt an innovation, because they are respected others will look more favorably on it.

Early Majority Are Careful.   Where the Innovators and Early Adopters are fairly quick to adopt, the *Early Majority* are more deliberate. They take time and give more consideration in making the adoption decision. They are connected to others but less likely to have positions of influence, as is characteristic of Early Adopters. The Early Majority represent a large proportion of the potential adopters. Rogers (2003) estimates that 34 percent of the potential adopters will have characteristics of the Early Majority. This makes them an important Target for those who want to see an innovation adopted by many individuals.

Late Majority Are Cautious.   The *Late Majority* are slow to adopt and tend to do so only when there is pressure from others or the need becomes very strong. They need more pressure to make the change. For example, if they are losing market share or can no longer afford to compete against the success of those who have already adopted, they will move toward making the change. They approach change with doubts and caution. Rogers (2003) estimates that in the typical population the Late Majority represents about 34 percent. However, they the Late Majority tend to want to avoid risk because the cost of failure will be much higher for them.

Laggards Resist the New.   This label brings with it an unfortunate negative connotation. However, as the name implies, *Laggards* are very slow, and even resistant, to the adoption of new ideas. They are more conservative, more provincial or isolated, with less education and more limited resources. They are traditional in outlook and take a very long time to make an adoption decision. In other words, they are resistant to change. As one of our colleagues once observed, "They would complain if you hung them with a new rope." Laggards are a cause and a victim of their circumstances. Since, in general, they are less well educated, more conservative, and less wealthy, change presents more risk. Since Laggards have fewer connections to others, they also will likely have less information and understanding about the potential benefits of the innovation and less resources to invest in making an adoption successful. The consequence of these characteristics and conditions is that Laggards are more likely to be trapped in place.

Pothole Warning

Do not assume that all Laggards can be ignored until they see the need to adopt the innovation.

Pothole Repair

Often persons with the characteristics of Laggards will have a responsible position and can undercut adoption by others. An exciting and regularly observed possibility is for some Laggards to become excited about the innovation.

THE FLOW OF INFORMATION ACROSS ADOPTER CATEGORIES

As already stated, the primary theme in the Diffusion Perspective is communication. Close attention is placed on understanding the ways and the hows of communication. Examining who communicates and how their communications are interpreted are important for change leaders to understand. These understandings can then be used to increase the *rate of adoption*. One important characteristic of adopters is *Opinion Leadership*. Another is understanding the way *communication flows* across the five Adopter Categories.

Opinion Leaders

In any social system or organization some people will be seen as the solid citizens. They are well respected and turned to when expert advise is needed. They are the trusted colleagues. In other words, they are the *Opinion Leaders*. These individuals have extra influence, although they tend to be more low profile. They probably have been in the system for quite some time, are successful in their own practices, and have had some leadership roles. At the same time, they tend to not be flashy and not apt to engage in change for the sake of change. When it is important to obtain sound insight or advice about what is happening in a particular situation, the Opinion Leaders are the ones who are sought out.

Opinion Leadership varies across the Adopter Categories. Innovators have some influence at home, but in many ways they are seen as the ones who are always ready to try crazy ideas. They are not always trusted to have the best advice. The Early Adopters are the strongest in Opinion Leadership. They are the ones who the other members of the system respect and to whom they turn. If they adopt an innovation and have favorable ideas about it, others will look more favorably on making the adoption decision. Innovators may be the first to introduce a new idea, but it is the Opinion Leadership of the Early Adopters that others follow.

Communicating Across Adopter Categories

A related insight from Diffusion research is the general pattern of flow of communication across the Adopter Categories. This can be thought about in terms of where people are most likely to get their information. (This is another way to think about Sources and Targets.) The Innovators obtain a lot of their information through their extensive external networks, whereas the Laggards have very limited sources of information. In between are the other Adopter Categories.

Each Adopter Category has more communication with its adjacent Adopter Categories than those farther away. There also is a directionality to the flow of communication that parallels the time of adoption. For example, the Early Majority learns from the Early Adopters. As adoptions spread within the Early Majority cohort, the Late Majority is learning from them. In other words, there is a general flow of communication, as well as adoptions, from Innovator, to Early Adopter, to Early Majority, to Late Majority, and finally to Laggards.

The Rate of Innovation Adoptions

Another theme within the Diffusion Perspective has to do with how quickly the adoption of an innovation spreads across a social system. We know of many innovations, such as all-day kindergarten, that have taken decades to be adopted by most states and schools, as well as other innovations, such as cell phones, that seem to be adopted by everyone within months. Studies of the rate of adoption document these differences. For example, Mort (1953) charted the adoption of kindergartens beginning in the early 1900s and found that it had taken 50 years for most states and school districts to adopt kindergartens. It should be noted that even now, another 50 years later, some states, such as Nevada, still do not have all-day kindergarten required for all children. Compare the rate of adoption of kindergarten with technologies such as cell phones or flat screen TVs. These innovations have been adopted rapidly worldwide. Still the Adopter Categories can be observed. For example, business executives were the first to adopt mobile phones back in the 1980s when the phones were provided by their companies. Today in some social systems, such as Hong Kong or Finland, the adoption rate can be over 100% due to some adopters having more than one phone: worldwide adoption within 30 years!

The S Curve Explains It All

Another of the many contributions of Ryan and Gross (1943) was the introduction of the S curve as a way to graphically chart the rate of adoption. Figure 10.3 is an example of the S curve and includes the typical distribution of adopters by category. Nearly all studies of the rate of adoption result in a curve of this shape. The difference from innovation to innovation will be in the steepness of the curve. In other words, as with the examples of kindergartens and cell phones, the rate of adoption across time can be charted as an S curve, but the amount of time can vary dramatically.

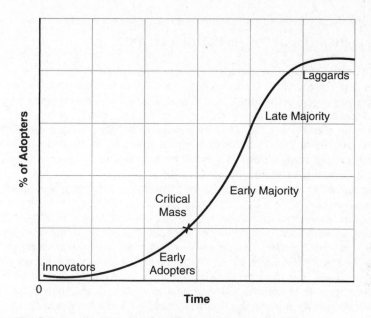

FIGURE 10.3   The S Curve for Rate of Adoption by Adopter Categories

As the S curve illustrates, adoption of an innovation starts slowly and then gradually picks up speed. The curve then progresses upward until nearly all of the potential adopters have adopted the innovation. The timeline for moving from few to most having adopted the innovation can vary from a few months, to years, to decades, to hundreds of years, if ever.

The other concept addressed in Figure 10.3 is the relationship between Adopter Categories and the rate of adoption. The Innovators are few (typically 2–3% of a population) so that the rate of adoption doesn't begin to accelerate until the Early Adopters accept the innovation. This is followed by periods of steady growth as the Early Majority and then the Late Majority adopt the innovation. As the S curve approaches 100%, the rate of adoption slows with gradual acceptance of the innovation by Laggards.

Critical Mass Signifies an Important Point.   One of the themes of the Diffusion Perspective is that communication about and adoption of an innovation flows across the Adopter Categories. A related assumption is that at a certain point, activity and rate of adoption are sufficient so that the process will become self sustaining. In other words the process will reach *critical mass*. Just as the atomic reaction in a nuclear bomb is self sustaining at a certain point, Diffusion theorists see a similar phenomenon happening with the adoption of an innovation. There is a point when enough adoptions have taken place and awareness of the innovation has spread far enough that further adoptions will occur without outside pressures. The actual point along the S curve at which critical mass occurs seems to range from 16% to 40%. Given the complexity of the change process in any system, it makes sense that the actual point of critical mass would vary. The key idea being introduced here is that at some point, according to Diffusion theorists, the continued adoption of an innovation within a social system should become self sustaining.

GUIDING PRINCIPLES OF THE DIFFUSION PERSPECTIVE

1. The Diffusion Perspective applies to all types of systems, including schools, businesses, and communities. A social system may be more local, such as the farmers in a geographic region or the employees in a school. A social system may be geographically dispersed, such as the participants in a Web chat room.
2. The amount of communication and the number of people engaged in making and receiving communications is a key to adoption rates. More communication and with more people will have a positive effect. Those with fewer connections and involvement will be slower to adopt.
3. Innovators are the first to adopt new ideas; however, they are less influential as Opinion Leaders. They certainly are Opinion Leaders, but the Early Adopters are most influential.
4. Perceptions of the innovation influence the rate of adoption. Innovations that are seen as having an advantage over current practice, not being complicated, being able to be sampled, and matching well with current values are more likely to be adopted.
5. Opinion Leaders are a key to the rate of adoption. Their views and adoption decisions influence others. Early Adopters are highest in Opinion Leadership.
6. Lines or channels of communication become important because those who have more access will have more and earlier information about the innovation.
7. Information about an innovation will travel fastest when there are more lines or channels of communication and more people. This is true within a building as well as across a region.

Implications of Adopter Categories for Facilitating Change.   Social systems and organizations will have individuals that represent each of the Adopter Categories. The meaning of wealth may differ. For example, the wealth of farmers might be indicated by the quantity of acreage they own, whereas wealth for a sales representative could be the quantity of technology (e.g. laptops, GPS systems, Web connections) used to reach potential customers. Still, change facilitators can use the Adopter Categories to identify Opinion Leaders and to think about which individuals are most likely to be first, second, or later to make an adoption decision. They also should realize that the rate of adoption will start slowly and with time increase, as illustrated in the S curve.

REFLECTION QUESTIONS

As you think about yourself and your colleagues, which Adopter Category best represents you? What are the indicators that lead you to make this conclusion?

OTHER DIFFUSION CONSTRUCTS: PERCEPTIONS OF THE INNOVATION AND CHARACTERISTICS OF CHANGE AGENTS

Two other important and useful sets of ideas from the Diffusion Perspective have to do with how the innovation may be viewed by adopters and the role of the change agent. Both of these ideas have important and useful implications for implementing change in organizations as well as other social systems.

Perceived Attributes of the Innovation

Instead of defining an innovation in terms of its function, or its pieces, or its intents, in the Diffusion Perspective the innovation is considered in terms of how it is *perceived* by prospective adopters. Regardless of whether the perceptions are accurate or inaccurate, understanding how the innovation may be viewed by adopters is important to understand. In many ways perception is reality. If an innovation is perceived to have certain attributes, then those perceptions must be considered as real and need to be addressed. There is general acceptance in the Diffusion Perspective of the following five perceived attributes of innovations.

Relative Advantage.   One obvious comparison prospective adopters make is to appraise the potential of the innovation to have an advantage over current practice. There could be a perception that the innovation will have greater outcomes, profits, or consequences when compared to what is being done currently. For example, a computer program that keeps an up-to-the-minute inventory based on today's sales could reduce warehousing costs. A particular hybrid wheat seed that is disease resistant could have higher yields. Teachers could perceive that a particular set of curriculum materials will lead to higher student test scores. Each of these examples is based on a perception of the innovation having an advantage over current practice. Relative advantage could be related to other factors besides effects. For example, the innovation may be cheaper to use in terms of money or time, or the innovation may present a potential increase in status. Perceptions that are favorable will tend to increase the rate of adoption. Inversely, the adoption rate will be slowed when the innovation is perceived as not being as good in some way as what is currently being done.

Compatibility.   The degree to which the innovation is perceived to be compatible with the adopter's values, needs, and concerns influences the adoption decision. Prospective adopters weigh the innovation in terms of how well it matches with what they see as important values and cultural norms. In some groups driving an SUV is still "in," whereas in others it would be seen as unacceptable. These are values-based decisions. Higher compatibility will increase the chances of an affirmative adoption decision, whereas perceptions of incompatibility will decrease the rate of adoption. One of the authors of this book had a Taiwanese graduate student drop his course on change "because the course was not taught by lecture." In hindsight, given the student's cultural background, it is easy to understand how he could have had the perception of incompatibility.

Complexity.   The importance of this perceived attribute is obvious. Innovations that are perceived to be very complex are likely to be adopted more slowly. Innovations that are perceived to be simple to implement and use will be more readily adopted. Technology innovations are an easy example to use to illustrate complexity. The earliest VCRs were complicated to use. A dozen steps were required to record a program, and failing to do any of the steps would mean that the desired program would not be recorded. Today's devices automatically analyze the programs watched and then record like programs in the future. Which form of technology will be perceived as less complicated? About which will adopters tell others "It is easy to use"?

　　Complexity misperception is a serious problem for educational innovations. All too often policymakers, education experts, and parents will perceive that a particular educational innovation is simple and will be easy to implement. However, teachers will perceive the same innovation as complex and difficult to use in the classroom. These types of misperceptions make for interesting case studies of change attempts.

Pothole Warning

It is all too easy for policymakers and leaders at the top of organizations to perceive that a particular innovation is uncomplicated, whereas those who have to implement it perceive that it is very complicated. If the innovation is perceived as simple, then there will be less understanding of the need for extensive implementation support.

Pothole Repair

Policymakers and leaders need to think more about how an innovation will be perceived. It might in fact be simple, but if it is perceived as complex this perception will need to be addressed. If it really is complex, more will need to be done to facilitate implementation.

Trialability.   Innovations that are easy to try out have an increased adoption potential—in other words, trialability. Test driving a hybrid car provides useful information. It is much more difficult to try out a new assembly-line process or a year-long science curriculum. To address this potential limitation, many innovation developers create samplers and trial activities. With other innovations it may be possible to test it in a limited way before making a 100% commitment. This happens when a farmer plants one field with new seed and the rest of the fields with regular seed. In schools, textbook adoption processes frequently include opportunities for some teachers to try out sample units. Being able to sample a component and experience success positively affects the adoption decision.

Observability.   Observability entails being able to see the innovation in use and to see the results. When observability is high, a favorable adoption decision is more likely. Some innovations are easy to see. A drive through the Midwest in summer presents an easy-to-see example of observability: cornfield rows that are posted with signs shaped like corn ears that designate the particular hybrid that has been planted, such as "DeKalb 6746." Farmers can stop, look over each row of corn, and see for themselves what each type of seed produces. The farmer is then in a better position to decide which seed to purchase next year. This is a classic example of observability. It is also a classic example of how the findings from Diffusion research can be used to increase the rate of adoption of an innovation.

Addressing Perceived Attributes of the Innovation

One of the generalizations derived from the Diffusion Perspective is that the more positive the perceptions of the innovation, the more likely the chances are of having a favorable adoption decision. We are talking about perceptions, not objective reality. If the perception is there, then it is a reality that should be considered. Each of the perceived attributes represents an area that can be anticipated and that can be addressed. To the extent perceptions are addressed, adoptions should be higher.

■ ■ ■ ■ ■ ■

VIGNETTE
HERE WE GO AGAIN!

THE BEGINNING

When Sara Johnson returned from her meeting at the district office with other building union representatives, she couldn't wait to spread the word. She immediately talked with her close colleague who also was very active in the union. The superintendent had had some sort of meeting with a nationally prominent professor from an out-of-state research university. Now the district was buying a new program, and soon teachers would be receiving special training. Sara did not see any reason why the district should be spending money on another program when teachers needed a raise. "Besides," said Sara, "today's kids just don't study. If they spoke English and did their homework, we wouldn't even be talking about changing the curriculum."

Sara did not hear that the visiting professor was the creator of a research-based curriculum program that was designed to increase the achievement of at-risk students in urban schools. All Sara heard was that teachers were going to have to change their teaching "one more time." Her primary concern had to do with whether or not teachers would be paid for the time spent in training. Having been a teacher in the district for 27 years, she was "fed up" with having to do things without real compensation.

Bev White, the literacy coordinator, had attended the meeting and was very excited about the new program. She saw it as a real possibility for helping at-risk kids succeed. She also liked that the plan included regular visits by the professor's staff to help teachers adopt this program. Bev immediately scheduled a meeting with the district literacy committee, which included teacher representatives from each building. Her first call was to Paul Borchardt, an outstanding literacy teacher in one of the most poverty-stricken parts of town. He listened carefully, asked a few questions, and agreed that this sounded like a good opportunity. Paul said that he would e-mail three of his fellow committee members and would tell several colleagues in his school over lunch.

AN ANALYSIS WITH NEXT STEPS

This vignette is unfolding in typical fashion. News about a meeting, a decision, and a new initiative are beginning to be communicated across a "user system." Different versions and different perceptions are being shared. Constructs from the Diffusion Perspective can be used to diagnose the current situation and in planning next steps.

The change agent in this case is the university professor and her associates. In another way, Bev White is an "internal" change agent. Bev will have day-to-day responsibility for districtwide implementation of the change. The Adopter Categories can be applied—but carefully. In some ways, the categories are too simplistic and it is too easy to label someone. Still, it sounds like Sara has some of the characteristics of Laggards. She and Bev have different perceptions of the innovation. Sara does not see anything wrong with current practice (relative advantage) and believes funds should be spent on teacher salaries instead of a new program (compatibility).

Paul seems to be an Early Adopter. Bev turns to him first, which suggests strength as an Opinion Leader, but Paul is careful although positive and ready to communicate with others. A beginning sociogram would have Sara and her fellow building representatives in one group, with Paul and the other literacy-building representatives in another group. Then there are Sara and her union interests.

The Diffusion Perspective can help formulate some questions at this point, too. Bev is connected to the district literacy committee, but what are her committee members' connections to their union building representative members? To what extent do Paul and his building union representatives network? What about Sara and the literacy-building representatives in her school?

(continued)

■ ■ ■ ■ ■ ▬▬▬▬▬▬▬▬▬▬▬▬▬▬▬▬▬▬▬▬▬▬▬▬▬▬▬▬▬▬▬▬▬▬

VIGNETTE CONTINUED

A lot of positive and timely communication to all teachers is also needed. Bev needs to get ahead of Sara's message to all teachers. Immediate communication with the principals is also needed. The communication channels depend on what is available. Maybe there is a listserv for teachers. Hopefully a principal meeting is taking place very soon during which the superintendent can explain his vision and agenda. Of course, these messages will need to be repeated and sent via multiple Media. For example, Bev could prepare a one-page handout that the superintendent could ask principals to share with their teachers.

The constructs of observability and trialability would be useful to consider. Perhaps one or two schools or classrooms could pilot the program. Other teachers could then see the program in action. Of course, the highways metaphor is an important consideration here. Paul's classroom would be a logical one to choose, but we don't know if he is on the "highway" or off the beaten path.

Identifying Early Adopters and getting them ready to consider and adopt the new approach will be another important part of the effort. Bev should be able to assume that the teachers on the district literacy committee will be excited about the new program. Bev should ask them to start communicating back in their buildings about the importance of this opportunity and to show that they personally are supportive.

From here out, communication must continue, and as adoptions begin, it is important that the early implementers have success. They will be communicating to the Early Majority and, in time, the Late Majority.

VIGNETTE CRITIQUE QUESTIONS

1. What about the fact that in most organizations, including schools, adoption of an innovation happens at the same time for everyone? The Diffusion Perspective assumes that individuals make the adoption decision at different times. When the district decides to adopt a curriculum, all teachers are expected to adopt it. Are these two views incompatible?
2. To what extent should constructs from the Diffusion Perspective be shared? Should Bev tell members of her committee that these constructs are being used? For example, sociograms could be constructed and used to plan communication activity. Who should see these? Also, in the case of sociograms, which individuals and groupings would you want to see charted?
3. In many ways, *Laggard* is a pejorative term. Still, the construct seems to be real. How can it be used in positive ways? In this vignette, Sara cannot be ignored, so what should be done?

THE ROLE OF CHANGE AGENTS

A very important role in the Diffusion Perspective is that of a change agent:

> A *change agent* is an individual who influences clients' innovation-decisions in a direction deemed desirable by a change agency. A change agent usually seeks to secure the adoption of new ideas, but he or she may also attempt to slow the diffusion process and prevent the adoption of certain innovations with undesirable effects. (Rogers, 2003, p. 366)

In much Diffusion work the change agent is an external innovation expert who engages with the client system to introduce and encourage adoption of the innovation. The change agent has expert knowledge about the innovation and its use. The change agent also needs to be expert in understanding how the Diffusion process works.

A good and very effective example of a change agent is the agricultural extension agent, who typically is housed at a state university that has an agricultural research station and related academic programs. These agents also staff county extension offices. Extension agents learn from university researchers and then travel around the state and introduce farmers to the latest findings and ideas about best practices. Pharmaceutical sales representatives serve in the same way with physicians. They are the *linking agents* who provide a personal connection between the researchers and the adopters. They are skilled at translating and applying what the researchers have been studying.

In addition to expert knowledge about the innovation and its use, change agents also possess appropriate interpersonal skills for interacting with clients. When potential adopters perceive a commonality with a change agent, the potential of a favorable adoption decision increases. The mode of attire, the kind of car, and even whether one smokes or drinks can make a difference in change agent effectiveness. Change agents may be more effective with some clients and have more difficulty in matching up with the values and interests of others. Patience and the skill to listen are other important characteristics.

Frequency of contact also becomes an important indicator of change agent effectiveness. More frequent contact should be associated with increases in adoption rates. However, it is possible to wear out one's welcome. Here again, becoming an effective change agent requires being sensitive to people and their needs, as well as being expert with the innovation.

REFLECTION QUESTIONS

In your work life, who are the change agents? How closely do they fit the description presented in this chapter?

SUMMARY

The Diffusion Perspective has a long and rich tradition of research and widespread application. Many of the constructs, such as the five Adopter Categories, have become standard content in the training of sales representatives and others who have change agent roles.

Diffusion constructs will be introduced to college students in business, education, nursing, communication, and other disciplines. In addition to viewing change as a communication process, the Diffusion Perspective focuses on the decision to adopt. Other perspectives focus less on this decision and emphasize other aspects, such as the process of implementation. Still, the Diffusion Perspective offers a number of well-tested and effective tools that can be applied by those who are engaged in facilitating change and those who are studying change processes.

DISCUSSION QUESTIONS

1. Use the Diffusion constructs introduced in this chapter to analyze the quotes that were introduced at the beginning of this chapter. Which Adopter Categories are represented? What should a change agent do after hearing each?

2. Choose an innovation that you, or others, are currently considering or have recently adopted. Use the perceived attributes to analyze the innovation and the various communications that took place as it was being adopted.

3. Think about a change agent you have experienced. Was this person housed inside or outside? What was the person's level of expertise with the innovation? What were the person's interpersonal strengths?

4. Think about a social system you know well, such as a church, family, community, or business. In that setting, who is an Opinion Leader? What characteristics are key to this person being an Opinion Leader? Which side of an adoption decision did he or she represent?

6. In the Diffusion Perspective, adoption of an innovation is typically seen as a decision that an individual makes. Farmers decide which corn seed to plant. It is an individual decision whether to buy a hybrid or an SUV. In organization settings, the adoption of a new idea is not an individual decision. To what extent do you think the organization context reduces the usefulness of Diffusion constructs, or does it?

FIELDWORK ACTIVITIES

1. Sociograms are fun to construct and a very useful tool for change agents. For a system where you have access, develop a sociogram of the interpersonal connections. Who sits together in meetings and at lunch? Who does the most text messaging? Which people are members of the same team or department? Which people seem to be isolated? If you were a change agent, which people would you want to target first, second, and last?

2. For a system where you have more knowledge, identify a person who is an Opinion Leader. Interview that person about how he or she sees his or her role in the school. Also interview two or three other people about this person as an Opinion Leader. First, ask them who they turn to; they may identify someone else. Then explore what they see as the key characteristics of the identified Opinion Leader(s) that makes him or her (them) trusted sources.

3. For a change effort that you are part of, use the five perceived attributes to analyze the innovation. Which attribute have favored adoption, and which have discouraged it? To what extent have the change agent(s) addressed these attributes?

4. Keep in mind that communication is done using a variety of Media. In the past, face-to-face interactions were primary. Today, e-mail, the Web, and Twitter are very important Media. Cell phones might be important in some settings. Use the coding system introduced in Table 10.1 to analyze one week's interventions. Reflect on the resultant pattern. What could be done to further increase communication effectiveness?

CONDUCT A STUDY

1. The extensive history of research using Diffusion constructs and tools makes it relatively easy to conceptualize new studies. Even a superficial review of the Diffusion literature will yield study questions and research methods that can be applied in new situations. For example, although the Adopter Categories are well established in the literature, very few studies have been

done with teachers or higher education faculty. The generally more difficult context of introducing change in secondary schools is especially in need of study.

2. Although there has been extensive study of the characteristics of the different Adopter Categories, less has been done in schools and higher education. These settings are different than a social system of farmers in that the leader(s) of the organization quite often make the adoption decision. All members of the organization then are expected to implement the innovation. An interesting study would be to explore more closely the characteristics of the different implementer groups. What are the characteristics of those who implement early as contrasted against those who implement later?

ADDITIONAL READING

Rogers, E. M. (2003). *Diffusion of innovations* (5th ed.). New York: Free Press.

   This book is the definitive resource for learning more about the Diffusion Perspective. All of the constructs and themes of Diffusion are described. Each chapter includes interesting examples of how each construct has been studied and applied. The rich history of Diffusion is reviewed. The last chapter explores the important topic of the potential for good as well as bad consequences of change efforts.

CHAPTER 11

ORGANIZATION DEVELOPMENT

Team Building, Action Research, and Process Consultants

Our team is really good at solving problems. We don't jump to conclusions and always begin with examining the symptoms.

—One member's view of how the team does its work

As a committee chair, she listens closely to what each member says and makes sure that everyone's views are heard. She never has a hidden agenda.

—One member's observation of the how the chair facilitates committee process

We never make a decision. There is a lot of talk and the meetings go on, and on, and on. There never is closure.

—View of another group effort

I like the way he restates what someone has said and makes sure that he understands what the person meant.

—Reflection about a team member's skill

This consultant comes in every month and leads training sessions. We don't deal directly with our work, but what we learn can be applied.

—View of the role of a process consultant and team training experiences

In our school everyone has the opportunity to present his or her view, but once we have consensus, everyone supports it. All team members have responsibilities for what happens after a decision is made.

—Assistant principal

A regular activity in all organizations is people working with others. Meetings, committees, and teams are important ways to organize tasks, assign responsibilities, and produce services and products. When these group efforts work well, a significant amount can be accomplished efficiently and effectively. Each group has a unique feel and approach to accomplishing its work. In some groups, members feel that their ideas are heard, agreements are made, and participants are satisfied with the results.

Unfortunately frustration is oftentimes greater than satisfaction in group work. A lot of talk and not much listening can happen, with the same points repeated and few agreements finalized. In a discussion, each person argues his or her point of view in an attempt to persuade; in a dialogue, there is give and take along with an effort to develop mutual understanding. Unfortunately, often group work entails extended discussion with little or no dialogue.

In this chapter, the Organization Development (OD) perspective will be introduced as a way of understanding the interpersonal processes and skills that can help group work be effective. A variety of methods and tools have been developed for assessing, intervening, and growing healthy processes, especially in teamwork. OD is viewed as a major approach for making long-term change in organizations.

FOCUS QUESTIONS

1. What is OD?
2. What are the key features of OD intervention strategies?
3. Do OD efforts focus only on groups?
4. What are the differences between organizational climate and organization culture?
5. What is the role of the consultant in OD?

WHAT IS OD?

The OD perspective focuses on the interactive *processes* of people in doing their work rather than on the substance of the work. The primary assumption about change in this perspective is that if the members of an organization develop more process skills, then the organization will be more successful in its core work. Understanding and becoming expert in the use of OD processes can be very helpful for those engaged in implementing change, whether they are team members, committee chairs, leaders, or consultants. Today widely arrayed OD strategies and consulting processes are applied in business and industry, in government, and in the military. Little has been done with OD in schools since the 1980s.

The foundations of the OD perspective can be traced back to World War II and the efforts to prepare teams of military personnel to accomplish various tasks and objectives. Psychologists identified the kinds of process skills that more effective teams used. They also identified skills of individual members that contributed to overall team effectiveness. Following the war, attention was given to how these types of analyses and skills could be used for personal growth and to improve teamwork in businesses.

The emphases within this, the OD perspective, have varied over time, but the primary goal has continued to be to help the members of a system/organization develop expertise and the capacity to use group and individual process skills to handle whatever changes come their way. Addressing this goal now includes cross-organization processes as well. One important caveat is that in the OD perspective, the various process skills and change foci are viewed as generic. The assumption is that individuals, teams, and systems/organizations will be better able to solve their specific problems when they have developed expertise in using generalized process skills. In contrast to the Diffusion Change Agent, OD consultants do not introduce solutions to particular problems and needs. Instead, their focus is on helping the members of the system/organization develop process skills that can be used again and again as specific problems and needs arise.

OD Definitions Across the Decades

Throughout the 1950s and 1960s, development of OD was parallel to development of the human potential movement. In both cases psychologists focused on the human side of change. In OD, the subjects were employees in organizations with an interest in improving performance; in the human potential movement, subjects were people interested in personal growth. Both movements used similar approaches. For example, rather than working with clients individually, trainers and psychologists worked with them in groups. Various types of group "exercises" were created. Each facilitated learning new skills and gathering insight into the causes of resistance to change.

Training and Planning.   The earliest methods employed to improve organization effectiveness were (a) personnel training and (b) long-range organization planning (French, 1971; McGill, 1977). The personnel training method that emerged as most important was the *basic skill training group,* also known as the *T-group,* laboratory training, and sensitivity training. The training design typically had participants engaging in group work with artificial (rather than job-specific) tasks. The training process emphasized collecting data and receiving feedback about one's own behavior and the behavior of the group. The training approach also emphasized using the feedback to better understand oneself and others. It was believed that feedback about participants' interactions in the laboratory setting provided rich personal learning experiences that could then be applied in the workplace. The training did not directly address the workplace; rather, it was assumed that the participants could make the job-related transfer.

The emergence of systems theory (see Chapter 9) in the 1950s also became a cornerstone of OD. In systems theory the members of one department in an organization were seen as one of many interconnected subsystems. Each of these subsystems affects others and is affected by others. An assumption in the OD perspective is that improving the knowledge and skill of a subsystem will lead to overall improvement in the organization. In other words, training that leads to behavioral change and improvements in the members of an organization will lead to overall improvement in the organization.

Changing OD Definitions.   As Hall and Shieh (1998) observed, one of the challenges in developing a clear definition of OD is that across the decades the definition has evolved. Definitions also vary from author to author. The following sample of definitions illustrate this theme:

> Organization development is an effort (1) planned, (2) organization-wide, and (3) managed from the top, to (4) increase organization effectiveness and health through (5) planned interventions in the organization's "processes," using behavioral-science knowledge. (Beckhard, 1969, p. 9)
>
> Organization development (OD) [is] a philosophy of and technology for producing organization change. . . . Growing out of the human relations tradition in the forties and fifties, it is

actually a pastiche of techniques developed in the behavioral sciences which focus on problems of organization learning, motivation, problem solving, communication, and interpersonal relations. (Kimberly & Nielsen, 1975, p. 191)

OD is a planned and sustained effort at school self-study and improvement, focusing explicitly on change in both formal and informal norms, structures, and procedures, using behavioral science concepts and experiential learning. It involves the school participants themselves in the active assessment, diagnosis, and transformation of their organization. (Schmuck, 1987, pp. 1–2)

Organization development is a systemwide application and transfer of behavioral science knowledge to the planned development, improvement, and reinforcement of organizational strategies, structures, and processes that lead to organization effectiveness. (Cummings and Worley, 2008, pp. 1–2)

The failure of OD proponents to agree on a common definition has limited understanding and made it extremely difficult to conduct studies of its effectiveness. Although different in vocabulary and emphasis, each definition and approach reflects the importance of personal and interpersonal relationships—and process skill development—for increasing organization health and effectiveness. For those interested in implementing change, the understandings, techniques, and strategies offered through the OD perspective can be very helpful as sources of interventions, even if the total perspective is not used in a particular setting.

REFLECTION QUESTION

Think about your experience in being part of a committee or team. What did people do that made positive and/or negative differences in the group's effectiveness?

GUIDING PRINCIPLES OF THE OD PERSPECTIVE

1. Developing organization members' interpersonal and group process skills is an important way to improve organizational effectiveness.
2. Organizations, groups, and individuals are important targets for developing process skills.
3. The context of OD process training is intended to be free of the organization's core technology. The assumption is that members can transfer the learning to the work setting.
4. The OD consultant comes from outside the organization.
5. The OD consultant does not introduce a specific innovation. The role is to help the organization develop more effective processes in order to be better at solving its problems.
6. Planned change is a sustained multiyear approach to improving an organization.
7. Assessment and feedback about process and skills are important activities and should be ongoing.
8. Survey feedback is an important tool for diagnosing and informing the consultant and organization members about the current state of the organization.
9. Assessing organizational climate and culture can be an important step.

OD Intervention Tools and Techniques

The OD approach employs a number of methods for developing individuals, groups, and organizations. In many ways, these techniques and tools provide an operational definition for OD. When used well, these become powerful interventions. When they have been used poorly, resistance develops, and OD as a change approach loses its credibility.

Survey Feedback.   An important theme in the OD perspective is collecting performance data and providing feedback to the participants—in other words, *survey feedback.* Floyd Mann at the University of Michigan is credited with developing this strategy (Mann & Likert, 1952). The main functions of survey feedback are to collect information about members' attitudes and opinions, to provide survey information to organization units as feedback, and to design corrective actions based on the feedback information. Various forms and formats can be used to collect the data, with questionnaires probably being the most frequently used. The regular use today of a continuum to rate each item on a questionnaire (i.e., *Likert scales*) is a direct descendant of the early survey efforts. Interviews, telephone surveys, and data about customer satisfaction or student performance are other examples of information sources. In the OD perspective, feedback of the survey data typically will be provided by an external consultant. The consultant will guide the participants in constructing an analysis and interpretation of the data. Following feedback, the consultant assists organization members in identifying steps that can be taken to improve—in other words, OD.

Exercises.   The training situation that has been used for more than 50 years in OD for development of new skills, as well as in creating opportunities for reflection on current practice, is the *exercise.* These will range in length from half an hour to several days. Each exercise is designed to help participants, individually and as groups, learn new skills and reflect on their learning. Standard components of each exercise include an introduction that poses a problem. Then the participants will engage in a set of activities, such as building a tower using paper and masking tape, or developing a consensus set of rankings in regard to a question or topic. At some point an assessment will be made of the participants' current knowledge and skill in relation to the exercise objective. Once the group work is completed, a debriefing and critique will focus on how the *process*—not the product—of the exercise unfolded and what was learned. Often there will be no "right" answer to the exercise; the focus will be on the participants' process skill development and reflections about how their work in this context-free situation transfers back to their work setting.

Building Consensus.   Making decisions in teams is one of the traditional OD skills. The preference is for the group to come to a "consensus" through dialogue that has all members understanding and supporting the decision. An expectation inherent in consensus decision making is that those who would have preferred a different decision still will support the one that has been agreed upon. Voting is discouraged. It is seen as reducing consensus and encouraging a minority view that may be unsupportive of the majority's decision.

A classic OD training exercise for developing skill in consensus decision making is called *Lost on the Moon.* Each group is given a handout with information (see Figure 11.1) and is asked to develop a consensus ranking of the items. In this case, there is a more valid ranking, but that is secondary to learning more about group decision making. This type of exercise is based in the OD assumption that teams make better decisions than individuals.

FIGURE 11.1   Problem Sheet for the Exercise *Lost on the Moon*

LOST ON THE MOON: PROBLEM SHEET

You are a member of a space crew originally scheduled to rendezvous with a mother ship on the lighted surface of the moon. Mechanical difficulties, however, have forced your ship to crash-land at a spot some 200 miles from the rendezvous point. The rough landing damaged much of the on-board equipment. Since survival depends on reaching the mother ship, the most critical items available must be chosen for the 200-mile trip. The following lists contains the 15 items left intact after landing. Your task is to rank them in terms of their importance to your crew in its attempt to reach the rendezvous point. Place number 1 by the most important item, number 2 by the second most important, and so on through 15, the least important.

_____ Box of matches

_____ Food concentrate

_____ Fifty feet of nylon rope

_____ Parachute silk

_____ Solar-powered portable heating unit

_____ Two .45 caliber pistols

_____ One case of dehydrated milk

_____ Two 100-pound tanks of oxygen

_____ Stellar map (of the moon's constellation)

_____ Self-inflating life raft

_____ Magnetic compass

_____ Five gallons of water

_____ Signal flares

_____ First-aid kit containing injection needles

_____ Solar-powered FM receiver/transmitter

Source: Based on J. Hall, "Decisions, Decisions, Decisions," *Psychology Today,* 5 (1971): pp. 51–54, 86, 88. For a full description of this exercise, consult a resource such as R. A. Schmuck & P. J. Runkel, *The Handbook of Organization Development in Schools and Colleges* (Prospect Heights, IL: Waveland Press, 1994).

Team Functioning.   Another area of skill development has to do with how well each member of a team understands the task and how they contribute to the effort of the whole. Ideally, team members do not divorce themselves from the task by not contributing or texting under the table. More effective team members strive to recognize the problems that other team members may be having. An exercise classic for learning about team functioning is *Five Squares*. Bavelas (1950) introduced the idea, and over time it has been adapted by many consultants and presenters, including Schmuck and Runkel (1994).

With the Five Square exercise, participants are organized so that each group has five members seated at a table and one or two others are designated as Observers. Each participant at a table receives an envelope with several cardboard pieces that are different in size and shape from what other participants have in their envelopes. The task of the group is to pass pieces to each other so that when the activity is completed each participant will have assembled in front of them a square. Several important process rules must be followed: (a) Participants may not talk or gesture; (b) participants may only pass pieces to others—they cannot take pieces; and (c) the activity is concluded only when all of the assembled squares are of the same size.

The Five Squares exercise has several process objectives. Participants certainly discover the importance of talking and taking, since they are not permitted to do either in this exercise. Participants often become frustrated at not being able to talk. When several groups are doing the activity, a sense of competition develops between the groups, which adds tension. Often one of the participants will pass all of his or her pieces to the other members and then sit back with folded arms. The group experiences added difficulty in completing the task when one member does this. The process observers will be taking notes throughout the activity, which often takes more than 30 minutes.

After the activity is completed, a debriefing about what has happened takes place. Participants are asked about their feelings and what the keys to success were. The experience will then be used as a metaphor to talk about how the members share and help each other in their workplace. For example, the observers, or the OD consultant, will ask about the person who withdrew: "Does this happen at work?" "How does this affect the ability of the team/department to accomplish its tasks?"

Pothole Warning

Simply taking an OD exercise because it is interesting and intervening with it has the potential to cause harm.

Pothole Repair

Individual OD exercises can be used as interventions; however, the reason for the use and how it is applied need to be carefully thought out and explained to the participants.

OD Exercises Are Job Context Free.   As has been pointed out, typically, OD exercises will not directly address job-specific tasks or problems. As with the two "classics" described here, exercises are designed using unfamiliar contexts and with materials and activities that are job neutral. The expressed intent is to remove the job-setting context so that it does not interfere with learning new skills. The explicit assumption is that once learned, the participants can make the transfer back to the work setting.

Finding and Sharing OD Exercises.   Many sources and types of OD exercises are available. One of the traditional strengths and significant norms of OD experts is their willingness to share exercises and to encourage others to add to the quality of each. Excellent beginning sources are the earlier publications of such experts as J. William Pfeiffer and John E. Jones in business, and Richard A. Schmuck and Matthew B. Miles in education. The Web is a very useful resource for finding exercises and learning about their applications. Reflecting the evolution in definition of OD, contemporary sources have a more holistic view of OD with more reliance on case studies; see, for example, *Organization Development: The Process of Leading Organizational Change* (Anderson, 2010).

REFLECTION QUESTIONS

Have you ever participated in an OD exercise? What did you learn from the experience? Will learning more about OD make a difference in your approach to participating in the future?

TEAM/GROUP AND INDIVIDUAL PROCESS SKILLS

The contributions of OD have been particularly strong in bringing about change through the identification of process skills and training for groups and individuals. Skills that were a primary focus of OD activity in its earlier days had to do with group work and team building. In most organizations, work is accomplished in departments, teams, or other grouplike arrangements. A number of important group skills and processes have been identified and have become the focus for training. Equally important is the identification of skills that individual members of a team can use to make group work more efficient and effective.

Implementing change in almost any setting entails people working in groups. With the advent of such innovations as total quality management and site-based decision making, not only is more work being done in groups, but those groups are expected to make group decisions. This can be a very frustrating and inefficient experience unless the members have developed skill in working as a team. The OD perspective offers a number of useful concepts and strategies that can greatly improve group functioning.

Team Decision Making

A key premise in the OD perspective is that, on average, groups will make better decisions than individuals. This is a disturbing idea for some, especially those who are more comfortable with the traditional chain of command and organizational chart perspective, which specifies that those at the top make the decisions and those below follow orders. In the OD perspective, decision making requires teams to develop skill in working together.

Brainstorming.   Another of the classic skills is *brainstorming*. Rather than leaping to a conclusion, effective groups first work through a process of generating alternatives ideas, some of which may represent out-of-the-box thinking. As with other OD skills, brainstorming has a set of rules, which include (a) there should be no value judgments, (b) all possibilities must be accepted and placed on the list, and (c) an agreed-on time limit applies to generating ideas.

> *Pothole Warning*
>
> *An important skill in brainstorming is for all participants not to indicate judgment or valuing of ideas by voice or nonverbal reaction. Such evaluative behaviors inhibit others from introducing ideas that might stretch the thinking.*

> *Pothole Repair*
>
> *Begin a brainstorming activity by reminding participants of the rules. List the rules on a slide or handout. If during brainstorming someone violates the rules, all should be reminded of the rules.*

Developing Consensus.   As described above, proponents of OD place major emphasis on groups achieving consensus in decision making. Voting and decisions being made by the formal leader are seen as last resorts. At the same time, reaching a decision by consensus does not mean that everyone's position will be supported; however, each position is to be heard and respected. Through discussion, a decision direction emerges that has wide support within the group. As this decision takes shape, an expectation is that, in the end, those whose points of view have received less support will still accept the decision of the group.

Problem Solving.   Another key OD process is *problem solving*. When a problem is introduced in a work setting, individuals and groups have a strong tendency to leap immediately to offering solutions. In the OD perspective, solving a problem begins with first asking questions about the facts and then defining the problem. In OD a number of steps to the problem-solving process have been identified, and many training exercises have been developed to help teams become better at problem solving. Figure 11.2 portrays some of the steps that can be included in problem solving. Note that problem solving is represented as a cycle. Usually solving one problem leads to new problems, so the steps may need to be repeated.

A number of training exercises may be used to facilitate a group in becoming more skilled in applying each of the steps in problem solving. For example, identifying symptoms and distinguishing these from solutions is an important early step. However, many symptoms are causes of other symptoms. This analysis could lead to the discovery that what initially was assumed to be one problem is in fact a "chain" of problems. Every identified problem in the chain is not of equal importance. The key is to select one of the problems that will make the biggest difference and to focus on "fixing" it.

Force-Field Analysis.   With this technique, two columns are presented on chart paper or with digital projection. In one column, participants list those forces that will be supportive of a certain action or solution. In the other column, forces that will inhibit implementation are listed. The next part of the problem-solving process entails selecting a solution (hopefully

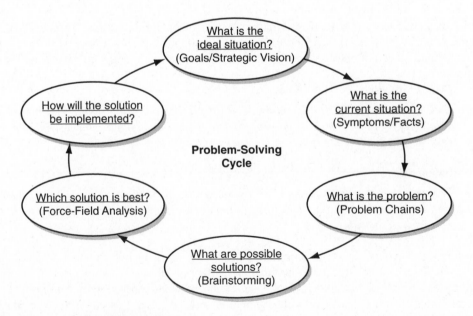

FIGURE 11.2   Problem-Solving Cycle

through consensus) and developing a plan to take advantage of the supportive forces and tactics for offsetting the potential effects of the inhibiting forces.

Meeting Skills.   So much time in organizations is spent in meetings that one would expect that there should be ideas about better ways to run them. Skills and procedures for making meetings more efficient and effective have been identified. A key to having effective meetings is the repertoire of process skills that each team member brings to group work. Here again OD training can be useful for developing whole group and individual skills.

Consideration of member skills is reflective of another OD value, *followership*. The designated leader of a team is expected to have certain skills. In addition, the OD perspective places expectations on the "followers." Rather than the leader being solely responsible for leading, skill and role expectations befall all members of the group. Team leadership is seen as a shared responsibility. A number of tools have been developed that all the members of a group can use to facilitate team work.

Individual Team Member Process Skills.   Over the years, OD experts have identified a number of process skills that individual members of groups/teams can use to increase effectiveness. Training exercises have been developed to assist in learning to use these skills. A wide variety of self- and group assessments that can be used to evaluate how well individuals and groups/teams are doing in using these skills are also available. Some of these skills are described in Figure 11.3.

Today's OD experts have refined the descriptions and use of individual skills. They also have created new training materials that help individuals and teams increase their effectiveness.

FIGURE 11.3   Individual Skills for Increasing Group/Team Effectiveness

Encouraging: Asking another to say more, participate, elaborate, and/or lead by being warm toward and accepting of their contributions.

Clarifying: Saying an idea or point in a new way and asking, "Is this what you mean?"

Consensus testing: Asking for an indication of where each member of the group is positioned at this time. This does not mean that it is his or her final position—it is just a check on where each person is right now.

Compromising: Offering a new position that takes into account points of disagreement and suggests a middle ground.

Gatekeeping: Inviting someone to contribute. This may be someone who has not said much or a person with relevant information.

Information seeking: Asking for information about the topic or a member's concerns.

Listening: Paying attention and carefully following a discussion.

Opinion giving: Presenting one's own position or feelings.

Paraphrasing: Restating what someone has said in order to be sure that there is shared understanding.

Perception checking: Asking a person if what you think he or she said is what the person intended to say.

Seeking opinion: Directly asking for an opinion.

Summarizing: At various points in a discussion, briefly reviewing the points that have been made so far and the flow of topics.

FIGURE 11.4   Advocacy Skill Steps and Examples

Make Your Thinking and Reasoning Visible

State your assumptions. "Here's what I believe about. . . ."

Describe your reasoning. "I came to this conclusion because. . . ."

Describe your feelings. "I feel _____ about this."

Distinguish data from interpretation. "These are the data I have as objectively as I can state them. Now here is what I think the data mean."

Reveal your perspective. "I'm seeing this from the viewpoint of _____ or _____ or _____."

Frame the wider context that surrounds this issue. "Several groups would be affected by what I propose. . . ."

Give concrete examples. "To get a clear picture, imagine that you are in school X. . . ."

Test Your Assumptions and Conclusions

Encourage others to explore your model, assumptions, and data. "What do you think about what I just said? Do you see any flaws in my reasoning? What can you add?"

Reveal where you are least clear. "Here's one area you might help me think through. . . ."

Stay open. Encourage others to provide different views: "Do you see it differently?"

Search for distortions, deletions, and generalizations. "In what I've presented, do you believe I might have overgeneralized, or left out data, or reported data incorrectly?"

Source: Garmston, Robert, & Wellman, Bruce. (2000). The Adaptive School Developing and Facilitating Collaborative Groups (4th ed.). Sacramento, CA 95762. Center for Adaptive Schools, www.adaptiveschools.com. Reprinted by permission.

For example, Garmston and Wellman (2008) provide training and consultation to school districts all around the United States. Their materials provide detail about the reasoning behind each skill and offer examples of ways to say things (see Figure 11.4).

REFLECTION QUESTIONS

Have you thought about your skill as a follower? Which skills do you use regularly in meetings?

USING OD TO CHANGE WHOLE ORGANIZATIONS

As the OD field has evolved over the last 50 to 60 years, one of the trends has been toward more systematic strategies for changing whole organizations. In its early days, "planned change" was a key purpose (for example, see Lippitt, Watson, & Westley, 1958). Proponents believed that organization change could be more successful when various processes were internalized as the regular way of working. Over time, the processes for organization change have become more complex and the view of the organization more holistic. Today, especially in business and industry, the range of models and strategies is quite wide. Still, core strategies continue to include addressing climate/culture, strategic planning, and process consultation. However, there have been significant increases in complexity and sophistication, as well as more rigorous research about their effectiveness.

Assessing and Developing Climate/Culture

Organizational climate is an important topic for survey feedback. Over the years, many questionnaires have been developed for surveying elements of climate. For example, questionnaires can be used to measure the values and norms organization members hold about such constructs as autonomy, reward orientation, the amount of communication, and feelings about colleagues ("We trust each other") and their clients ("*Those* kids can't learn this"). The OD consultant can then work with the organization to help it become clear about its explicit and implicit assumptions. Targets can be set and action plans developed for improving one or more aspects of climate as measured with the survey.

Pothole Warning

Many climate questionnaires have little or no indications of statistical quality. If used, the resultant findings from data analyses may be misleading.

Pothole Repair

It is best to obtain information about reliability and validity of any climate questionnaire before deciding to use it. If a questionnaire with uncertain psychometric qualities is used, be sure to provide caveats of caution in drawing inferences from data analyses.

Organizational Climate Defined.   The earlier efforts to define and measure organizational climate became quite confused. Many climate surveys were developed. Few had systematic estimates of reliability and validity. Often there would be little obvious connection between the survey items and the construct being measured. For example, measuring the average size of offices might be associated with a scale called task specialization. Quite literally, consultants would create climate surveys on the plane and apply them the next day. Very little research documented that the various climate measures did measure elements of climate (i.e., validity) and that the measures did this consistently (i.e., reliability).

A very important conceptual and empirical analysis of the early climate measures was reported by James and Jones (1974). In the introduction to their article, they observed, "Organizational climate research occupies a popular position in current industrial and organizational psychology. However, conceptual and operational definitions, measurement techniques, and ensuing results are highly diverse, and even contradictory" (p. 1096). Actually, given the state of practice at that time, James and Jones were kind in their appraisal of the state of climate measurement.

The first need was for clarity in definition of what was being measured. James and Jones proposed that three separate constructs were being addressed under the organizational climate umbrella:

1. *Situational variables* are attributes of the organization that are relatively stable over time, that require multiple measures, and that represent an objective view. These are organizational characteristics that influence the behavior of individuals and are true for the organization as a whole. Table 11.1 is how James and Jones (1974) summarized the situational components. Situational variables can be measured objectively, almost as if they were facts about a particular organization.

TABLE 11.1 Defining Organizational Climate as Situational Variables

CONTEXT	STRUCTURE	PROCESS	PHYSICAL ENVIRONMENT	SYSTEMS VALUES AND NORMS
Goals and objectives	Size	Leadership	Physical space characteristics (temperature, lighting, sound, etc.)	Conformity
Ownership and control	Centralization of decision making	Communication	Personnel protection	Rationality
Charter (diversity of mission)	Configuration	Control	Remoteness	Predictability
Dependence	Specialization	Conflict resolution	Environment hazards	Impersonality
Age	Standardization of procedures	Change	Space restrictions and confinement	Loyalty
Function	Formalization of procedures	Coordination	Endurance demands	Reciprocity
Level of technology	Interdependence of subsystems	Selection	Environmental stresses	Adherence to chain of command
		Socialization		Local (cosmopolitan) orientation
		Reward		Programmed (unprogrammed) approaches to problem solving, etc.
		Decision making		
		Status and power Relationships		

Source: L. James, and P. Jones, "Organizational Climate: A Review of Theory and Research." *Psychological Bulletin,* 81, 12, (1974): 1096–1112. Copyright © 1974 by the American Psychological Association. Reprinted by permission.

2. *Psychological climate* is an individual's perceptions of characteristics of the organization. Each person will have his or her own view of the organization. The factual situation may be different from an individual's perceptions, but the individual's perceptions are reality for him or her.

3. *Organizational climate* is the summary of the individual perceptions of particular characteristics of the organization. At its simplest, organizational climate is the average of all the psychological climate scores.

As useful as the James and Jones (1974) definitions are, they also raise questions. For example, when there is wide variation in individuals' perceptions, what is the true picture of organizational climate? Still, the definitions continue to be useful in clarifying designs and uses of climate surveys and related feedback activities.

Climate Versus Culture.   As the 1990s were unfolding, a new term, *culture,* became popular to use in survey feedback. This trend was taking place at the same time as the rise in use of qualitative research methods. Both trends were foreshadowed by the writings of Schein (1985) and others. Qualitative research methods emphasize the importance of in-depth observations in the field, developing rich narrative descriptions, and then looking for themes. These are the preferred methods for studying the culture of an organization.

A problem with climate surveys is that a standard set of items is used across organizations and an established a priori scoring procedure is used to determine scale/construct scores. Organization culture proponents assume that each setting will be unique in some ways and that a standardized questionnaire will miss some of the important local themes. There also is a risk that, as a consequence of a climate survey including a standard set of scales, one or another of the scale constructs could receive emphasis in a feedback session when it really is of minor relevance to a particular organization.

Interviewing to Assess Organization Culture.   Assessing culture requires extensive time inside the organization. It also requires being especially observant and sensitive to how participants interpret symbols and ascribe meaning to actions and events. There is a delicate balancing task for the culture observer. He or she must enter the setting and be able to distinguish between seeing things as they are in some sort of objective view and learning how members of the organization interpret the same phenomenon. The culture observer also has to be able to understand the biases the participants bring to the setting. Many observers fall into the trap of interpreting things from their experiences, rather than hearing the meanings and interpretations constructed by the organization members.

Interviews are one of the key tools for assessing organization culture. Special interview questions need to be developed. These will be open ended and address key elements such as the role of the leader(s), the perceptions of colleagues, and the explanations for how things are accomplished. This is what Spradley (1979) calls an *ethnographic* interview.

Examples of Organization Culture.   A research team in Belgium under the leadership of Roland Vandenberghe (Staessens, 1993) developed a set of questions for the team's studies of school organization culture. A sampling of their questions is presented in Figure 11.5. The findings from their research clearly illustrate that *organization culture is a social construction.*

FIGURE 11.5 Example Organization Culture Interview Questions

SEEKING MEANING OF THE BEHAVIOR AND ACTIVITIES OF THE PRINCIPAL FOR TEACHERS

- Do you have many contacts with your principal? What do you talk about?
- Can you tell me what is of great importance to your principal?
- To which matters does your principal pay little or no attention?
- What does your principal expect from you as a teacher?
- What does your principal expect from you as a member of the team?
- What is the importance of your principal in your school?

DISCOVERING THE EXISTENCE OR THE FUNCTIONING OF A GOAL CONSENSUS OR SHARED VISION

- What does the staff consider as very important in this school?
- Why is this considered important?
- How can I see that this is important?
- Does everyone in the school consider this matter as important, or is this only true for a few teachers?
- How would you characterize your school during a conversation with parents?
- What exactly makes your school different from other schools?
- What are some of the stories, expressions, or slogans that are used to express what is considered as very important?

DISCOVERING THE VALUES AND NORMS THAT ARE CONSTRUCTED IN THE PROFESSIONAL CONTACTS BETWEEN TEACHERS

- How often is there a staff meeting in your school? What themes are discussed at these meetings?
- During lunch and at other times do you talk about work?
- Do you ever look in on a colleague's classroom? How often does that happen? What makes you do that? Do you discuss it afterward?
- When you think over all the contacts with colleagues you have just described, can you say which contacts are most precious to you? Why?
- Are there things in this school that you are not able to talk about?
- Are there ever conflicts between staff members? What are they about?

Source: Based on Staessens, K. (1990). *De professionele cultuur van basisscholen in vernieuwing: Een empirisch onderzoek in V.L.O.-Scholen* [The professional culture of innovating primary schools: An empirical study of R.P.S.-Schools]. Unpublished doctoral dissertation, University of Leuven, Leuven, Belgium. For more information, see Staessens, K. (1993). Identification and description of professional culture in innovating schools. *Qualitative Studies in Education,* 6, 2, 111–128.

The type of culture and its shape are the result of individual and interactive interpretation and construction of meaning. This research team identified three culture types:

The Family-School There is an informal culture of congeniality, with an aversion to official and structural matters. The basic assumption is "We are a great group with good intentions. We can trust the spontaneous development of matters." Teachers don't talk about their classroom work or subject matter, or visit each other's classrooms. The principal can be characterized as a "grandfather figure." "If you have problems, you can call on me."

The School as a Professional Organization   Teachers are expected to be part of the team. There is a basic philosophy about teaching and learning that is pervasive. "We devote our heart and soul to our work." It is taken for granted that by working hard together a great deal can be achieved. Teachers characterize the principal as an architect. Teachers can always call on the principal for help with their professional problems, and the principal puts forward his/her own ideas. "The school is his hobby."

The Living-Apart-Together School   "A ship without a compass." Teachers lack a vision about the future. Teachers speak in individual terms rather than as "we." The principal is often not present at school or functions in an invisible way. Teachers say, "Whether the principal is present or not, it really doesn't matter much."

As these example cultures imply, leadership, teacher consensus about school goals, and the shared values and norms can be quite different.

Comparing Measurement of Climate and Culture.   As with other OD tools and strategies, potential strengths and weaknesses are inherent in choosing to apply a climate survey or to do the more in-depth fieldwork that is required to develop a picture of organization culture. Climate surveys are economical to use, and the resultant information can be informative. The feedback session could include each respondent receiving feedback about his or her scores (psychological climate). The individual scores could then be compared to the average for all respondents (organizational climate). This type of process can reveal to the individual how closely his or her perceptions are in agreement with others and provide everyone with information about the shared perceptions.

Assessing organization culture begins with extensive observation, interviews, and analysis of documents and artifacts. The resultant identification of themes will be rich and grounded in the uniqueness of the particular organization. The feedback process requires special skills and should come from a consultant who is trusted. In the feedback process the resultant themes are introduced along with examples of evidence that illustrates how the themes were identified. Some of the themes would likely overlap some organizational climate survey scales, whereas others would be unique to that organization.

Strategic Planning

Strategic planning has become a very comprehensive and extended process that is used regularly by businesses, institutions of higher education, school districts, and governments. The goal is to envision the ideal future for the organization and to identify the strategies and steps for achieving the vision. School improvement processes and plans are an example of strategic planning. Developing a full strategic plan can take several years. Once developed, it must be reviewed regularly and updated as progress is made or the situation changes. Typical process steps and products are presented in Figure 11.6.

Making Strategic Planning Real.   The strategic planning process is a very effective way to involve all members of an organization, as well as outsiders, in learning about and contributing to an organization's agenda for the future. The ideas of the many will be developed into the plan by

FIGURE 11.6 Strategic Planning Process Steps and Components

THE STRATEGIC PLANNING PROCESS

- A process consultant
- A designated leader, coordinator
- A strategic planning committee
- Retreats and workshops, including process training
- Surveys of organization members, customers, clients, consumers, and policymakers
- Top-down and bottom-up contributions
- All organization unit's activities and aspirations nested inside the organization's plan
- Championing of the plan by the top executive leaders and governing board
- Multiyear timeline

STRATEGIC PLAN COMPONENTS

- *Beliefs:* Statements of core values and assumptions about the organization, its members, its clients, and how things work
- *Vision Statement:* A Sentence or single paragraph that describes an ideal view of the world that the organization serves (in some cases this will be an ideal view for the organization)
- *Goals:* General statements of the desired accomplishments for the organization over the next 6 months to 5 years
- *Mission statement:* An outline of the purposes and contributions of this organization that will contribute to achieving the vision
- *Strategies:* A set of plans, resources, and activities that will be used in combination with others to accomplish each goal
- *Action plan:* The specific objectives, tasks, activities, assignments, and timeline for the work that will be done
- *Indicators:* Areas of evidence that could be used to benchmark progress toward accomplishing objectives, strategies, and goals
- *Measures:* The specific pieces of evidence that will be collected and used to make judgments about progress
- *Cost-benefit analysis:* An analysis of the direct cost (time, dollars, and other resources) to do a task, which is compared to the potential gains (tangible and intangible) and can be used to judge the potential "return on investment"
- *Opportunity cost:* An examination of the other tasks, activities, and accomplishments that will not be done, or done with less priority, in order that those identified in the plan can be done

having a strategic planning committee, which is led by a key organization executive. At intervals, drafts of the plan are circulated and feedback considered. The final plan, once accepted by the top executives and governing board, should be referred to constantly and be the basis for making major decisions. Many of the individual and group OD process skills, such as brainstorming and consensus decision making, become important to having a strategic planning process go well. Ideally, the resultant plan is a 3- to 5-year map for organization change and growth.

When a strategic planning process is introduced, the first response of many is "So what?" These people might attend the planning retreats and offer cursory feedback about the drafts but make no real commitment to the plan. For many, a strategic plan does not become real until the time when "real" decisions are made based on the plan. For example, if the decision on next year's department budget is heavily influenced by what the department submitted in its plan, the following year all departments will take the strategic planning process more seriously. If the plan is used only as a public relations document, then it will have little effect on changing the organization.

Providing Indicators/Evidence Is Important.   A component of strategic planning that has become increasingly important is the "indicators and measures." In the past, clarifying assumptions and developing a vision statement had the most emphasis. There also tended to be a lot of discussion about the differences between vision (the ideal world) and mission (steps for moving toward the ideal) statements. More recently, the plan for action and the timeline have been key topics in the planning process. Now the key focus is on what evidence has been and will be collected to indicate that there was change and, hopefully, improvement. Having evidence and making decisions based in evidence is becoming the critical component of strategic planning.

> *Pothole Warning*
>
> *Frequently strategic planning processes get drawn out to the point that some of the participants become very frustrated. Intervention Mushrooms (see Chapter 8) may start growing with themes such as "This is a waste of time" and "Every meeting is the same stuff."*

> *Pothole Repair*
>
> *Leaders need to continually monitor the pace of the planning process and anticipate the possible growth of themes of frustration. Also, tension may develop between the slower pace desired by the OD consultant and the participants who desire to "get on with it."*

Action Research.   A useful strategy for engaging teams in learning more about their work is action research (Eden and Huxham, 1996). This strategy begins with an individual or team identifying a question about their practice. It could be teachers wondering if a certain instructional approach is serving English language learners, or administrators questioning the effectiveness of a particular schedule. In action research the team begins by agreeing on the question to be studied. They then identify the type of data that will be collected to answer the question. The team then collects data, analyzes the data, and shares the findings with colleagues. This strategy reflects many of the attributes of OD. The focus is on collecting data, a team works on the problem, the skills of team work and data analysis are applied, and the findings are used to examine current practices.

REFLECTION QUESTIONS

Use the items in Figure 11.6 to examine what is done in your organization to plan for the future. Has your organization developed a strategic plan? How often is the plan reviewed? What are the key indicators used to judge progress?

■ ■ ■ ■ ■ ■

VIGNETTE

THE STRATEGIC PLANNING RETREAT DAY

Paul had been looking forward to this day. Representatives from every department were meeting in a large conference room at the country club. Paul thought, "This is a good location. Plenty of coffee, and everyone had to check cell phones at the door. We need to come up with some new directions today. What we have been doing will not carry us into the future." As Paul entered the room he saw the two consultants, CarolAnn and Art, talking with President Schneider. The usual chart paper and felt-tipped pens were in place, and tables were arranged so that eight people could sit in a group.

The day began with introductions. President Schneider said how important this day was, but that he had to leave for another meeting. The strategic planning committee members were introduced, and it was announced that each of them would chair one of the breakout groups. José, who is in charge of planning, led a discussion of the advance readings. Each of the articles related to some aspect of the problems and issues being faced by other like organizations as well as this one.

The agenda for the morning was to work in groups and do a SWOT Analysis. The consultants introduced the meaning of SWOT:

Strengths: What is the organization currently doing well?

Weaknesses: What are the weaknesses in what the organization is currently doing?

Opportunities: What are the needs that we could address?

Threats: Are there things within our organization or in the situation outside that are hurting our efforts?

The consultants emphasized the importance of keeping an open mind; this is a time to think differently and to introduce new ideas. They also emphasized the importance of everyone participating, "since the best ideas and decisions come out of people working together."

The consultants then reminded everyone of the rules for brainstorming:

1. Set a time limit (10 minutes).
2. Produce ideas as fast as you can.
3. Do not evaluate the ideas.
4. The priority is on producing as many ideas as possible.
5. It can be helpful to build on what someone else has said.
6. Someone needs to record all ideas.

As practice, each table had to brainstorm which animal, bird, or plant should be adopted as the organization's mascot.

Then each group began work on its SWOT analysis by spending 10 minutes brainstorming the *strengths* of the current situation. Then they did the same with *weaknesses* and *opportunities*. Paul saw what he thought were some good ideas being introduced, especially about opportunities. He had one frustration, though. Sally just did not understand the rules of brainstorming. She constantly kept lobbying for her single solution to everything: "We need to hire more staff. We just can't get everything done."

Following the brainstorming, each group had 10 minutes to report the results. There was a surprising amount of overlap, which the two consultants pointed out. Then each group was asked to do a force-field analysis of *threats* (the *T* in *SWOT*). As Paul heard Sally point out that staffing was a threat, he thought of several threats to add to the list, but he held his breath. As a way of developing

■ ■ ■ ■ ■

VIGNETTE CONTINUED

group consensus, the consultants asked the members of each group to place a red dot by the threat that they saw as most serious and an orange dot by the second most serious threat. They also were asked to place a green dot by the one opportunity that they thought would really move the organization ahead. (This is a way to show visually those items for which a consensus is developing. It also is a way to reduce attention on some items that have only one or two individuals as advocates.) The consultants then asked each group to report out its top three threats and its highest-rated opportunity.

The afternoon session started with a discussion of imagination and the importance of thinking "out of the box." A very interesting video was used to illustrate how easy it is to jump to conclusions that are based in wrong interpretations of the situation. Most of the afternoon was spent in each group preparing a presentation of the new strategic direction that it thought should be the way to go. Each group was challenged by the consultants to make their presentation interesting and to stretch the thinking of everyone. A part of their task was to develop a 3- to 5-year timeline with benchmarks for when each task would need to be completed. They also had to name roles and functions that would need to be established.

Following the group reports, members of the strategic planning committee and Vice President Young asked questions and offered additional ideas that they had been considering. The day ended with the consultants explaining that over the next two days the strategic planning committee would be working with all of the notes, charts, and ideas that had been introduced during the day. One important task was to collect and compile data related to each of the four topics (strengths, weaknesses, opportunities, and threats). The strategic planning committee would then send out a draft of its report. In 6 weeks a half-day retreat would be held to review and further refine the plan. At some point the plan would also need to include "indicators" and "measures." The strategic plan would then go to the board and be used in making budget decisions for the next several years.

VIGNETTE CRITIQUE QUESTIONS

1. Which activities and processes described in this vignette are reflective of OD? What do you see being the process objective of each?
2. What individual and group process skills were employed in this vignette?
3. What would you predict to be the participants' reactions when President Schneider announced that he would not be there? How could the reaction be different depending on the culture of the organization? How would perceptions be different if President Schneider had stayed and participated?

OD PROCESS CONSULTANTS

Introducing an organization to OD and assisting members in developing skills to move through a multiyear process, such as is required for strategic planning, is the job of the OD consultant. Most OD consultants come from outside the client organization. The range of expertise of OD consultants is wide. They have to be expert in consultation and training, and they must be able to diagnose problem areas and avoid inserting their own agendas. Particularly important are the interpersonal skills of the consultants. Their continued credibility is dependent on how well they can communicate with and be seen as supportive by all members

IMPLICATIONS FOR LEADERS FACILITATING CHANGE

1. Everyone—consultants, leaders, and followers—will be more effective as they come to understand and develop skill in using OD processes.
2. The many methods, exercises, and survey feedback techniques of OD can be applied on a small scale as well as in sustained, whole-organization, planned change efforts.
3. Understanding problem solving can be very useful since so many people jump to solutions without first identifying the facts/symptoms and describing the problem.
4. OD exercises and methods for analyzing and improving group decision making can be used by any team/department/unit.
5. The OD perspective addresses conflict resolution through a variety of strategies as well as the role of the consultant. The strategies can help organizations reduce conflict and/or develop positive ways of dealing with conflict.
6. OD is an excellent source of interventions for facilitating change, even when OD itself is not being used as the change model.

of the organization. To be effective, they must be equally comfortable and eloquent in communicating with managers and workers. Since they are introducing processes and skills, rather than dealing directly with the production of the organization, they must be able to help members understand why skills and understandings of processes are important.

OD Consultants at Work

OD consultants bring to the organization a repertoire of process skills and understanding of an organization's interpersonal dynamics. They understand goal setting, communication, problem solving, decision making, conflict resolution, and the skills that groups and individuals need to function effectively. They also bring with them a set of interventions. These include feedback surveys, exercises, training protocols, and skill in coaching individuals and groups at all levels of the organization.

Planned Change Steps.   In its totality, OD is viewed as a way of accomplishing *planned change*. In the OD perspective a set of process steps has been identified for accomplishing change in organizations. There is a sequence to how change works, and with each step the consultant provides relevant process training and consultation. The external OD consultant serves as coach, guide, and trainer to the organization as it addresses a need and moves through the steps entailed in changing.

From the consultants' view, planned change includes the following steps (Rothwell, Sullivan, & McLean, 1995):

1. *Entry:* In many ways, beginning a relationship involves a courtship. The prospective client is reading the actions of the consultant closely and carefully. The consultant also is engaged in an early assessment of the organization. Both are asking questions: Can I

trust and work with this person? Do I have the right resources to offer? Several contacts will be made before an agreement is struck, which will likely cover the first steps. Long-term commitment has to be earned.

2. *Start-up:* The first steps are careful steps. The consultant has to be a fast learner. There are bound to be mixed signals and individual perceptions that only represent part of the picture. All of the actions of the consultant are watched closely. Keys to success include identifying shared values, recognizing that the consultant has expertise, and seeing the consultant becoming sensitive to organization politics and building linkages with key Opinion Leaders.

3. *Assessment and feedback:* Obtaining systematic information about the current situation is important. Before deciding on a course of action, the consultant and client need to share an evidence-based understanding of where things are now. As important as gathering information is, giving feedback is even more critical. The feedback needs to be based in the assessment and presented in ways that are seen as accurate. The resultant dialogue leads to consensus about the problem and the needed change. The assessment also provides the baseline for future measurement of change.

4. *Action planning:* To accomplish change, actions must be taken. The process of developing the action plan should include as many of the members of the organization as possible. A change strategy needs to be selected. The plan needs to be affordable, doable, and supported by top executives.

5. *Interventions:* To accomplish the change, interventions likely will be needed at three levels: whole organization, groups, and individuals. Whole organization interventions might include strategic planning, a reorganization of production tasks, or a change in the reward system. Group and team interventions include interpersonal communication, decision making, and team skill in meeting roles and responsibilities. Addressing how individuals work in organizations could be done through self-study and reflection as well as interpersonal process skill development.

6. *Evaluation:* Collecting and using evidence is a continuing part of the OD process. Each intervention activity can be evaluated and used to refine the next steps. Evaluations should be done across time so that there are regular snapshots for viewing progress and identifying emerging areas of need. Evidence should be collected at the end to judge how successful the process has been.

7. *Adoption:* Outcome(s) have become a staple in group work and are ingrained in the organization culture. This does not mean a rigid adherence to a certain way of doing things, however. The new way continues when there are changes in key personnel and the client is no longer dependent on the presence of the OD consultant.

8. *Separation:* The consultant is no longer needed for the change to be sustained, or the consultant role is reduced to occasional appraiser of continuation of the change.

OD Consultant Issues.   As with all change perspectives, OD presents a number of issues and potential problems. One is the extent of knowledge and skill required of the OD consultant. For example, each of the OD processes and related intervention exercises is interesting. However, processing the exercise sessions is a delicate matter and requires a high level of skill. Consultants also must be skilled at working with all levels of an organization. The consultant is likely to be contracted by a top-level executive, but he or she must also be able to

USING OD CONSTRUCTS AND TOOLS TO ASSESS AND STUDY IMPLEMENTATION

OD offers a wealth of concepts, models, and measures that can be used in evaluation, implementation assessment, and research studies. The 60-year history of OD ensures that the core concepts are grounded in the reality of changing organizations. An important caveat for researchers is that most of the measures used in OD do not have information available about their psychometric qualities. Historically, OD was an applied field. Until recently there was little research, and what there was had questionable quality. For example, the effectiveness studies would be conducted by the consultant (potential for bias), reliability and validity of the measures were not established (reduction in confidence of findings), no comparison data were available from a like group or organization (any changes in scores could be due to some other undocumented intervention), too many of the studies were based on participant and consultant self-report (potential for bias), and few of the studies reported direct data about increases in effectiveness or productivity in the organization's core technology.

Even with the limits of the past, the potential of OD to be used in evaluation, assessment, and research is very high. (See, for example, Volume 14 of *Research in Organizational Change and Development* by Pasmore & Woodman, 2003.) Today's research, especially in business, organization, and industrial psychology, is rigorous. Theories, models, and constructs are well defined, and the study designs include systematic controls.

Study possibilities abound. For example, OD concepts related to group decision making and problem solving are ripe for use in education. Most public schools are required to develop school improvement plans each year. This is intended to be a schoolwide and community-involving effort. Many schools have difficulty with the process. Intervention studies using OD methods and techniques could be conducted to see if the school improvement process improves and the quality of the plans is enhanced. In higher education, parallel dynamics engage with strategic planning.

Studies of organizational climate and culture could use concept definitions identified in the various measures that OD consultants have developed. For the quantitatively inclined, factor analytic studies similar to those of James and Jones (1974) could be conducted to test for the existence of constructs and to develop research verified measures. Of course, those with a qualitative bent should become immersed in an organization for the purpose of describing elements of culture that support or inhibit planned change efforts.

work with sales representatives in regional offices as well as workers on the assembly-line floor. This requires flexibility and genuine comfort in working with diversity.

Since OD consultants come from outside, they have to earn their continuing involvement. Their contract can be terminated at any time. They must work well with the executives. They also should continually remind themselves that their primary client is the organization, not just the top executive(s). They must do all of this while maintaining confidentialities with everyone. Consultants will have knowledge of impending strategic decisions and various employee personal problems. They must be responsible to the people, the organization, and the planned change effort.

REFLECTION QUESTIONS

What about you serving as an OD consultant? Which of the skills do you already possess? Where would you have the most difficulty in being effective?

SUMMARY

OD represents a different perspective for understanding and implementing change. The focus on process, the role of the external process consultant, and the planned change steps represent a systematic approach to change. The OD perspective does not focus directly on the core technology of the organization or implementation of a particular innovation. There is an avoidance of expertise or offering of assistance in whatever the organization's product or service may be. Instead, the OD perspective focuses on the personal and interpersonal dimensions of people in organization settings. A core assumption of OD is that the members of the organization will be better able to solve their technology problems as they become more skilled in the "technology" of OD.

DISCUSSION QUESTIONS

1. Have you ever participated in an OD planned change effort? What was it like? What processes were used?

2. Have you ever participated in an OD training exercise? What skills were being developed? Did you find that you were able to bring the skill back to your work setting? Why or why not?

3. Planned change efforts using strategies such as strategic planning and school improvement are designed to involve everyone in reviewing the current situation and setting an agenda for the future. As a leader, how would you see using OD concepts and methods to involve everyone?

4. Participants in OD are often slow to see any connection between the time spent in doing exercises and doing their job. What do you think about the OD reasoning of not using the work context in process skill development? What would be gained or lost from embedding the training in the work context?

5. The OD consultant represents himself or herself as not bringing a solution to any particular problem and not representing a certain direction for the organization. By comparison, the change agent in the Diffusion Perspective openly represents and advocates for adoption of a specific innovation. In many ways OD and the consultant are innovations that must be adopted. To what extent do you think that OD and the consultant are innovations? With OD, what is the innovation(s)?

FIELDWORK ACTIVITIES

1. Observe several meetings of a group. This could be a committee, a department, a team, or a complete staff. Use the skills list presented in Figure 11.3 to observe the group's process. Which skills do individual members of the group apply? How are decisions made? Does the

leader make them, or are they made by consensus or voting? Would other skills, if used, help the group in accomplishing its tasks?

2. Go to the Web or one of the suggested readings and select a training exercise that you could process for a group. Work closely with a colleague or your instructor on all that is entailed in serving as the process consultant for the selected exercise. Develop a feedback form to evaluate your role in leading the exercise and your skill as the consultant. Select a group of colleagues or fellow students and try facilitating a session. At the end, be sure to critique the exercise and your role as the process consultant.

3. Examine a strategic plan, school improvement plan, or similar product from a whole-organization planned change effort. Interview several of the participants. Ask them to reflect on the process, as well as the product. Who led the work? Were decisions made by voting, consensus, or the leader? Was there a process consultant? If so, what role did that person play? Develop an analysis of the OD processes that were in place. Were any introduced by the leader or consultant? In hindsight, what other skills might have been of help if employed?

CONDUCT A STUDY

1. Many interesting and useful action research studies can be imagined. For example, if a particular team or committee wanted to improve its functioning, a study could be made of the process skills currently used. With agreement to do action research, the list of individual process skills outlined in Figure 11.3 could be used to develop a checklist. Then a colleague who is not a member of the group could observe several meetings and use the checklist to tally skills use. Subsequent analysis and discussion of the checklist data could be used to identify skills that are frequently used and some for which an OD exercise might provide useful training.

2. OD theory, constructs, and tools could be used to study planning processes. For example, each year most schools must complete a school improvement plan. Studies could be done of the extent to which different OD constructs, skills, and tools are used. A major source of variation across schools is the extent to which the school improvement plan (SIP) is used to make decisions throughout the year. Examining differences among schools, or other organizations, that are associated with more and less use of the plan could be informative.

ADDITIONAL READINGS

Carter, L., Giber, D., & Goldsmith, M. (Eds.). (2001). *Best practices in organizational development and change: Culture, leadership, retention, performance, and coaching.* San Francisco: Jossey-Bass/Pfeiffer.
    Case studies along with assessment instruments and evaluation tools are described as they are being used with a variety of companies. The cases are organized around five topic areas: (a) OD and change, (b) leadership development, (c) recruitment and retention, (d) performance management, and (e) coaching and mentoring.

Clegg, S. R., Hardy, C., Lawrence, T., & Nord, W. R. (2006). *The SAGE handbook of organization studies.* Thousand Oaks, CA: Sage.
    Although not an OD book, this edited volume is an excellent resource for those who are interested in contemporary models, research, and thinking about organizations. The chapters in this handbook document the increased rigor in thinking, theory building, and research that is true of OD and the extensive

field of organization studies. Chapter titles reflect new ways of thinking about organization change—for example "Creative Deconstruction," "Diverse Identities in Organizations," "Metaphors of Communication and Organization," and "Organizing for Innovation."

French, W. L., & Bell, C. H. (1998). *Organization development: Behavioral science interventions for organization improvement* (6th ed.). Upper Saddle River, NJ: Prentice-Hall.

> For a traditional view of OD, how it works, and keys to its success, this is the book. The authors are long-time scholars and practitioners in the field of OD. The history, current practices, and examples of efforts to make long-range change in organization culture and social processes are described. In many ways this book reflects the dynamic and evolving nature of OD, from its earlier human potential days to today's context of globalization and contemporary innovations such as total quality management.

Gallos, J. V., & Schein, E. H. (Eds.) (2006). *Organization development: A Jossey-Bass reader.* San Francisco: CA: Jossey-Bass

> The authors for each chapter in this book of readings and the editors are major names in the field. The early chapters present the history of OD. There are readings that describe various theories and others that explore interventions. Separate readings explore intervening with small and large groups. Other readings address intervening on whole organizations.

McLean, G. N. (2006). *Organization development: Principles, processes, performance.* San Francisco, CA: Berrett-Koehler.

> The author brings systems theory to understanding and applying OD. Chapters progress from implementing OD at the individual level, to teams, to organizations, to community wide and national levels. The final chapters address two important topics that are often neglected: reasons for separation from the organization, and ethics.

PART V

COMBINING VIEWS
AND TOOLS

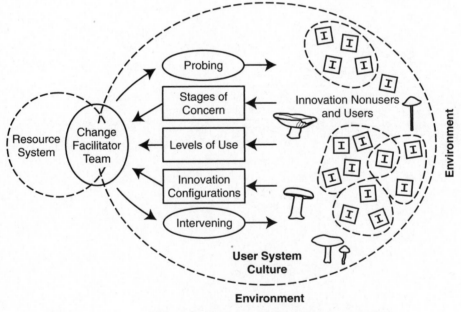

THE CONCERNS-BASED ADOPTION (CBAM)

ORGANIZING FRAMEWORK

This organizing framework brings together in one place many of the key constructs and ideas presented in Chapters 1 through 11. The details of individual implementation along with the grouping and networking of individuals are represented. The important roles of change facilitators to diagnose the current state of implementation and to make interventions are identified. Also included are symbols of Mushrooms to remind us of the uncontrolled but very important social construction of meaning that all change process participants contribute.

CHAPTER 12

Chapter 12 presents several examples of how the perspectives, constructs, tools, and techniques introduced in Chapters 1 through 11 can be applied. Some of the examples come from research and evaluation studies, and others are drawn from the "real world" of implementing change. Another of the main change perspectives is emphasized, the Concerns-Based Adoption Model (CBAM). This perspective uses many of the constructs and tools introduced in the preceding chapters.

The intents of this chapter are four:

1. Illustrate how some of the ideas and tools introduced in the earlier chapters can be used to facilitate and to evaluate change initiatives
2. Report on more of the research and evaluation studies that have incorporated change process constructs and measures
3. Stimulate further thought and reflection about how the change process works, especially the importance of leaders and leadership
4. Emphasize the importance of continually keeping in mind the ethics of change agentry—in other words, when do efforts to facilitate change become manipulation?

In addition, the reader needs to keep in mind that there is more—more to be read and more to be learned about how better to facilitate the implementation of change at the individual, organization, and social system levels.

IMPLEMENTING CHANGE

Assessing and Facilitating the Process from Individuals to Whole Systems

We have spent all this time implementing this program. How do we know if it is making a difference?

—School district superintendent after 3 years of curriculum reform

We are getting a new principal. I wonder what she will be like?

—One teacher talking to another

The evidence is clear. When this approach is fully implemented, outcomes go up. But teachers hate it. Should we insist on its use?

—District office administrator

The preceding chapters have introduced a rich set of principles, constructs, tools, and perspectives. Each can be of assistance in understanding, facilitating, evaluating, and researching change efforts. Across the chapters the unit of change—that is, the "implementer"—ranges from the individual(s) to groups, to whole organizations, to considerations of change across large social systems. Facilitating change has different scope and depth depending on the size and type of change unit. Implementing a change with a few individuals is vastly different from accomplishing a companywide change or changing a state or nation.

The chapters have been organized to move from the individual to the large-scale system. Chapter 1 introduced a set of Change Principles that should be accepted as givens. These are basic facts and realities that apply to any change effort. The metaphor of an Implementation Bridge is helpful for visualizing the principle that *change is a process*. Chapter 2 addressed the importance of developing a special form of organization culture, *Professional Learning Communities*. Change will be more successful in organizations with a PLC. Chapters 3, 4, and 5 described three "Diagnostic Dimensions" (*Innovation Configurations, Stages of Concern,* and *Levels of Use*). Each of these offered a frame of reference for assessing how far across the bridge each implementer has progressed. Each also can be used in planning for facilitating change.

The next set of chapters examined the importance of leadership, especially the *Change Facilitator Style* of the leader. The actions taken to facilitate change, in other words *interventions,* are initiated by many Change Facilitators. Another intervention species is socially constructed *Intervention Mushrooms.* These can be toxic or nutritious for a change effort.

The first eight chapters were based in one of the established change perspectives, the *Concerns-Based Adoption Model (CBAM),* first proposed by Hall, Wallace, and Dossett in 1973. The final three chapters broadened the view of change by introducing three other widely used perspectives: Systems, Diffusion, and Organization Development (OD). Each of these perspectives has an extensive history of theory, research, and application. In total they represent many constructs and tools that can be used to understand, evaluate, and facilitate change efforts.

Another significant characteristic of the constructs and tools presented in this text is that all are *evidence-based.* The information and ideas introduced in each chapter are not groundless generalities and platitudes. They have been conceived through research and deal with the realities of implementing change on the ground. Each chapter references some of the extensive research verifying and supporting the introduced constructs and their applications. Each chapter provides illustrations of how each construct and its tools can be used to increase change process success.

In this chapter, illustrations of how the various constructs and tools can be used *in combination* will be described. This chapter's topics will unfold along the same lines from individual(s), to groups, to organizations, and finally to large systems. Also, success entails more than having implementers move across the Implementation Bridge; the ultimate purpose of a change initiative is to *increase outcomes.* In this chapter research examples and issues related to linking extent of implementation to outcomes are presented. The final, and not to be underrated, topic will be *ethics of change agentry.* All of the constructs, tools, and applications introduced in this text can be picked up and used in responsible, or malevolent, ways. Users and recipients of use of these constructs and tools must continually reflect on the question "Is this an appropriate action to take?"

FOCUS QUESTIONS

1. What are the different units of change?
2. How can combinations of the three Diagnostic Dimensions (Innovation Configuration [IC], Stages of Change [SoC], and Levels of Use [LoU]) be used to measure movement across the Implementation Bridge?
3. The CBAM change perspective integrates many constructs. What are its features?
4. What research designs should be used when the phenomenon of implementation is taken into consideration?
5. What are the relationships between school principal Change Facilitator (CF) Style and student test scores?
6. When change process constructs are used as a heuristic, what are some of the questions that can be generated?
7. How do the various constructs apply to large system change, or do they?
8. Are there guidelines or questions to ask to ensure that those facilitating change are being responsible and ethical?

UNITS OF CHANGE RANGE FROM THE VERY LARGE TO THE VERY SMALL

An important question to answer early in a change effort is this: What is the unit of change? Is it an entire system or organization, certain departments, or particular individuals? The answer to this question tells a lot about what should be the target(s) of interventions. Regardless of the answer, without exception some individuals will be expected to implement change. Systems and organizations may adopt change, but individuals implement it. The question about the unit of change is important since interventions have to be targeted toward someone(s), a team, and/or a whole entity. The larger the unit, the more targets for interventions. The four basic units of change are the individual, teams, an entire organization, and large systems (see Figure 12.1).

The System as the Unit of Change

Oftentimes, large systems such as the farmers in Iowa (Chapter 10), a national company, the statewide delivery of a service, or a school district are targeted for change. For example, a corporation may determine that the introduction of a new product line requires the attention of the entire nationwide company. A state identifies an approach to Response to Intervention (RTI)

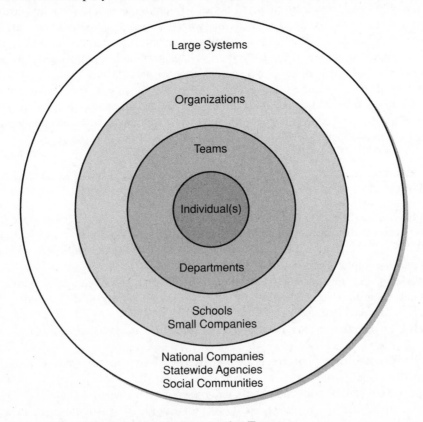

FIGURE 12.1   Units of Change, Potential Intervention Targets

that should be used in all districts and schools. A school district develops a new administrator evaluation program and a performance pay plan for teachers that are closely connected to student outcomes. Each of these initiatives includes the expectation that the "smaller" units will be implementing the change. If they do not, there will not be systemwide change.

The assumption is often made in large-scale change initiatives that all parts of the system must do the same thing and at the same time. For example, the federal education mandates around No Child Left Behind (NCLB) treated all states, school districts, and schools equally in terms of expectations and consequences for lack of performance. In this "one size fits all" approach, all subparts or subsystems of the system are given the same directives, rules and regulations, and consequences. In contrast to what was stated in Chapter 1, Change Principle 9, there seems to have been a belief that a "mandate" intervention is all that is needed for change to occur. Although the whole system is being targeted, the thinking behind the approach is not systemic.

A systems approach would build in adjustments for various subsystems. With NCLB, for example, adjustments would have been made for Connecticut and California which have been focusing their testing around growth. Other adjustments could be based on the distribution of English Language Learners, the extent of teacher professional development, and the extent of already in place state-required testing. When the entire system is the target and no differentiated support is provided for subsystems, the likelihood is strong that change will be uneven. As became clear with NCLB, some subsystems (e.g., states or schools) will implement the change quickly, and others will lag far behind.

An entire system can change, if, as in the example of the Instituto Tecnológico y de Estudios Superiores de Monterrey (ITESM) effort, a clear goal is stated and held to, there are wide-ranging and multiple years of professional development, and administrators provide support and assistance (see Chapter 9 on systems thinking). Along the way systemic thinking and adaptations based on the interactions and needs of each subsystem (i.e., campus) are necessary. Without guiding and supporting interventions customized for each subsystem, it is nearly impossible to achieve systemwide change. A small percentage of individuals who may already have the capacity to enact the identified change will proceed, whereas most others will become Late Majority adopters at best.

One of the key strategies for having successful change across a large system is to differentiate professional development and support for the leaders of the various subsystems. Leader training and development should be different from that provided to the front-line implementers. The leaders must be skilled in guiding and providing support and assistance to the implementers, rather than being seen as implementers of the change themselves. A systemic approach will include differentiations in interventions based in considerations of each leader's CF Style.

Pothole Warning

Many policymakers and organization leaders assume that proclamations and directives will accomplish change.

Pothole Repair

Regardless of the unit of change, the importance individuals make to change success must be understood.

An Organization as the Unit of Change

An organization as the unit of change could be a particular business site, such as the local fast-food restaurant or a specified school within a district. Each of these units does not operate independently of the system of which it is a part, but each organization can have its own change initiatives. Some changes may be initiated from the executive level, whereas others will start from lower levels within the organization. Most of these changes are likely intended to improve services, products, and outcomes. In each case, the executive leader (e.g., the school principal and department or team leaders) will have particular CF Styles (Chapter 6). The overall plan for implementing change should take these characteristics into consideration. All the organization leaders will have some responsibility for rallying the "troops" and convincing them that the change is important and beneficial. However, each will do it on their own. Initiation of a change effort should include explanation of why the need for change, what the change entails, and professional development to create the capacity to perform the change (SoC must be addressed). As implementation progresses, many more interventions will be needed that address the whole organization. The entire organization should receive the same messages that focus overall on what the change is and how it will work. Interventions must address the subunits, the individual departments, or teams. Other interventions will be needed to attend to individual members of each team/department.

Teams or Divisions as the Unit of Change

A smaller intervention unit is that of teams and departments. The OD perspective (Chapter 11) provides interventions, such as training exercises, to help these units develop problem-solving and group-work process skills. Innovation-related interventions that address the whole group and others unique to individuals will be needed. As was stated previously, when a whole organization or system is implementing change some customized intervening still will need to be done for each team/group. For example, the marketing division will need support and assistance that differ from the sales division. The district office curriculum department staff will need different interventions than will the accountability department. At this unit of change level the interventions can be tailored in more personalized ways and still address attaining the desired outcomes. It should be feasible for the leader to meet with the members and solicit their ideas for support and assistance in implementing the change.

The Individual as the Unit of Change

Regardless of the overall scale of change or how large or small the units of intervention, implementation of the innovation is accomplished at the individual level. In some way each change perspective addresses the role of the individual in implementing change. The Diffusion perspective identifies five Adopter Categories. The OD perspective emphasizes process skills, whereas the cornerstone of the Concerns-Based model are the three Diagnostic Dimensions (SoC, LoU, and IC). Nearly all—if not all—change initiatives should take into account the role of the individual. As has been emphasized at several points in this text, change is not accomplished until each person implements the innovation.

REFLECTION QUESTIONS

In your experience, which units of change have you seen emphasized? Which should have received more emphasis?

THE CHANGE PERSPECTIVE OF THE CONCERNS-BASED ADOPTION MODEL

CBAM was first proposed by Hall, Wallace, and Dossett in 1973. Key elements of this change perspective have been introduced throughout this book. The three Diagnostic Dimensions (Chapters 3, 4, and 5) of the CBAM focus closely on the process and elements of implementation. CBAM incorporates elements of each of the other major perspectives that were introduced in Chapters 9, 10, and 11. In the graphic representation of CBAM (Figure 12.2), the larger system view is acknowledged, as are the three Diagnostic Dimensions and the importance of change facilitation leadership. Interventions, including Mushrooms, are part of CBAM as well.

CBAM Addresses the Individual

As the name implies, the CBAM perspective begins with emphasizing the importance of understanding and addressing the personal side of change. Each person differs measurably in terms of their understanding and skill to implement change (LoU), willingness to change (SoC), and fidelity to the developer's vision (IC). Some will change readily, others will come to understanding and be willing to implement a change over time, and some will never reach full acceptance. Some will become confident and competent users of ideal configurations quite quickly. Others will struggle. Understanding and addressing these differences are important to overall implementation success. Regardless of how big or small the overall unit of

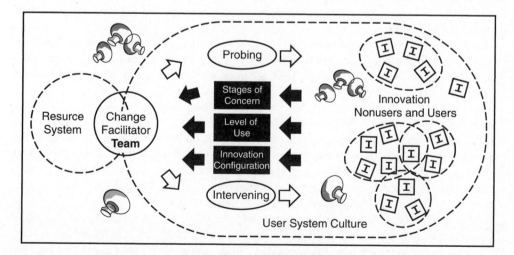

FIGURE 12.2   The Concerns-Based Adoption Model (CBAM)

change, the three Diagnostic Dimensions of the CBAM perspective (see Figure 12.1) can be used to account for and address individual differences.

Pothole Warning

Too many see SoC, LoU, and IC as being of use only with individuals.

Pothole Repair

Yes, SoC, LoU, and IC are described and apply to individuals. However, the information from individuals can be aggregated for groups and whole system assessments.

CBAM Addresses Teams and Groups

In the CBAM perspective diagnostic information about individuals can be aggregated for teams, departments, whole organizations, and across large systems. For example, in most projects the individual SoC profiles will be combined to develop a group SoC profile. With a large sample of respondents, subgroup SoC profiles can be identified as well.

SoC Whole Group Profiles: Laptop Computers for Teachers.   In the state of Victoria, Australia, the Ministry of Education decided to provide each teacher with a laptop computer. As part of the initiative an evaluation team was contracted to monitor implementation (Matthews, Marshall, & Milne, 2000). One of the assessment measures was the SoC Questionnaire (SoCQ). Figure 12.3 is the SoC group profile for the study sample of 704 teachers.

This profile compares well with the theoretical SoC Wave Motion (see Figure 4.3) that depicts the ideal flow of concerns as implementers move from nonuse to early implementation. The group laptop SoC profile indicates a combination of Self and Task concerns being intense, which reflects what the researchers had been finding through interviews. Some teachers were still not doing much and uncomfortable with what they should be doing (Stage 1 Informational and Stage 2 Personal) while others were trying out many of the programs and potential uses (Stage 3 Management) but not yet skilled or certain about how they would be used on a regular basis.

An atypical point on the group SoC profile is the higher Stage 5 Collaboration concerns. Upon further investigation this was explained by the fact that for 6 years the state department of education "has encouraged teachers to work together and to support one another" (Matthews & Hall, 1999, p. 3).

SoC Subgroup Profiles.   With a large sample of individual data it can be important to search for subgroups of individual SoC profiles that have common characteristics. For example, in the laptop study six subgroups were identified. Each fit within the overall Self–Task early implementation theme but varied in which SoC were most intense. Some were very high on Stage 1 Informational, and another subgroup had very intense Stage 2 Personal concerns. Two of the subgroups had "tailing up" on Stage 6 Refocusing.

All these data reflect the importance of understanding the current status of individual implementers and aggregating to assess the overall status of groups and the whole system. With this diagnostic information, interventions can be prepared that are customized for each subgroup as well as for the whole.

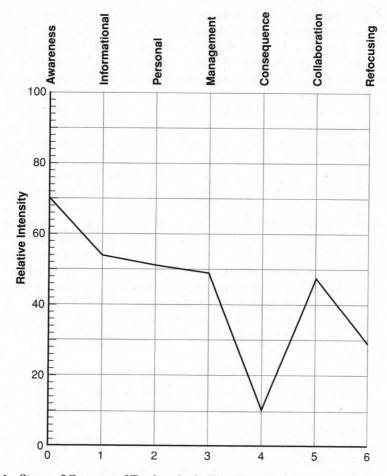

FIGURE 12.3   **Stages of Concerns of Teachers in the First Use of Implementing Laptop Computers**

REFLECTION QUESTION

Given the information from the Australian SoC implementation assessment of teachers using laptops, what would you recommend be included in the next phase of change facilitating interventions?

The Implementation Bridge: Using LoU and IC to Assess Change Progress

Collecting implementation data at any point in time represents a snapshot of current status. One-time data collection does not tell us what the situation was in the past. Information from a snapshot most certainly can be used as diagnostic information for planning future interventions. Ideally, multiple snapshots will be accrued across time. Then movement across the Implementation Bridge can be charted. The following example comes from a study where LoU and IC were measured at the end of the first and second years of implementation.

A School District Superintendent Wants to Know.   One school system with a history of making concerted efforts to improve schooling and to evaluate the results is the U.S. Department of Defense Dependents Schools (DoDDS). This is the system of school districts spread around the world to provide schooling for the children of members of the U.S. military. In one of the DoDDS school districts in Germany, the superintendent made a concerted effort to support the implementation of a dramatically different approach to teaching mathematics. The curriculum innovation was based on the standards for teaching and learning developed by the National Council for the Teaching of Mathematics (NCTM). The approach required teachers to make a dramatic change in their teaching. Rather than teaching rules for computation, the new teaching strategy was constructivist: Teachers should pose mathematical problems, and the students should construct answers using their own approaches. Rather than the teacher explaining the one correct way, students must explain their reasoning and how they got their answers.

This approach represented a major change for many veteran teachers. Understanding this, the superintendent developed an implementation support strategy that was centered on employing three master teachers as districtwide specialists. The change facilitators designed workshops, presented demonstration lessons, consulted with teachers, and paced the implementation effort. In addition, the superintendent understood that change is a process, not an event (Change Principle 2), so the commitment to having three math specialists was kept in place for 3 years (Johnson, 2000).

Given the size and seriousness of the investment plus the political risk, since focusing on mathematics for 3 years meant that a number of other areas were not as high on the priority list, led the superintendent to ask her question: How can I know if this investment is making any difference?

Assessing Implementation.   The Implementation Bridge metaphor made sense to the superintendent and the other district leaders. The decision was made to assess the extent to which teachers were moving across the bridge by measuring teacher's LoU (Chapter 5) and for each classroom completing an Innovation Configuration (IC) Map (see Chapter 3).

Action Research Can Happen.   An added dimension to this effort was that the change process researchers and the school district staff collaborated in design and conduct of the study. School district administrators and lead teachers were engaged in data collection, data analysis, interpretation of findings, and report writing. It was a true example of action research (Eden & Huxham, 1996). The research questions were developed by the district, and researchers and practitioners collaborated in conducting all aspects of the study. In addition, the data about implementation were used as diagnostic information for further facilitating implementation, as well as for answering the superintendent's question.

Two Snapshots Are Better Than One.   To document change, extent of implementation must be measured a minimum of two times. In the districtwide mathematics implementation project, extent of implementation was done at the end of the first and second years of the effort. The school district staff, including the superintendent, were trained to research criteria in conducting and rating LoU interviews. Each year they, along with the researchers, collected data on over a hundred teachers representing all schools and across Grades K–8 (Thornton & West, 1999).

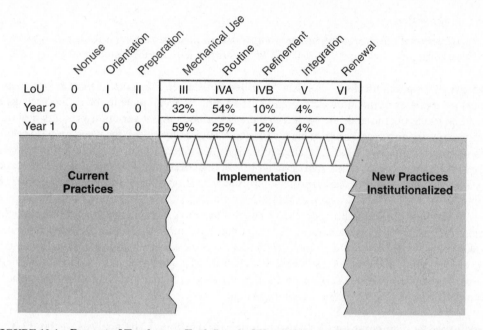

FIGURE 12.4   Percent of Teachers at Each Level of Use (LoU) of a Standards-Based Mathematics Curriculum.

LoU Is One Indicator.   The LoU data for the first 2 years of the implementation effort are summarized in Figure 12.4. Three key findings were as follows:

1. Each year all teachers sampled were users at some level of the new approach. No teachers were rated at LoU 0 Nonuse, I Orientation, or II Preparation.
2. The year 2 pattern of an increasing proportion of teachers being at LoU IVA Routine Use or higher was a clear indication that teachers were moving further across the Implementation Bridge (Thornton & West, 1999).
3. Even after 2 years of systematic support, one third of the teachers were still at LoU III Mechanical Use.

Another Indicator: Innovation Configurations.   The LoU data documented that teachers were engaged with using the innovation, but these data do not inform about the pieces, features, and functions of the innovation that were being used. Answering this question is the purpose of IC Mapping. For the math study, an IC Map was developed. A component of this map was presented as Figure 3.4 OLINK. The IC Map was used to observe and document classroom practices as well as a guide for targeting teacher training, coaching, and professional development (Alquist & Hendrickson, 1999).

Pothole Warning

Do not trust what an implementer says he or she is doing with an innovation, including responses on paper-and-pencil or Web-based surveys.

Pothole Repair

Determining what actually is being implemented must be checked through direct observations, review of artifacts, and carefully constructed interview questions.

Fidelity of Implementation.   As was described in Chapter 3, in an IC Map the key operational *components* of the innovation are identified. For each component, the different ways it could be made operational, the *variations,* are described. The *a* variation presents a word-picture description of best practice; the *b* variation is slightly less ideal; the *c* variation is acceptable but not exciting; and the *d, e,* and *f* variations describe practices that are different from what is expected as part of the innovation—in this case, traditional practice. Based on classroom observation and interviewing, the appropriate variation of each component is circled on the IC Map.

Computer clustering procedures can be employed to group classrooms according to the extent of fidelity of implementation. IC Maps that have more *a* variations circled represent high fidelity, whereas those with many *d, e,* and *f* variations represent limited fidelity and/or use of something other than the innovation. When IC Map data are placed on the Implementation Bridge (see Figure 12.5), those configurations of practice that include more *a* and *b* variations will be placed further across the bridge.

Fidelity of Implementation of a Mathematics Innovation.   The analysis of the IC Map data for the mathematics study revealed a wide range of configurations, including some classrooms that were all *a*'s and *b*'s, and other classrooms with more *c*'s and *d*'s. In the *d/e* classrooms many of the IC Map components indicated that traditional practices were still prevalent. One overall finding was that by the end of the second year of implementation effort, less than one third of the classrooms exhibited implementation with high fidelity. This is

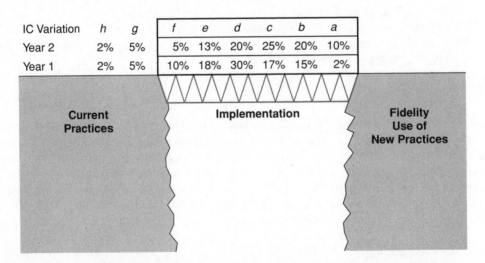

IC Variation	h	g	f	e	d	c	b	a
Year 2	2%	5%	5%	13%	20%	25%	20%	10%
Year 1	2%	5%	10%	18%	30%	17%	15%	2%

Current Practices   Implementation   Fidelity Use of New Practices

FIGURE 12.5   IC Map Data for the First 2 Years of Implementation of a Standards-Based Mathematics Curriculum

IMPLICATIONS FOR EVALUATORS, RESEARCHERS, AND LEADERS FACILITATING CHANGE

1. The unit of change can range from large social systems to individuals. Some interventions are needed that address each unit of change.
2. In the CBAM, systemic thinking is employed as change facilitators regularly assess SoC, LoU, and IC and then provide relevant interventions to individuals, subgroups, and the whole system.
3. Impact concerns (Stage 4 Consequence, Stage 5 Collaboration, and Stage 6 Refocusing) will be found regularly in organizations that have a PLC type of organization culture. In these settings there will be fewer Toxic Intervention Mushrooms.
4. When Self concerns are high, any indications of uncertainty and/or misleading information contribute to the rapid germination and growth of Toxic Mushrooms.
5. The design of evaluation and research studies should not implicitly assume use and nonuse; this must be checked at the individual level in *both* treatment and comparison groups.
6. Studies of outcomes should incorporate assessment of extent of implementation in treatment as well as any comparison groups.
7. Studies of outcomes should include more than effects of individual implementers. They should address the role and potential for effects of the leaders.

not an unusual finding and should again remind leaders and evaluators that implementing complex innovations takes time and extended support.

REFLECTION QUESTION

There are three ways to assess implementation (SoC, LoU, and IC). Which would you want to use in your next change initiative?

The Bottom-Line Question: What Is the Relationship Between Extent of Implementation and Outcomes?

As important as facilitating implementation and assessing the extent of implementation are, the ultimate purpose is to see improvements in outcomes. With changes in curriculum, instruction, and schools, the bottom line has to be determining what has happened with student learning. This question cannot be answered until the new way is fully implemented. Unless the implementers have worked through the mechanical problems of use, have implemented fidelity configurations, and have reduced Self and Task concerns, any assessment of student effects will be incomplete and probably misleading.

Pothole Warning

Assuming that no nonusers are in randomly assigned treatment groups and no users are in randomly assigned control groups is a mistake.

Pothole Repair

Use/nonuse must be documented at the individual unit level within both the treatment and control groups.

Which Research Design Is Best?

As change process researchers, the authors of this text strongly recommend a paradigm shift when it comes to selecting a research design. The traditional treatment and control group designs rarely, if ever, make sense in schools—or, for that matter, in other organization settings.

Problems With Treatment-Control Group Designs.   Beginning in 2000 the U.S. Department of Education strongly advocated for rigorous research. The basic criterion for rigorous research—the "gold standard"—was to randomly assign subjects to treatment and control groups. For example, teachers in the treatment schools would be trained and given the special program. Teachers in the control schools would not be trained in the program. Then the researchers would examine test results from the two sets of schools to see if students in the treatment schools had significantly higher scores.

Consideration of the constructs, measures, and study findings described in each chapter of this text point out why this traditional research design makes little sense. As was just described with the mathematics study, teachers in the treatment schools will be implementing the program with varying degrees of use and fidelity. Also as was described in Chapter 5, if LoU and IC are measured it is quite possible that some teachers in the treatment schools will not be using the innovation. It also is quite possible that some teachers in the comparison schools will be using some practices that are quite similar to those associated with the innovation. They are similar components in operation but may have different names.

Traditional treatment–control group research designs have very limited applicability when humans are the innovation users. All sorts of variations in implementation can be imagined when SoC, LoU, IC, and the Implementation Bridge are taken into consideration. At its most absurd, the "gold standard" research paradigm demands that one group of kids be taught and another group not be taught to read. In reality, no matter the subject area, it is likely that members of the comparison group will have some sort of practices in place that address the targeted student outcomes. When change process research and theory are taken into consideration, a different research design makes more sense.

Comparing Degrees of Implementation.   A more logical approach to research and evaluation studies is to compare higher to lower fidelity implementations. In practice this entails assessing how far across the bridge each implementer has moved and comparing outcomes each is obtaining. This is the approach used in the mathematics study referenced previously in this chapter (George, Hall, & Uchiyama, 2000). In that study higher fidelity configurations and higher LoU were associated with significantly higher student test scores.

If some sort of dichotomy needs to included (because that is what the grant office expects), then compare those who have moved all the way across the bridge (LoU IVA Routine and above) with those that have not stepped on the bridge (LoU 0 Nonuse, I Orientation, and II Preparation). In a summative study LoU III Mechanical users should be left out of the analysis. If a quality IC Map has been constructed, the right-hand component variations—the d's, e's, and f's—will represent traditional practices. Comparisons of outcomes can then be made between a–b configurations and d–e configurations. Either way the Implementation Bridge offers a research design that is based in the realities of implementation.

REFLECTION QUESTIONS

Which research design do you believe should be used in studies? Is the gold standard or extent of implementation making more sense?

LEADERSHIP IS A VERY IMPORTANT FACTOR

In Chapter 6 three different behavioral profiles of leaders—CF Styles—were described. Initiators have a vision; they push and have passion for their school. Managers focus on following the rules, having clear procedures, and controlling budgets. Most Responders are friendly, and all want everyone to get along. Chapter 6 presented research findings about the relationships between principal CF Style and teacher implementation success. Two additional themes about the importance of leadership are introduced here: (a) the relationship of leadership to student outcomes and (b) themes to consider when there is leader succession.

Relationships Between CF Style and Student Outcomes

There is a rich history of research and evaluation studies that draw causal connections between what teachers do and how much students learn. A less studied and less considered question is to inquire about the possibility of there being a pass-through relationship from the effects of the principal. We know that there are significant relationships between principal CF Style and teacher implementation success. Do you suppose there could be relationships between principal leadership and student learning? Or are all of the outcomes dependent directly on what individual teachers do? We now have the first study that addressed this question.

Principal CF Style and Student Test Scores.   The one study that has examined this relationship was described briefly in Chapter 6. In that study, 27 elementary school principals in one urban school district were assessed for CF Style. Fourth-grade student test scores on the Connecticut Mastery Tests (CMT) for Direct Assessment of Writing, Editing and Revising, Reading Comprehension and Mathematics were used as the indicators of student outcomes. Students CMT scores from fourth grade were compared with the scores they obtained near the end of fifth grade (Hall, Negroni, & George, 2008). Statistically significant relationships were found between the principal's CF Style categorical ratings and student achievement on three of the four tests. The researcher's summary of the study findings was presented in Table 6.1.

A Summary Systemic Framework.   The authors of the principal CF Style by student outcomes study developed a framework to summarize the various relationships that have been identified and studied. Figure 12.6 presents this framework. In it multiple pathways and relationships indicate what is known about the relationships among teacher implementation success, principal CF Style, and student outcomes. In many ways this figure represents the *systems view* that was addressed in Chapter 9.

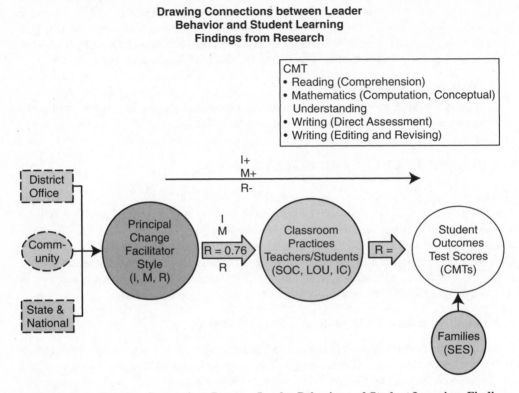

FIGURE 12.6   Drawing Connections Between Leader Behavior and Student Learning: Findings from Research

Clearly teachers have direct effects on student learning. Several studies have documented that principal leadership affects teacher success in implementing change. In addition, schools are systems. The findings from the more recent study suggest that there are pass-through student learning effects based on how principals lead change efforts. Another potential implication of these findings is that individual teachers are not isolated islands in affecting student learning. A schoolwide impact is related to principal leadership—in other words, no teacher is an island but rather each is part of an organization called a school. There are individual and whole system effects of their efforts.

Principal CF Style and School Organization Culture

As was described in Chapters 2, 8, and 11 the participants in an organization share their beliefs, views, and interpretations of events and actions. One result is the shared themes of Intervention Mushrooms. Another is identification of what is important. Still another is the implicit rules about how things really get done within the organization. In many ways these themes and elements are the characterization of the organization's culture.

One of the authors of this text, along with several colleagues, including some doctoral students, have developed a set of descriptions of how the organization culture of a school is related to the principal's CF Style. This set of ideas is presented in Table 12.1. As can be inferred from these descriptions, the themes, what is valued, and how things work within each of these cultures differ dramatically. In the Responder CF Style school the culture is balkanized. A small group of teachers runs the school. These teachers have all the supplies and control the agenda. The teachers who are not members of the controlling clique are left out: "Where did you get that paper? There is none in the supply closet." The Manager CF Style school culture is organized and efficient: "Everyone will have the same amount of supplies." In the Initiator CF

TABLE 12.1   Indicators and Relationships Between Principal CF Style and Organization Culture

	CF STYLE		
ELEMENTS OF CULTURE	**RESPONDER**	**MANAGER**	**INITIATOR**
Culture Name	*Balkanized*	*Efficient*	*Strategic*
Indicators of Culture	Individuals are isolated, with a clique running the school. Principal decision making is influenced most through personal contact.	Principal controls through literal interpretation of rules and procedures and allocation of resources. Schedules, procedures, and tasks are clearly spelled out.	Efforts are integrated from top to bottom with clear connections between day-to-day activities and principal's vision. Leadership is shared with those who support the vision.
Myths and Stories	Gossip about adults Frustrations and complaining about what adults don't do	Stories about obtaining and using resources and when someone did not follow the rules	Student successes, sharing resources, and exchange of ideas about instruction
Symbols	Adult centered; some have a lot, others little.	Published rules and procedures; plenty of supplies	Data walls; student progress monitoring student work and learning
Center of Action	Taking care of *me* Protecting one's classroom	*Controlling* tasks and resources *Following* rules and procedures	(Teaching and *Learning*) Collective effort and continuing improvements
Who gets what	First come, first served: attending to the loudest voices	Equality: All receive the same.	Equity: Each receives what he or she needs based on job tasks.
Theme	"Us. vs. Them" A few have everything, others have what's left.	"We are very busy." More resources will be needed to do more things.	"We are a team." All continually working to improve learning for all students.

Style school, distribution of resources is based on function and need: "Since she is teaching ESL she should have the white board, while math teachers need document projectors."

CF Style, Organization Culture, and Leader Succession

An additional application for this framework about the relationship of CF Style to organization culture is in considering factors related to leader succession. Interesting predictions can be made about what will happen when a particular leader leaves and is replaced by another. For example, when an Initiator replaces a Responder the clique that had been getting its way will no longer be able to do so. The Initiator will take control of resource allocations, schedules, and school priorities. The clique no longer can run the school. The clique's typical reaction is to complain to parents, district administrators, and maybe members of the school board about how bad the new principal is doing. The first year or two can be rough as new norms and procedures are established. Similar scenarios can be envisioned for other combinations of leader successions.

> ### REFLECTION QUESTIONS
> **What kinds of changes in organization culture have you observed when there was a change in the leader? What was the CF Style of the departing leader, and what was the CF Style of the incoming leader?**

FINAL REFLECTIONS ABOUT IMPLEMENTING CHANGE

As this final chapter comes to a close, we offer several points of reflection. Some relate to facilitating change, others to studying change processes, and some hint at current dilemmas the authors face.

Ethical Issues in Facilitating Change

As architects and creators of the CBAM model, and as researchers and writers about PLCs and systemic change, we worry about how the constructs, measures, and ideas described in this book will be used by well-meaning, and perhaps not so well-meaning, persons in the field. Do they fully understand the constructs? Do they have skills sufficiently adequate to interpret results from use of the measures, and will their responses—interventions—be valid and appropriate?

Understanding the Constructs.   We receive frequent phone calls from individuals who have modest knowledge of SoC, LoU, IC, CF Styles, and PLCs. They tend to have high levels of enthusiasm and want permission to use one of the constructs and its related measure. It is worrisome to us that some of these people are trying to use the concepts and measures without a deep and full understanding of what they are measuring. How will they use these measures and their results with people when they are not knowledgeable and skilled? We ask them to obtain and study the technical manuals. We encourage them to talk with us again about their interests in using the ideas for facilitation change and for research and evaluation. We also encourage participating in training workshops and becoming certified.

Responsible Use.   It is even more troubling to receive phone calls of inquiry from people who have administered the SoCQ, or one of the other measures, and don't know how to score it or interpret the results. It is important, we believe, to be sure the various instruments and techniques are used responsibly. But the dark side is not knowing about the many others who have not contacted us or accessed the technical resources. On the surface, constructs such as SoC and PLC appear deceptively simple, but, in truth, they are quite complex. The ethical dilemma for us, and the construct/measure users, is how to determine and ensure that each has sufficient knowledge and skill to use the constructs and measures responsibly.

Support at All Levels of the Organization.   Many change efforts fail because facilitation and assistance are not provided to all members of the organization, whether they be in executive, management, or staff positions. Support must come from the top of the organization to the middle managers as well as to the front-line implementers. In the case of educational change, this means that principals of the schools that are expected to change will need professional development in order to exercise their facilitation role successfully. All too frequently, principals and other middle managers are left in that space between the executive or policy level that requests change and the level of staff that will need to implement the change. Frequently, these leaders are without the tools or skills to do the job of supporting and assisting the staff well. Promoters of change should pay closer attention to the need to develop and support the middle managers who are the key to implementation success.

What About the Ethics of Change Agentry?

This is a question that we always raise with our students and clients. One way we phrase it is to ask "When does change facilitation become manipulation?" After all, we are talking about tools and techniques to get people to change. Unfortunately, little has been said or written about this important issue. Early in our work, we asked the late Matt Miles (1979) to write a paper and provide us with a seminar on ethics. His thoughts and wise counsel have stayed with us. For example, in reflecting on OD consultants, he pointed out critical issues related to the accountability of OD change agents:

> To whom are OD change agents accountable? At one level, as Bermant and Warwick (1978) point out, they are personally accountable for their actions, like any person in society. They should not lie, cheat, steal, or engage in similar socially reprehensible actions. And they are legally accountable in a very general sense, not only for misdemeanors and felonies, but for items like breach of contract. However, I have never heard of malpractice litigations being threatened against an OD practitioner (though it has occurred for encounter group leaders).
>
> In any case, litigation is a gross tool for insuring ethical behavior by practitioners. The most central form of accountability is that which OD consultants have toward their sponsors, who are paying the bill, in several senses. Sponsors can terminate contracts, or at least revise them, if the program is not functioning as intended. . . . Finally, there is professional accountability for OD practitioners, for which at present there are no formal structural supports comparable to those in medicine, law, accounting, and psychology. (Miles, 1979, pp. 8–9)

Matt Miles wrote these words more than 30 years ago. Unfortunately, the situation remains the same today. Maintaining ethical behavior is still mainly a personal responsibility.

Ethical Behavior from a Concerns-Based Perspective.   In the Concerns-Based perspective, *good* and *bad* are primarily defined in terms of what Change Facilitators do and do not do in relation to the present state of their clients. It is neither good nor bad for individuals to have certain concerns profiles, LoU, or IC. What *is* good or bad are the types of interventions that are made in response to each diagnostic profile. All interventions need to be *Concerns-Based.* They need to be related to the concerns of the clients, not the Change Facilitators.

Wrong Interventions.   As a simple example, consider a teacher with high Stage 2 Personal concerns. We have heard administrators and others say to these individuals something like "You should be concerned about students, not yourself." This is a wrong intervention from a Concerns-Based perspective, for its single effect will be to further raise the teacher's Personal concerns. "Good" interventions acknowledge the Personal concerns, attempt to provide additional information to increase understanding, and are supportive by providing stability.

Deliberate Manipulation.   At many points in this text your authors have emphasized the importance of being Concerns-Based. Still there will be times when inappropriate interventions are made either out of ignorance or innocence and, in some cases, malevolence. Unfortunately, examples are many of deliberate efforts to mislead. Further, it seams that the larger the system, the easier it is to manipulate its members.

A classic example unfolded in the summer of 2009 around President Obama and Congress' efforts to change health insurance law. Over the congressional summer recess, public forums were held around the country. This intervention strategy was intended as a way to hear from voters and to explain elements of the draft bills. Keep in mind the context at that time. It was the low point of the Great Recession, the stock market had plunged, and many people had lost their jobs. Stage 2 Personal concerns were high.

The public forums turned into orchestrated shouting matches, and code words such as *death panels* were used to misrepresent the real wording in the draft bills. In a few weeks Toxic Mushrooms were seeded and grew large across the nation. This anecdote is offered here as another ethical reminder: The use of disinformation and taking advantage of personal fears in times of uncertainty cannot be tolerated.

Continue Asking the Ethics Question.   Our point here is that the CF bears major responsibility for everyone achieving implementation success. In the Japanese management model, if an employee is not doing well, the manager has failed. Failure in a change effort is mainly in the hands of the leaders. Making Concerns-Based interventions increases the likelihood of success for the implementers and the facilitators. The question we frequently ask our students bears repeating: "When does change facilitation become manipulation?"

The responsible change facilitator frequently remembers to ask this important question:

"Is what I am doing right and best for everyone?"

SUMMARY

In this book we have presented key concepts about change, especially as they relate to people and how the process unfolds in organizational settings. Many additional ideas, research findings, and stories could be discussed, but it is time for you, the reader, to use what you have learned. Whether you are a potential user of an innovation, a key Change Facilitator, a leader, or a researcher, the constructs and tools presented here should be of help. We offer one brief caveat and one of our favorite phrases in the way of conclusion.

The Caveat

We have touched on the ethics of being a Change Facilitator. Here we offer a different emphasis. As dramatic as it may sound, the information presented in this book and similar texts can be used in very inappropriate and inexcusable ways. In fact, the tools and findings from research in the social sciences are in many ways far more dangerous than what the physicists were doing underneath the football stadium at the University of Chicago in 1940, since social scientists are talking about how to change people, organizations, and social systems. In addition, there are no rules of access to the information. Anyone can choose an idea out of this book, some questionnaire, or any other piece of work, and do with it what he or she pleases. No codes of conduct are in place, no security clearances. What happens from here depends on the integrity and professionalism of the user.

We ask that you think often about whether you are being responsible in what you do. Fortunately, the first concerns that are aroused when there is change are Self concerns. To a large extent, people begin a change process by protecting themselves. Only when the innovation and change facilitators are perceived to be safe will people move to implement the change. Your job is to make sure that Self concerns are respected and that the abusive intentions and actions of others are challenged. Change success is achieved when Self and Task concerns are resolved and, ideally, when Impact concerns are aroused.

A Final Phrase

An important perspective to keep in mind when engaged in the change process is summarized in one phrase:

The road to success is always under construction.

DISCUSSION QUESTIONS

1. What has been your experience with moving across the Implementation Bridge? When was the bridge long? When was it shorter? What explains the differences in the sizes of the bridges?

2. Do you think the gold standard (randomly assigned treatment and control groups) research design should be required in evaluation studies? Why? Why not?

3. The importance of leadership to success in implementing changes has been emphasized again in this chapter. In what ways do you see leaders making a difference?

4. This chapter concluded with a discussion of ethics in change agentry. Do you think this is an important topic or something that is obvious and does not need to be addressed? Why? Why not?

5. In the next change initiative that you are a participant, which constructs and tools will you want to be sure to incorporate?

FIELDWORK ACTIVITIES

1. There are bound to have been some research or evaluation studies conducted in the organization where you currently work. Seek out the report for one of these studies. Examine the report to see how implementation was addressed. What was the research design? Was the extent of implementation documented? Was there an assumption that implementation was dichotomous (use/nonuse), or was there a view similar to having an Implementation Bridge?

2. For a recent change initiative in an organization or a larger social system, interview a range of participants to obtain their views of the initiative. Focus on their understanding of the various interventions that were made. Develop a case study description of the overall initiative. As part of your case provide an analysis of at least one Positive and one Toxic Intervention Mushroom. Then pull back and reflect on the whole initiative. Was the change initiative successful, or was it a failure? What were the key strategies and themes that contributed to success (or failure)? Also, did all the leaders and Change Facilitators perform in ethical ways?

CONDUCT A STUDY

1. Design a program evaluation study that includes assessing extent of implementation. Use one, two, or all three of the CBAM Diagnostic Dimensions (SoC, LoU, IC). Be sure to keep in mind that the leaders and facilitators of the change effort will be very interested in having access to the information. They need all sorts of ideas about how best to facilitate further movement across the Implementation Bridge. Be sure to plan for confidentiality and providing implementation assessment information in understandable ways.

2. Effects on outcomes is the bottom-line study question for most change initiatives. Studies that address this question should take into account extent of implementation by individuals. In addition, research reported in this chapter suggests that studies must take into account the role and style of the leaders. More studies are needed that explore the relationships between the style of the leader, the extent of implementation, and outcomes.

ADDITIONAL READINGS

Bolman, L. G., & Deal, T. E. (2008). *Reframing organizations: Artistry, choice and leadership* (4th ed.). San Francisco, CA: Jossey-Bass.

    This text is a useful primer for learning more about leaders and leadership. The extensive literature of research and theory about organizations, leaders, and leadership is organized around four frames: Structural, Human Resource, Symbolic, and Political. Each frame is described and illustrated with interesting anecdotes and examples from businesses and other types of organizations.

Rossi, P. H., Lipsey, M. W., & Freeman, H. W. (2004). *Evaluation: A systematic approach* (7th ed.). Thousand Oaks, CA: Sage.

    Many texts address the theories and practices of program evaluation. This text covers the key steps and components that should be part of evaluation studies. Various examples are drawn from evaluation studies to illustrate each component. Chapter 6 addresses "assessing and monitoring program process"—in other words, this chapter is about documenting implementation.

■ ■ ■ ■ ■ ▬▬▬▬▬▬▬▬▬▬▬▬▬▬▬▬▬▬▬▬▬▬▬▬▬

STAGES OF CONCERN QUESTIONNAIRE (SoCQ)

Three technical manuals are available for use in measuring Stages of Concern. The appropriate manual should be studied before any efforts to assess Stages of Concern. Each of these manuals is available from the Southwest Educational Development Laboratory in Austin, Texas, http://www.sedl.org.

STAGES OF CONCERN QUESTIONNAIRE SoCQ (FORM 075)

George, A. A., Hall, G. E., & Stiegelbauer, S. M. (2006). *Measuring implementation in schools: The Stages of Concern Questionnaire*. Austin, TX: Southwest Educational Development Laboratory.

CHANGE FACILITATOR STAGES OF CONCERN QUESTIONNAIRE CFSoCQ

Hall, G. E., Newlove, B. W., George, A. A., Rutherford, W. L., & Hord, S. M. (1991). *Measuring change facilitator stages of concern: A manual for use of the CFSoC Questionnaire*. Austin, TX: Southwest Educational Development Laboratory.

OPEN-ENDED CONCERNS STATEMENTS

Newlove, B. W., & Hall, G. E. (1976). *A manual for assessing open-ended statements of concern about the innovation* (Report No. 3029). Austin: The University of Texas at Austin, Research and Development Center for Teacher Education. (ERIC Document Reproduction Service No. ED 144 207).

Questionnaire should only be used after studying the technical manual.

Stages of Concern Questionnaire

Name (optional): _____

The purpose of this questionnaire is to determine what people who are using or thinking about using various programs are concerned about at various times during the adoption process.

The items were developed from typical responses of school and college teachers who ranged from no knowledge at all about various programs to many years' experience using them. Therefore, **many of the items on this questionnaire may appear to be of little relevance or irrelevant to you at this time.** For the completely irrelevant items, please circle "O" on the scale. Other items will represent those concerns you do have, in varying degrees of intensity, and should be marked higher on the scale.

For example:

This statement is very true of me at this time.	0	1	2	3	4	5	6	(7)
This statement is somewhat true of me now.	0	1	2	3	(4)	5	6	7
This statement is not at all true of me at this time.	0	(1)	2	3	4	5	6	7
This statement seems irrelevant to me.	(0)	1	2	3	4	5	6	7

Please respond to the items in terms of **your present concerns,** or how you feel about your involvement with _____. We do not hold to any one definition of the innovation so please think of it in terms of your own perception of what it involves. Phrases such as "this approach" and "the new system" all refer to the same innovation. Remember to respond to each item in terms of your present concerns about your involvement or potential involvement with the innovation.

Thank you for taking time to complete this task.

0	1	2	3	4	5	6	7
Irrelevant		Not true of me now		Somewhat true of me now		Very true of me now	

Circle One Number For Each Item

1. I am concerned about students' attitudes toward the innovation.	0 1 2 3 4 5 6 7
2. I now know of some other approaches that might work better.	0 1 2 3 4 5 6 7
3. I am more concerned about another innovation.	0 1 2 3 4 5 6 7
4. I am concerned about not having enough time to organize myself each day.	0 1 2 3 4 5 6 7
5. I would like to help other faculty in their use of the innovation.	0 1 2 3 4 5 6 7
6. I have a very limited knowledge of the innovation.	0 1 2 3 4 5 6 7
7. I would like to know the effect of reorganization on my professional status.	0 1 2 3 4 5 6 7
8. I am concerned about conflict between my interests and my responsibilities.	0 1 2 3 4 5 6 7
9. I am concerned about revising my use of the innovation.	0 1 2 3 4 5 6 7
10. I would like to develop working relationships with both our faculty and outside faculty using this innovation.	0 1 2 3 4 5 6 7
11. I am concerned about how the innovation affects students.	0 1 2 3 4 5 6 7
12. I am not concerned about the innovation at this time.	0 1 2 3 4 5 6 7
13. I would like to know who will make the decisions in the new system.	0 1 2 3 4 5 6 7
14. I would like to discuss the possibility of using the innovation.	0 1 2 3 4 5 6 7
15. I would like to know what resources are available if we decide to adopt the innovation	0 1 2 3 4 5 6 7
16. I am concerned about my inability to manage all that the innovation requires.	0 1 2 3 4 5 6 7
17. I would like to know how my teaching or administration is supposed to change.	0 1 2 3 4 5 6 7
18. I would like to familiarize other departments or persons with the progress of this new approach.	0 1 2 3 4 5 6 7

0	1	2	3	4	5	6	7
Irrelevant		Not true of me now		Somewhat true of me now			Very true of me now

Circle One Number For Each Item

19. I am concerned about evaluating my impact on students.	0 1 2 3 4 5 6 7
20. I would like to revise the innovation's approach.	0 1 2 3 4 5 6 7
21. I am preoccupied with things other than the innovation.	0 1 2 3 4 5 6 7
22. I would like to modify our use of the innovation based on the experiences of our students.	0 1 2 3 4 5 6 7
23. I spend little time thinking about the innovation.	0 1 2 3 4 5 6 7
24. I would like to excite my students about their part in this approach.	0 1 2 3 4 5 6 7
25. I am concerned about time spent working with nonacademic problems related to the innovation.	0 1 2 3 4 5 6 7
26. I would like to know what the use of the innovation will require in the immediate future.	0 1 2 3 4 5 6 7
27. I would like to coordinate my efforts with others to maximize the innovation's effects.	0 1 2 3 4 5 6 7
28. I would like to have more information on time and energy commitments required by the innovation.	0 1 2 3 4 5 6 7
29. I would like to know what other faculty are doing in this area.	0 1 2 3 4 5 6 7
30. Currently, other priorities prevent me from focusing my attention on the innovation.	0 1 2 3 4 5 6 7
31. I would like to determine how to supplement, enhance, or replace the innovation.	0 1 2 3 4 5 6 7
32. I would like to use feedback from students to change the program.	0 1 2 3 4 5 6 7
33. I would like to know how my role will change when I am using the innovation.	0 1 2 3 4 5 6 7
34. Coordination of tasks and people is taking too much of my time.	0 1 2 3 4 5 6 7
35. I would like to know how the innovation is better than what we have now.	0 1 2 3 4 5 6 7

STAGES OF CONCERN (SoC) SCORING DEVICE

Stages of Concern Quick Scoring Device

The Quick Scoring Device can be used to hand score the Stages of Concern Questionnaire (SoCQ) responses and to plot an individual profile. It is especially useful when only a small number of questionnaires need to be processed or when computer processing is not available. By following the step-by-step instructions, the SoCQ responses are transferred to the device, entered into seven scales, and each scale is totaled. Then the seven raw scale score totals are translated into percentile scores and plotted on a grid to produce the individual's SoCQ profile.

Instructions

1. In the box labeled A, fill in the identifying information taken from the cover sheet of the SoCQ.

2. In the table labeled B on the Scoring Device, transcribe each of the 35 SoCQ circled responses from the questionnaire (raw data). Note that the numbered blanks are not in consecutive order.

3. Row C contains the Raw Scale Score Total for each stage (0–6). Take each of the seven columns (0–6) in Table B, add the numbers within each column, and enter the sum of each column (0–6) in the appropriate blank in Row C. Each of these seven Raw Scale Score totals is a number between 0 and 35.

4. Table D contains the percentile scores for each Stage of Concern. For example, find the Raw Scale Score Total for Stage 0 from Row C ("12" from the example) in the left-hand column in Table D, then look in the Stage 0 column to the right in Table D and circle that percentile rank ("69" in the example). Take the raw score for Stage 1 ("31" in the example) to Table D and locate that numeral in the left hand Raw Score Total column. Move across in the percentile table to the Stage 1 column and circle the percentile value ("98" in the example). Do the same for Stages 2 through 6.

5. Transcribe the circled percentile scores for each stage (0-6) from Table D to Box E. Box E now contains seven numbers between 0 and 99.

6. Box F contains the SoCQ grid. From Box E, take the percentile score for Stage 0 ("69" in the example) and mark that point with a dot on the Stage 0 vertical line of the SoCQ grid. Do the same for Stages 1–6. Connect the points to form the SoCQ profile.

You can now check your own scoring by using the blank profile sheet (see Appendix C). You will want to make copies of the blank scoring device before writing on it. Reproduce the data in the example by recording the original data from the completed SoCQ.

Stages of Concern Quick Scoring Device

SoCQ 075

A

Date: _____

Site: _____ SS#: _____

Innovation: _____

B

Individual Item responses (fill in the blanks with average of other item on that scale)

Stage	0	1	2	3	4	5	6
	3 ___	6 ___	7 ___	4 ___	1 ___	5 ___	2 ___
	12 ___	14 ___	13 ___	8 ___	11 ___	10 ___	9 ___
	21 ___	15 ___	17 ___	16 ___	19 ___	18 ___	20 ___
	23 ___	26 ___	28 ___	25 ___	24 ___	27 ___	22 ___
	30 ___	35 ___	33 ___	34 ___	32 ___	29 ___	31 ___

C Raw Score Totals ___ ___ ___ ___ ___ ___ ___

E Percentile Scores ___ ___ ___ ___ ___ ___ ___

F

RELATIVE INTENSITY (0–100) plotted against SoC Stages:
UNCONCERNED (0) — INFORMATION (1) — PERSONAL (2) — MANAGEMENT (3) — CONSEQUENCE (4) — COLLABORATION (5) — REFOCUSING (6)

D Percentiles

Raw Scale Score	Stage 0	Stage 1	Stage 2	Stage 3	Stage 4	Stage 5	Stage 6
0	0	5	5	2	1	1	1
1	1	12	12	5	1	2	2
2	2	16	14	7	1	3	3
3	4	19	17	9	2	3	5
4	7	23	21	11	2	4	6
5	14	27	25	15	3	5	9
6	22	30	28	18	3	5	11
7	31	34	31	23	4	7	14
8	40	37	35	27	5	10	17
9	48	40	39	30	5	12	20
10	55	43	41	34	7	14	22
11	61	45	45	39	8	16	26
12	69	48	48	43	9	19	30
13	75	51	52	47	11	22	34
14	81	54	55	52	13	25	38
15	87	57	57	56	16	28	42
16	91	60	59	60	19	31	47
17	94	63	63	65	21	36	52
18	96	66	67	69	24	40	57
19	97	69	70	73	27	44	60
20	98	72	72	77	30	48	65
21	99	75	76	80	33	52	69
22	99	80	78	83	38	55	73
23	99	84	80	85	43	59	77
24	99	88	83	88	48	64	81
25	99	90	85	90	54	68	84
26	99	91	87	92	59	72	87
27	99	93	89	94	63	76	90
28	99	95	91	95	66	80	92
29	99	96	92	97	71	84	94
30	99	97	94	97	76	88	96
31	99	98	95	98	82	91	97
32	99	98	96	98	86	93	98
33	99	99	96	99	90	95	99
34	99	99	97	99	92	97	99
35	99	99	99	99	96	98	99

Concerns Based Systems International

LEVELS OF USE OF THE INNOVATION (OPERATIONAL DEFINITIONS)

Two technical manuals have been prepared to assist in becoming prepared to conduct Levels of Use (LoU) Interviews. No one should assume that they have become reliable and valid LoU Interviewers from studying only these manuals. For research and evaluation studies, only certified LoU Interviewers should be used. These individual have been through the established training program that was presented by a trainer approved by one of this text's authors. Also, it is not possible to measure LoU with questionnaires and online surveys. The only two methodologies are ethnographic observation and the established LoU Interview protocol.

Each of these manuals is available from the Southwest Educational Development Laboratory in Austin, Texas, http://www.sedl.org/.

LEVELS OF USE TECHNICAL MANUALS

Hall, G. E., Dirksen, D. J., & George, A. A. (2000). *Measuring implementation in schools: Levels of use.* Austin, TX: Southwest Educational Development Laboratory.

Loucks, S. F., Newlove, B. W., & Hall, G. E. (1975). *Measuring levels of use of the innovation: A manual for trainers, interviewers, and raters.* Austin: The University of Texas at Austin, Research and Development Center for Teacher Education. Available from the Southwest Educational Development Laboratory, Austin, TX.

CATEGORIES

SCALE POINT DEFINITIONS OF THE LEVELS OF USE OF THE INNOVATION	KNOWLEDGE	ACQUIRING INFORMATION	SHARING
Levels of Use are distinct states that represent observably different types of behavior and patterns of innovation use as exhibited by individuals and groups. These levels characterize a user's development in acquiring new skills and varying use of the innovation. Each level encompasses a range of behaviors, but is limited by a set of identifiable Decision Points. For descriptive purposes, each level is defined by seven categories.	That which the user knows about characteristics of the innovation, how to use it, and consequences of its use. This is cognitive knowledge related to using an innovation, not feelings or attitudes.	Solicits information about the innovation in a variety of ways, including questioning resources persons, corresponding with resources agencies, reviewing printed materials, and making visits.	Discusses the innovation with others. Shares plans, ideas, resources, outcomes, and problems related to use of the innovation.
LEVEL 0 NON-USE State in which the user has little or no knowledge of the innovation, no involvement with the innovation, and is doing nothing toward becoming involved.	Knows nothing about this or similar innovations or has only very limited general knowledge of efforts to develop innovations in the area. 0	Takes little or no action to solicit information beyond reviewing descriptive information about this or similar innovations when it happens to come to personal attention. 0	Is not communicating with others about innovation beyond possibly acknowledging that the innovation exists. 0
DECISION POINT A	*Takes action to learn more detailed information about the innovation.*		
LEVEL 1 ORIENTATION: State in which the user has acquired or is acquiring information about the innovation and/or has explored or is exploring its value orientation and its demands upon user and user system.	Knows general information about the innovation such as origin, characteristics, and, implementation requirements. I	Seeks descriptive material about the innovation. Seeks opinions and knowledge of others through discussions, visits or workshops. I	Discusses resources needed in general terms and/or exchanges descriptive information, materials, or ideas about the innovation and possible implications of its use. I
DECISION POINT B	*Makes a decision to use the innovation by establishing a time to begin.*		
LEVEL II PREPARATION State in which the user is preparing for first use of the innovation.	Knows logistical requirements, necessary resources and timing for initial use of the innovation, and details of initial experiences for clients. II	Seeks information and resources specifically related to preparation for use of the innovation in own setting. II	Discusses resources needed for initial use of the innovation. Joins others in pre-use training, and in planning for resources, logistics, schedules, etc., in preparation for first use. II
DECISION POINT C	*Changes, if any, and use are dominated by user needs. Clients may be valued, however management, time, or limited*		
LEVEL III MECHANICAL USE State in which the user focuses most effort on the short-term, day-to-day use of the innovation with little time for reflection. Changes in use are made more to meet user needs than client needs. The user is primarily engaged in a stepwise attempt to master the tasks required to use the innovation, often resulting in disjointed and superficial use.	**KNOWLEDGE** Knows on a day-to-day basis the requirements for using the innovation, is more knowledgeable on short-term activities and effects than long-range activities and effects, of use of the innovation. III	**ACQUIRING INFORMATION** Solicits management information about such things as logistics, scheduling techniques, and ideas for reducing amount of time and work required of user. III	**SHARING** Discusses management and logistical issues related to use of the innovation. Resources and materials are shared for purposes of reducing management, flow and logistical problems related to use of the innovation. III
DECISION POINT D-1	*A routine pattern of use is established. Changes for clients may be made routinely, but there are no recent changes outside*		
LEVEL IV A ROUTINE Use of the innovation is stabilized. Few if any changes are being made in ongoing use. Little preparation or thought is being given to improving innovation use or its consequences.	Knows both short- and long-term requirements for use and how to use the innovation with minimum effort or stress. IVA	Makes no special efforts to seek information as a part of ongoing use of the innovation. IVA	Describes current use of the innovation with little or no reference to ways of changing use. IVA
DECISIONS POINT D-2	*Changes use of the innovation based on formal or informal evaluation in order to increase client outcomes. They must be recent*		
LEVEL IV B REFINEMENT State in which the user varies the use of the innovation to increase the impact on clients within his/her immediate sphere of influence. Variations are based on knowledge of both short- and long-term consequences of client.	Knows cognitive and affective effects of the innovation on clients and ways for increasing impact on clients. IVB	Solicits information and materials that focus specifically on changing use of the innovation to affect client outcomes. IVB	Discusses own methods of modifying use of the innovation to change client outcomes. IVB
DECISION POINT E	*Initiates changes in use of innovation based on input of and in coordination with what colleagues are doing.*		
LEVEL V INTEGRATION State in which the user is combining own efforts to use the innovation with related activities of colleagues to achieve a collective impact on clients within their sphere of influence.	Knows how to coordinate own use of the innovation with colleagues to provide a collective impact on clients. V	Solicits information and opinions for the purpose of collaborating with others in use of the innovation. V	Discusses efforts to increase client impact through collaboration with others on personal use of the innovation. V
DECISION POINT F	*Begins exploring alternatives to or major modifications of the innovation presently in use.*		
LEVEL VI RENEWAL State in which the user reevaluates the quality of use of the innovation, seeks major modifications of or alternatives to present innovation to achieve increased impact on clients, examines new developments in the field, and explores new goals for self and the system.	Knows of alternatives that could be used to change or replace the present innovation that would improve the quality of outcomes of its use. VI	Seeks information and materials about others innovations as alternatives to the present innovation or for making major adaptations in the innovation. VI	Focuses discussions on identification of major alternatives or replacements for the current innovation. VI

Procedures for Adopting Educational Innovations Project. Research and Development Center for Teacher Education, University of Texas at Austin, 1975, N.I.E. Contract No. NIE-74-0087.

CATEGORIES

ASSESSING	PLANNING	STATUS REPORTING	PERFORMING
Examines the potential or actual use of the innovation or some aspect of it. This can be a mental assessment or can involve actual collection and analysis of data.	Designs and outlines short- and/or long-range steps to be taken during process of innovation adoption, i.e., aligns resources, schedules activities, meets with others to organize and/or coordinate use of the innovation.	Describes personal stand at the present time in relation to use of the innovation.	Carries out the actions and activities entailed in operationalizing the innovation.
Takes no action to analyze the innovation, its characteristics, possible use, or consequences of use.	Schedules no time and specifies no steps for the study or use of the innovation.	Reports little or no personal involvement with the innovation.	Takes no discernible action toward learning about or using the innovation. The innovation and/or its accouterments are not present or in use.
0	0	0	0
Analyzes and compares materials, content, requirements for use, evaluation reports, potential outcomes, strengths and weaknesses for purpose of making a decision about use of the innovation.	Plans to gather necessary information and resources as needed to make a decision for or against use of the innovation.	Reports presently orienting self to what the innovation is and is not.	Explores the innovation and requirements for its use by talking to others about it, reviewing descriptive information and sample materials, attending orientation sessions, and observing others using it.
I	I	I	I
Analyzes detailed requirements and available resources for initial use of the innovation.	Identifies steps and procedures entailed in obtaining resources and organizing activities and events or initial use of the innovation.	Reports preparing self for initial use of the innovation.	Studies reference materials in depth, organizes resources and logistics, schedules and receives skill training in preparation for initial use.
II	II	II	II

experimental knowledge dictate what the user does.

ASSESSING	PLANNING	STATUS REPORTING	PERFORMING
Examines own use of the innovation with respect to problems of logistics, management, time schedules, resources and general reactions of clients.	Plans for organizing and managing resources, activities, and events related primarily to immediate ongoing use of the innovation. Planned-for changes address managerial or logistical issues with a short-term perspective.	Reports that logistics, time, management, resource organizations, etc., are the focus of most personal efforts to use the innovation.	Manages innovation with varying degrees of efficiency. Often lacks anticipation of immediate consequences. The flow of actions in the user and clients is often disjointed, uneven and uncertain. When changes are made, they are primarily in response to logistical and organizational problems.
III	III	III	III

the pattern.

ASSESSING	PLANNING	STATUS REPORTING	PERFORMING
Limits evaluation activities to those administratively required, with little attention paid to findings for the purpose of changing use.	Plans intermediate and long-range actions with little projected variation in how the innovation will be used. Planning focuses on routine use of resources, personnel, etc.	Reports that personal use of the innovation is going along satisfactorily with few if any problems.	Uses the innovation smoothly with minimal management problems; over time, there is little variation in pattern of use.
IVA	IVA	IVA	IVA
Assesses use of the innovation for the purpose of changing current practices to improve client outcomes.	Develops intermediate and long-range plans that anticipate possible and needed steps, resources, and events designed to enhance client outcomes.	Reports varying use of the innovation in order to change client outcomes.	Explores and experiments with alternative combinations of the innovation with existing practices to maximize client involvement and to optimize client outcomes.
IVB	IVB	IVB	IVB
Appraises collaborative use of the innovation in terms of client outcomes and strengths and weaknesses of the integrated effort.	Plans specific actions to coordinate own use of the innovation with others to achieve increased impact on clients.	Reports spending time and energy collaborating with others about integrating own use of the innovation.	Collaborates with others in use of the innovation as a means of expanding the innovation's impact on clients. Changes in use are made in coordination with others.
V	V	V	V
Analyzes advantages and disadvantages of major modifications or alternatives to the present innovation.	Plans activities that involve pursuit of alternatives to enhance or replace the innovation.	Reports considering major modifications to present use of the innovation.	Explores other innovations that could be used in combination with or in place of the present innovation in an attempt to develop more effective means of achieving client outcomes.
VI	VI	VI	VI

Reprinted from Hall, G.E., Loucks, S.F., Rutherford, W.L. & Newlove, B.W. Levels of Use of the Innovation: A framework for analyzing innovation adoption. *The Journal of Teacher Education.* 1975. 26(1), 52–56

SIX DIMENSIONS OF CHANGE FACILITATOR STYLE

Cluster I: Concern for People

The first cluster of CF Style behaviors deals with how the principal, as the change facilitator, addresses the personal side of change. People have feelings and attitudes about their work and about how a change process is going. They have personal needs, too. Day to day, facilitators can monitor, attend to, and affect these concerns and needs in different ways and with different emphases. For example, it is possible to spend little time directly addressing the feelings of others or to become preoccupied with listening and responding to each concern that is expressed. The emphasis can also be on attending to individual concerns as they are expressed daily or on focusing on the more long-term needs of all staff, with attention to individual concerns on an as-needed basis.

The Concern for People cluster is composed of two dimensions that weigh the degree to which the moment-to-moment and daily behaviors of a facilitator emphasize *social/informal* and *formal/meaningful* interactions with teachers. The Social/Informal dimension addresses the extent to which the facilitator engages in informal social discussions with teachers.

Social/Informal   This dimension addresses the frequency and character of the facilitator's informal social discussions with teachers and other staff. Many of these discussions may not be even remotely related to the work of the school or a specific innovation. Facilitators who emphasize this cluster engage in frequent social inter-actions. They attend to feelings and perceptions by emphasizing listening, understanding, and acknowledging immediate concerns, rather than providing answers or anticipating long-range consequences. There is a personable, friendly, almost chatty tone to the interactions. When concerns are addressed, it is done in ways that are responsive rather than anticipatory.

Formal/Meaningful   This dimension addresses brief, task-oriented interactions that deal with specific aspects of the work and the details of the innovation implementation. Facilitators are centered on school tasks, priorities, and directions. Discussions and interactions are focused on teaching, learning, and other substantive issues directly related to use of the innovation. Interactions are primarily intended to support teachers in their school-related duties, and the facilitator is almost always looking for solutions that are lasting. The interactions and emphases are not overly influenced by superficial and short-lived feelings and needs. Teaching and learning activities and issues directly related to use of the innovation are emphasized.

Cluster II: Organizational Efficiency

The work of the organization can be facilitated with varying degrees of emphasis on obtaining resources, increasing efficiency, and consolidating or sharing responsibilities and authority. Principals can try to do almost everything themselves, or they can delegate responsibility to others. System procedures, role clarity, and work priorities can be made more or less clear, and resources can be organized in ways that increase or decrease availability and effectiveness. In this cluster the principal's administrative focus is examined along two dimensions— *trust in others* and *administrative efficiency.*

Trust in Others   This dimension examines the extent to which the facilitator assigns others tasks of locating resources, establishing procedures, and managing schedules and time. When there is delay in making decisions, administrative systems and procedures are allowed to evolve in response to needs expressed by staff and to external pressures. The assumption is that teachers know how to accomplish their jobs and that they need a minimum of structuring and monitoring from the principal. As needs for additions or changes in structures, rules, and procedures emerge, they are gradually acknowledged and introduced as suggestions and guidelines rather than being directly established. Formalizing procedural and policy change is left to others and to time.

Administrative Efficiency   This dimension addresses the extent to which establishing clear and smoothly running procedures and resource systems to help teachers and others do their jobs efficiently is a priority. Administration, scheduling, and production tasks are clearly described, understood, and used by all members of the organization. Emphasis is placed on having a high level of organizational efficiency so teachers can do their jobs better. As needs for new structures and procedures emerge, they are formally established.

Cluster III: Strategic Sense

To varying degrees, principals are aware of the relationship between the long-term goals and their own monthly, weekly, daily, and moment-to-moment activities and those of their school. Some principals are more "now" oriented and treat each event in isolation from its part in the grand scheme, while others think and act with a vivid mental image of how today's actions contribute to accomplishing long-range aspirations. Some reflect about what they are doing and how all of their activities can add up, while others focus on the moment. Principals also vary in the degree to which they encourage or discourage the participation of external facilitators and in how they prescribe their role in the schools. This cluster examines the principal's strategic sense according to two dimensions: *day-to-day* and *vision and planning.*

Day-to-Day   At the high end of this dimension, there is little anticipation of future developments, needs, successes, or failures. Interventions are made in response to issues and needs as they arise. Knowledge of the details of the innovation is limited, and the amount of intervention with teachers is restricted to responding to questions and gradually completing routine steps. Images of how things could be improved and how more rapid gains could be made are incomplete, limited in scope, and lacking in imagination. There is little anticipation of longer term patterns or consequences. External facilitators come and go as they wish and spend an extraordinary amount of effort advising the principal.

Vision and Planning   The facilitator with a high emphasis on this dimension has a long-term vision that is integrated with an understanding of the day-to-day activities as the means to achieve the desired end. The facilitating activity is intense, with a high degree of interaction related to the work at hand. There is depth of knowledge about teaching and learning. Teachers and others are pushed to accomplish all that they can. Assertive leadership, continual monitoring, supportive actions, and creative interpretations of policy and use of resources to reach long-term goals are clear indicators of this dimension. Also present is the ability to anticipate the possible systemic effects of interventions and the broader consequences of day-to-day actions. Effects are accurately predicted, and interventions are made in anticipation of likely trends. Moment-to-moment interactions with staff and external facilitators are centered on the present work within a context of the long-range aspirations. The focus is on completing tasks, accomplishing school objectives, and making progress. External facilitators are encouraged to be involved in the school according to the principal's perception of their expertise and value.

For additional information, see G. E. Hall and A. A. George, "The Impact of Principal Change Facilitator Style on School and Classroom Culture," in H. Jerome Freiberg (Ed.), *School Climate: Measuring, Improving and Sustaining Healthy Learning Environments* (Philadelphia and London: Falmer Press, 1999), pp. 165–185.

CHANGE FACILITATOR STYLE QUESTIONNAIRE (CFSQ)

An important resource related to use of the Change Facilitator Style Questionnaire is Hall, G. E., & George, A. A. (1999). The impact of principal Change Facilitator Style on school and classroom culture. In H. J. Freiberg (Ed.), *School climate: Measuring, improving and sustaining healthy learning environments.* Philadelphia: Falmer Press.

School: _____ **Date:** ___/___/___

Change Facilitator Style Questionnaire
(CFSQ)

On the following page is a list of short phrases that describe different activities, goals, and emphases that leaders can exhibit. Studies have shown that different people place different emphases on each of these behaviors and that an overall pattern or style is unique to each.

This questionnaire is a way to estimate the emphasis that is given to different leadership activities. One of the key uses of this questionnaire is to help leaders analyze and reflect on what they are doing. There is no right or wrong way; rather, there are variations in emphases and patterns that may be worth considering.

In this instance, consider the leadership/facilitating activities of your principal.

Note that some of the items in this questionnaire refer to how this person is working in relation to a particular program or innovation. For these items, please think about *your principal's role with facilitating change in the school.*

Also, some of the items are similar to other items. This is done deliberately in a questionnaire of this type. By having similar items, each item can be less complex, and it is possible to complete the questionnaire in a minimum amount of time.

Having each item rated on a continuum is important, too. For most facilitators/leaders, most items will apply; what constitutes the difference is the amount of emphasis or de-emphasis a particular leader gives to each type of activity.

Please read each phrase and use the following scale points to rate the degree of emphasis given to each by your principal.

1	2	3	4	5	6
Never True Not True	Rarely True	Seldom True	Sometimes True	Often True	Always or Very True

Change Facilitator Style Questionnaire

Please indicate how accurately each statement describes your principal:

1 Never True Not True	2 Rarely True	3 Seldom True	4 Sometimes True	5 Often True		6 Always or Very True	
1. Is friendly when we talk to him or her				1	2	3	4	5	6
2. Knows a lot about teaching and curriculum				1	2	3	4	5	6
3. Procedures and rules are clearly spelled out				1	2	3	4	5	6
4. Discusses school problems in a productive way				1	2	3	4	5	6
5. Seems to be disorganized at times				1	2	3	4	5	6
6. Shares many ideas for improving teaching and learning				1	2	3	4	5	6
7. Plans and procedures are introduced at the last moment				1	2	3	4	5	6
8. Keeps everyone informed about procedures				1	2	3	4	5	6
9. He or she is heavily involved in what is happening with teachers and students				1	2	3	4	5	6
10. Propose loosely defined solutions				1	2	3	4	5	6
11. Is primarily concerned about how teachers feel				1	2	3	4	5	6
12. Asks questions about what teachers are doing in their classrooms				1	2	3	4	5	6
13. Has few concrete ideas for improvement				1	2	3	4	5	6
14. Provides guidelines for efficient operation of the school				1	2	3	4	5	6
15. Supports his or her teachers when it really counts				1	2	3	4	5	6
16. Allocation of resources is disorganized				1	2	3	4	5	6
17. Efficient and smooth running of the school is his or her priority				1	2	3	4	5	6
18. Uses many sources to learn more about the new program or innovation				1	2	3	4	5	6
19. Being accepted by teachers is important to him/her				1	2	3	4	5	6
20. He or she sees the connection between the day-to-day activities and moving toward a longer term goal				1	2	3	4	5	6
21. Knows very little about programs and innovations				1	2	3	4	5	6
22. Is skilled at organizing resources and schedules				1	2	3	4	5	6
23. Has an incomplete view about the future of his or her school				1	2	3	4	5	6
24. Attending to feelings and perceptions is his or her first priority				1	2	3	4	5	6
25. Explores issues in a loosely structured way				1	2	3	4	5	6
26. Chats socially with teachers				1	2	3	4	5	6
27. Delays making decisions to the last possible moment				1	2	3	4	5	6
28. Focuses on issues of limited importance				1	2	3	4	5	6
29. Takes the lead when problems must be solved				1	2	3	4	5	6
30. Has a clear picture of where the school is going				1	2	3	4	5	6

CHANGE FACILITATOR STYLE SCORING DEVICE

The responses for an individual can be scored using the CFSQ Quick Scoring Device. When there are multiple respondents, the first step is still to score each individual's responses. For more than one respondent, the individual raw scale scores can be summed and the average determined. The average score can then be converted using the same percentile table.

Instructions

1. In the box labeled A fill in the identifying information taken from the CFSQ cover sheet.
2. In the table labeled B on the Scoring Device, transcribe each of the 30 CFSQ circled responses from the questionnaire (raw data). Note that the numbered blanks are not in consecutive order.
3. Total the raw scores for each column in Box B. Place them along the row labeled Total Scores.
4. Table C contains the percentile scores for each of the six Change Facilitator Style dimensions. Take the first column's (S/I) Total Score from Box B and find it within the Raw Scale Score column of Table C. Look across to the first column ("S/I") and determine the percentile equivalent. For example, if the Raw Score was 20, then the Percentile Equivalent for S/I would be 27. Write the percentile score underneath the S/I column in the row labeled Percentiles under Box B.
5. Repeat step 4 for each of the remaining five columns. Be sure to identify the corresponding column in Box C when identifying the percentile.
6. The CFS Self Scoring Chart on page 298 is provided so that bar graphs can be shaded to represent the height of each percentile column.
7. Interpretation of the resultant bar graphs should be guided by referring to the Six Dimensions of Change Facilitator presented in Appendix E. The higher the graph, the more of that aspect of change leadership the respondent(s) views the leader to exhibit.

Change Facilitator Style Questionnaire Scoring Device

A

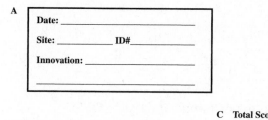

Date: _____

Site: _____ ID#_____

Innovation: _____

_____

B

S/I	F/M	TiO	AE	DtD	V&P
1 ___	4 ___	5 ___	3 ___	10 ___	2 ___
11___	6 ___	7 ___	8 ___	13 ___	9 ___
19 ___	12 ___	16 ___	14 ___	21 ___	18 ___
24 ___	15 ___	25 ___	17 ___	23 ___	20 ___
26 ___	29 ___	27 ___	22 ___	28 ___	30 ___

C   Total Scores   ___ ___ ___ ___ ___ ___

Percentiles   ___ ___ ___ ___ ___ ___

D

Raw Scale Score	Percentile equivalent					
	S/I	F/M	TiO	AE	DtD	V&P
5	1	1	6	1	7	1
6	1	1	10	1	13	1
7	1	1	15	1	19	1
8	1	1	21	1	26	1
9	1	1	28	1	33	1
10	2	1	35	1	42	1
11	2	1	42	1	50	1
12	3	2	49	1	57	1
13	4	2	55	1	64	2
14	5	3	60	2	69	2
15	7	4	66	2	76	3
16	9	5	71	3	80	3
17	12	6	77	5	85	4
18	16	8	81	7	88	6
19	20	12	86	9	91	7
20	27	16	90	12	95	10
21	34	21	92	18	97	14
22	43	28	95	24	99	19
23	52	36	97	31	99	26
24	62	45	98	40	99	33
25	71	56	99	50	99	42
26	81	66	99	60	99	53
27	87	75	99	71	99	63
28	92	85	99	79	99	72
29	97	93	99	87	99	84
30	99	99	99	99	99	99

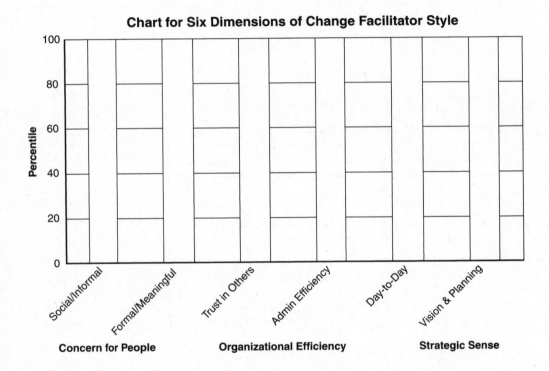

Chart for Six Dimensions of Change Facilitator Style

Shade each of the bar graphs to the height of the corresponding Change Facilitator Style Questionnaire percentile score.

EXAMPLE INTERVENTIONS FOR EACH STAGE OF CONCERN

Many possible interventions can be used to address each Stage of Concern (SoC). Interventions that are concerns-based can make a significant positive difference. However, there also are interventions that are likely to be inappropriate. The following are examples of each for each SoC.

<u>Stage 0 Unconcerned</u>. At this stage the types of interventions that may be appropriate certainly depend upon the context. For example, is it the very beginning of a change process, or are many others already using the innovation? Also, is use of the innovation required or even desirable? The following interventions might be relevant.

Appropriate Interventions

    a. Acknowledge that little concern about the innovation is legitimate and okay.
    b. Share some general information about the innovation in the hopes of arousing some interest in it.
    c. Suggest and describe how the innovation might be related to an area that the person(s) is concerned about.
    d. Decree that use of the innovation is required.
    e. Encourage the person(s) to talk with others who are interested in or using the innovation.

Inappropriate Interventions

    a. Communicating lack of concern to others, thereby discouraging their interest.
    b. Continuing to accept/tolerate a lack of concern while others are engaged.

<u>State 1 Informational</u>. Interventions should be designed to provide general descriptive information. Too much detail will not be useful. "Buying them the book" will not lead to their reading all of it. Interventions for this stage should be spread over time and through varied medium and context.

Appropriate Interventions

    a. Share general descriptive information about the innovation through one-legged interviews, e-mail, brochures, short media presentations, and discussions during staff meetings.
    b. Provide information contrasting what the individual is presently doing with potential advantages of use of the innovation.

    c. Express enthusiasm for consideration of the innovation.

    d. Hear from others who are excited about what they are doing with innovation.

    e. State realistic expectations about the benefits, costs, and effort needed to use the innovation.

Inappropriate Interventions

    a. Support travel to a site where the innovation is in use (unless there is careful construction of questions about what to ask before the trip).

    b. Provide in-depth and detailed information at a single time.

    c. Do not provide information about expectations and what use of the innovation will entail.

<u>Stage 2 Personal</u>. Change facilitators need to be extra sensitive in working with persons who have intense Personal concerns. It is quite easy to further raise their Personal concerns. Also, frequently intense Personal concerns are not innovation related. They could be job related (Will I have job next year?) or non–work related (My daughter is going through a divorce). The key to resolution of Personal concerns is to have more information. However, when people have intense Personal concerns, they are not as open to or trustful of the information that is provided. When Personal concerns are clearly innovation related, the following types of interventions may be useful:

Appropriate Interventions

    a. Establish rapport and be empathetic about their feelings of uncertainty.

    b. Be encouraging and offer assurance of their adequacy to engage with the innovation.

    c. Encourage innovation use gingerly; do not push unnecessarily.

    d. Clarify how the innovation relates to other priorities that potentially could conflict in terms of energy and time demands.

    e. Emphasize understanding of personal feelings, and deemphasize talk about the innovation.

    f. Be consistent in what is said about expectations and what is entailed in use of the innovation.

Inappropriate Interventions

    a. Ignore Personal concerns and focus only on presenting advantages of the innovation.

    b. Direct the person(s) to "get rid of those Personal concerns—you should be concerned about students."

    c. Provide inconsistent information over time.

    d. Call a staff meeting so that personal concerns can be shared.

<u>Stage 3 Management</u>. Interventions should focus on the "how-to-do-its." All-day, full-group trainings may not be the most effective method since many Task concerns are idiosyncratic. At one research site, the leaders created informal after-school "comfort and caring" sessions, during which experienced innovation users could provide advice and assistance that addressed specific Management concerns.

Appropriate Interventions

a. Provide answers in ways that address the person-specific "how-to" issues that are causing concern.
b. Provide a Web site with answers to the frequently heard Management concern questions.
c. Provide assigned time for a respected and expert innovation user to meet with and coach those who have Task concerns.
d. Demonstrate or provide a (video) model for effective use of the innovation, or provide "hands-on" materials for practice.
e. Send e-mails that provide planning tips, and pace what implementers should be doing "this week."
f. Establish a buddy system/consulting pair or support group.

Inappropriate Interventions

a. Provide a lecture or all-day training on philosophy and theory behind the innovation.
b. Assume there will be no Task concerns, and don't plan any supports or other interventions to address their resolution.
c. Introduce another major innovation before Management concerns about the first innovation are reduced.

Stage 4 Consequence. Facilitators enjoy persons with Consequence concerns. The concerns of such individuals are targeted toward Impact and how quality of use of the innovation can be enhanced. Persons with Impact concerns appreciate recognition and encouragement for their efforts to improve outcomes.

Appropriate Interventions

a. Recognize, encourage, and reinforce their ideas and activities.
b. Drop by and inquire about their ideas for refinements and how things are working.
c. Share a journal article or book that is related to their efforts.
d. Provide a professional development session that introduces and supports ways to enhance innovation use.
e. Encourage the person(s) to reach out to others. They could help by suggesting "how-to-do-its" for those with Task concerns or could develop a collaborative effort with a colleague(s) who also has Impact concerns.

Inappropriate Interventions

a. Fail to encourage Impact concern innovation users by spending all the time attending to those with Self and Task concerns.
b. Do not follow up to see what has happened with their efforts to refine use and enhance outcomes.
c. Reward those with less quality of use of the innovation and not those with Consequence concerns.

Stage 5 Collaboration. The arousal and sustaining of Impact concerns about working with one or more colleagues in relation to use of an innovation is the ultimate. Leaders should do all they can to facilitate the arousal of Collaboration concerns and to support innovation implementers working together.

Appropriate Interventions

   a. Encourage through advocacy and action the arousal of Collaboration concerns.

   b. Arrange a meeting between interested individuals so that there can be an exchange of ideas.

   c. Change schedules, room assignments, and other structures so that those who want to collaborate can do so.

   d. Create opportunities for them to circulate outside their present situation and work with others who have similar ideas.

   e. Celebrate their collaborative efforts.

Inappropriate Interventions

   a. Ignore Stage 5 Collaboration concerns and assume they can work it out on their own.

   b. Change schedules and structures in ways that support those with Self and Task concerns and at the same time reduce the potential for collaboration.

   c. State that "We can't do that. The bus schedule can't be changed."

Stage 6 Refocusing. Individuals at this SoC are self-starters and certainly have their own goals in mind. They have strongly held ideas about ways that the change process and/or the innovation should move in new directions. If the institutional change effort is moving in a direction antagonistic to their opinions and concerns, some fairly directive actions may be necessary to outline the limits within which they may deviate from the main steam. If their ideas are consistent with furthering use of the innovation and vision for the organization, then encouragement to "go ahead" is appropriate. However, there also should be regular monitoring for unexpected creative adaptations.

Appropriate Interventions

   a. Inquire about how well their ideas match with the vision or strategic directions outlined in the School Improvement Plan (SIP).

   b. Encourage the person(s) to take action while staying within the vision and strategic direction.

   c. Provide the person(s) with resources to access other materials and ideas that could help advance the overall effort.

   d. Encourage the person(s) to test their idea to see if it can increase outcomes.

Inappropriate Interventions

   a. Don't check to see what the person(s) is up to.

   b. Permit them to share their ideas with others who have Self or Task concerns.

   c. Put them in charge of facilitating others' implementation of the innovation. (However, in a few major change efforts we have seen this strategy lead to the Refocusing concerned person owning success of the change process and becoming a very effective leader.)

REFERENCES

Ackoff, R. L., & Emery, F. G. (1972). *On purposeful systems.* Chicago: Aldine-Atherton.

Allen, R. (2003, November). Building school culture in an age of accountability: Principals lead through sharing tasks. *Education Update, 45*(7), 1, 3, 7–8.

Alquist, A., & Hendrickson, M. (1999). Mapping the configurations of mathematics teaching. *Journal of Classroom Interaction, 34*(1), 18–26.

Anderson, B. (1993, September). The stages of systemic change. *Educational Leadership, 51*(1), 14–17.

Anderson, D. L. (2010). *Organization development: The process of leading organizational change.* Thousand Oaks, CA: Sage.

Argyris, C. (1982). *Reasoning, learning, and action: Individual and organizational.* San Francisco: Jossey-Bass.

Argyris, C., & Schon, D. (1978). *Organizational learning.* San Francisco: Jossey-Bass.

Banathy, B. H. (1973). *Developing a system's view of education: A systems models approach.* Palo Alto, CA: Fearon.

Banathy, B. H. (1995). A systems view and systems design in education. In P. M. Jenlink (Ed.), *Systemic change: Touchstones for the future school.* Arlington Heights, IL: Skylight Professional Development.

Banathy, B. H. (1996). *Designing social systems in a changing world.* New York: Plenum.

Bass, M., & Bass, R. (2008). *The Bass handbook of leadership: Theory, research, and managerial applications.* New York: Free Press.

Bavelas, A. (1950). Communication patterns in task-oriented groups. *Journal of Acoustical Society of America, 22,* 725–730.

Beckhard, R. (1969). *Organization development: Strategies and models.* Reading, MA: Addison-Wesley.

Bermant, G., & Warwick, D. P. (1978). The ethics of social intervention: Power, freedom and accountability. In G. Bermant, H. C. Kelman, and D. P. Warwick, *The ethics of social intervention* (pp. 377–418). Washington, DC: Hemisphere.

Blake, R. R., and Mouton, J. S. (1964). *The managerial grid.* Houston: Gulf.

Bobbett, J. J., Ellett, C. D., Teddlie, C., Olivier, D. F., & Rugutt, J. (2002). *School culture and school effectiveness in demonstrably effective and ineffective schools.* Paper presented at the annual meeting of the American Education Research Association, New Orleans.

Bolman, L. G., & Deal, T. E. (2008). *Reframing organizations: Artistry, choice and leadership* (4th ed.) San Francisco, CA: Jossey-Bass.

Bond-Huie, S., Buttram, J. L., Deviney, F. P., Murphy, K. M., & Ramos, M. A. (2004, November). *Alignment in SEDL's Working Systemically Model.* Austin, TX: Southwest Educational Development Laboratory.

Boyd, V. (1992a). Creating a context for change. *Issues . . . About Change, 2*(2), 1–10.

Boyd, V. (1992b). *School context: Bridge or barrier for change.* Austin, TX: Southwest Educational Development Laboratory.

Note: Copies of key papers and reports related to the Concerns Based Adoption Model, and the technical manuals for measuring Stages of Concern, Levels of Use, and Innovation Configurations can be obtained from the Southwest Educational Development Laboratory in Austin, Texas. The authors can be contacted about the various reports and manuals as well as consultation in their use.

Boyd, V., Fuentes, N., Hord, S. M., Mendez-Morse, S., & Rodriquez, D. (1993). *Leadership for change.* Austin, TX: Southwest Educational Development Laboratory.

Boyd, V., & Hord, S. M. (1994). *Principals and the new paradigm: Schools as learning communities.* Paper presented at the annual meeting of the American Educational Research Association, New Orleans.

Bridge, C. A. (1995). *The progress of implementation of the K–3 primary program in Kentucky's elementary schools.* Paper presented at the annual meeting of the American Educational Research Association, San Francisco.

Caine, R. N., & Caine, G. (1997). *Education on the edge of possibility.* Alexandria, VA: Association for Supervision and Curriculum Development.

Capra, F. (1997, April). *Creativity and leadership in learning communities.* Lecture presented at Mill Valley School District.

Charters, W. W., Jr., & Jones, J. E. (1973). On the risk of appraising nonevents in program evaluation. *Educational Researcher, 2*(11), 5–7.

Checkland, P. (1981). *Systems thinking: Systems practice.* New York: Wiley.

Cheung, D., Hattie, J., & Ng, D. (2001). Reexamining the Stages of Concern Questionnaire: A test of alternative models. *Journal of Educational Research, 94*(4), 225–236.

Cheung, D., & Yip, D. (2004). How science teachers' concerns about school-based assessment of practical work vary with time: The Hong Kong experience. *Research in Science & Technological Education, 22*(2), 153–169.

Chin, R., & Benne, K. D. (1969). General strategies for effecting changes in human systems. In W. G. Bennis, K. D. Benne, & R. Chin (Eds.), *The planning of change* (2nd ed., pp. 32–59). New York: Holt, Rinehart and Winston.

Christou, C., Eliophotou-Menon, M., & Philippou, G. (2004). Teachers' concerns regarding the adoption of a new mathematics curriculum: An application of CBAM. *Educational Studies in Mathematics, 57*(2), 157–177.

Clune, W. (1993). Systemic educational policy: A conceptual framework. In Susan H. Fuhrman (Ed.), *Designing coherent education policy: Improving the system.* New York: Jossey-Bass.

Cowan, D., Joyner, S., & Beckwith, S. (2008). *Working systemically in action: A guide for facilitators.* Austin, TX: Southwest Education Development Laboratory.

Cummings, T. G., & Worley, C. G. (2008). *Organization development and change* (9th ed.). Mason, OH: South-Western Publishing.

Danek, J., Calbert, R., & Chubin, D. (1994, February). *NSF's programmatic reform: The catalyst for systemic change.* Paper presented at Building the System: Making Science Education Work Conference, Washington, DC.

Darling-Hammond, L. (1996). The quiet revolution: Rethinking teacher development. *Educational Leadership, 53*(6), 4–10.

Deal, T. E., & Kennedy, A. A. (1982). *Corporate cultures: The rites and rituals of corporate life.* New York: Addison-Wesley.

Deal, T. E., & Peterson, K. D. (1990). *The principal's role in shaping school culture.* Washington, DC: U.S. Department of Education.

Dunn, L., & Borchardt, P. (1998). *The Essential Curriculum.* Kansas City, MO: The Teel Institute.

Eden, C., & Huxham, C. (1996). Action research for the study of organizations. In S. R. Clegg, C. Hardy, & W. R. Nord (Eds.), *Handbook of organization studies* (pp. 526–542). Thousand Oaks, CA: Sage.

English, F. W. (2004). *The SAGE handbook of educational leadership: Advances in theory, research, and practice.* Thousand Oaks, CA: Sage.

Entrekin, K. M. (1991). *Principal change facilitator styles and the implementation of consultation-based prereferral child study teams.* Unpublished doctoral dissertation, Temple University.

Fiedler, F. E. (1978). The contingency model and the dynamics of the leadership process. In L. Berkowitz (Ed.), *Advances in experimental and social psychology* (pp. 59–112). New York: Academic Press.

Floden, R., Goertz, M., & O'Day, J. (1995, September). Capacity building in systemic reform. *Phi Delta Kappan, 77*(1), 19–21.

French, W. (1971, August). *A definition and history of organization development: Some comments.* Proceedings of the 31st Annual Meeting of the Academy of Management, Atlanta, GA.

French, W. L., & Bell, C. H. (1998). *Organization development: Behavioral science interventions for organization improvement* (6th Ed.). Upper Saddle River, NJ: Prentice-Hall.

Fullan, M. (1993). Innovation, reform, and restructuring strategies. In G. Cawelti (Ed.), *Challenges and achievement of American education, ASCD 1993 Yearbook.* Alexandria, VA: Association for Supervision and Curriculum Development.

Fuller, F. F. (1969). Concerns of teachers: A developmental conceptualization. *American Educational Research Journal, 6*(2), 207–226.

Fuller, F. F. (1970). *Personalized education for teachers: An introduction for teacher educators.* The University of Texas at Austin, Research and Development Center for Teacher Education.

Fuller, F. F., & Bown, O. H. (1975). Becoming a teacher. *Teacher education 1975.* Chicago: The National Society for the Study of Education.

Gallos, J. V., & Schein, E. H. (Eds.) (2006). *Organization Development: A Jossey-Bass Reader.* San Francisco: CA: Jossey-Bass

Garmston, R., & Wellman, B. (2000). *The adaptive school: Developing and facilitating collaborative groups.* El Dorado Hills, CA: Four Hats Seminar.

Garmston, R., & Wellman, B. (2008).

George, A. A., Hall, G. E., & Stiegelbauer, S. M. (2006). *Measuring implementation in schools: The Stages of Concern Questionnaire.* Austin, TX: Southwest Educational Development Laboratory.

George, A. A., Hall, G. E., & Uchiyama, K. (2000). Extent of implementation of a standards-based approach to teaching mathematics and student outcomes. *Journal of Classroom Interaction, 35*(1), 8–25.

Gonzalez, C. E., Resta, P. E., & De Hoyos, M. L. (2005). *Barriers and facilitators on implementation of policy initiatives to transform higher education teaching-learning process.* Paper submitted for presentation at the annual meeting of the American Educational Research Association, Montreal.

Hall, G. E., Dirksen, D. J., & George, A. A. (2006). *Measuring implementation in schools: Levels of Use.* Austin, TX: Southwest Educational Development Laboratory.

Hall, G. E., & George, A. A. (1988). Development of a framework and measure for assessing principal Change Facilitator Style. Paper presented at the American Educational Research Association Annual Meeting. (ERIC Document Reproduction Service No. ED 336 401).

Hall, G. E., & George, A. A. (1999). The impact of principal Change Facilitator Style on school and classroom culture. In H. J. Freiberg (Ed.), *School climate: Measuring, improving and sustaining healthy learning environments.* Philadelphia: Falmer Press.

Hall, G. E., George, A., & Rutherford, W. L. (1979). *Measuring stages of concern about the innovation: A manual for use of the SoC Questionnaire* (Report No. 3032). Austin: The University of Texas at Austin, Research and Development Center for Teacher Education. (ERIC Document Reproduction Service No. ED 147 342).

Hall, G. E., & Hord, S. M. (1984). A framework for analyzing what change facilitators do: The Intervention Taxonomy. *Knowledge: Creation, Diffusion, Utilization, 5*(3), 275–307.

Hall, G. E., & Hord, S. M. (1987). *Change in schools: Facilitating the process.* Albany, NY: SUNY Press.

Hall, G. E., & Hord, S. M. (2006). *Implementing change: Patterns, principles, and potholes*, 2nd ed. Boston: Pearson/Allyn and Bacon.

Hall, G. E., Hord, S. M., & Griffin, T. H. (1980). *Implementation at the school building level: The development and analysis of nine mini-case studies* (Report No. 3098). Austin: The University of Texas at Austin, Research and Development Center for Teacher Education. (ERIC Document Reproduction Service No. ED 207 170).

Hall, G. E., & Loucks, S. F. (1977). A developmental model for determining whether the treatment is actually implemented. *American Education Research Journal, 14*(3), 263–276.

Hall, G. E., Loucks, S. F., Rutherford, W. L., & Newlove, B. W. (1975). Levels of Use of the Innovation: A framework for analyzing innovation adoption. *The Journal of Teacher Education, 26*(1), 52–56.

Hall, G. E., Negroni, I. A., & George, A. A. (2008). Examining relationships between urban principal leadership and student learning. Paper presented at the annual meeting of the American Education Research Association, New York City.

Hall, G. E., Newlove, B. W., George, A. A., Rutherford, W. L., & Hord, S. M. (1991). *Measuring change facilitator stages of concern: A manual for use of the CFSoC Questionnaire.* Austin, TX: Southwest Educational Development Laboratory.

Hall, G. E., & Rutherford, W. L. (1976). Concerns of teachers about implementing team teaching. *Educational Leadership, 34*(3), 227–233.

Hall, G. E., Rutherford, W. L., Hord, S. M., & Huling, L. L. (1984). Effects of three principal styles on school improvement. *Educational Leadership, 41*(5), 22–29.

Hall, G. E., & Shieh, W. H. (1998). Supervision and organizational development. In G. R. Firth & E. F. Pajak (Eds.), *Handbook of research on school supervision.* New York: Simon & Schuster Macmillan.

Hall, G. E., Wallace, R. C., & Dossett, W. A. (1973). *A developmental conceptualization of the adoption process within educational institutions* (Report No. 3006). Austin: The University of Texas at Austin, Research and Development Center for Teacher Education. (ERIC Document Reproduction Service No. ED095126)

Hargreaves, A. (1997). Rethinking educational change: Going deeper and wider in the quest for success. In A. Hargreaves (Ed.), *ASCD yearbook: Rethinking educational change with heart and mind* (pp. 1–26). Alexandria, VA: Association for Supervision and Curriculum Development.

Hargreaves, L., Moyles, J., Merry, R., Paterson, F., Pell, A., & Esarte-Sarries, V. (2003). How do primary school teachers define and implement "interactive teaching" in the National Literacy Strategy in England? *Research Papers in Education, 18*(3), 217–237.

Heck, S., Stiegelbauer, S. M., Hall, G. E., & Loucks, S. F. (1981). *Measuring innovation configurations: Procedures and applications* (Report No. 3108). Austin: The University of Texas at Austin, Research and Development Center for Teacher Education. (ERIC Document Reproduction Service No. ED 204 147).

Hersey, P., Blanchard, K. H., & Johnson, D. E. (2000). *Management of organizational behavior: Leading human resources* (8th ed.). Upper Saddle River, NJ: Prentice-Hall.

Hord, S. M. (1992a). *Facilitative leadership: The imperative for change.* Austin, TX: Southwest Educational Development Laboratory.

Hord, S. M. (1992b). *Voices from a place for children.* Austin, TX: Southwest Educational Development Laboratory.

Hord, S. M. (1993). *A place for children: Continuous quest for quality.* Austin, TX: Southwest Educational Development Laboratory.

Hord, S. M. (Ed.). (2004). *Learning together, leading together: Changing schools through professional learning communities.* New York: Teachers College Press.

Hord, S. M., & Hirsh, S. A. (2008). Making the promise a reality, Chapter 2. In A. Blankstein, P. D. Houston, & R. W. Cole (Eds.), *Sustaining professional learning communities.* Thousand Oaks, CA: Corwin Press.

Hord, S. M., & Hirsh, S. A. (2009, February). The principal's role in supporting learning communities, *Educational Leadership, 66*(5), 22–23.

Hord, S. M., & Huling-Austin, L. (1986). Effective curriculum implementation: Some promising new insights. *The Elementary School Journal, 87*(1), 97–115.

Hord, S. M., Rutherford, W. L., Huling-Austin, L. L., & Hall, G. E. (2004). *Taking charge of change.* Austin, TX: Southwest Educational Development Laboratory.

Hord, S. M., Stiegelbauer, S. M., Hall, G. E., & George, A. A. (2006). *Measuring implementation in schools: Innovation configurations.* Austin, TX: Southwest Educational Development Laboratory.

Hougen, M. C. (1984). *High school principals: An analysis of their approach to facilitating implementation of microcomputers.* Doctoral dissertation, The University of Texas at Austin.

House, E. R., Steele, J., & Kerins, C. T. (1971). *The gifted classroom.* Urbana, IL: Center for Instructional Research and Curriculum Evaluation, University of Illinois.

James, L. R., & Jones, A. P. (1974). Organizational climate: A review of theory and research. *Psychological Bulletin, 81*(12), 1096–1112.

Jehue, R. J. (2000). *Development of a measure for assessing military leaders' change facilitator styles.* Unpublished doctoral dissertation, University of Northern Colorado.

Jenlink, P. M. (1995). *Systemic change: Touchstones for the future school.* Arlington Heights, IL: Skylight Professional Development.

Johnson, M. H. (2000). A district-wide agenda to improve teaching and learning in mathematics. *Journal of Classroom Interaction, 35*(1), 1–7.

Joyce, B., Wolf, J., & Calhoun, E. (1993). *The self-renewing school.* Alexandria, VA: Association for Supervision and Curriculum Development.

Kimberly, J. R., & Nielsen, W. R. (1975). Organization development and change in organizational performance. *Administrative Science Quarterly, 20,* 191–206.

Knapp, M. S., Copland, M. A., & Talbert, J. E. (2003, February). *Leading for learning: Reflective tools for school and district leaders.* Seattle: University of Washington, Center for the Study of Teaching and Policy.

Koon, S. L. (1995). *The relationship of implementation of an entrepreneurial development innovation to student outcomes.* Doctoral dissertation, University of Missouri–Kansas City.

Kourilsky, M. L. (1983). *Mini-society: Experiencing real-world economics in the elementary school classroom.* Menlo Park, CA: Addison-Wesley.

Kuhn, T. S. (1970). *The structure of scientific revolutions.* Chicago: The University of Chicago Press.

Laszlo, E. (1972). *The systems view of the world.* New York: Braziller.

Lee, V. E., Smith, J. B., & Croninger, R. G. (1995, Fall). Another look at high school restructuring. *Issues in restructuring schools.* Madison: Center on Organization and Restructuring of Schools, School of Education, University of Wisconsin.

Leithwood, K., Louis, K. S., Anderson, S., & Wahlstrom, K. (2004). *How leadership influences student learning.* Minneapolis, MN: Center for Applied Research and Educational Improvement, University of Minnesota; Toronto, ON: Ontario Institute for Studies in Education.

Leithwood, K. A., & Montgomery, D. J. (1982). The role of the elementary school principal in program improvement. *Review of Educational Research, (52)*3, 309–339.

Lieberman, A. (1995). Practices that support teacher development: Transforming conceptions of professional learning. *Phi Delta Kappan, 76*(8), 591–596.

Likert, R. (1967). *The human organization: Its management and value.* New York: McGraw-Hill.

Lippitt, R., Watson, J., & Westley, B. (1958). *The dynamics of planned change.* New York: Harcourt Brace.

Little, J. W. (1982). Norms of collegiality and experimentation: Workplace conditions of school success. *American Educational Research Journal, 19*(3), 325–340.

Little, J. W., & McLaughlin, M. W. (1993). *Teachers' work: Individuals, colleagues and contexts.* New York: Teachers College Press.

Loucks, S. F., Newlove, B. W., & Hall, G. E. (1975). *Measuring levels of use of the innovation: A manual for trainers, interviewers, and raters.* Austin: The University of Texas at Austin, Research and Development Center for Teacher Education. Available from the Southwest Educational Development Laboratory, Austin, TX.

Machiavelli, N. (2005). *The prince.* P. E. Bondanella, Ed., Trans. New York: Oxford University Press. (Original work published 1532.)

Mann, F. C., & Likert, R. (1952, Winter). The need for research on the communication of research results. *Human Organization, 11*(4), 15–19.

Matthews, R. J., & Hall, G. E. (1999, November). *Cohort 1: Baseline Data.* Melbourne, Victoria, Australia: Consultancy and Development Unit, Faculty of Education, Deakin University.

Matthews, R. J., Marshall, A. K, & Milne, G. R. (2000, April). *One year on: Report of the notebook evaluation.* Burwood, Victoria, Australia: Deakin University.

McGill, M. E. (1977). *Organization development for operating managers.* New York: AMACOM.

McGregor, D. (1960). *The human side of management.* New York: McGraw-Hill.

McLaughlin, M. W., & Talbert, J. E. (1993). *Contexts that matter for teaching and learning.* Stanford, CA: Center for Research on the Context of Secondary School Teaching, Stanford University.

Miles, M. B. (1979). Ethical issues in OD. *OD Practitioner, 11*(3), 1–10.

Mort, P. R. (1953). Educational adaptability. *School Executive, 71,* 1–23.

National Staff Development Council. (2001). *National Staff Development Council's standards for staff development, revised.* Oxford, OH: National Staff Development Council.

Newlove, B. W., & Hall, G. E. (1976). *A manual for assessing open-ended statements of concern about the innovation* (Report No. 3029). Austin: The University of Texas at Austin, Research and Development Center for Teacher Education. (ERIC Document Reproduction Service No. ED 144 207).

Northouse, P. G. (Ed.) 2007. Leadership: Theory and Practice. Thousand Oaks, CA: Sage.

Novak, A. (1992). *The entrepreneur's Fast Trac II handbook.* Denver, CO: Premier Entrepreneur Programs.

Pasmore, W. A., & Woodman, R. W. (2003). *Research in organizational change and development* (Vol. 14). Greenwich, CT: JAI Press.

Persichitte, K. A., & Bauer, J. W. (1996). Diffusion of computer-based technologies: Getting the best start. *Journal of Information Technology for Teacher Education, 5*(1–2), 35–41.

Rogers, E. M. (2003). *Diffusion of innovations* (5th ed.). New York: The Free Press.

Rood, M., & Hinson, R. (2002). *Measuring the effectiveness of collaborative school reform: Implementation and outcomes.* Paper presented at the annual meeting of the American Evaluation Association, Washington, DC.

Rosenholtz, S. (1989). *Teacher's workplace: The social organizations of schools.* New York: Longman.

Rossi, P. H., Lipsey, M. W., & Freeman, H. W. (2004). *Evaluation: A systematic approach* (7th ed.). Thousand Oaks, CA: Sage.

Rothwell, W. J., Sullivan, R., & McLean, G. N. (1995). *Practicing organization development: A guide for consultants.* San Francisco: Jossey-Bass Pfeiffer.

Roy, P., & Hord, S. (2003). *Moving NSDC's staff development standards into practice: Innovation configuration, Volume 1.* Oxford, OH: National Staff Development Council.

Ryan, B., & Gross, N. C. (1943). The diffusion of hybrid seed corn in two Iowa communities. *Rural Sociology, 8,* 15–24.

Sashkin, M., & Egermeier, J. (1992). *School change models and processes: A review of research and practice.* Paper presented at the annual meeting of the American Educational Research Association, San Francisco.

Schein, E. (1985). *Organizational culture and leadership: A dynamic view.* San Francisco: Jossey-Bass.

Schein, E. (1992). *Organizational culture and leadership: A dynamic view* (2nd ed.). San Francisco: Jossey-Bass.

Schiller, J. (1991a, Winter). Implementing computer education: The role of the primary principal. *Australian Journal of Educational Technology, 7*(1), 48–69.

Schiller, J. (1991b). Implementing computer education: The role of the primary principal. *Australian Journal of Educational Technology, 14*(4), 36–39.

Schiller, J. (2002). Interventions by school leaders in effective ICT implementation: Perceptions of Australian principals. Special issue: "Leadership of Information Technology in Education." *Journal for Information Technology for Teacher Education, 11*(3), 289–301.

Schiller, J. (2003, July/August). The Elementary School Principal as a Change Facilitator in ICT Integration. The Technology Source Archives at the University of North Carolina. Retrieved March 17, 2010, from http://technologysource.org/article/elementary_school_principal_as_a_change_facilitator_in_ict_integration

Schmoker, M. (1997). Setting goals in turbulent times. In A. Hargreaves (Ed.), *ASCD yearbook: Rethinking educational change with heart and mind.* Alexandria, VA: Association for Supervision and Curriculum Development.

Schmuck, R. A. (1987). *Organization development in schools: Contemporary conceptual practices.* Eugene: Center on Organizational Development in Schools, Oregon University. (ERIC Document Reproduction Service No. ED 278 119).

Schmuck, R. A., & Runkel, P. J. (1994). *Handbook of organization development in schools* (4th ed.) Prospect Heights, IL: Waveland Press.

Schneider, M., & Somers, M. (2006). Organizations as complex adaptive systems: Implications of Complexity Theory for leadership research, *The Leadership Quarterly, 17,* 351–365

Senge, P. M. (1990). *The fifth discipline: The art and practice of the learning organization.* New York: Doubleday/Currency.

Shieh, W. H. (1996). *Environmental factors, principal's change facilitator style and implementation of the cooperative learning project in selected schools in Taiwan.* Unpublished doctoral dissertation, University of Northern Colorado.

Smith, J., & O'Day, J. (1991). *Putting the pieces together: Systemic school reform.* CPRE Policy Brief. New Brunswick, NJ: Eagleton Institute of Politics.

Spradley, J. P. (1979). *The ethnographic interview.* New York: Holt, Rinehart and Winston.

Staessens, K. (1990). *De professionele cultuur van basisscholen in vernieuwing. En empirisch onderzoek in v.l.o.-scholen.* [The professional culture of innovating primary schools. An empirical study of R.P.S.-Schools.]. Unpublished doctoral dissertation, University of Leuven, Leuven, Belgium.

Staessens, K. (1993). Identification and description of professional culture in innovating schools. *Qualitative Studies in Education, 6*(2), 111–128.

Stiegelbauer, S. M., Tobia, E. F., Thompson, T. L., & Sturges, K. M. (2004). *Building capacity in low-performing settings: Using research and data-based planning as a tool for system-wide change.* Paper presented at the annual meeting of the American Educational Research Association, New Orleans.

Tarde, G. (1903). *The laws of imitation.* (Trans. Elsie Clews Parson). New York: Holt (reprinted 1969, Chicago: University of Chicago Press).

Thornton, E., & West, C. E. (1999). Extent of teacher use of a mathematics curriculum innovation in one district: Years 1 and 2 Levels of Use (LoU). *Journal of Classroom Interaction, 34*(1), 9–17.

Timar, T., & Kirp, D. (1989, March). Education reform in the 1980s: Lessons from the states. *Phi Delta Kappan, 70*(7), 504–511.

Trice, H. M., & Beyer, J. M. (1993). *The cultures of work organizations.* Englewood Cliffs, NJ: Prentice-Hall.

Trohoski, C. G. (1984). *Principals' interventions in the implementation of a school health program.* Unpublished Ph.D. thesis, University of Pennsylvania.

Van den Berg, R., & Vandenberghe, R. (1981). *Onderwijsinnovatie in verschuivend perspectief.* Amsterdam: Uitgeverij Zwijsen.

Vandenberghe, R. (1988). *Development of a questionnaire for assessing principal change facilitator style.* Paper presented at the annual meeting of the American Educational Research Association, New Orleans. (ERIC Document Reproduction Service No. ED 297 463).

Weick, K. E. (1976, March). Educational organizations as loosely coupled systems. *Administrative Science Quarterly, 21*(1), 1–19.

Wheatley, M. J. (1992). *Leadership and the new science: Learning about organization from an orderly universe.* San Francisco: Berrett-Koehler.

Wheatley, M. J., & Kellner-Rogers, M. (1996). A *simpler way.* San Francisco: Berrett-Koehler.

Yuliang, L., & Huang, C. (2005). Concerns of teachers about technology integration in the USA. *European Journal of Teacher Education, 28*(1), 35–48.

Zmuda, A., Kuklis, R., & Kline, E. (2004). *Transforming schools: Creating a culture* of *continuous improvement.* Alexandria, VA: Association for Supervision and Curriculum Development.

INDEX